TONY'S
TEN
YEARS

TONY'S
TEN
YEARS

Memories of the Blair Administration

ADAM BOULTON

**SIMON &
SCHUSTER**

London · New York · Sydney · Toronto

A CBS COMPANY

First published in Great Britain in 2008 by Simon & Schuster UK Ltd
A CBS COMPANY

Copyright © 2008 by Adam Boulton

1 3 5 7 9 10 8 6 4 2

Simon & Schuster UK Ltd
1st Floor
222 Gray's Inn Road
London WC1X 8HB

www.simonsays.co.uk

Simon & Schuster Australia
Sydney

A CIP catalogue for this book is available
from the British Library.

ISBN: 978-1-84737-242-0 (Hardback)
ISBN: 978-1-84737-432-5 (Trade paperback)

Typeset in Bembo by Ellipsis Books Limited, Glasgow
Printed and bound in Great Britain by
CPI Mackays, Chatham, ME5 8TD

CONTENTS

To all my girls

FOREWORD

I started working as a political journalist in Britain twenty-five years ago. The rise of New Labour and Tony Blair's subsequent premiership have been the biggest story of my career so far. As prime ministers, Margaret Thatcher and John Major occupied me for just as long, but back in 1983 that Conservative era was already an open book. New Labour was indeed something new. It was the story of my time. We may never have joined up or even voted for it, but all those of my generation who were actively involved in politics in the period just gone by have been shaped by New Labour and have, in turn, played some part in shaping *Tony's Ten Years*.

That is why I wanted to write this book. Neither to praise Tony Blair nor to dismantle him but to bear witness to the epoch we have just lived through. To try to shed some light on the phenomena of that time and the man with whom it is inextricably identified. To me, there is no point in getting angry about what we have just been through or grieving about it. It is already in the past, closed with crisp finality by its eponymous hero, who wasted no time in moving on to an afterlife – in the Middle East, the Catholic Church, Africa, the climate debate or the million-dollar lecture and memoir circuit.

Before first-hand memory fades, it seemed worth trying to recall some key themes, moments and motivations of Blair's career as seen from the front-row seat which I have enjoyed as a political editor. This is a book of memories, principally my own, built up from the thousands of conversations and interviews, both on and off the record, which I have had over the past quarter of a century. Memories are not a diary and this book is not about my life, but it is formed from my recollections of what I saw and heard and of what people said to me at the time.

I have talked to many people who worked with and for Tony Blair, and of course to Blair himself. Most of those conversations took place during my professional and personal life over the years, rather than as explicit research for this book. This reflects my normal working practices. I do not believe that there is some talisman, Holy Grail or golden nugget of information jealously hidden away which makes everything comprehensible. History and journalism are built up by keeping your eyes and ears open, and your wits active.

Obviously if you cover politics at first-hand for a long time, you get to know many of the protagonists quite well, both those who are elected and those who are appointed to work for them. Along with your own colleagues, these people make up the milieu in which you spend the majority of your waking hours. Whatever their party political affiliations, such individuals become your close acquaintances, if not your friends. Over this past period, electoral success and the exercise of patronage meant that New Labour has outnumbered any other political faction.

Some argue that intimacy with politicians blunts the critical faculties of political journalists. Sometimes it can, but not, I would claim, in my case. I view politics with detachment because it is the way my mind works. Once the big fundamental of democratic liberty has been established, I can see both sides of the argument as to how it should be managed. Football commentators can tell you about the strengths and weaknesses of teams without supporting, or being known to support, any particular club. They know that talented players can be horrible people and vice versa; that the most successful teams can be charmless or even a bad advert for the game. My approach to politics and politicians is similar to that of a sports commentator to his subject.

My starting point is that politics matters because governments set the rules by which we are all forced to live, and that whatever their allegiances, the vast majority of politicians are well intentioned and want to make the world a better place. Like the rest of us they can be prone to vanity, sloth, careerism, selfishness, deceitfulness and stupidity. They are different because they are generally more pompous, bossy and status conscious, with a much higher tolerance for the boring than any journalist. Politicians also believe that they are right most of the time.

However, the explicit certainties of politicians are counterbalanced by a paradox, which sets them apart from most of us: they are all gamblers, who blithely subject their entire careers to the hazard of public elections every few years. Even when circumstances can be managed by being elected to a (never totally) 'safe' seat, the chance to put opinions into practice still depends on the *Zeitgeist*. A career can be stillborn if the spirit of the times keeps a politician's party out of government during his or her prime.

This risk-taking persona is well camouflaged by the blue and grey suits of male politicians and the chainstore Chanel-style suits of the women. Nor is it readily apparent in the mealy-mouthed compromises which politicians often settle for. But in fact the two are bound up with each other. As John Major, perhaps the archetype of the grey politician, once explained to me: by nature, a true politician will do anything to get re-elected – including breaching electoral law, shaving the corners off core beliefs and donning subfusc so as to look bland to the greatest possible share of the electorate.

To a politician, what matters is winning. That's why they can generally persuade themselves that they have been right all along even if the end result is rather different from what they proposed at the outset. Journalists work in the opposite way: we happily pass through all shades of grey but we like our conclusions to be seen as definitive, there in black and white.

The television satirists of *Have I Got News For You* made much of the guest list at my wedding to Anji Hunter in 2006. Tony Blair, Alastair Campbell, Charles Clarke, Derry Irvine, Tessa Jowell, Michael Howard and Sir Menzies Campbell were amongst the thirty or so politicians, out of more than 300 people, who were invited that day. On the programme I retorted that they were mostly my wife's

xii TONY'S TEN YEARS

friends. That was true. But they were also people alongside whom I had spent my adult life, as we grew older together. It has been much easier in my second marriage to acknowledge those associations than it was in my first marriage to try to ignore them.

Reader, I married one of them! Next to Tony Blair himself, his close friend and long-serving amanuensis, Anji Hunter, is perhaps the most elusive character of the Blair drama. A figure of fascination to many more than just me because of her charm, beauty, intelligence, charisma and upper-middle-class Scottish background, Anji has always declined to record her memories. And anyone who is hoping this book represents her memoirs by proxy should disabuse themselves.

I am ashamed to say that I am a little deficient in the 'rat-like cunning' which the late Nicholas Tomalin prescribed as necessary for a career in journalism. Whenever the phone rang on Blair business during our relationship, my rule was to leave the room and shut the door behind me. I was not very interested in their partisan plotting. Undoubtedly, I know some of the key figures better now that I am Anji's consort but that is about it. She has not read what I've been writing. As she herself proudly put it, 'Thank God I had nothing to do with this book!'

Would that writing this had been as easy as transcribing Anji's thoughts. Instead, while breathing in my own professional and political ambiance, I have tried to assemble my ideas on the past ten years of government in Britain by exploring the narrative of the hundred days around Tony Blair's final exit from power.

There were many unique aspects to Tony Blair's decade as Britain's prime minister: he was the first Labour leader to win three general elections in a row; the first modern prime minister to bring up a young family in Downing Street; the first prime minister since the Victorian period to deliver a decade of unbroken economic growth; the first prime minister to be questioned by the police in a criminal investigation; the first prime minister to give his press secretary the power to command civil servants; the first prime minister since Churchill to send Her Majesty's armed forces to fight and die on three continents.

However, the most original feature of Blair's premiership was its final year – the way he left office. Prime ministers have often resigned mid-term before. In fact, since 1945 as many have made their exit from the top office that way (Churchill, Eden, Macmillan, Wilson, Thatcher) as were given the *coup de grâce* by the electorate (Attlee, Douglas-Home, Heath, Callaghan, Major). Political pressure, sickness and personal whim all played a part in these 'voluntary' exits but the departures were mostly melancholy and hurried affairs – until Tony Blair.

The corrosive dynamic of his rivalry with Gordon Brown meant that Blair always lived politically under the shadow of 'how long'. From the beginning of his party leadership, he contrasted his own recognition that he wouldn't go on for ever with Margaret Thatcher's unrelenting 'on and on'.

Blair's political quietus was undoubtedly forced by the attempted coup against him of September 2006 but, uniquely, he succeeded in orchestrating his own departure. In effect, he was able to use the year from that September for a long goodbye, during which he moved from prime minister to embryonic elder statesman. No other outgoing British leader has had the luxury, or perhaps the self-absorption, to use an orderly exit from the job of prime minister like a second-term US president – to round off neatly and to attempt to write the first draft of history on his own years in power.

This final stage had two overlapping phases – the period when he was in power, still the active prime minister; and the period when he was bidding his farewells. The first phase dominated the eight months from September until Blair set in motion the formal process of leaving office in early May 2007. During it he attempted to bed in irrevocably his domestic agenda of public service reform and to ensure that Gordon Brown remained faithful to New Labour. Blair continued to attempt to wield executive power to achieve his aims to the very end, until he left Downing Street on 27 June 2007.

By then, the other phase of the long goodbye had already begun: the lap of honour. This was the time when Blair self-consciously revisited the issues and places which he clearly considered would define him: among them Northern Ireland, Africa, Washington, Iraq, Prime Minister's Questions, schools and hospitals. He also made a number of reflective speeches on his time in office and the lessons he drew from it. 'The Blairwell Tour' earned him a prize for 'Resignation of the Year' at The Spectator/Threadneedle Parliamentary Awards (in his absence, my wife collected the trophy for him).

Blair's biographers often like to dwell on his success as a schoolboy actor. At Fettes he had his best roles in *Journey's End*, *Captain Brassbound's Conversion* and *Julius Caesar*, but never played *Macbeth*. Even so, Malcolm's description to Duncan of the execution of the Thane of Cawdor offers an apposite cliché in this case: 'Nothing in his life became him like the leaving it.' Of course, Blair's departure was not his death, nor did he confess treason, implore pardon or set forth a deep repentance – much to the disappointment of his growing band of critics over Iraq.

Considering the opponents ranged against him, Tony Blair's carefully controlled exit was both graceful and typical of a leader who had always recognised the importance of presentation – a man who never shied from expressing what he was trying to do.

This book takes those final three months – the almost hundred days of May, June and July 2007, which witnessed Blair's carefully planned departure and the transition to Prime Minister Gordon Brown – as its narrative spine. From what happened during those months, I set out to explore some of the themes of the preceding ten years and earlier, just as Blair did when he was stepping down.

I have borrowed my subtitle, though nothing else I'm afraid, from John Updike's novel *Memories of the Ford Administration*, because this book is made up of memories of Tony Blair. The loaded word is 'administration', a term that is usually applied with reference to presidents; 'government' or 'premiership' does for prime ministers. But as the MP Graham Allen has pointed out from a parliamentary perspective in his *The Last Prime Minister*, and as I will often suggest in these pages, there was much that was presidential about Tony Blair.

Lots of books have been written about the Blair era. Many more are to come – including Tony's own memoirs. This is my own, first-hand contribution.

Westminster, April 2008

1

POWER

1 MAY

Within the next few weeks I won't be prime minister of this country.
Tony Blair, Edinburgh, 1 May 2007

Marking the decade

The ten years were up. But still nobody knew exactly when they would be over for Tony Blair.

Precisely a decade ago there had been no doubt. Even before the results were declared in 1997, there had been no false modesty, no need to prevaricate – everyone knew Tony Blair was about to become prime minister. But on May Day 2007 the only known fact was that Blair had promised the previous September to be gone within a year. The general assumption was that he would give some indication of his plans around his tenth anniversary in office because in practice he would have to step down before the approaching long summer parliamentary recess. The Labour Party would then have time to elect a new leader before the annual party conference in September 2007.

A decade earlier 71 per cent of eligible British voters had gone to the polls. Tony Blair had spent 1 May 1997 in his Sedgefield constituency, briefly crossing the playing fields in Trimdon with his family to vote before returning home to plan for the future and prepare for government – two activities beloved of rising politicians. This amounted to planning and appointing his cabinet team over the phone from Myrobella, his constituency base, aided by Anji Hunter and Alastair Campbell, and bickering privately with his wife, Cherie, about who would have, or not have, which role in his equally important 'kitchen cabinet'.

By definition a general election is a public event, with the outcome declared within hours. Usually departures from Downing Street are sudden and brutal, the voters' or party's sentence of execution duly carried out without appeal on the doorstep of Number 10. Not this time. Uniquely, Tony Blair managed to take control of his own exit timetable and to divorce it from any electoral process. He also chose to keep the precise date a secret.

Even on this milestone day Blair decided to keep the nation, and more particularly the media, guessing. The advance spin from his advisers was that this would be a working day like any other with no news conference or public celebrations to mark what had been achieved during Blair's decade in power. So Britain's veteran prime minister pretended that 1 May 2007 was indeed a working day like any other. He began in London before moving on to Scotland for a campaigning visit. The prime minister had long fallen out with the '24/7 media', as he would make explicit in his Reuters speech a month later. He had no desire to be seen feeding 'the feral beast', even though 'Blair Decade Special' supplements were pouring from the presses and airwaves alike.

The prime minister made the announcement of his departure bathetically in the least combative and most inconsequential forum he could find – the breakfast television studio of GMTV, just across the river from Downing Street on London's South Bank. Fiona 'Fifi' Phillips (a sometime Chequers dinner-party guest along with her husband, Martin Frizzell, editor-in-chief of the show) and her firm-jawed co-presenter, Andrew Castle, were informed, 'I'll make an announcement next week.' This all but non-announcement was significant for two reasons: it made it clear that Blair did not plan to announce his departure when the local election results came in that Friday; it also relaxed Gordon Brown.

Blair's statement that he would begin the countdown to his departure in the middle of May made it certain that power would indeed be handed over by the time Parliament rose in July. Some Blairites hankered for delay, postulating that he could linger over the summer and yet still honour his commitment to be gone by the start of the Labour Party conference at the end of September. But even the dilatory Labour leadership timetable would not stretch from May to September. Brown now knew that he would be prime minister before July was out: the public statement of intention long demanded by him had finally been made on the GMTV sofa.

Just to make sure that there would be no further misunderstanding with Brown, Blair gave his clearest pronouncement so far on his succession later that day in Scotland. His campaigning for Labour candidates to the Holyrood Parliament was overshadowed when he told his audience of party activists in Edinburgh, 'Within the next few weeks I won't be the prime minister of this country. In all probability, a Scot will become prime minister of the United Kingdom . . . That's someone who has built one of the strongest economies in the world and who, as I've always said, will make a great prime minister.'

Since announcing his intention to be gone within a year at the Labour conference in Manchester in the autumn of 2006, Blair had refused to repeat his endorsement of Brown – 'he would make an excellent prime minister' – that had punctuated their tortured relationship for more than ten years. In Manchester it would have been difficult to back Brown, thanks to the tale of Cherie Blair's overheard stage whisper against the chancellor, even if Tony Blair had felt inclined to do so after that September's attempted coup against him orchestrated by Brown allies. But now, on the day he took the decisive step towards the exit, he was finally giving his clear endorsement, while sticking to his pledge not actually to name his successor.

There was, however, one other Scotsman still notionally in the frame as a potential challenger to Brown. The home secretary, John Reid, had not yet officially withdrawn from possible contention. Reid was working class, Catholic, populist and self-confident compared to the withdrawn, cautious, Presbyterian, middle-class Brown, and the two men had a long-standing political enmity. It seemed implausible that Reid could ever have mustered the support to beat Brown, but he was a 'big beast' who would have made the leadership a real contest. Reid, however, had just signalled that he was unlikely to be a candidate. In a coded utterance on the BBC's *Sunday AM* just two days before, he had pleaded for party unity: 'there will not be a fracturing beyond this election, there will be a coming together of the Labour leadership'. The next day Tessa Jowell, the culture secretary, gave an uncharacteristically pointed speech calling for an end to tribalism. The mobile phone lines had been busy and now Jowell and Reid, the two most prominent standard bearers of Blairism still active, were admitting that they would carry his torch but not challenge the transition from Blair. A week or so later, the offer of the chairmanship of his beloved Celtic Football Club convinced John Reid that he would spend much of the Brown era away from Westminster, and certainly out of the cabinet frontline.

In the end – because nobody ever really trusted what anyone else said in private – the manner of Tony Blair's departure was decided in the way New Labour had always done business – a double bind in which private negotiations and understandings were backed up by public declarations from which inferences could be drawn.

The problem for Blair and his advisers was that the 'ten years' anniversary, which they wanted to celebrate, had become unavoidably linked to his departure, which they naturally wanted to play down. After Iraq, and with tricky regional elections underway, they were also aware that there was a limited public appetite for ten years' jubilation. The compromise was the business-as-usual, taking-it-all-in-my-stride demeanour forced on the prime minister.

Framing the legacy

In truth, both Blair and the Blairites did not really want the moment to pass unnoticed or unspun. Much thought had in fact been given to the exit strategy.

As far back as the spring of 2006, Ben Wegg-Prosser, the head of the Strategic Communications Unit and former aide to Peter Mandelson, had produced a memo, 'Reconnecting with the Public – a New Relationship with the Media', with detailed proposals for Blair's activities during the 'final phase'. This document was subsequently leaked to the *Daily Mirror* at the beginning of that September, coinciding with the attempted coup against Blair by some MPs.

The document from BWP, also known as 'Benjie', was much mocked for its hubris and concentration on presentation: 'We know what works well: strong policy focused events which have substance, striking pictures, words from TB and real people involved.' Wegg-Prosser was ambitiously proposing that 'TB . . . needs to go with the crowds wanting more. He should be the star who won't even play that last encore,' after a series of nationwide visits during which 'he needs to embrace open spaces, the arts and businesses, he needs to be seen to be travelling on different forms of transport. He needs to be seen with people who will raise eyebrows . . . carefully positioned as someone who while not above politics, is certainly distancing himself from the political village.'

Escaping from the village was also tied to the media opportunities that the outgoing prime minister was to embrace. Political journalists were to be avoided, replaced by disc jockeys and appearances on such shows as the BBC's sanctimonious *Songs of Praise*, and *Blue Peter*, its flagship children's programme. Blair's appearance on *Blue Peter* had already been filmed by the time the contents of the memo became known, and the BBC's younger viewers subsequently learned, amongst other trivia, that the prime minister's nickname for Downing Street was 'The Tardis', given its surprising size. But the 'Vicar', as *Private Eye* dubbed him, never made it to *Songs of Praise*. The producers had insisted that it would have to be a joint appearance with Gordon Brown and that had proved impossible to arrange.

Wegg-Prosser also betrayed some important anxieties about Blair's 'place in history'. Iraq was 'the elephant in the room, let's face up to it . . . Most importantly, are we up for it? Is TB up for it?' There seemed to be even some question as to how prominent concrete

domestic achievements could or should be in 'the triumph of Blairism':
'his genuine legacy is not the delivery, important though that is, but
the dominance of New Labour ideas'.

Number 10 sought to play down the leak, claiming that 'nobody
senior' had seen or acted upon the memo. Initially no one would
admit authorship of it. The *Daily Mirror* carefully spread the blame:
'among the Downing Street aides involved with the document are
Ruth Turner, Dave Hill, Liz Lloyd, John McTernan'. Philip Gould
(by now Lord Gould), Blair's public opinion analyst, was also fingered.
He had previous form, having authored another embarrassing memo
about the prime minister's desire to be associated with 'eye-catching
initiatives'.

However, Wegg-Prosser cheerfully acknowledged his work shortly
after he left Number 10, a few weeks before Blair's own departure,
to pursue internet business opportunities in Moscow with his
Russian wife, Yulia. In the meantime, his proposals bore some fruit.
Blair cut down his contacts with the pack of political journalists.
His last monthly news conference took place on 17 April 2007,
more than two full months before he quit. Instead a team was set
up, comprising Wegg-Prosser, Deputy Chief of Staff Liz Lloyd and
political researcher Catherine Rimmer, to manage the so-called
'Legacy Project' to ensure that Blair's exit from office was given a
well-known on sympathetic terms. They organised special access
for selected well-known journalists and writers including Martin
Amis for the *Guardian*; Robert Crampton for *The Times*; Roger
Cohen, the London-born *New York Times* columnist, writing for
Men's Vogue (covering the American market); Will Hutton and
Andrew Rawnsley for Channel 4; and David Aaronovitch for the
BBC. But even these privileged few were kept at arm's length. This
satisfied the Blair team's desire to control, but it did not get their
message across for them.

Opposition leaders, however, were ready with their own tenth
anniversary tributes on 1 May. While on the local election trail, David
Cameron impudently raised the state of the National Health Service
in a speech at a hospital in Crewe:

'Tony Blair's time as prime minister started with great hope but ended with disappointment. It is clear he has done some good things like make the Bank of England independent. But ten years ago he promised "twenty-four hours to save the NHS". Today, community hospitals face closure, the NHS faces more job losses than ever, maternity units are under threat, it is difficult to find an NHS dentist and junior doctors are being treated appallingly. Tony Blair will be remembered as a successful party leader but not as a good prime minister.'

The former Liberal Democrat leader, Paddy Ashdown, who had been so disappointed after 1997 by Blair's unconsummated flirtations with partnership, was scarcely more generous: 'Tony Blair will go down as a good, but not great prime minister.' As his diaries showed, Ashdown had been seduced by Blair's talk of a 'progressive century' during which the parties of the centre-left – Labour and the Liberal Democrats – could combine to keep the Conservatives out of power. In 1997 Blair would have been prepared to do the deal, but Labour won too big. With a majority of 179 it was simply not possible, even for Blair, to tell his party that they needed to share power. In deference to Ashdown and Roy Jenkins (the Labour cabinet minister turned SDP founder turned Liberal Democrat whom Blair regarded as a mentor), the prime minister would eventually commission Jenkins to make recommendations on electoral reform – only to leave them not taken up. Even if it was not reciprocated in the end, Blair's admiration for Ashdown remained warm. He backed him as UN high representative in the former Yugoslavia and praised his work there. But even after Blair's resignation Ashdown shrunk from the Labour embrace, declining Gordon Brown's offer to make him Northern Ireland secretary in his first cabinet.

If the record was to be put straight and the Blair ten years commemorated properly, the Blairites always knew they would have to do the job themselves. Following the Wegg-Prosser leak disaster, Blair had begun to outline his own summary of achievements. As so often before, he worked on this document by hand during spare hours at Chequers and then had it typed up and circulated to his advisers – both those formally still on the payroll and those, like Campbell and Hunter, now off it. In the early days this would all have been done by faxes, reams of which were fired off most Sunday evenings, but now email certainly did its bit to save the environment or, at any rate, fax paper.

A draft circulated in April 2006 contained sixteen points. The introductory paragraph was a first-hand exposition of the paradoxes and reconciliations which drove Blair's politics:

1. A basic philosophy – the new Labour essence – that sought to overcome the traditional right–left divide ie the right understands the economy, the left, social justice. In place of this, recognising that the development of human capital is key, New Labour put economic prosperity and social justice as partners not opposites. We supported aspiration and compassion. This changed the basic parameters of British politics with the Tories having to say the same.

The same philosophical juxtapositions recurred in the remaining points, even as he tried to reconcile seemingly opposing approaches. Tony Blair was convinced of his own righteousness and asserted it provocatively. The document showed that the verbless sentences which made up so much of his public rhetoric were indeed his natural style of self-expression.

2. A nation, open, at ease with globalisation, prepared to compete on its merits not its history.
3. Public Service Reform. We recognised the under-investment but combined the values of public service – equal access and equity – with the virtues of the market – breaking up the monolith, diversity of supply, consumer choice, flexibility.
4. We have redrawn the boundaries of the liberty debate: socially liberal, pro gay rights, anti-discrimination; but hard and intolerant of anti-social behaviour and lawlessness. People may question the success in implementing the policy but the essential liberty/security paradigm is widely accepted.
5. A society at ease with itself. Immigration an issue but still racially and ethnically tolerant. Minimum wage. Gay rights.

6. Economic Prosperity for all, through stability, high employment and bringing children and pensioners out of poverty. Good relationship with business as well as brining [sic] in work/life balance changes. New agenda on social exclusion.

7. Massive constitutional reform. Devolution. London. FOI [Freedom of Information]. ECHR [European Court of Human Rights]. Party funding. First House of Lords reform etc.

8. Northern Ireland – a changed part of the UK.

9. A new doctrine of interventionism in international policy: Kosovo; Sierra Leone; Iraq; Afghanistan, on the one hand; Africa, climate change, Palestine, on the other. An agenda in which hard and soft power has been combined. Again, it may not always have been to people's liking, but it was and is a coherent and radically different approach to international relations.

10. We took Britain's two key alliances – Europe and America – and kept them both strong. In Europe the UK went from the Beef War and isolation, to leading the debates on European defence, economic reform, energy, enlargement, and did the budget deal. The American alliance has been very controversial. But no doubt of its strength. And eg on G8 Gleneagles summit; WTO; or MEPP [Middle East Peace Process], has given UK a chance to influence policy.

11. A renaissance in British cities.

12. Science – stem cell, bioscience and the new creative industries. All new British success stories. Art and culture flourishing.

13. Africa and Climate change. Real progress on two major issues, G8 Gleneagles set a new standard in international negotiation.

14. Party transformed from election losing (4 in a row) to winning (3 in a row). Cl IV changed governing philosophy, our Bad Godesberg. Became a modern social democratic party.

15. Britain became definably, in many different facets, a modern country, finally over the Empire hangover, able to combine modern attitudes with great traditions (monarchy etc) in a way that gave Britain a new image for new times eg.

16. The Olympics!

Blair's catalogue of achievements was manifestly designed for eventual public consumption. He grasped for 'eye-catching initiatives' such as cities, science, culture and the Olympics without offering corroborative details and didn't even bother to stake claims about education and health, which got barely a mention. Leaving Scotland and Wales out of 'massive constitutional reform', while including the never-loved Freedom of Information Act and European Convention on Human Rights, was a revealing slip as Labour worried about its fate in the local elections. Significantly, 'liberty' does not warrant a capital 'L'.

Blair's own thoughts seeded such glossy publications as the brochure produced and circulated by David Blunkett titled 'Then and Now: A Country Transformed', released on 1 May, and a twenty-four-page brief prepared for the Parliamentary Labour Party, 'Ten Years of Labour Government'.

In spite of his two forced resignations from the cabinet, David Blunkett remained one of Blair's most loyal colleagues. His document was printed on a background of positive newspaper headlines and covered the 'five key areas of education, employment, health, crime and the economy'. Once more, this analysis showed why Blunkett had been such a 'key supporter of the project'. Unlike the prime minister, Blunkett, or 'Blunks' as Blair called him, came from an impoverished working-class background, but he shared with Blair the experience of having lost a parent during his formative years – a statistically prominent feature of many successful politicians.

Just before Christmas 1959 when Blunkett was only twelve, his father – a foreman for the East Midlands Gas Board – fell into a vat of boiling water after a fellow worker failed to repair a safety device. Arthur Blunkett managed to save himself from drowning but his horrific injuries led to his death a month later. He was sixty-seven years old. Despite having specifically asked Arthur to stay on beyond the usual age of retirement to train up new recruits, the Gas Board refused to compensate the family. It argued that such money was intended to replace lost potential earnings during a working life and that Arthur Blunkett had in effect already reached the end of his. Doris Blunkett was left with no other option but to bury her husband in an unmarked grave. This tragedy and its shattering effect on the family proved a particularly cruel blow to a child already dealing with the challenge of blindness. When he started to earn money – ironically enough from 1967 to 1969 he worked as a clerk typist for the same Gas Board that had treated his family so shoddily – one of David Blunkett's first actions was to erect a headstone for his father's grave.

Blunkett was born Labour, rising to become council leader of 'the People's Republic of Sheffield'. But, like Blair and Neil Kinnock, Blunkett was a pragmatist. He was less interested in ideology than in delivering material services and opportunity to all. He was a vital ally to Kinnock in the battle against the Militant Tendency, and he shared Blair's conviction that education needed reform – believing that if it wasn't working it was worth trying alternatives. Like Blair, Blunkett also understood the importance of the media and was happy to 'sup with the devil' in pursuit of a good editorial. Like Blair, Blunkett enjoyed the trappings of success, but unlike him he was brought down twice as a minister by his links to smart friends. Unlike Blair though, his experiences at the hands of the press over the ten years did not seem to have embittered him towards journalists. 'Then and Now' was media-friendly verbally and visually (as befitted a former cabinet minister employed to write a lucrative column for the *Sun*).

The PLP brief was a list of typically staccato and sketchy bullet points ranging over twenty-two policy areas: economy, welfare, education, health, families, law and order, immigration and asylum, public realm [i.e. physical infrastructure], cities, science, open and outward culture ('1997: Inheritance. Public life at top overwhelmingly dominated by white middle-class males . . .'), social exclusion, constitution [Wales and Scotland are listed as the main items now], Northern Ireland, transport, rural affairs, arts, foreign policy [with just passing references to Iraq and Afghanistan and no mention of the Middle East], Europe, Africa, climate change and finally the Labour Party itself.

Just in case MPs and peers missed 'the line to take', each of the twenty-two sections detailed above was subdivided further under five separate headings – '1997: Inheritance, Our approach, Key moments', and '2007: Passing On and In Summary'.

The document was packed with 'killer' statistics and factoids: '58 consecutive quarters of growth . . . employment is at record levels . . . 600,000 kids lifted out of poverty . . . Failing schools – 1570 turned around . . . Waiting lists cut and on track for 2008 – the problem of 1997 cured.'

But occasionally the claims looked a little thin or even bombastic. For example under the section for arts, the sub-section '2007: Passing On' states simply:

- Golden Age of Arts
- Highest ever arts audiences (museums, theatre, film)
- Envy of the World (outstripped New York and Paris)
- Boom in regional theatre (reaching all classes)
- Areas regenerated by arts venues (eg Sage)

Accompanying this document came a typed letter from Tony Blair, topped and tailed in his own hand: 'Dear Colleague . . . Yours sincerely, Tony Blair'. In it he was more defensive and frank about the 'difficulties and troubles' prompting his departure from both the premiership and the Labour leadership. After short paragraphs on the economy and public services, he at last referred to the controversy which did more than any other to drive him out:

> 9/11 fundamentally changed the world. We are still dealing with its impact, most obviously in both Afghanistan and Iraq. The strong views which the war in Iraq generated are still felt today. As I have said before, history will make its own judgement on our policy but the priority for the moment has to be to support the long-term reconstruction of the country and improving security, which we are doing with a UN mandate.

In the weeks remaining to him, Blair was to use the instruments of power to try to shore up his claims to have transformed Britain during his ten years and above all to justify his actions in the Middle East.

As for officially marking the decade, after leaving the GMTV sofa

Tony Blair paid a brief, anti-climactic visit to Labour Party headquarters, before boarding his flight to Edinburgh.

During Blair's years as leader, Labour HQ had drifted around central London according to the aspirations and available funds of the New Labour cadre. Blair's team were desperate to abandon Walworth Road, the ramshackle cluster of converted town houses in Elephant and Castle lent by the trade unions, which witnessed many of the clashes and demonstrations of the Kinnock years. By the 1997 general election campaign the party had taken down the newly carved 'John Smith House' plaque and moved with it north of the river to occupy two floors of Millbank Tower. The modernist skyscraper on the Embankment would become synonymous with New Labour and the awesome organisational power which delivered the landslide victories of 1997 and 2001. Millbank was a business office building and so symbolised Blair's break with the smoky union rooms and factory stacks of the past – but it was also expensive. As the Labour Party's cash troubles mounted, it downscaled its premises. On 1 May 2007, therefore, it was a temporary HQ in an anonymous suite of rented offices on Victoria Street that the party leader visited.

A solitary television camera team was invited along to take pictures, which it would then 'pool' (make available on an unrestricted basis) with all the other news broadcasters. Such pools were usual practice for most prime ministerial engagements, and especially the brief public handshakes, 'grip and grins', with visiting politicians. Blair's ten year anniversary, however, was not official government business. It was a party political event which in the glory days gone by would have been celebrated with balloons, bands and boasts. Not now. Instead the pictures simply showed the staff cheering in the nondescript office surroundings and the leader thanking them for their hard work. How very different from ten years before . . .

Downing Street

Tony Blair's first triumphant arrival in Downing Street on the morning of 2 May 1997 as the newly elected prime minister provided the defining images of the Blair premiership which would last for the next decade: the well-prepared, flag-waving crowds of supporters and their children lining the road on either side beyond the security gates; the new prime minister and his young family posing on the step. The iconic pictures would be used and parodied throughout the ten years and beyond. No subsequent satire of prime ministerial power was complete without a version of the walk to the door of destiny. As the years passed, the Blairs restaged and updated this family photo at key junctions in their political life – twice more to mark the victories of 2001 and 2005, and finally in 2007 when they left Downing Street for the last time.

With the efficiency which was characteristic of those early days, New Labour commissioned its own photographer to record the ascent to power. The pictures taken by the respected photojournalist Tom Stoddart captured the excitement of the new, younger faces as they took office, including two striking women, Anji Hunter and the flame-haired Jan Royall (who would one day become Gordon Brown's chief whip in the Lords), striding purposefully towards Number 10. Later in 1997 the Labour Party produced a Christmas card showing Tony and Cherie in front of the door with the caption 'Christmas came early this year'; Derek Draper's book cover used the same picture and the door numbers 1 and 0 to spell out his title – *Blair's 100 Days*. A talented and mouthy young moderniser and activist from the University of Manchester, Draper would go on to be one New Labour acolyte who fell by the wayside. He started the Blair years as an over-confident special adviser to Peter Mandelson MP (the pair were often lampooned as Dastardly and Muttley). By 1998 he had moved on to become a private lobbyist, later finding himself at the heart of one of the first New Labour scandals after boasting to an undercover reporter about his connections: 'There are seventeen people who count [in this government]. And to say I am intimate with every one of them is the understatement of the century.' Draper subsequently suffered a semi-public series of personal breakdowns. He eventually retrained as a psychotherapist and married the GMTV presenter Kate Garraway. *OK!* magazine secured the rights to their wedding in 2005 and duly published a twenty-two-page glossy spread.

There was no leisurely transition period for the incoming Blair administration. The morning after the vote the defeated Tory leader John Major was out of 10 Downing Street and Tony Blair was in. As a television reporter facing the famous shiny black door that morning, I was feeling a little fragile. I had had no sleep, having just co-anchored an overnight election results special. Unlike the partisans around me, I knew the people on both sides well. I could empathise with both groups as I gave my commentary and it was difficult not to get caught up in the competing emotions. The stoic desolation of John Major and the more tearful aides behind him as he told the cameras 'when the curtain comes down it is time to leave the stage'; the triumphant excitement of Tony Blair and the many hundreds more supporters now crowding Downing Street.

It was 2 May 1997 – a day of fulfilment for Labour: the party was back in power after eighteen years, with the biggest majority since Baldwin's national government coalition of 1935. The party was satisfied and quiescent, enabling Blair to embark on an extended honeymoon during which he faced little effective opposition.

Blair was not interested in venerating Labour or Britain's history. As the slogan had it, he was much more concerned with 'the future not the past'. Even before he arrived in Downing Street, his team had introduced an innovation – a victory party across the river at the Festival Hall. As the twilight brightened, Blair declared 'a new dawn has broken, has it not?'

The Blairs did not move into Downing Street immediately. The small flat at the top of Number 10, traditionally occupied by the prime minister, could not accommodate a family of five. Gordon Brown, who never moved full time into his official quarters until becoming prime minister, gave up his claim to the chancellor's accommodation next door and a bigger apartment was fashioned for the Blairs above Numbers 11 and 12 Downing Street. These delayed domestic arrangements eventually provided evidence that the nation suffers from false-memory syndrome. A tousled Mrs Blair was not caught on camera answering the door in a shorty nightie to accept a flower delivery the morning after Labour came to power. On Friday 2 May she accompanied her husband into Number 10, but that night she returned with her family to their Richmond Terrace home in Islington. The flower delivery was filmed the following Saturday morning.

However, Tony Blair showed no hesitation in taking up the reins of power once inside Downing Street. There was uncertainty amongst his aides about what job each of them would get since Mrs Blair did not invite everybody to the celebratory lunch she organised. And it quickly became clear that 'the boys' had been rather more self-interested than 'the girls' by quietly negotiating their titles and salaries in advance. But though Blair could be careless with the people who worked for him, he had no doubt what he wanted. He set out to transform the way government would work.

Blair was preoccupied with establishing systems which would 'deliver' the policy outcomes he wanted. He tried to turn his government into an American-style administration in which he, and his chosen appointees, would wield executive power to take decisions. He created a series of posts with *West Wing* titles: chief of staff for Jonathan Powell and director of communications for Alastair Campbell, while Anji Hunter became special assistant for presentation and planning, a post which was upgraded to director of government relations after the 2001 election. Hunter did not take special powers; her responsibility was dealing with people on behalf of Blair, both internally to the cabinet and the Labour Party and externally to business, media and other opinion-formers. No previous prime minister had ever seen the need for three such powerful surrogates.

Hunter and Campbell had recruited a cadre of twenty- and thirtysomething political appointees to work with them. The future foreign secretary, David Miliband, was head of the Policy Unit, which also included another future cabinet minister, James Purnell; Andrew Adonis, the future schools minister; and Pat McFadden, the future local government minister. Kate Garvey was appointed diary secretary, along with Liz Lloyd – who would stay with Blair to the end, working first on home affairs then on African development – and Sarah Hunter, a clever protégée of Derry Irvine, the new Lord Chancellor. Campbell appointed Tim Allan as his deputy. Allan came from the BBC and his job at Number 10 seemed to consist of knowing which buttons to press at the Corporation. When Allan moved on to the private sector he was replaced by another BBC old hand, Lance Price.

Blair's innovation was to have his political appointees working in tandem with civil servants in carefully specified areas of responsibility. Post-9/11 this dual structure would emerge as a faultline in government, but at the time it was introduced, the civil servants were complacent or even enthusiastic about it. Many of them – such as Jeremy Heywood and Alex Allan, at senior level, and Magi Cleaver, operationally – had careers which thrived under Blair. There was no wholesale clearout of the civil service after 1997, although it is fair to say that Campbell used the first term to carry out a pretty comprehensive overhaul of communications officers. When Blair was elected, it was considered – rightly or wrongly – that John Major had been an indecisive and ineffective prime minister. While some civil servants were almost queuing up for the smack of firm government, the strongest resistance came from the top departmental permanent secretaries – the 'Sir Humphreys' – and their shop steward, the cabinet secretary. Blair had prickly working relationships with his first two cabinet secretaries, Robin Butler and Richard Wilson. Things improved in 2002 with the appointment of Andrew Turnbull, who was an enthusiastic admirer of Blair's delivery systems. Having worked closely with John Major, Blair's last cabinet secretary, Gus O'Donnell, managed the transition to Gordon Brown, whom he had previously served as permanent secretary at the Treasury. O'Donnell was well placed to fine-tune relations between those elected to office and permanent government as represented by the civil service.

In his report published in July 2004 on the use of intelligence and the Iraq War, Robin Butler would articulate the most precise criticisms yet of Blair's style, summarised as 'sofa government'. The inquiry team was concerned that the 'informality' of government procedures reduced the 'scope for informed collective political judgement' – a reference to cabinet decision-making. Physically at least, Blair certainly spent more time working from a sofa than any previous prime minister. When he first entered Downing Street he was still hesitant about some of the trappings of rank and decided that he didn't need a big office (even though, unlike Major, he was reluctant to work at the cabinet table). He took a small room overlooking the Downing Street garden at right angles to the Cabinet Room. For the sun-loving prime minister this had the advantage of immediate access to French windows and a veranda. But after a few months, he ejected the permanent secretaries from their large room overlooking Horse Guards Parade and opening directly into the Cabinet Room, and kept this 'den' for the remainder of his time in Downing Street.

Both rooms had pretty much the same layout – a pair of sofas facing each other across a fireplace and other furniture scattered around in the corners. There was always a bowl of fruit. A flat-screen television was attached to the wall as soon as they appeared on the market. Blair never used a typewriter or computer. He preferred to work sitting on one of the sofas leaning forward to a coffee table to write with a fountain pen in his clearly legible longhand. He used the large desk in a corner more and more in his final years as prime minister as his eyesight weakened. Working meetings took place with staff informally perched on the furniture. For journalists summoned in for a briefing, it was a disarmingly casual environment. According to my BBC 'oppo' Nick Robinson, I called the prime minister a liar during a session when he was briefing us on cancer treatment statistics. After a lifetime at the starchier end of the civil service, Butler must have felt equally disorientated, even if his main complaint was that decisions taken informally were not fully minuted.

Blair was not a bully and he didn't shout. Like many politicians, he was good with names, good at greeting the Downing Street staff. They in turn liked him. His public school good manners could set people at ease but, with the more bumptious, a quick joke would soon put them in their place. He allowed his advisers to be extraordinarily blunt and informal with him. Campbell and Hunter were both known to talk over the prime minister and to give him instructions which sounded like orders in front of third parties. But they weren't the only ones. Blair grasped a demotic mood which wanted to make punchbags of politicians and he was quite prepared to stand and take abuse, as he showed when assailed by members of the public while campaigning.

At his news conferences and in interviews, he would frequently engage in barbed exchanges. Yet this did not diminish his authority. Without consciously asserting himself, he had an easy physical presence and assurance which conveyed that he was the prime minister and he mattered, even when in groups with other national leaders. He didn't pander to what was going on around him and remained a little aloof from it. This meant that whatever was being said to him, however and by whoever, he reserved the right to disagree. Verbal challenges would be countered with a quizzical look, or on occasion a stern one. By staying engaged and polite, he could rise above the arguments swirling around him. Campbell blustered, but Blair commanded when he had to. He was also able to express himself directly and simply. He seldom felt the need to demonstrate his superiority, so he was never afraid to ask the simple questions such as 'Why are we doing this?', 'What's the problem?' or 'What is so-and-so up to?' He was also very happy to invite people in to give their advice, and then completely ignore their views. It was no secret that he would work round people or opinions which obstructed him. For all the informality and smiling invitations into his big tent, few were left in any doubt that he knew what he wanted and had a steely determination to obtain it.

Not all of Blair's attempts to shake up protocol succeeded that first summer. The request to 'Call me Tony' was adopted by politicians but not by officials. The Blairs' efforts to liven up Downing Street hospitality were ultimately unsuccessful. During his first July in power, the Blairs threw a reception which was immediately likened to Harold Wilson's parties in the swinging sixties. This was largely because Wilson had then invited the Beatles and now their self-proclaimed heirs Oasis were on the guest list. The invocation of 'Cool Britannia' was inevitable (again the phrase itself was a sixties throwback, first coined by the Bonzo Dog Doo-Dah Band and recycled as the competition-winning name of a Ben and Jerry's ice-cream flavour in 1996, before being emblazoned on the cover of *Newsweek* that same year). But the controversial guest lists were actually an attempt to make the parties more interesting. Rather than invite people by profession and host a reception, say, for diplomats, or journalists, or the voluntary sector, Blair's team tried to mix it up by asking three representatives from each group: three trade unionists, three showbiz stars, three ambassadors and so on. Instead of seeing the familiar faces from their usual social circuit, most of the guests enjoyed mixing with people from other spheres of life.

My wife at the time, Kerena Mond, and I attended the second – it turned out to be the last – of these parties during that summer. Our eclectic fellow guests included the then general secretary of Unison, Rodney Bickerstaff; Alan Rusbridger, the editor of the *Guardian*; the band M People (whose song 'Moving On Up' had been used as a New Labour campaign anthem) and the comedian Harry Enfield. Everyone seemed to interact happily, although the trade unionists remarked that they were simply pleased to be allowed back into the building after eighteen years of having the door closed to them. Tony and Cherie Blair claimed that they were far more interested in meeting the spouses than the 'names'.

The presence of celebrities led to more media interest than Downing Street receptions usually elicited. Extensive coverage was given to colourful remarks reportedly made to the prime minister by Noel Gallagher and Enfield. There was much argument about who was invited, and few would-be guests appeared to understand the principle of working through a list. The Cool Britannia parties became more trouble than they were worth and Blair reverted to royal-style, safe receptions for categories of guests.

2 MAY

Ten years on, such fripperies were far from the minds of the Labour Party leadership and those members of the Blair team who were still by his side. In 2007 2 May was given over to apprehension. It was the eve of the elections to the Scottish Parliament, Welsh Assembly and many English councils. It was also, potentially, the eve of the day when Tony Blair would finally have to set in train his departure from office. He had insisted that he would clarify his plans 'next week' and his staff officially denied that he would have anything to say immediately after the results were known, but there was still the possibility that a cataclysmic performance by Labour would force the decisive resignation of a party leader who was already on the way out.

For anything other than an unexpected victory, Tony Blair was lined up to take the blame. His resignation announcement could not come too soon for some. Douglas Alexander, the Brown loyalist put in charge of the Scottish campaign, had even suggested that Blair should step down in April in the midst of the election battle, just days before polling, as a way of boosting the Labour vote. At least for the time being though, Blair was still in power and had to take another session of Prime Minister's Questions.

Upon becoming prime minister he halved his obligatory attendances in Parliament by changing PMQs to a once-a-week event. By his own admission, he was interested in exercising power rather than discussing it. He seldom voted and came to the Commons mainly to make statements on his intentions rather than to debate policy. Number 10 Downing Street was his White House, his HQ, and he made sparing use of his prime ministerial suite in the Commons corridor behind the Speaker's Chair overlooking New Palace Yard. It was convenient for some private meetings away from the television cameras and especially for seeing MPs quickly without palaver, while flattering them that the mountain had come to Mohammed. Even so, Blair was a very effective Commons performer – witty and quick to grasp an argument.

The Prime Minister's Questions he now faced in the week of his tenth anniversary in power turned out not to be as awkward for him as Labour's expected rout in the Scottish poll suggested they could have been. The main opposition leaders, Cameron and Campbell, also had a problem because the big winner on Thursday night was likely to be neither the Conservative nor the Liberal Democrat parties but a foe they shared with Blair – Alex Salmond, the leader of the Scottish National Party. In these circumstances, neither of Blair's main opponents was bold enough to use his time during PMQs for open electioneering. Instead, both Cameron and Campbell reached for the single greatest controversy of Blair's ten years – Britain's involvement in the Iraq War.

The Tory leader began by asking for a public inquiry into the big news story of the week so far – the conviction of five British-born men for planning terrorist attacks, following the police investigation codenamed 'Operation Crevice'. Cameron's mention of 'intelligence failures' slyly echoed the controversies which followed the Iraq invasion in 2003 – but he did no further damage. The Liberal Democrat leader was more blunt, picking up on an interview by the former secretary of state for defence, Geoff Hoon (who was moving rapidly into the Brown camp and would be rewarded by the new prime minister with a return to the cabinet as chief whip). Campbell wanted to know who would take responsibility for 'serious errors in the planning for post-war Iraq'. He answered his own question: 'The president made the decisions, the prime minister argued the case, the chancellor signed the cheques and the Tories voted it through.'

Blair was untroubled by either assault, although his explanations for Iraq did not cite the alleged threat of 'Weapons of Mass Destruction', his legal *casus belli* at the time of the invasion. Instead, he explained: 'the reasons why things are so difficult and challenging in Iraq is that we have al-Qaeda on the one hand – an outside terror organisation committing appalling acts of carnage . . . – and Iranian-backed Shi'a extremists on the other . . . I believe that our job is to stand up against terrorism.'

Gordon Brown was not in the chamber to celebrate Blair's decade in power. The chancellor was attending to European business in Brussels before flying directly on to Scotland to campaign.

Two Commons heavyweights, however, Dennis Skinner and Ian Paisley, came in behind the prime minister with helpful questions. Both men were well known for their fierce independence but both had eventually been recruited into Blair's big tent. By now Paisley was less than a week away from becoming first minister of Northern Ireland – a present neither giver nor receiver had expected to be handed over nine years previously when Paisley's DUP boycotted the Good Friday negotiations. His question was to ask Blair to support the European Union bounty heading in Northern Ireland's direction. This was not a difficult task for the prime minister. As for the left-wing ex-miner Skinner, the 'Beast of Bolsover' had been surprisingly cuddly towards his middle-class leader throughout Blair's tenure. Some accused Skinner of having gone soft with age and serious illness, but his reply to his detractors was succinct. He argued that the Labour government had delivered under Blair's leadership on the basic issues such as schools and hospitals: if his own excellent treatment under the NHS was part of that delivery then so what? Skinner's 'question' didn't really seek an answer; it was more an opportunity to bring up the single biggest failure of the last Conservative government and to remind the television audience that David Cameron had been Chancellor Norman Lamont's special adviser at the time of the Black Wednesday economic disaster in 1992. The ever-reliable David Blunkett simply offered congratulations to Blair on 'his tremendous vision and leadership'.

Rising again from the opposition front bench following this unabashed praise, Cameron struggled to unsettle Blair by citing his endorsement of Brown the day before: 'He has told us who is going to wear the crown; can he tell us who wielded the knife?' All he got back was a litany of Blair and Brown achievements: 'economic stability through the independence of the Bank of England; record investment in public services; better maternity leave and maternity pay; more support for pensioners; the repeal of Section 28; a ban on tobacco advertising; and, of course, the minimum wage. What do they have in common? The right hon. Gentleman's party voted against them.' Blair had managed to put tribute to his ten years firmly on the record: *Hansard*, the official account of British parliamentary proceedings, would record for posterity Blair's own version of his achievements.

2

DEVOLUTION

3 MAY

*. . . there are two kinds of people in politics: those who stand aside
and commentate and those who get their hands dirty and do.*

Tony Blair, Belfast, 8 May 2007

London and Livingstone

Since there were no local elections in London on 3 May 2007,
Tony Blair did not participate as a voter in the last British election
of his premiership. As prime minister his practice was to vote for
himself in his Sedgefield constituency in general elections and to
vote in London, as a council-tax payer, in the council and mayoral
elections. But on a day when 'election purdah' dictated relatively
little party political activity, the London media provided the best
Blair story, exposing in the process one of the least attractive aspects
of the Blair operation.

Editions of the *Evening Standard* splashed with the front-page
headline 'BLAIR QUITS TO MAKE MILLIONS', elaborating on an earlier
News of the World report that Blair would give up his seat in Parliament
as soon as he stepped down as prime minister and start making
money. The idea had also been foreshadowed in Ben Wegg-Prosser's

'triumph of Blairism' memo, which spoke of the need for 'careful' handling of Blair's departure as an MP from his constituency in County Durham.

Of course all this speculation had the merit of turning out to be true. On 27 June Blair confirmed that he had applied for the Chiltern Hundreds thus disbarring himself from being an MP. Up until that point both Blair and his spokespeople denied both that he would step down as an MP and that he would become the Middle East envoy for the Quartet (UN, EU, US and Russia) – the reason subsequently given for his resignation. Blair himself explicitly told me that it was his intention to serve on as an MP when I asked him about it at a news conference following the *News of the World* report.

So why weren't they straight about leaving Westminster? The job of MP is not bonded labour and many honourable members have stood down mid-term. Blair's disingenuousness had two explanations beyond an all-too-frequent default *modus operandi*. Firstly, he did not want to spark an extended and potentially politically dangerous by-election campaign in Sedgefield. Secondly, he was breaking with the precedent of other departing prime ministers.

Margaret Thatcher had served as an MP to the end of the full session after she was deposed in 1990; so had Harold Wilson after his resignation in 1976. Jim Callaghan and John Major both continued to serve as MPs after losing office at a general election (Callaghan for two further terms, becoming the longest-serving member of the House in the process, and Major for a single term). Ted Heath stayed on as an MP for nearly three decades after 1974, eventually becoming Father of the House.

But not Tony Blair. He left Parliament for good the day he ceased to be national leader. Of course this very much underlined the presidential style of his premiership, and as he admitted himself at his final appearance in the chamber, he had never relished parliamentary scrutiny – generally preferring statements, in which he faced only brief questions, to the full ordeal of a debate.

For Blair, the purpose of politics was the acquisition and exercise of political power. He frequently conceded that he had not enjoyed being leader of the opposition because it was 'about saying not doing'. On the day he became prime minister he recast these words: 'Enough of talking. It is the time to do.' And once inside Number 10, he stated that, like Thatcher, he did not intend to waste time holding lengthy cabinet discussions. Blair seldom enjoyed argument, unless convinced that he was demonstrably and absolutely right – as in his dealings with 'old' Labour and the trade unions. No respecter of traditions, the public school boy rebel never enjoyed the formalities of parliamentary debate – although, ever the barrister, he could wield them very efficiently to his advantage. For such a man, once he resigned as prime minister there was little point in remaining as an MP, however much he flattered those he left behind that their calling was 'noble'.

The status of 'political civilian' also freed Blair up from the obligations of disclosure of interests laid on both MPs and peers, obligations which the successive Blair governments themselves had made considerably more onerous. The desire to replenish family funds as private citizens was certainly one factor in the distaste both John Major and Ted Heath expressed for becoming members of the House of Lords. There is little doubt that both men were the record out-of-office earners amongst post-Second World War prime ministers.

Blair also expressed the view that he couldn't see himself joining the Lords in spite of his enthusiasm for sending others to the Upper House. He did not take up any lucrative new employment immediately on leaving office. But he had already burdened himself with the expenses of his new Connaught Square home and adjoining mews house, and a five-person office whose running costs would far exceed the allowances made to ex-prime ministers, (by spring 2008 Blair's staff had swollen to more than twenty). The job of Middle East envoy did not pay a salary, although considerable funds for travel, staff and office expenses were provided. The ex-prime minister even declined a fee for speaking at a media conference in Idaho attended by Rupert Murdoch and other moguls.

None of this was on Blair's agenda in the first week of May. As party leader his task was to support Labour's council election candidates so he found himself on breakfast television saying that it was a bad idea for local councils to move from weekly to fortnightly refuse collections. Fortuitously the mayor of London, Ken Livingstone, chimed in with agreement. Livingstone had chosen the seventh anniversary of his victory to announce that he would indeed stand for re-election in a year's time for a consecutive third term (despite originally stating in 1998 that he would serve for only one). Given the long history of difficult relations between them, Blair probably wasn't too bothered that he would have to delay the pleasure of voting for Livingstone – if he so chose – until May 2008.

As the last leader of the Greater London Council before Margaret Thatcher abolished it, Livingstone had obvious qualifications to run as Labour candidate in the first mayoral contest in 2000. But having secured a London referendum vote for a mayor, the Blair team had devoted much of his first term to trying to ensure that Livingstone would not be elected, even though he was a Labour MP at the time. This was because Livingstone had been an outspoken opponent of New Labour. (In spring 2008 he was caught on camera boasting that his proudest moment had been 'taking on and smashing the New Labour machine in 2000 . . . and just grinding them into the dust'. He later claimed his comments had been an April Fool joke.) As a member of the Campaign Group, Livingstone frequently rebelled against the Labour whip. He also had a particular antipathy towards Blair and most of his team. 'John Smith used to talk to me. He was always polite but Blair just ignores me, pretends I don't exist,' he once complained to me.

In 1996, two years after Blair became leader of the opposition, Livingstone published a pseudonymous attack on him in the left-wing magazine *Tribune* in which he predicted that Blair would be ousted in favour of Robin Cook. In the article Livingstone claimed Blair was out of touch with his party, his shadow cabinet and the trade unions – citing as one reason for the disenchantment the leader's decision to send his son to a voluntary-aided Catholic comprehensive. Blair was highly sensitive to any mention, let alone criticism, of his children. But it was typical of Livingstone to devote as much effort to personal vituperation as to political argument. He had a fondness for exaggerated statements and *ad hominem* attacks.

Or as he put it himself when making a comparison with Blair: 'He does not like the everyday venalities of politics and I do.'

(Shortly after Rupert Murdoch established Sky News in 1989 and I became its political editor, I tried to interview Livingstone. 'Oh, you've joined the Nazis,' he sneered. He boycotted our channel for some weeks after that but it didn't last long. As a Londoner born while memories of the Blitz were fresh, Livingstone was particularly fond of Second World War imagery. I was not surprised some years later when Mayor Livingstone was reprimanded for likening an *Evening Standard* reporter, who was Jewish, to a concentration camp guard.)

In the run-up to the 2000 contest, Blair's dependable director of government relations, Anji Hunter, was just about the only member of the Number 10 inner circle who had retained links to Livingstone. Blair flatly refused to endorse him, declaring he would be 'a disaster for London'. Blair had not been outspoken when he was a tyro politician but now he recalled bitter memories from the seventies and eighties to justify his opposition to Livingstone: 'My problem with him is that while I was growing up in the Labour Party, and he and Arthur Scargill and Tony Benn were in control of the Labour Party, they almost knocked it over a cliff into extinction.'

Labour had no obvious candidate to run instead, but every trick and manipulation was deployed to stop Livingstone. A little-known London MP and junior minister, Nick Raynsford put himself up. I asked him if he would withdraw should Frank Dobson, the former health secretary, stand. Raynsford flatly denied it. Within days campaign manager Raynsford opened Dobson's launch news conference with the words, 'Everyone always knew I would back Frank if he stood.'

Dobson, who had given up his cabinet seat with reluctance, was no match for Livingstone. And, although he had a long record of service as a London councillor and MP, he was somewhat hampered by having a distinctive Yorkshire accent. Livingstone saw his opportunity and announced that he would stand as an independent. He was expelled from the Labour Party, but was elected London mayor with ease.

This was the first sign of an unforeseen consequence of the devolved elections Blair was introducing: voters tended to favour colourful personalities over machine politicians. The former police chief Ray 'Robocop' Mallon would become directly elected mayor in Middlesbrough on the same night that H'Angus the Monkey, aka Stuart Drummond, the mascot for the local football club, took power in Hartlepool. Although they were not directly elected, the same impetus helped drive Rhodri Morgan, Alex Salmond, Ian Paisley and Martin McGuinness to the top in their national elections.

Livingstone did not turn out to be a disaster for London. By the end of his first term he was near certain of re-election. Blair buckled. 'Predictions have not turned out to be correct,' he said paraphrasing Keynes. 'I think if the facts change you should be big enough to change your mind.' Even so, deploying a formula he would later adapt to John 'Thumper' Prescott, Blair confided that 'Ken being Ken', he didn't expect future relations would always run smoothly.

In January 2004, four months before the London election, Labour's National Executive Committee voted to readmit Livingstone to the party before he had served the customary five-year exclusion period. The only votes against came from Michael Cashman, an *EastEnders* star turned modernising MEP, and Dennis Skinner, the outspoken left-wing MP for Bolsover, who had never liked Livingstone and felt he was being given preferential treatment compared to other Labour expellees.

In Livingstone's second term, the Labour prime minister and the Labour mayor could at last work together openly. Even though Livingstone still made it clear that his preference was for Gordon Brown (a remarkable endorsement given the fierce disagreement he had had with the chancellor over the financing of the London Underground). Livingstone and Blair's greatest joint success was London's bid to host the 2012 Olympic Games – even if future taxpayers do not come to see it that way.

In July 2005, on the eve of hosting the G8 summit at Gleneagles, Blair flew a twenty-eight-hour round trip to Singapore to spend thirty-six hours lobbying for Britain as the International Olympic Committee met to make their final decision. Mayor Livingstone had already arrived, but this was one New Labour spin operation to which he did not object. The London bid's style was familiar to me as a seasoned Blair-watcher, but it was very different from the efforts mounted by Madrid, Paris, New York and Moscow. Unlike President Chirac, who arrived bombastically to take part in the final French presentation, the British politicians – Blair, Livingstone and Culture Secretary Tessa Jowell – stayed in the background.

The main British presentation was left to Sebastian Coe, the former Olympic gold medallist and ennobled Conservative politician. He in turn shared frontline duties with a number of other prominent sports stars including David Beckham and Sir Steve Redgrave – just as New Labour presentations were often sprinkled with big names from outside politics. But the democratisation did not end there. If in doubt, Blair was prone to make public appearances surrounded by a group of photogenic and ethnically diverse children – London's Olympic bid followed exactly that pattern, giving great prominence to a score of young athletes of the future. This theme was picked out in the London presentation video which began, not with shots of the City's gleaming glass towers, but with poor children in Africa underlining the global and social inclusivity of the British approach.

Meanwhile, Blair was at his most charming and unassuming. He put himself at the disposal of the pack of self-important specialist hacks who are often influential in bureaucracies such as the Olympic organisation. Even more crucially, he spent a whole day privately meeting as many international delegates as he could in hotel rooms, one on one. Unlike most leaders, Blair lobbied wholeheartedly while cheerfully admitting that there was no certainty of success. 'I think we're in with a chance and I want to do all I can,' was all he would say both in public and in private. This was the same rare spirit – both optimistic and self-sacrificial – with which he had thrown himself into international diplomacy in Northern Ireland, after 9/11, and which he proposed to George Bush that he should adopt in the Middle East during their 'Yo Blair' conversation.

For the 2012 Olympics bid it worked. Inevitably there were allegations that skulduggery and stupidity by members of the Olympic Committee delivered the vote to London by a fluke. That was not how it felt in Singapore. What seemed like an irresistible momentum had built up behind London's bid in the few hours following Blair's arrival. Against typecasting, the mayor of London had been the straight man. There is no doubt that his commitment to put the pockets of London council-tax payers at the disposal of the Olympics, coupled with guaranteed lottery funds, gave the British bid a financial solidity which no other city was able to match. The Olympic success created a bond between Blair and Livingstone; they now had something nice to say about each other whenever they had to.

As he later recalled, Blair flew back to the G8 in Scotland in triumphant spirits – only to have them dashed, along with the excitement of all Londoners, the very next morning, 7 July, by the bus and Tube bombers.

Livingstone continued to make use of the New Labour spin machine as its practitioners moved out into the private sector. The mayor of London's loyal in-house director of communications was Joy Johnson, a former TV producer, who quit the Labour Party press office shortly after Blair and Campbell took over because she was too out of step with the centrist drift. But as his out-of-house PR consultancy, Livingstone retained Freud Communications, the most Blairite agency. His Freud account executive was Kate Garvey who had also worked as 'events organiser' for Blair until 2006. A typical Freud stunt was to publicise Livingstone's extensive trip to India by floating a giant model of the Taj Mahal down the Thames and past Parliament.

In May 2007, his announcement of a bid for a third term offered Livingstone a platform to give his considered verdict on the outgoing prime minister. 'One of the biggest successes is bringing peace to Northern Ireland,' the now very experienced office-holding politician ventured, 'the most catastrophic error is the war in Iraq. It has, in a sense, created a whole new generation of terrorists.'

As Labour leader, Blair had set out to bury Livingstone. He had not bargained on the cheeky chappie being mayor of London, comfortably placed to give Blair the last rites.

4 MAY

Results

Tony Blair didn't bother to stay up for the results of the local elections. Not least because the Scottish outcome would not become clear until Friday afternoon thanks to the two simultaneous elections being held there (for councils and Parliament), the complicated voting system, and the untried automated counting machines.

The results were as bad as expected, although not as bad as Labour spin doctors had suggested they would be in a classic attempt to lower expectations so that the real result could be presented as some kind of success. In Scotland the Labour Party failed to top the poll for the first time since 1959; in Wales it had its lowest share of the vote for almost ninety years; and in England Labour ended up with fewer councillors and councils under its control than at any time since the early 1970s.

According to an authoritative analysis carried out by the Local Government Elections Unit for the *Sunday Times*, the outcome could be extrapolated into a general election result giving the Conservatives 40 per cent (+1 per cent on 2006 local elections), Labour 26 per cent (no change) and the LibDems 24 per cent (-2 per cent). In the Westminster Parliament such a result would have put David Cameron and the Tories in power with a majority of fifty-four seats. The Conservatives exceeded even their own expectations in terms of council seat gains (almost 900) and made a modest advance at the constituency level in both Scotland and Wales.

David Cameron boasted of gains in the North where his party had last performed well during the Tories' national hegemony under Margaret Thatcher and John Major – in such places as Blackpool, Chester and South Ribble. Equally, Labour fell back in towns such as Brighton and Hove, southern parts that it had seemed only Tony Blair could reach for them. Labour lost around 550 councillors, a fifth of its total strength. In the English shires the casualty rate rose to about one in three. There were now more than ninety councils with not a single Labour member sitting on them – a massive erosion to the local power base built up during the party's resurgence in the 1990s.

For the second time in a week, Tony Blair went to Labour's London HQ to give his reaction in another tightly controlled 'pool' interview. In this instance only a BBC crew and reporter James Landale were invited to Victoria Street.

The Blair team had already slackened the tension by making it clear in advance (during his GMTV appearance on Tuesday) that the prime minister would not be confirming his departure timetable. Instead Blair asserted boldly that the election results provided a 'perfectly good springboard to win the next general election'.

On the face of it this was a laughable claim and Blair was duly mocked by his many critics within and outside the Labour Party. But as so often during his leadership, there were some tactically astute calculations behind the bravado. As he was to remind Cameron at the subsequent PMQs, 'it's the general election that matters'. His comments projected forward to the next, genuinely pivotal, moment in British politics. They implicitly placed this year's exceptionally poor result in the long list of false dawns when opposition parties have prospered in mid-term contests but failed to cash in on the success at the following general election.

Blair's comments were also analytically astute. The Conservative performance by no means guaranteed that Cameron would follow Brown through the door of Number 10. The Tories had only just hit the critical 40 per cent mark – seen as the minimum share of the national vote likely to be needed to win an overall majority in the House of Commons. This was far short of Labour's performance prior to Blair's election. Labour took 47 per cent of the local vote in 1995 and 44 per cent in 1996. The electoral bias also favours Labour because its support is more evenly distributed across the nation than that of the Conservatives. In these local elections Cameron had succeeded in obtaining the sort of lead (14 per cent) required for an overall Conservative majority, but once again the Tories had failed to make inroads in the symbolically important northern metropolises of Manchester, Liverpool and Newcastle.

Hardly a 'springboard' therefore, but it did not require a leap of faith to envision Labour recovering from these mid-term blues, especially after changing its unpopular leader. Subsequent opinion polls during the summer of 2007 gave Blair's analysis at least some credibility.

Scotland

The result from north of the border was more serious. New Labour had brought the Holyrood Parliament into existence; now it had lost the third election held to fill it, overtaken by its most hated rival in Scotland, the SNP. The Scottish Nationalist leader, Alex Salmond, had done all he could to make the Scottish election personal to Blair. As the results came in Salmond deployed characteristic matter-of-fact verbal brutality and pointedly remoulded one of Blair's most famous sayings. 'New politics is dawning in Scotland,' he gloated.

Like most other Scots, Salmond regarded Blair as a renegade Scotsman. But Blair had never embraced this allegiance. Even though he was born in Scotland and educated at Fettes College in Edinburgh, he always insisted that he was English because of his parentage. This was precisely the opposite tack from that taken by his friend and former aide Alastair Campbell. Campbell was born and raised in England, but declared himself Scottish, even playing the bagpipes, wearing kilts and calling his sons Callum and Rory. When asked who they supported in football and rugby home internationals, Blair backed England while Campbell plumped for Scotland (probably because this annoyed his friends).

Anthony Charles Lynton Blair was born in Edinburgh on 6 May 1953, but neither of his parents, Leo and Hazel, claimed to be Scottish. Hazel Corscadden came from Protestant Irish stock; Leo had grown up in a Glasgow tenement but his natural parents were English. They were itinerant music-hall entertainers: Charles Leonard Augustus Parsons, stage name Jimmy Lynton, and Mary Augusta Ridgway Wilson, stage name Celia Ridgway. The unmarried partners gave Leo up for adoption by a Scottish couple, James and Mary Blair. Parsons and Wilson later married but Mary Blair refused to give up Leo or to let him have contact with them. So Leo Blair was raised by working-class Scottish communists on 'Red Clydeside', rather than by middle-class English actors – his natural mother's family were Sussex landowners.

Leo kept his adoptive surname and passed it on to his children but gave his second son middle names drawn from his father – his first name and his stage surname. Tony Blair knew his adoptive grandmother (she died just after he graduated from Oxford), but his instinct for avoiding trouble meant that he mostly steered clear of his ancestry. It was easy to see why. Shortly after he became Labour leader, his background seemed to offer irresistible copy to inquisitive reporters and Leo was eventually reunited with Pauline, an unknown half-sister. Blair did not want to follow John Major in being characterised by his colourful music-hall backstory, even if Leo Abse and other psychological profilers inevitably speculated on where his acting talent came from.

Blair's rare attempts to exploit his Scottish roots fared poorly. There was a major flare-up with the Scottish media during one campaigning visit when a radio phone-in revealed that Blair didn't know that 'scheme' was the Scots expression for 'council estate'. Alastair Campbell retaliated by branding the local media 'unreconstructed wankers'. 'Unreconstructed' because the Scottish political press corps had not adopted New Labour's reform agenda.

In January 2006, Blair went to Glasgow as part of his 'Respect' campaign against anti-social behaviour. The prime minister hosed off some graffiti and compared the present day unfavourably with the moral standards of the past. 'If you go back to my parents' generation, my father growing up in Glasgow in a poor community,' Blair opined, 'he didn't have as much money as we have, he didn't have the same opportunities, he didn't have travel or communications, but people behaved more respectfully to one another and people are trying to get back to that and most people want it.' The words were scarcely out of his mouth before local old codgers emerged to declare that Blair didn't know what he was talking about. They claimed that, far from fostering a sense of community, the dingy streets of Glasgow in those days witnessed sectarian punch-ups between Protestants and Catholics, and that Mary Blair was just the type of woman to daub the walls with left-wing slogans (similar to the graffiti her adoptive grandson was now trying to expunge).

Like son, like father. Leo moved away from his adoptive Glasgow roots as soon as he grew up. No Communist Party for him; he became an active Conservative. When Tony was only two, Leo, Hazel and their two sons left their modest, genteel bungalow in the Edinburgh suburb of Newington for Australia and then County Durham. As an adult Tony Blair was much happier to bring up these two territorial associations. Australia was the inspiration for his tendentious and unsuccessful campaign to 'rebrand Britain' as 'a young country'. Durham Cathedral Choir School allowed him to claim personal ties with nearby Sedgefield, his future parliamentary constituency.

In 1966 Blair returned to Scotland at the age of thirteen for a five-year stint as a boarder at Fettes public school, though this was more a continuation of his journey into the English upper-middle class than a rekindling of Scottish identity. Precise location mattered little in the softly spoken network of Britain's privately educated elite which Blair was now joining.

Fettes may have been located in Scotland, but its ethos was not exclusively Scottish. Some of its old boys, such as Blair's lifelong friend Nick Ryden, stayed north of the border, but many others followed Blair's path. Unlike its rival Scottish public schools Glenalmond and Loretto, Fettes did not favour bagpipes and tartan. In the New Labour government old boys from those establishments – Charlie Falconer from Glenalmond and Alistair Darling from Loretto – had distinct Scottish identities and accents, but at the age of thirteen Tony Blair was already beginning his journey south.

In practice, Fettes gave Blair the keys to university at Oxford, professional training in the London Inns of Court and an English seat in the Westminster Parliament. This was clearly demonstrated in the contrasting life stories of Blair and the man who would succeed him as prime minister. Tony Blair and Gordon Brown were born less than a hundred miles from each other, but their lives and identities diverged radically. Brown grew up in Scotland with two Scottish parents; he went to local schools, followed by Edinburgh University; worked as a journalist in Scottish television and had always represented a Scottish seat. Brown was Scottish; Blair passed for English in an understated sort of way.

Blair seemed to know instinctively that his scope for operation would be less confined if he identified with the – English – majority rather than with the – Scottish – minority. His personal ambivalence towards Scotland was reflected in his political approach to Wales, Scotland and Northern Ireland. Blair was never a passionate devolutionist, but, in a slightly aloof, disinterested sort of way, he saw no reason why 'they' shouldn't forge individual political identities if they wanted to. Scottish devolution was part of the unfinished agenda Tony Blair had inherited from John Smith. In honouring it Blair also brought to it his own independent analysis. Firstly, devolution would go ahead only by consent; referendums would be fought and won in the place to be devolved. Secondly, devolution would be symmetrical: a version of what was on offer to Scotland would be offered to Wales, Northern Ireland and even English cities and regions.

The Scottish Labour hierarchy, including Gordon Brown, did not see things from the same perspective, even though they had mostly come round to devolution. To them Scotland was a special case. They considered that Blair was behaving rather cavalierly towards what was a national power base. In the 1997 landslide Labour had taken fifty-six out of a total of seventy-two seats in Scotland. Blair approached the referendum campaigns and the elections which followed with typical gusto, but he did not have a sustained interest in Scottish affairs, as was shown by his casual approach to the post of Scottish secretary and by his failure to pressure any of the many talented Labour politicians at Westminster to transfer to Holyrood – with the exception of the unfortunate Donald Dewar.

In both Scotland and Wales, Blair's impatience with local sensitivities led him to attempt hastily to impose reforming Labour leaders in his own image. But he was unsuccessful. In Scotland, Donald Dewar died in harness; Henry McLeish fell in a petty expenses scandal, and in any case neither he nor his successor, Jack McConnell, had sufficient stature to be credible. From Blair's point of view Wales was an equally sorry story. Ron Davies succumbed to scandal (a rather juicier one than McLeish's); and the decent Alun Michael could hardly bring himself to carry out a job he didn't believe in. His successor, the left-wing intellectual Rhodri Morgan, was popular but hardly to Blair's taste.

Blair found Wales an irritant, not least because it almost upset his plans for symmetrical devolution. Wales's referendum was agonisingly close, provoking him to exclaim 'Fucking Welsh' as the results came in, according to *The Spin Doctor's Diary*, the book published in 2005 by Lance Price, who was a Downing Street press officer at the time. Amazingly, the publication of Price's book prompted an official Welsh Police inquiry into allegations of anti-Welsh racism by the prime minister. This came to an end only when Chief of Staff Jonathan Powell informed the police that he had no recollection of Blair ever having made such a remark.

Blair's consuming mission was to expand Labour Party support into areas it had never reached before, such as the prosperous middle ground, often referred to as Middle England. The danger was that the Labour heartlands might be left feeling neglected, or even shunned.

Scottish Labour adopted a sniffy attitude to 'New' Labour from the outset. It saw little need for reform of the public services in a country heavily dependent on them, both as services and for employment. There are well-rehearsed arguments about who subsidises whom, but the fact remains that, per capita, expenditure from the Exchequer is higher for the Scots and Welsh than it is for the English. Not surprisingly, at home the Scots had more faith in social solidarity, believing that the state and public authorities should play a significant role in shaping the lives of citizens.

Why change? Labour had dominated Scottish elections since the 1940s. For fifty years Scotland had never given the Conservatives a majority and so, it was claimed, it had never elected Margaret Thatcher, believing – unlike her – that there was 'such a thing as society'. In return, right-wingers sneered that Scotland was prey to welfarism because all enterprising Scots left their homeland to seek their fortunes elsewhere. Tony Blair was often seen simply as one such 'Scotsman on the make', in J. M. Barrie's phrase.

In practice the Scottish elections were a test for the UK's two most prominent Scots-born politicians: Tony Blair and Gordon Brown. But by definition Scottish elections were for Scottish politicians, fought by local candidates under local leaderships. Westminster politicians had to lurk in the background.

Had Blair not already agreed to step down by September 2007, his attitude might have been different since he would have had more to lose. As it was, he took an early decision to cede the running of the campaign to the Brownites, deferring to their strategy. Jack McConnell – once a Blairite 'fixer', now first minister and leader of the Scottish Labour Party – was nominally in charge, with the assistance of John McTernan, Blair's political secretary, who was loaned from Number 10. But the real control rested with the Brown camp (McTernan had a foot in both camps). The campaign chairman was Douglas Alexander, secretary of state for Scotland (and transport) – a long-time Brown devotee. Alexander's sister, Wendy, was deputy party leader (in Scotland). Alexander was supported by two other Scottish-based cabinet ministers, Alistair Darling and Des Browne, who were both due for promotion under the expected incoming leader.

Tony Blair did not wish to stand accused of turning his back on the supersensitive Scottish Labour Party. He campaigned vigorously in Scotland during the early months of 2007. But he was barely welcome. There were many who felt that his presence, or even any reminder of his existence, would be counter-productive in the effort to win votes. Other Blairite ministers with Scottish links, such as Tessa Jowell and Charlie Falconer, also hit the campaign trail, while carefully liaising with Alexander.

However, their obedient efforts did not stop Alexander from blaming Blair's unpopularity for Scottish Labour's poor performance in the pre-election opinion polls. In desperation, or possibly Brownite self-interest, he even suggested that Blair should bring forward his retirement date to before the Scots voted on 3 May. Blair ignored the suggestion. In truth it was difficult to argue that the Scottish campaign had been a referendum on Blairism because it was the very devolutionary reforms which his government had brought in that enabled Scotland to deviate from his model for the rest of Britain. During most of his administration Scotland had had its own leadership, a Labour–LibDem coalition since 2000, which pursued policies different from his own, notably on university fees and long-term care for the elderly.

So when the election went wrong in Scotland, Blair did not dwell on the poor result. He had done what was asked of him and deferred to Brown – now he could shrug it off. His only bitterness was reserved for Alex Salmond. Blair simply ignored him. He refused to speak to the new first minister either in person or on the phone for his remaining two months in office. Salmond was probably the only member of the newly elected Holyrood Parliament with a UK-wide stature. He was a witty and skilful debater and an MP who had long dominated the nationalist faction at Westminster. But Blair was furious because Salmond had placed the allegations against Labour over the 'cash for peerages' scandal at the centre of his campaigning – even though it had no relevance to Scotland. The Metropolitan Police investigation had come about in response to a complaint from an SNP MP, Angus MacNeil.

Scotland had a nationalist minority government and was disenchanted with Labour, but that was now Brown's problem. After polling day Labour's hope was that the result somehow would not stand and that the Scottish electorate would be given the chance to come to its senses. Scottish Labour tried to pretend that it hadn't happened or at least that the election could be run again. It was argued that Labour had lost by only one seat (forty-seven SNP to forty-six Labour) and that this might easily be reversed in a rerun of the election. Labour consulted its lawyers.

Amidst comparisons with events in the state of Florida in 2000, there were some grounds for a recount. The election had been shockingly badly planned and conducted. Voters had been asked to cast their votes on a newly designed ballot paper, expressing preferences both for candidates and parties; they had also taken part in two elections, council and parliamentary, voting by crosses in one case and number ranking in the other. Then ballots had been counted by new, untested electronic machines. Not surprisingly there had been a record number of spoilt and disallowed ballot papers – a massive and unprecedented 140,000 in total, representing approximately 10 per cent of all the votes cast. In some constituencies discarded ballots far outnumbered the winning majority. There were tales of ballots being thrown out because they got soaked while being transferred by boat from islands; one hundred more votes were counted out in Arran than were counted in in Irvine and Labour's majority in Airdrie and Shotts was smaller than the number of discounted ballots. But Labour pinned its main hope on its painful loss in Cunninghame North, where the former junior minister Allan Wilson had been defeated by forty-eight votes, while some 1,000 or so had been disallowed.

Other parties, especially smaller ones which had lost seats, also complained that the election had been unfair. But it was far from clear which party would benefit from a full recount, were such a thing feasible, or even a rerun election. By the end of May Labour had dropped its legal case, suggesting instead that the matter would be best dealt with by the Electoral Commission. When its report came out it pointed the finger of blame back at Scottish Labour's two most senior politicians, Scottish Secretary Douglas Alexander and First Minister Jack McConnell, suggesting that they had attempted to manipulate the rules of the elections for party advantage. The commission concluded: 'The Scotland Office and the Scottish Executive were frequently focused on partisan political interests in carrying out their responsibilities, overlooking voter interests and operational realities within the electoral administration timetable.'

Labour's next hope (endorsed by their former coalition partners, the Liberal Democrats, who effectively ruled out working with the SNP) was that Salmond would fail to form a government or that any minority administration would collapse in its early months. Neither of these outcomes would have been as satisfactory, however, because the fixed-term constitution for Holyrood, put in place by Blair's government, allowed for a rerun of a botched election but provided for an early election outside the normal four-year cycle only if at least eighty-six MSPs demanded one.

In reality, Salmond formed a minority government and the SNP topped the opinion polls in Scotland for the rest of 2007. Douglas Alexander gave up his Scottish responsibilities when Gordon Brown promoted him to international development secretary, as well as putting him in charge of Labour's general election campaign. (He was one of the 'young turks' who tried to press Brown into a snap election in the autumn of 2007, with disastrous consequences for his leader. Brown drew back at the last moment and claimed, unconvincingly, that he had not been influenced by Labour's drop in the polls.) McConnell took leave of absence to concentrate on development interests in Africa. He was appointed British High Commissioner in Malawi from 2009. Douglas Alexander's sister, Wendy, took over as leader of Scottish Labour. In November 2007, she became mired in the maelstrom surrounding 'Donorgate' after admitting that her leadership campaign had unlawfully accepted a £950 donation from a non-UK resident. She resigned in June 2008 after being suspended for a day by Holyrood's Standards Committee.

None of these sorry events for Scottish Labour were of concern to Blair. (Although they had greater significance than is generally assumed in persuading Brown against an early general election.) Blair's legacy in the land of his birth was devolution. Despite this historic constitutional gift, Scotland and Scottish Labour had remained resolutely unBlairite. Tony Blair would not be defined by Scotland.

Northern Ireland was different.

8 MAY

Northern Ireland

The Good Friday Agreement of April 1998 was the high point of Tony Blair's first year in office, though he could never have reckoned that it would take so long to enact as to become also one of the climaxes of his last few months in power. As with almost every other step along the way, this final one came later than it should have done. But for once the delay was fortuitous and Blair embraced it as the prelude to pressing the button on his official departure timetable. The significant portion of his legacy that Northern Ireland would make up was emphasised by the fact that this was his last important constitutional act before he began to dissipate his powers.

Appropriately for an act of devolution, Blair and his Irish counterpart Bertie Ahern were technically no more than bystanders witnessing the ceremony which took place on 8 May at Stormont, Northern Ireland's imposing Parliament building, which stands high on a hill in a parkland estate on the outskirts of Belfast. True, they had created the conditions for devolution by changing the constitutional law in their two countries, but that work was long done and finished. The British cabinet minister Peter Hain had formally cleared the way for the re-establishment of devolution the day before.

The ceremony at Stormont was in fact the fourth attempt since 1998 to establish a viable devolved government. Blair and Ahern were there to attend the swearing in of an 'executive' comprising a first minister, a deputy first minister and ten departmental ministers. The intricate cross-meshing of the Belfast Agreement, the Good Friday Agreement's official title, ensured both that the two main unionist parties and the two main nationalist parties were represented in the executive and that neither side could govern without the consent of the other.

This was power-sharing by proportional representation, rather than the Protestant majoritarian government of the past, which had been one of the causes of the Troubles. The difference over the ten years was that on each side of the religious divide the more moderate constitutional party had been eclipsed by its hard-line rival. When the first attempt had been made to establish an executive in June 1998, David Trimble of the UUP was elected first minister and Seamus Mallon of the SDLP was deputy, but their power bases had shrunk in the two Assembly elections since then. By May 2007 their voting strength entitled the UUP to just two seats and the SDLP to a single one on the twelve-member executive. The DUP and Sinn Fein held all the rest.

To the amazement of practically everyone, and the disgust of quite a few, Northern Ireland's two leaders now were some of the Troubles' hardest men: First Minister Ian Paisley of the DUP, the one-time organiser of the Protestant workers' strike, famed for saying 'No' and 'Never', and Deputy First Minister Martin McGuinness, hero of Free Derry and generally considered to be an experienced terrorist and member of the IRA's Army Council.

As was so often the case in Northern Ireland, however, menace lurked in the background that morning and with the demonstrators representing those who had been bereaved by the violence of the Troubles outside the building. The ceremonial itself was an almost cosy affair with an emotional performance provided by The Sky's the Limit, a group of young people with Down's Syndrome. After Paisley and McGuinness had made their pledges of office in the Assembly chamber, the main official act for the top politicians was a cup of tea in the first minister's parlour. They had to perch on the furniture, but this homely Ulster tea ceremony avoided any awkwardness. The Reverend Doctor Paisley was a celebrated teetotaller. If the toasts had come any later in the day, some might have felt champagne, or some other manifestation of 'the Devil's Buttermilk', was called for. Amidst the smiles and tinkling cups, Paisley confined himself to a gentle dig at Blair, remarking that while he was over eighty and just beginning his time in office, the prime minister – a much younger man – would soon be stepping down.

Throughout his premiership Blair was seldom happier than with a cup or mug of tea – whether the one imprinted with a family photo he clutched the day he announced his son Leo's birth, or the embossed china brought in rather stagily to punctuate his press conferences. Anyone tasked with making the prime ministerial brew quickly learned to abide by the simple formula: milk, no sugar and as strong as possible.

Blair returned to the theme of tea when the leaders went downstairs to the Great Hall for the formal speeches, as he praised his indispensable political counterpart during the peace process, An Taoiseach: 'During the past decade relations between Britain and Ireland have been transformed . . . that in no small part has been due to Bertie Ahern. No other prime minister, I suspect, has shared as many cups of tea with me as we toiled through the long hours of negotiation, but Bertie has always been there – willing to surmount yet another obstacle.'

Blair's speech was an unembarrassed celebration of his personal credo that political power should be applied to difficult but achievable ends: 'Northern Ireland was felt synonymous with conflict. It was felt intractable. The Troubles. Not so much a dispute as a fact of life. Irreconcilable differences. People felt it could not be done; even sometimes that it should not be done – the compromises involved were too ugly. Yet, in the end, it was done.'

After the Belfast Agreement was secured in 1998 Blair had flown to the Middle East. Now he signalled again that he had not lost those ambitions for peace two months before he was to take up the post of the Quartet's Middle East envoy: 'This holds a lesson for conflict everywhere. To define the right political framework since only through politics can come peace that lasts.'

The speech was a virtuoso demonstration of the politician's art, as it congratulated the people for what the politicians had steered them into: 'The people of Northern Ireland have taken responsibility for the future. That is what the people voted for and that is what has happened.' He then dealt with the nub of the deal – equality and mutual respect before the law for the two communities, unionist and nationalist, Protestant and Catholic. And in a revealing glimpse of his own optimistic philosophy, he then equated fairness directly with the more mundane reason for ending the Troubles – the desire to restore normal life to the people of the province: 'Normal life, and normal politics, can seem a small ambition to anyone who has not lived through the abnormality of a society living daily on the edge.'

Blair did not miss the opportunity to schmooze the key politicians in Northern Ireland, but it was schmooze with insight: 'I recognise the leadership of Gerry Adams and Martin McGuinness. History has cast republicans and British prime ministers in two very different camps. Long ago I lost count of the times I was told they would not or could not commit to peace. But from the first meeting I had with them, I believed they were genuine.' I remembered speaking to the prime minister shortly after the first time he met with the Sinn Fein leadership in the autumn of 1997. He said then that he believed they had blood on their hands (in spite of their claims not to have been active members of the Provisional IRA) but that he also believed they were committed to finding a settlement even though it would fall short of their goal of a united socialist Ireland.

Adams and McGuinness had been in some way part of the official search for a solution in Northern Ireland ever since being invited to secret talks in the late Paul Channon's Cheyne Walk home by the Heath government. Ian Paisley was not seen as a peacemaker, although he had always condemned sectarian violence and was never directly linked to it. There seemed to be no room for compromise in his defence of 'the Protestant people of Northern Ireland'. Successive British prime ministers came to detest 'Dr No'. Until Blair. In spite of Paisley's refusal to take part in the Belfast Agreement, and his active attempts to wreck it, Blair built up a cordial relationship with the DUP leader. Paisley once loudly protested that Major had kicked him out of Number 10 without even allowing him to use 'the little room' to gather his thoughts. But Blair gave 'Mamie', Paisley's wife Eileen, a seat in the House of Lords and sent the couple a leather-bound photo album for their golden wedding anniversary (An Taoiseach also gave them an expensive gift).

Paisley's age and increasing frailty may have mellowed him. After his most serious illness he told reporters at the Leeds Castle talks in 2004 that he had 'just passed through the Valley of Death' and emerged wanting to make peace. In fact, he had also fallen victim to Blair's charm and tenacity. Perhaps this was because Blair respected, or at least entertained, Paisley as a man of faith, when other politicians regarded him simply as a religious bigot.

Unlike others, Blair respected Paisley's sincerity. His last winter holiday as prime minister had been spent at the Miami home of the former Bee Gee Robin Gibb. It had been far from ideal. On holiday Blair was careless of his surroundings and his choice of hosts – provided there was sun and seclusion. Gibb had sun but not seclusion: paparazzi, some of them in boats, could easily pry on to Gibb's beachfront lawn and terrace. Blair hid behind an improvised screen of potted plants, only to spend much of his time on the telephone to Ian Paisley. On Boxing Day 2006, the pair shared at least nine calls as Blair cajoled Paisley into a public meeting with Gerry Adams, the president of Sinn Fein. Although Adams chose not to join the executive himself, because of his pan-Irish image in contrast to McGuinness's strong local identity, a constructive encounter between the two party leaders was the essential prelude to setting up a successful initiative. The meeting – and press pictures of the two men sitting side by side at the apex of a diamond-shaped table – eventually took place on Monday, 26 March 2007, although the DUP exacted a price of further prevarication, delaying the establishment of the executive until May.

And on that sixty-second anniversary of VE Day, there was now no turning back for the new first minister, however grudging his speech. He stated that he believed Northern Ireland had come 'to a time of peace', a reference drawn from King Solomon in the Old Testament. And as usual for the preacher-politician, his words were shot through with biblical references from his very first breath: 'How true are the words of Holy Scripture, "We know not what a day may bring forth." If anyone had told me that I would be standing here today to take this office, I would have been totally unbelieving. I am here by the vote of the majority of our beloved province.' There was no direct reference from Paisley to his new partners, although McGuinness publicly sent his good wishes. Instead Paisley argued that Northern Ireland could have 'settled the matter' more quickly without outside interference. His most conciliatory words were also salutary, a tribute to 'Ulster's honoured and unageing dead – the innocent victims, that gallant band, members of both religions, Protestant and Roman Catholic . . .' Gerry Adams led the applause.

Blair and Ahern were centre stage at Stormont to soak up the congratulations, but for once many of the fathers of the Agreement were absent. It was a melancholy day rather than a triumph, a celebration perhaps for those who were taking office but for almost all other participants and onlookers a time to remember decades of frustration and grief with wary impatience. Most notably there was no role for John Hume and David Trimble, the two local politicians who won the Nobel Peace Prize for their contribution to the Agreement – both had been consumed by the revolution they had wrought. Trimble, now a Conservative member of the House of Lords, was absent altogether. His position as first minister and the pre-eminence of his Ulster Unionist Party had both been bitter sacrifices to the rise of Paisley and his one-time rejectionist DUP.

His fellow Nobel Laureate, John Hume, was reported to be one of the celebrants. If so he was an onlooker – I didn't see him. Without the rancour of Trimble, Hume had been willing to see the SDLP, a party he helped to create, largely superseded by Sinn Fein as the price of peace. There was no place at the top table either for Seamus Mallon, long-suffering deputy both to Hume within the SDLP and to Trimble as first minister.

Blair would accept no blame for the eclipse of the SDLP and Ulster Unionists. In his view it was their own fault. In the case of the nationalist party, Blair claimed he had repeatedly asked them to move into government without Sinn Fein but they always refused to do so. As for David Trimble, 'he simply refused to sell the deal'. Trimble himself argued that it was Blair who did not deliver on his handwritten note, going ahead with the full release of republican prisoners without tying it to the reciprocal decommissioning of arms by the IRA.

Bill Clinton sent his apologies and a message of goodwill. There would have been no peace had he and his successor George W. Bush not put a choke hold on the IRA. Absent too were the foreign statesmen who had made their contribution to ending the violence: former US Senator George Mitchell, first brought in by Major to explore decommissioning and then kept on by Blair to broker the talks; Canadian General John de Chastelain; Finnish troubleshooter Martti Ahtisaari; and South African ANC leader Cyril Ramaphosa, who managed and witnessed the weapons decommissioning process.

Former Taoiseach Albert Reynolds was amongst the VIPs but former prime minister John Major wasn't. Instead he uttered a typically mundane comment, which nonetheless captured the moment: 'I don't think the people of Northern Ireland have any appetite whatsoever to go back to the situation that was there before.' As Blair generously acknowledged in his speech at Stormont it had been during Major's time that 'we saw the first steps to peace'. And indeed John Major had devoted great energy to seeking a settlement, working closely with Albert Reynolds, a similarly low-key politician whom Major had got to know when they were both finance ministers. The previous generation of prime ministers, Margaret Thatcher and Garret

FitzGerald, had also helped to pave the way, with the Anglo-Irish Agreement. But even if they had been up for it, Thatcher never gave the impression that she wished to work in partnership with either FitzGerald or the prime minister with whom he alternated, Charles Haughey.

Britain's Conservative politicians were always conflicted over granting any form of self-government to the province; both Thatcher and Major were passionate defenders of 'the Union'. Until the Troubles of the 1970s the Conservative and Unionist Party had formally united the Tories with Ulster Protestants. All of which made it difficult for Major to develop a positive rationale for the pursuit of peace.

From the British mainland perspective Major appeared to be motivated as much by defeatism as by any high-minded principle. The IRA's mainland campaign against high-profile targets and plate-glass towers such as the Baltic Exchange was extremely damaging in economic terms. Just as Major was taking over from Margaret Thatcher in November 1990, the then Northern Ireland secretary, Peter Brooke, made a crucial concession to the nationalists, stating that Britain had no 'selfish, strategic or economic interest' in Northern Ireland. A few months earlier Brooke had declared that the IRA could not be defeated by military means; instead he proposed a ceasefire and talks.

And, as it turned out, Major's peacemaking efforts would be stymied, towards the end of his term by a pragmatic revival of the old Unionist alliance because of the prime minister's dependence on the votes of UUP MPs to maintain his parliamentary majority at Westminster. By that and by recurring republican violence. One Saturday afternoon in October 1993 I happened to be with Major at a Commonwealth conference in Cyprus, when he was given news of the Shankill Road bombing. He was visibly shaken, even asking me: 'What can I say?' This latest republican atrocity was the last thing John Major wanted to hear because weeks later the news broke that his government had opened back-channel negotiations directly with the IRA.

Major did not allow himself to be put off by the wave of tit-for-tat sectarian violence which the bombing provoked. Instead, in

December 1993 he and Albert Reynolds issued the 'Downing Street Declaration', in which Dublin matched London's expression of disinterest by accepting that a United Ireland could be achieved only on the basis of consent by the two populations, North and South. In other words Unionists had a veto so long as they could command a majority in the North.

In August 1994 Major got his reward: the Provisional IRA announced 'a complete cessation of military hostilities'. In October the Combined Loyalist Military Command also announced a ceasefire. But it proved impossible to reach an agreement on the decommissioning of IRA arms – their opponents' precondition for beginning talks. The IRA bombing of London's Docklands in February 1996 killed two people and ended John Major's ceasefire. And that June an IRA bomb destroyed much of Manchester's city centre.

Major's argument for seeking peace in Northern Ireland was heartfelt and typical of his moderate, almost suburban, view of politics. He was genuinely affronted that security constraints and sectarian strife meant that the people of Belfast, say, could not live ordinary lives like those in Birmingham, Brighton or Bromley. Tony Blair shared these sentiments as he explained on his last official visit to Stormont. But whereas Major's vision for Northern Ireland was passive, Blair had two strong interests, religion and devolution, much more consistent with an active stance to seeking a solution.

Unlike Major, Blair could argue that devolved government for Northern Ireland was of a piece with the devolution New Labour had already installed in Scotland, Wales and London. As far as the home nations went, the installation of the potentially stable Paisley–McGuinness-led executive was the final piece in the jigsaw. Where Major spoke as a citizen yearning for the people of Northern Ireland to share humdrum lives, Blair presented a related argument as a politician. He would tell the crowds repeatedly during his walkabouts at the time of the Good Friday Agreement that he wanted to come back and argue with them – but next time about schools and hospitals, as he did anywhere else in Britain.

Amongst modern British prime ministers Blair was unique in having a profound interest in and respect for religion. And he had ties to both sides of Ulster's sectarian divide. His grandfather on his mother's side had been an Orangeman and Blair spent childhood summers at Rossnowlagh in County Donegal. 'One of the things I felt very strongly was that there was a strong emotional pull on this because of my Irish background,' he told the *Ulster News Letter* whose new offices he opened on this last prime ministerial visit to Belfast in May 2007. 'I remember very vividly at the time that I stopped coming to Ireland for my holidays, specifically partly because of the Troubles.' But on the other side of what he called 'a very curious background', Blair also claimed links to the nationalist side: 'I married a Catholic who also had Irish blood in her too.' In fact Cherie came from Liverpool, the closest English city to Northern Ireland, and its most sectarian.

In essence, any lasting deal in Northern Ireland would depend on two interlocking agreements: agreement by both the Catholic and Protestant communities genuinely to share power with each other on a fair basis, and agreement by both sides to give up, or at least suspend, their core political goals – remaining an inalienable part of the UK on one side and a United Ireland on the other. This was a classic conundrum for a 'triangulator' (someone who uses the tactic of outmanoeuvring his opponents by incorporating their position first – used to great effect by the Clinton administration) such as Blair who had already made 'the Third Way' his guiding tenet. Neither side would get what they wanted. Both would feel pain. But both might just end up in a better place than they were to begin with. On Northern Ireland Blair was also lucky in having the friendship and support of the two other most important 'outside' politicians. President Bill Clinton, the triangulators' triangulator, who also claimed to hail from Ulster Protestant stock, and An Taoiseach Bertie Ahern, who was impatient to recalibrate along non-confrontational lines Ireland's vital relations with its nearest and most important neighbour.

Blair basically had no alternative but to act on Northern Ireland. Labour's policy had long had a green tinge. Before Blair its manifestos had advocated a United Ireland. As late as 1992 the party was still stating that 'in the long term, we want to see a united Ireland achieved by consensus and without violence'. This was a 'loony left' policy which Blair recognised as totally incompatible with the mainstream majority he was courting. In opposition, he had replaced the veteran republican Northern Ireland spokesman Kevin McNamara with the pragmatic moderniser Mo Mowlam.

In spite of Major's efforts, the Northern Ireland peace process was in tatters by the spring of 1997. The IRA ceasefire had broken down and England was again living with the threat of terrorist attack. In April, the month before Blair was elected, the Grand National was targeted and there were hoax bomb alerts on major motorways. But within three months of Blair becoming prime minister, the IRA restored its ceasefire on 20 July. In October Blair held his first meeting with the Sinn Fein leader Gerry Adams, who had just won back his seat as a Westminster MP.

Labour's 1997 election slogan, 'Things can only get better,' may have been aimed at cleansing the memory of eighteen Tory years, but nowhere was it more applicable than Northern Ireland. The Celtic mindset in general, and the Irish in particular, tended to view English politicians as arrogant and demanding and the tired, sceptical Northern Irish public was used to being governed by a series of patrician, aloof-seeming ministers and secretaries of state.

But Blair and Mowlam appeared different and cut across that. Rather than trying to play the two communities off against each other (with a default unionist position) they engaged both unionists and republicans at the same time.

To the wider community, Blair was that youngish guy who was changing Britain. They saw him as someone who genuinely seemed to care. When things went wrong they blamed their own politicians, seldom him. Mowlam's straight-talking style sat easily with the Ulster craic. She may have annoyed them at times, but they didn't think they were being talked down to. Mo Mowlam certainly had problems with unionist gentlemen who were inclined to take offence at any hint of vulgarity from a lady, be it removing her wig, swearing or making 'wanker' hand signals. But they also respected her courage, most notably the visit she paid to loyalist inmates inside the Maze prison in January 1998 to urge support for the negotiations.

In contrast to previous Conservative governments, the fresh Labour administration skilfully managed to balance gestures to one side with gestures to the other. In January 1998, for example, nationalists were granted a public inquiry into the shootings by British troops on Bloody Sunday in 1972.

All this political foreplay culminated in the second week of April. Politicians and media gathered at Government Buildings in Stormont, where the sides had been brought together for two days 'to do the deal', with the deadline set for 5 p.m. on Maundy Thursday. Government Buildings had none of the splendour of the other landmarks of the estate – the Parliament building and Stormont Castle, a former stately home. They were a humble cluster of mid-twentieth-century buildings in scrubby woods at the foot of Stormont Hill, which until recently had been used as Ministry of Agriculture laboratories and offices.

The whole complex was surrounded by a high chain-link fence, which added to the impression that the politicians were interned behind it. Most of them ended up spending at least a couple of nights sleeping in their makeshift offices. (One of Blair's favourite anecdotes from the talks tells of how he returned to his room for a few minutes' snooze only to find the Ulster Unionist MP Ken Maginnis in his bed. 'I'll do a lot for the peace process but I won't give my bed up to Ken Maginnis' was his punchline. He repeated this story to Martin Amis, one of the celebrity authors commissioned to cover the final days. Amis didn't get it. 'Is Ken Martin McGuinness's brother?' he asked to the delight of his colleagues and competitors in the business-class cabin. They were equally amused when Amis asked, 'What is this erm thing?' A reference to the ERM, the European Exchange Rate Mechanism.)

The media were outside, pressed right up against the fence. Our accommodation was more basic still: parked cars to sleep in (for those of us in the twenty-four-hour news business), portaloos and a wind swept and rain-battered marquee. From raised platforms live cameras pointed round the clock into the car park in front of Government Buildings.

Brinksmanship always played a big role in Northern Irish negotiations. The local delegations preferred to travel on foot in packs of as many supporters as possible. This was meant to be an often necessary demonstration of their solidarity. Such huddles marched up to the entrance of talks venues. Or came back from inside to brief the public, in neighbourly fashion, over the fence. On the first day of the Good Friday talks Martin McGuinness and Gerry Adams led a march round the grounds of Stormont, complete with banners and band, fetching up at the gates of Government Buildings. At strategic points over the following days the two Sinn Fein leaders went for walks in the car park – useful shots for the cameras and a sign that they were still engaged in the talks. Leaving, or not arriving with the others, were signals of discontent. The Ulster Unionist John Taylor didn't turn up with his delegation and announced that he 'wouldn't touch the agreement with a ten-foot barge pole'. He was later won back by the prime minister's handwritten pledges to Unionists. Taylor's UUP colleague, Jeffrey Donaldson, walked out and drove away around teatime on Thursday. I noted it as a sign of dissent, only to be subjected to vociferous lobbying on his behalf that he was simply tired and wanted to see his family. Donaldson was absent when the Agreement was signed and sometime later defected to Ian Paisley's DUP.

Ian Paisley's speciality was not going into meetings. During previous Anglo-Irish talks at Dublin Castle, I once watched him circle the compound, passing several entrances he could have used, until he found a suitably ominous portcullis through which, hands gripping the bars, he could bellow that the people of Ulster were being excluded while their futures were negotiated away. Paisley's party opposed and boycotted the talks in April 1998 but that didn't mean they stayed away. Paisley appeared several times to denounce what was going on and to claim airtime for his cause. One midnight he turned up with a particularly boisterous torch-lit parade. There was a moment of insight into his true nature when he batted away a question from a well-known local female journalist: 'Woman, know your place!' the reverend thundered. 'Why aren't you at home tending your family?'

There was no such abrasiveness in his inaugural speech as first minister, as he indulged his orotund reminiscences of those times:

I remember well the night the Belfast Agreement was signed. I was wrongfully arrested and locked up on the orders of the then secretary of state for Northern Ireland [Mo Mowlam, never his favourite minister]. It was only after the Assistant Chief of Police intervened that I was released. On my release I was kicked and cursed by certain loyalists who supported the Belfast Agreement. But that was yesterday, this is today and tomorrow is tomorrow.

The Good Friday negotiations were a rare moment of symbiosis between the politicians and the media. The various delegations often communicated with each other through the live reports which we were filing from the other side of the fence – almost all their offices were equipped with satellite and terrestrial TV.

The Troubles helped develop a cadre of reporters from north and south of the border of extraordinarily high quality. They were sensitive to every nuance and also had close and intimate professional relationships with the various political factions. Both local politicians and journalists were generously ready to share their thoughts with visiting reporters from national news networks such as myself. The advantages we had were twofold: a detachment which sometimes helped us distinguish the wood from the trees and a detailed knowledge of what made the Blair team tick. This could have some bizarre consequences. According to one of my BBC rivals, I 'briefed on behalf of Alastair Campbell' during the Good Friday negotiations. The reality is that he briefed me for Sky News over the phone, and asked me to convey what he had said to my colleagues because he was unable to come outside in person. I thought I was behaving honourably by passing on his briefing. Information sometimes flowed too well for the politicians' liking. During negotiations it is vital to control the process as well as the policy which will eventually emerge, but even the British government was not always able to do this. For example, the night before the Good Friday Agreement my Sky News colleague Gary Honeyford revealed the details of 'the institutions', the bureaucratic framework for the new Northern Ireland. This time Alastair Campbell did leave the building to berate him.

For most people of my generation, the Northern Irish Troubles were something we had grown up with. Living in Westminster, I had heard the start of the mainland bombing campaign and seen the immediate aftermath of those attacks and several afterwards. As a political journalist, I was in Brighton on the morning of 12 October 1984; I knew politicians and had acquaintances who had been maimed in terror attacks. Like every other citizen I had seen the wastepaper bins and phone kiosks disappear from stations and streets for fear that they could harbour bombs. None of these experiences was exceptional, but they did mean that I sympathised with the efforts of Major, Reynolds, Blair and Ahern in search of a just peace settlement which could return everyone's lives to normality. By the scale of most conflicts, Northern Ireland's death toll of some 3,000 over thirty years was modest. But the point was well made that for the size of Northern Ireland's population, this equated to over 100,000 deaths in mainland Britain or nearly half a million in the US, sobering in comparison to even such a horror as 9/11.

Tony Blair liked to describe himself as a 'big picture' politician, a man who preferred to get to grips with the elemental issues affecting ordinary people's lives rather than obsessed with the incremental point-scoring and positioning of tribal party politics. He had a quick grasp of detail but only so that he could make it serve his wider goals. I found it easy to understand Blair's attitude since it resonated with my own approach to political journalism.

It is wrong to describe them as 'favourite' stories because of the grave consequences for the people directly involved, but the three events which I had found most compelling to cover since 1982 were important 'big picture' dilemmas in which two opposing sides, each with a legitimate case, confronted each other: nationalists and unionists in Northern Ireland, pit communities and Thatcherite economic realists during the 1984–5 miners' strike, republicans and monarchists following the death of Diana in 1997. In each case, history and livelihoods were at stake with many of the onlooking public as passionately partisan as those directly involved. They provided rich raw material for a journalist, and demanded empathy and detachment from a politician such as Blair with an urge to conciliate.

Blair seems to have found these three aspects of contemporary British history as compelling as I did; he either shaped or was shaped by each of them. His entire economic and political strategy could be seen as a response to the miners' strike, as he tried to address the issues of a largely post-industrial Britain, the balance between the public and private sectors and the role of the trade unions within the Labour movement.

His two most memorable quotations of the ten years – both widely mocked – dealt with Princess Diana and Northern Ireland. Nobody ever summed up better than him the unstable cocktail of passions exploded by Diana's untimely death: 'She was the people's Princess.'

But you had to laugh at his Good Friday week soundbite: 'This is no time for soundbites – but I feel the hand of history on our shoulders, I really do.' It was clearly a moment when Tony Blair allowed his own verbal felicity and thespian skills to embarrass him – except for the awkward fact that he was right. It was a time for complex negotiations and agreements which could not possibly satisfy conflicting slogans such as the loyalist and republican rallying cries of 'No Surrender' and 'Chucky', or rather 'Tiocfaidh ar la', 'Our day will come'. It was also a historic moment in that decisions were possible which would change for ever the course of Irish politics.

Of course Blair delivered a soundbite while he was saying it was no time for them, but this echoed the double-speak which characterised the long route to a deal, in which 'no' never quite meant 'no' and 'yes' was hardly ever definitive. Even the humour, conscious or not, captured the curious mood of the Irish confrontation, where increasingly banter, smiles and familiarity from sectarian leaders suggested that an accommodation might one day be possible. Only in Northern Ireland could the Sinn Fein delegation have become known as 'Gerry and the Peacemakers' (a parody of the name of a sixties pop group), or the publicly harmonious relationship between First Minister Paisley and Deputy McGuinness earn them the nickname 'the Chuckle Brothers' (a children's slapstick comedy duo).

Blair's sense of drama contributed to the success of the process. He also had a sense of place – and given his love of the sun, an admirable tolerance for wet weather – which ensured that the key decisions about Northern Ireland were made on Northern Irish soil. Previous Anglo-Irish discussions relating to the North had mainly taken place in London or Dublin. Downing Street, and especially its out-of-sight side doors, continued to be essential for ongoing negotiations throughout the ten years as did An Taoiseach's base, the 'Charles Mahal' (the splendidly renovated government offices, nicknamed in honour of Charlie Haughey, the prime minister who had ordered the work). For open discussions Blair used imposing neutral venues such as Leeds Castle, Weston Park and St Andrews, but in the end it all came back to the territory.

Blair never missed the chance for a telling backdrop, however. Most dramatically of all, in April 2007 Blair and Ahern chose Armagh as the place for Britain and Ireland to sign off on the Stormont ceremony. Though the event was more symbolic than spectacular, the echoes of history were deliberate and deafening. The two prime ministers met at Navan Fort, which is believed to be the oldest site of habitation on the island. Over time it became the seat of Irish kings, including Brian Boru. And during the Troubles the border area of County Armagh was known as 'bandit country'. where army observation towers – eventually dismantled as part of the peace deal – tried to keep track of paramilitary operations.

The Good Friday Agreement was another moment when 'yes' did not mean 'yes', and would not mean 'yes' for another nine years, in spite of a 71 per cent 'yes' vote in the referendum which followed and victory for the UUP and SDLP in the first Assembly elections. Within days the Provisionals had put out an unequivocal statement: 'There will be no decommissioning by the IRA.' On the loyalist side there was violence at Drumcree during the marching season. And then in August the breakaway 'Real IRA' killed twenty-nine people in the Omagh bombing, the worst single atrocity of the Troubles.

Omagh was the low point for Blair and Northern Ireland, as the Warrington bombing in 1993 had been for John Major. In the same way he had during the Lenten negotiations on the Belfast Agreement, Blair continued to expend enormous energy and give great attention to detail on Northern Ireland. He was the single essential driving force; he never gave up, nor, mixing metaphors, did he ever allow 'the dreary steeples of Fermanagh and Tyrone' as Churchill put it, to be put on the bureaucratic back-burner.

Many other officials contributed to the settlement. Securing a deal exhausted four Northern Ireland secretaries – Mo Mowlam, Peter Mandelson, John Reid and Peter Hain – and as many permanent secretaries. Blair had two constant allies in his private office: his chief of staff, Jonathan Powell, who conducted many of the background talks, especially with the men of violence, and who undertook the drafting of agreements, and Tom Kelly, first Northern Ireland and then prime minister's spokesman, who, as a resident Ulsterman and former BBC journalist, took a warm personal interest.

Blair was also fortunate in his close alliance with Bertie Ahern. Ahern was fiercely intelligent and equally dogged. As a formidable Dublin street-level politician he was able to deliver his party, Fianna Fáil, and the people in support of the Agreement. Like Blair, Ahern was very much a modern European politician, impatient with the traditional image of his country abroad – from *The Shadow of a Gunman* to 'diddly-diddly' pubs. While no puritan himself (his marital arrangements and the bars he haunted on weekend evenings were well known), Ahern was proud to be the first European leader to introduce a smoking ban in public places and to refuse to extend licensing hours during the Irish football team's run in the World Cup in 2002. Ahern was similarly disdainful of the IRA, to the extent that one of his regular political problems was to explain why he flatly refused to deal with Sinn Fein TDs in the Irish Parliament while simultaneously urging that Sinn Fein should take up a share of power in the North.

Ahern yearned to set aside the old territorial disputes and to develop a new closer alliance with Britain. Both he and Blair laid out similar visions for this during a remarkable post-Good Friday visit to Dublin by the British prime minister which included an address by Blair to the Dáil. But practical development of such visions had to be postponed – one casualty of the delayed settlement. The British-Irish Council, effectively 'a council of the Isles', which brought together Ireland with the devolved nations of Britain and governments from the Channel Islands and the Isle of Man, was only a token gathering by 2008. Any development was left to Ahern's successors. Like Blair, Ahern achieved three general election victories, surviving a number of party financing scandals, and declared that his third term would be his last. But unlike Blair, Ahern's own departure from office in the spring of 2008 was rapid and undignified, prompted by his legal attempts to limit the work of a public inquiry probing allegations of planning corruption in the 1990s.

Ahern made an enormous contribution to securing the settlement but he was not vital to it like Blair. This is because the Irish state was essentially taking from the process, while Britain was effectively giving or giving way. Ahern did win a referendum in which Ireland gave up its constitutional claim on the North, but it did so without giving up its moral claim – precisely the selfish claim which the Major government abandoned for Britain. A United Ireland may never happen but the Belfast Agreement is a one-way street which potentially permits it to happen. There is no balancing possibility of closer links to the UK which could exclude Ireland and the nationalist community.

The circumstances for an agreement were favourable before Blair was elected in that the IRA had already offered one ceasefire, but he had the personal qualities – application, patience, ruthlessness and above all pragmatism – to carry it off.

For the remainder of his term in office, political progress in the form of Protestant–Catholic negotiations and the establishment and suspension of devolution were locked in a jerky 'excuse me' dance with paramilitary events related to violence and decommissioning. In 2000 and 2001 there were rocket attacks and the BBC bombing in London, IRA men arrested in Colombia and sectarian clashes outside Holy Cross Primary School. The winter of 2004–5 was worse with the £26 million stolen from the Northern Bank and Robert McCartney beaten to death outside a bar, both put down to the IRA. And just a year before the Stormont ceremony, there was the killing of Denis Donaldson, formerly a senior member of Sinn Fein, in what appeared to be an IRA execution. Donaldson was subsequently revealed to have been a British spy.

Blair did not allow any of this to put him off. Things kept breaking down and he kept holding them together. It was all process, process, process. He repeatedly retrenched, banked what had been agreed thus far and waited for a more propitious time to move on. Deadlines were missed and commitments ignored, but always there seemed to be a way out. The rules could be bent and any real problems were dealt with by organising another round of talks, preferably in a luxurious setting. He used any and all devices to keep the appearance of momentum.

Onlookers were often bewildered. The BBC's Northern Ireland political editor Stephen Grimason was once moved to comment: 'The wheel's still turning, but the hamster's dead.' Fortunately for Blair the hamster resurrected. But it took a long time.

Finally, in 2007 Blair at last got the two essential ingredients for a deal. The agreement of Ian Paisley to enter into a power-sharing government in response to the IRA both putting its weapons beyond use and declaring that it had ceased to exist (as anything other than 'the old boys' association' that Paisley had already deemed acceptable).

Tony Blair had won the day with his chat-show smile and his seeming impartiality, although his every action had been hallmarked with pragmatism and sophistry. For example, during the Good Friday talks, he tried to overcome unionist fears by writing pledges on a blackboard at the University of Ulster promising that Sinn Fein wouldn't be in government until the IRA disarmed. This briefly bolstered David Trimble and kept the process afloat. But, when events dictated, he welcomed Sinn Fein into government before the IRA gave up its weapons. Blair had the ability to send out messages which appeared to mean something but were completely ephemeral. In particular, Trimble felt that Blair's pronouncements, whether written or verbal, were not acted on. In other contexts such slippery politics may be deplored, but in Northern Ireland the British prime minister was using techniques which the locals well understood. Blair's skills enabled him to keep the two sides sweet and on board the peace process even though they were filled with mistrust of each other. He also demonstrated that he was prepared to take the casualties and sacrifice others in the process.

The Northern Ireland Blair left behind was profoundly different from the one he had inherited ten years before. The Ulster Unionist Party, which had dominated politics since the province was established in the 1920s, was all but destroyed. Similarly, the main nationalist party, the SDLP, was allowed to atrophy. The Royal Ulster Constabulary had been dismantled, replaced by the new Police Service of Northern Ireland. Normal rules of justice had been suspended, with the early release from prison of terrorist convicts. The Irish state had a constitutional role in the affairs of the North. And all this was accompanied by a gradual dwindling of terrorist violence, even if, as the Israelis loved to point out, more 'peace walls' than ever are being constructed to separate divided communities.

For most people in Northern Ireland Blair's peace process had been protracted, painful, frustrating and, at times, frankly boring. Even as the economy flourished (in no small part because of investment from the South) and house prices boomed, many in the North had been affected negatively, or at least felt they had lost something they once cherished.

There was no Nelson Mandela moment on 8 May 2007. Blair and Ahern weren't even centre stage. No statues of Tony Blair were planned in the province. The mood was no different in Scotland, Wales or London. Tony Blair was right; sometimes you don't get thanked for the most important things you do.

3

HOME FRONT

10 MAY

This country is a blessed nation.
The British are special. The world knows it. In our innermost
thoughts, we know it. This is the greatest nation on earth.

Tony Blair, resignation speech,
Trimdon Labour Club, 10 May 2007

Sedgefield

'We're all in tears except guess who?' Hilary Coffman, one of Blair and New Labour's most loyal servants, texted friends from Sedgefield on the day the prime minister declared officially that he was stepping down.

This latest in his series of final bows was not an opportunity which the veteran attention-seeker was going to miss.

Suspense had been deliberately built up. No formal details were ever given to the media of when, where and how Tony Blair would make his resignation statement. Naturally news organisations managed to work it out for themselves, and the Blair team would have been upset if they hadn't. But the fiction which Downing Street wished to communicate was that this was a solemn, almost private moment rather than the long awaited and skilfully planned appointment on the news agenda which in fact it was.

With maximum theatricality, Tony and Cherie and their aides made the journey north from London to his constituency in Sedgefield, deliberately mirroring the journey south which he had taken in the small hours of 2 May 1997 to become prime minister. On both occasions they flew by private jet, although the incoming plane had had to land at Luton airport, whereas the outgoing one had the full facilities of RAF Northolt for their departure from London. In another significant difference television cameras and a 'friendly' reporter (Robert Harris had filled the role in 1997) were not invited on board for this final journey.

Tony Blair was heading to Trimdon Labour Club for his statement. The humble stand of shacks on the green of a one-time mining village whose historic importance went back further than the ten years was where Blair had declared his official candidacy for the Labour leadership on 11 June 1994 after John Smith's death.

A 'normal' Downing Street cabinet meeting preceded the flight to Sedgefield at which Tony Blair had surprised no one by spelling out his intentions. Jack Straw, the leader of the House, and 'available man' of the New Labour years, had some words prepared. He found it 'a very poignant day indeed' for anyone who had worked through the dark days before 1997. Blair, he believed, had rescued the Labour Party, made it electable and ensured its values were in tune with the British people. Straw argued that Blair's place in history was 'up in the top rank of any prime minister in the last two centuries'.

Gordon Brown took longer to record his tribute. A television camera was summoned to the Treasury and kept waiting for more than two hours. Eventually, the chancellor made his comments. He spoke looking away from the lens as if answering a question, but in fact no reporter had been admitted. It was simply a faked interview.

Sedgefield is a 99 per cent white, solid Labour, working-class constituency on the northeastern spine of England, close to the old cities of Durham, Darlington, Bishop Auckland and the larger conurbations of Newcastle, Middlesbrough and Sunderland. The last coal pits in County Durham did not close until the 1990s but the local mines were in decline long before the miners' strike of 1984–5. In the Sedgefield area, Trimdon and Trimdon Grange collieries and Fishburn coking works had shut by the time Blair became MP. Employment in the constituency was mainly in the service industries, with some light industry, high tech and agriculture. The biggest population centre was the new town of Newton Aycliffe, home to the Flymo lawnmower factory, a Tesco superstore and a decaying 1960s shopping centre.

Tony Blair was the most important parliamentary representative the people of Sedgefield had ever had. And the constituency had been good to him, respectful of his national-scale ambitions. Blair would visit the constituency regularly once a month, not always staying the night in Myrobella, the former pit overseer's house which he and Cherie had bought as their local base. The house took its name from the plum trees in the garden.

For most of their time in Downing Street, Myrobella was the only home the Blairs owned. They bought the four-bedroomed brick detached house in 1983 for £30,000, as soon as Blair became MP. On top of their parliamentary salaries MPs are entitled to significant allowances to subsidise the expenses of a second home. Blair took full advantage of these but he also used the house as his constituency office. As in their London homes, the Blairs paid little attention to the furnishings. For many years a second-hand sofa took pride of place in the house – a hand-me-down from Pat Phoenix, the actress and *Coronation Street* sex symbol in her role as Elsie Tanner, who married Cherie's actor father, Tony Booth, shortly before her death in 1986.

In his early years as MP Blair assiduously held constituency surgeries at Myrobella, flanked by his agent, John Burton – a job which Burton took over on his own for the most part after Blair became party leader along with many of the other duties usually performed by a constituency MP. Once Blair became prime minister, the taxpayer spent more than £2 million on security. The house next door was purchased as a police base. Surveillance cameras, lights and security screens were installed outside. A local footpath near the house was closed and scrubland cleared of bushes. Roads around the property were sealed off by five-bar gates. Durham Police provided a security detail totalling two sergeants and twenty-two armed constables. The performance of their duties was not without incident: a police Alsatian savaged local sheep and an officer once discharged his weapon when startled by a pigeon.

There was always a sense of the young squire up from town mucking in with his political tenants whenever Blair returned to his constituency. There he was referred to in conversation as 'the prime minister', rather than the over-familiar 'Tony' or over-respectful 'Mr Blair'. Even so, the young squire delivered for his community. He put Sedgefield firmly on the map of modern politics by inviting foreign leaders such as presidents George W. Bush and Jacques Chirac and the French Prime Minister, Lionel Jospin. Blair often drew the inspiration for his delivery-based retail politics from his constituency. He would return to Sedgefield frequently to launch pet schemes, always well funded at the pilot stage. Sedgefield became a living laboratory for New Labour, and it did well out of it. Blair's decade in power witnessed massive investment in local schools and health services.

There was even some truth in Downing Street's claim that the outgoing prime minister would end the day 'having a beer with his mates' in the Trimdon Labour Club. Blair was a social chameleon who never really seemed to be entirely at home anywhere, but over twenty-four years he and his constituency activists had grown familiar with each other. The bred-in-the bone loyalists at the club respected him. On this most emotional of days they could be relied upon to be kind and not to intrude too much.

Blair's decision to give up being the constituency MP was pragmatic. The seat had served its purpose as the springboard for his political career. However, he chose to maintain a version of the practical and sentimental personal attachment which he had nurtured since 1983. In deference to what he took to be the local allegiance, he professed to support Newcastle United, dutifully pronouncing it with a northern short 'a', though he failed to pass this enthusiasm on to his elder sons, who favoured Liverpool (their mother's home town) and Manchester United (Alex Ferguson was a strong Blair supporter and generous with tickets). In fact, many in the constituency, including

Labour agent John Burton, were unimpressed by Blair's support for Newcastle, since they backed Sunderland instead.

Burton was famously the decisive figure in selecting Blair as prospective parliamentary candidate and *de facto* MP in waiting in a very safe Labour seat when Blair came in search of one of the few remaining chances to fight the 1983 general election. Both have repeatedly told the story of how their bond was sealed when Blair visited on 11 May, just four weeks before polling on 9 June. The prospective candidate agreed to sit politely through the UEFA European Cup Winners' being shown live on television before discussing his ambitions. The British team, Aberdeen, beat Real Madrid 2–1 in extra time. 'Unfortunately it was a draw at full time and he sat there for two and a half hours, I think,' said Burton.

Burton and Blair have often been contrasted as chalk and cheese: the northern working man born into the Labour Party, and the metropolitan lawyer who 'chose Labour'. In practice, Blair had just enough connection to the area to be a credible candidate. He had lived in County Durham and gone to junior school there – albeit private pre-prep and choir schools. He hadn't gone south until university – Fettes is a lot closer to Sedgefield than Eton.

Much more importantly, Burton and Blair shared a similar outlook: from different approaches both were committed to Labour and to making it electable again. Any conversation with Burton about Labour in the 1980s would contain the phrase 'We can't go on like this.' For the last three decades of the twentieth century Sedgefield had experienced what change meant. Its pits closed, so did nearby heavy industries on Tyneside and Teeside, while agriculture shrank. Ordinary working people in the constituency were in need. To both men the theological debates gripping Labour – between Bennites, Militants and the rest – were middle-class games irrelevant to the essential political task of looking after people.

Although Blair was a product of the educated, upper-middle classes, he sympathised instinctively with Burton's preoccupations. A key factor in his rise to power was his recognition that there were many other 'John Burtons' still active but disillusioned within the Labour Party. New Labour was constructed by identifying these like-minded people and building a network around them. Other ambitious young Labour politicians also found the Northeast fertile ground on which to take root, amongst them Mo Mowlam, Peter Mandelson, Stephen Byers and local lad Alan Milburn. After Blair became leader, this core group led the campaign to replace Clause IV of the Labour Party constitution. The removal of the time-honoured commitment to 'common ownership of the means of production, distribution and exchange' was the standard they planted to mark out the territory they had gained.

Acknowledgements of this shared history ran through Blair's calculated, yet personal and emotional speech at Trimdon Labour Club to a crowd of family, friends and supporters, some tearful, others cheering:

> It's a great privilege to be here with you again today and to thank you all for such a wonderful and warm welcome.
>
> I'd just like to say, also, if I might, just a special word of thanks to John Burton.
>
> John has been my agent here for many years now. He's still the best political adviser that I've got.
>
> He's . . . he's all the years I've known him he's been steadfast in his loyalty to me, to the Labour Party and to Sunderland Football Club, not necessarily in that order.
>
> You know it's been my great good fortune at certain points in my life to meet exceptional people and he is one very exceptional person. And also if I may refer to my wife, friend and partner, Cherie.
>
> And the children of course. Euan and Nicky and Kathryn and Leo who make me never forget my failings . . . but give me great love and support.
>
> So I have come back here, to Sedgefield, to my constituency, where my political journey began and where it is fitting it should end.
>
> Today I announce my decision to stand down from the leadership of the Labour Party. The Party will now select a new Leader.
>
> On 27 June I will tender my resignation from the office of Prime Minister to the Queen.

I have been prime minister of this country for just over 10 years. In this job, in the world today, that is long enough, for me but more especially for the country.

Sometimes the only way you conquer the pull of power is to set it down.

It is difficult to know how to make this speech today. There is a judgment to be made on my premiership. And in the end that is for you, the people, to make.

I can only describe what I think has been done over these last 10 years and, perhaps more important, why.

I have never quite put it like this before.

I was born almost a decade after the Second World War. I was a young man in the social revolution of the 60s and 70s.

I reached political maturity as the Cold War was ending, and the world was going through a political, economic and technological revolution.

I looked at my own country, a great country – wonderful history, magnificent traditions, proud of its past, but strangely uncertain of its future, uncertain about the future, almost old-fashioned.

All of that was curiously symbolised in its politics.

You stood for individual aspiration and getting on in life, or social compassion and helping others. You were liberal in your values, or conservative.

You believed in the power of the state or the efforts of the individual. Spending more money on the public realm was the answer, or it was the problem.

None of it made sense to me. It was 20th Century ideology in a world approaching a new millennium.

Of course people want the best for themselves and their families, but in an age where human capital is a nation's greatest asset, they also know it is just and sensible to extend opportunities, to develop the potential to succeed, for all – not an elite at the top.

People are, today, open-minded about race and sexuality, averse to prejudice and yet deeply and rightly conservative with a small 'c' when it comes to good manners, respect for others, treating people courteously.

They acknowledge the need for the state and the responsibility of the individual.

They know spending money on our public services matters and that it is not enough. How they are run and organised matters too.

So 1997 was a moment for a new beginning, for sweeping away all the detritus of the past.

Expectations were so high, too high – too high in a way for either of us.

Now in 2007, you can easily point to the challenges, the things that are wrong, the grievances that fester.

But go back to 1997. Think back. No, really, think back. Think about your own living standards then in May 1997 and now.

Visit your local school, any of them round here, or anywhere in modern Britain.

Ask when you last had to wait a year or more on a hospital waiting list, or heard of pensioners freezing to death in the winter, unable to heat their homes.

There is only one government since 1945 that can say all of the following: 'More jobs, fewer unemployed, better health and education results, lower crime, and economic growth in every quarter,' – this one.

But I don't need a statistic. There is something bigger than what can be measured in waiting lists or GSCE results or the latest crime or jobs figures.

Look at our economy – at ease with globalisation, London the world's financial centre. Visit our great cities and compare them with 10 years ago.

No country attracts overseas investment like we do.

Think about the culture of Britain in 2007. I don't just mean our arts that are thriving. I mean our values, the minimum wage, paid holidays as a right, amongst the best maternity pay and leave in Europe, equality for gay people.

Or look at the debates that reverberate round the world today – the global movement to support Africa in its struggle against poverty, climate change, the fight against terrorism.

Britain is not a follower. It is a leader. It gets the essential characteristic of today's world: its interdependence.

This is a country today that for all its faults, for all the myriad of unresolved problems and fresh challenges, is comfortable in the 21st Century, at home in its own skin, able not just to be proud of its past but confident of its future.

I don't think Northern Ireland would have been changed unless Britain had changed, or the Olympics won if we were still the Britain of 1997.

As for my own leadership, throughout these 10 years, where the predictable has competed with the utterly unpredicted, right at the outset one thing was clear to me.

Without the Labour Party allowing me to lead it, nothing could ever have been done.

But I knew my duty was to put the country first. That much was obvious to me when just under 13 years ago I became Labour's Leader.

What I had to learn, however, as prime minister was what putting the country first really meant.

Decision-making is hard. Everyone always says: 'Listen to the people.' The trouble is they don't always agree.

When you are in opposition, you meet this group and they say: 'Why can't you do this?' And you say: 'It's really a good question. Thank you.' And they go away and say: 'Its great, he really listened.'

You meet that other group and they say: 'Why can't you do that?' And you say: 'It's a really good question. Thank you.' And they go away happy you listened.

In Government, you have to give the answer – not an answer, the answer.

And, in time, you realise putting the country first doesn't mean doing the right thing according to conventional wisdom or the prevailing consensus or the latest snapshot of opinion.

It means doing what you genuinely believe to be right.

Your duty is to act according to your conviction.

All of that can get contorted so that people think you act according to some messianic zeal.

Doubt, hesitation, reflection, consideration and re-consideration, these are all the good companions of proper decision-making. But the ultimate obligation is to decide.

Sometimes the decisions are accepted quite quickly. Bank of England independence was one, which gave us our economic stability.

Sometimes, like tuition fees or trying to break up old monolithic public services, they are deeply controversial, hellish hard to do, but you can see you are moving with the grain of change round the world.

Sometimes, like with Europe, where I believe Britain should keep its position strong, you know you are fighting opinion, but you are content with doing so.

Sometimes, as with the completely unexpected, you are alone with your own instinct.

In Sierra Leone and to stop ethnic cleansing in Kosovo, I took the decision to make our country one that intervened, that did not pass by, or keep out of the thick of it.

Then came the utterly unanticipated and dramatic − September 11th 2001 and the death of 3,000 or more on the streets of New York.

I decided we should stand shoulder to shoulder with our oldest ally. I did so out of belief.

So Afghanistan and then Iraq – the latter, bitterly controversial.

Removing Saddam and his sons from power, as with removing the Taleban, was over with relative ease.

But the blowback since, from global terrorism and those elements that support it, has been fierce and unrelenting and costly. For many, it simply isn't and can't be worth it.

For me, I think we must see it through. They, the terrorists, who threaten us here and round the world, will never give up if we give up.

It is a test of will and of belief. And we can't fail it.

So, some things I knew I would be dealing with. Some I thought I might be. Some never occurred to me on that morning of 2 May 1997 when I came into Downing Street for the first time.

Great expectations not fulfilled in every part, for sure.

Occasionally people say, as I said earlier: 'They were too high, you should have lowered them.'

But, to be frank, I would not have wanted it any other way. I was, and remain, as a person and as a prime minister, an optimist. Politics may be the art of the possible – but at least in life, give the impossible a go.

So, of course the vision is painted in the colours of the rainbow, and the reality is sketched in the duller tones of black, white and grey.

But I ask you to accept one thing. Hand on heart, I did what I thought was right.

I may have been wrong. That's your call. But believe one thing if nothing else. I did what I thought was right for our country.

I came into office with high hopes for Britain's future. I leave it with even higher hopes for Britain's future.

This is a country that can, today, be excited by the opportunities, not constantly fretful of the dangers.

People often say to me: 'It's a tough job' – not really.

A tough life is the life the young severely disabled children have and their parents, who visited me in Parliament the other week.

Tough is the life my dad had, his whole career cut short at the age of 40 by a stroke. I have been very lucky and very blessed. This country is a blessed nation.

The British are special. The world knows it. In our innermost thoughts, we know it. This is the greatest nation on earth.

It has been an honour to serve it. I give my thanks to you, the British people, for the times I have succeeded, and my apologies to you for the times I have fallen short. Good luck.

It was a unique and emotional event and even this most loyal of audiences didn't know quite how to respond when Blair ended. As he would in the House of Commons in a few weeks' time, he finished softly, with a catch in his throat. When he at last stepped back from the microphone there were an agonising few seconds of delay before the applause began.

Unlike his farewell conference speech in Manchester the previous autumn, the Sedgefield resignation statement was not a lecture. It was reflective and contained no recommendations for the future beyond 'good luck'. Instead, along with the brief and familiar litany of achievements, this speech amounted to a revealing self-analysis, sometimes conscious, at others less so, as debatable ideas were taken as given – are 'people today' really 'conservative with a small "c" when it comes to good manners'?

For Blair's deputy, John Prescott, New Labour amounted to placing 'traditional values in a modern setting'. Blair picked up and used this phrase often, but in this resignation speech a more characteristic lack of sentimentality for the past – his critics would call it a lack of a sense of history – was on display as he discarded it without a backward glance: 'almost old-fashioned', '20th Century ideology', 'detritus of the past'.

An outing of his passion for reconciling apparent opposites, such as liberal/conservative and state/individual, was as inevitable as the rock star's encore, whatever Ben Wegg-Prosser had planned. As prime minister, Tony Blair exasperated people who came to lobby him by giving the impression that he agreed with them. In the speech he was frank about this technique. Briefly he almost sounded like a modern Machiavelli as he explained how he entertained points of view but never actually committed himself to them. In Sedgefield, Blair ascribed this approach to the period of opposition, ever faithful to his belief in the dichotomies of opposition/government, saying/doing, question/answer. But a more objective view would admit that he continued this approach into many of his dealings in government.

'And you say: "It's really a good question. Thank you." And they go away and say: "It's great, he really listened." You meet that other group and they say: "Why can't you do that?" And you say: "It's a really good question. Thank you.'"

But as Blair admitted in the speech, sometimes an answer cannot be avoided, even if talking about it at length can: 'And so Afghanistan and then Iraq – the latter, bitterly controversial.'

Blair's political career pivoted on the Middle East and external events which were 'utterly unanticipated and dramatic' as he described 9/11. Without the September 2001 attacks he would never have placed himself so irrevocably 'shoulder to shoulder' with President George W. Bush. Without the post-invasion setbacks in Iraq, it's questionable whether Blair would have declared his intention in the autumn of 2004 not to fight a fourth general election. In the summer of 2006, his refusal to condemn Israeli retaliation on Lebanon as 'disproportionate' fuelled the September rebellion against him by Labour MPs.

In Sedgefield he refused to engage in argument with the simple assertion: 'Hand on heart, I did what I thought was right.' He did not bother with the claims over weapons of mass destruction in Iraq, which nearly destroyed his government, leading to the suicide of the weapons inspector Dr David Kelly and the inquiries by Lords Hutton and Butler. Instead, his justification to Trimdon Labour Club was crude and therefore perhaps genuine. Sometimes, he argued, it's right to use military force. Fighting terror, removing Saddam Hussein and the Taliban were necessary and 'right'.

Test-bed in the North

Sedgefield was the appropriate place for Tony Blair to make this final speech of self-exculpation, or at any rate self-explanation. It was a test-bed where he discovered his purpose in politics: improving the lot of ordinary people. Sedgefield also had the advantage of being profoundly unconcerned by the metropolitan obsessions and rivalries which preoccupied much of modern politics and which had brought the Labour Party to the brink of destruction in the late 1970s and early 1980s, as the left-wingers such as Tony Benn and Militant tried to capture the soul of the movement.

Blair was not the only middle-class aspirant politician to be attracted to the verities of the Northeast. After the 1983 election, I asked Peter Mandelson what he was going to do next. He said he wanted to become an MP. He was from London, had served as a councillor in London, and London had been the powerbase of his famous grandfather Herbert Morrison. But Mandelson looked horrified when I asked if he wanted a London seat. 'Good Lord, no! London is a nest of vipers. I'll look for somewhere quiet and sensible in the Northeast or something.' In the 1997 general election Peter Mandelson was duly returned as member for Hartlepool, a constituency adjacent to Sedgefield.

Blair's utilitarian approach to politics and 'delivery' was first expressed in the five-point pledge card drawn up for the 1997 election campaign. Its whole focus was on the basic concerns of ordinary citizens about schools, health, crime, jobs and earnings. The pledge card crudely offered voters a menu of what they would get in exchange for their votes:

- Cut class sizes to 30 or under for 5-, 6- and 7-year-olds
- Fast-track punishment for persistent young offenders
- Cut NHS waiting lists
- Get 250,000 under-25-year-olds off benefit and into work
- No rise in income tax rates, cut VAT on heating to 5 per cent and inflation and interest rates as low as possible.

This clear deal was successively blurred in Blair's two subsequent general election manifestos, as the burdens and compromises of office took hold. In 2001 the five pledges were restated in terms of the inputs (which government can make) rather than the outputs which it cannot guarantee: numbers of new teachers and doctors rather than directly stated improvements in school and healthcare performance. By 2005, specific promises were obscured by a mass of verbiage and assertions about Labour's record of achievement, and a partisan statement of 'the choice' to be made by voters in each area, but the philosophical approach to the democratic contract established between the governed and the governing was the same. This was centred entirely on what material benefits would be delivered or, as a Labour slogan put it in both the second and third Blair campaigns, 'a lot done, a lot still to do'.

In his own constituency, Blair pointed to material benefits delivered, even if local schools and public services subsequently demonstrated new problems thrown up by the new arrangements.

Throughout his time in power, both in opposition and government, schools were the favourite location for Tony Blair's public appearances. He visited many hospitals too, but they carried with them the inevitable downer of association with sick people. Doctors, nurses, patients and carers could sometimes bite back at the prime minister, spoiling a PR opportunity, whereas the worst he got from photogenic bright-eyed, hopeful young people was a bit of sassy cheek.

New Labour used schools for any announcement linked to the future, not just for educational matters. Blair launched his 2001 re-election campaign at St Saviour's and St Olave's, a girls' comprehensive in Southwark, South London – an event to savour since it was combined with another Blair theme, religiosity, as the Labour leader attended a school service and was pictured worshipping in front of a stained-glass window. In his final months, the prime minister almost seemed to return to classrooms and young people for a rejuvenating shot in the arm. After the attempted coup of September 2006, Blair chose, inappropriately, to announce that he would be gone within a year at a North London school. In April 2007, he tracked back to Hackney Downs for a nostalgic relaunch of policy, all pinks and poster children, at the shiny new Mossbourne Community Academy which his government had instigated on the site of one of the worst-performing schools in Britain. And, weeks after his Sedgefield speech, his last official visit as prime minister would be to a West London Catholic primary school, Larmenier and Sacred Heart, this time to publicise an eco-friendly walk-to-school scheme in the non-partisan company of Arnold Schwarzenegger, muscular movie star turned governor of California.

Over the ten years, Sedgefield schools hosted more than their fair share of prime ministerial events – including the post-holiday news conference in September 2003 at Sedgefield Community College during which he tried to stem the rising tide of criticism over the Iraq War, to the background accompaniment of tennis balls thwacking in the courts just outside.

Many of the local schools were transformed by Blair's policies. In 1997 only a quarter of pupils at the main comprehensive in his constituency got five or more A to C grades at GCSE. Today, Sedgefield Community College is 'a specialist sports college . . . supported by HSBC, the world's local bank'. Over three quarters of pupils now achieve the top GCSE grades. Another school, Ferryhill Business and Community College, became the first in Britain to have its own television station.

A peculiarly Blairite set of issues was played out at Hurworth School, the top performer in his constituency. Darlington Council and the school clashed over plans to merge it with a less successful one as part of a new academy. Parents and governors sidestepped the threat by voting for foundation status. As a foundation, Hurworth continues its high performance as a 'Maths and Computing College'.

The member for Sedgefield was not keen to become publicly involved with another high-performing school in nearby Middlesbrough, but he left no doubt of his private support. The media were not informed in advance, and so were not on hand in strength to record the occasion, but the prime minister still turned up to open the new King's Academy in the city. The result of the enforced merger of two 'failing' schools, King's was the second of a proposed six schools in the Northeast to be run and partly funded by the family trust of Sir Peter Vardy, owner of the locally headquartered Reg Vardy car dealership set up by his father. The trouble with Sir Peter was that he was a Christian fundamentalist who became the focus of the debate over the teaching of creationism. Vardy denied any association as 'stark raving crazy', although the head of science at one of his academies was discovered to be a director of the 'Truth in Science' project which had distributed controversial 'intelligent design' teaching packs to every school in the country.

Blair's attitude set him instinctively at odds with many in his party, not least Alastair Campbell's formidable partner, Fiona Millar, who worked for a period at Number 10 for Cherie Blair. They believed that the goal should be universal and uniform provision – so all schools were good and all schools were effectively the same, even if that meant closing down private education or faith schools. Blair put into practice for himself and his family a totally contrary doctrine. He chose faith schools for all four of his children, at some distance away from his own home. Other senior Labour figures did likewise. Charlie Falconer had to be made a Lord because he refused to remove his children from private school as the price of a safe seat. Harriet Harman's choice of a selective grammar school for her younger son undoubtedly contributed to the bad-mouthing which led to her sacking as a cabinet minister (her elder son went to the grant-maintained Brompton Oratory – the same school attended by Nicky and Euan Blair). And in 2007, Ruth Kelly came under attack for placing her son with special needs in a private school.

Within the middle-class circles of New Labour, where parents chose to send their children to school was the issue which, more than any other, led to broken friendships and screeching across the dinner tables of North London. The newscaster Jon Snow and Alastair and Fiona organised a drop-in children's ice-skating club for friends and acquaintances on Sunday evenings at the Islington Sobell Leisure Centre. If voices were ever raised, it was because a sheepish parent had disclosed education plans which did not fit in with the comprehensive model. Blair, himself privately educated and not averse while in Downing Street to using masters from nearby Westminster public school to tutor his children, profoundly deplored these arguments and consistently supported opting-out colleagues when they came under attack.

Not that any of the arguments were relevant to Sedgefield – the Northeast remained one of the poorer parts of Britain, where the task was to improve standards across ordinary schools. City academies certainly played their part. This was one aspect of Blairite policy which Gordon Brown's supporters seemed to carp at but which Brown was to continue as prime minister. To universal surprise, including that of the minister in question, he kept on the controversial Schools Minister (Lord) Andrew Adonis, who planned to set up 400 academies by the end of the Blair–Brown third term.

Many local educationalists in the Northeast applauded the improvements witnessed over the Blair decade. David Heaton retired as principal of Queen Elizabeth Sixth Form College in Darlington around the same time as Blair resigned. His tribute was fulsome: 'Tony Blair made a huge difference. After 1997, the funding position changed almost overnight and the college was in a position to do things we couldn't have done before. There was a massive improvement. He doesn't always get the credit he deserves.' At York University, Professor David Jesson pointed out that teachers had benefited as well as pupils: 'No one ever thinks they have enough, but this government has overseen a substantial improvement.' Between 1997 and 2007 education spending went up 53 per cent; in County Durham it went up 55 per cent per pupil. A Durham University team published an audit of the Northeast over Blair's ten years, somewhat irrelevantly titled after Harold Macmillan, *Never Had It So Good?* On education, this concluded 'extra spending has funded more teachers, numerous initiatives, and new buildings. FE colleges have been rebuilt and the region's universities expanded. Performance at GCSE has been improving faster in the region than nationally – the gap has narrowed. In 2005/6 57.3 percent achieved five or more "good" GCSEs, only just below the national rate of 58.5 percent.'

Nationally, however, and in the Northeast, the government fell short of many of the targets it boldly set itself back in 1997 when the party manifesto declared: 'We will make education our number one priority.' For example, the original pledge of smaller class sizes was hit early, but then the effort fell back. As Blair left office, there were 29,000 children aged between five and seven in classes of over thirty.

Blair was sensitive to the possibility of recidivism, and he established regular 'stock takings' where spending ministers were pitched against a 'delivery unit'. But the traffic light categorisation of achievements never managed to switch all lights to green. The targeting approach was accused of being too bureaucratic, allowing quantitative targets to distort and even obstruct real qualitative improvements in public services. Blair and Campbell themselves quietly dropped the publication of an annual report monitoring their delivery of manifesto pledges after just two years. Yet Blair never abandoned the target/ delivery approach with its emphasis on outcomes rather than the priorities of the provider. And he determinedly, if not always convincingly, rebutted charges that the measurements (or 'metrics') had been tampered with or dumbed down to make the government look good.

There was a central failing of his education policies that Blair freely acknowledged, witnessed in his own constituency and revisited again and again as prime minister. The Durham University study put it succinctly:

> Too many young people are still achieving little at school and may be increasingly marginalised. Raising aspirations, especially of the most disadvantaged and hardest to reach, is evidently an issue . . . Overall crime rates have fallen – and there has been a greater reduction in the North East than nationally . . . Violent crime has been increasing both nationally and regionally . . . the public are especially concerned about drug offences and anti-social behaviour. Alcohol is an important factor . . .

Blair could have written the report. Before 'education, education, education', his favourite slogan was famously 'tough on crime and tough on the causes of crime' – even though it was Gordon Brown who coined it for him. When he was shadow home secretary, many of Blair's views were forged from what he witnessed as an MP in his own constituency. Phil Wilson was one of the sharers in Blair's ten years. He followed Blair to Labour HQ and Downing Street as an aide and researcher, and in July 2007 he succeeded him as Labour MP for Sedgefield. In 1997 he was a local party worker and volunteer already confident enough to speak for the incoming prime minister. 'Tony Blair knew from Sedgefield that law and order was a working-class issue,' Wilson told a *New Statesman* journalist exploring the rise of 'Sedgefield Man'. Blair himself, in an article for the *Observer* entitled 'My Vision for Britain' on 10 November 2002, directly attributed his priorities as shadow home secretary to his local experiences:

I had seen from my own Sedgefield constituency the destructive impact of lawlessness on local communities. As the 1980s had progressed I sensed increasingly that the task of the centre-left was not to replace crude individualism with an overbearing paternalistic state. It was to rebuild a strong civic society where rights and duties go hand in hand. Crime and anti-social behaviour is a Labour issue. In many of the poorest parts of Britain, in many traditional Labour areas, it is the issue.

So in the years which followed, Sedgefield and the Northeast would pioneer a succession of New Labour's anti-crime initiatives which ratcheted up the 'Respect' agenda in favour of the victim while restricting the civil liberties of the potential offender. New Labour habitually packaged each project with a name which could have been taken from George Orwell's 'Newspeak'; 'Community Patrols' made up of concerned citizens; 'Community Support Officers', quickly trained, uniformed auxiliaries to regular police officers; 'Acceptable Behaviour Orders', the first step towards ASBOs ('Anti-Social Behaviour Orders'), which enabled communities to impose criminal sanctions on nuisance behaviour that otherwise would not have been against the law; and in 2004, 'Streetsafe', launched by the prime minister himself at Hardwick Hall, the local luxury hotel – a variation of 'zero tolerance' aimed at street criminals such as drug dealers, car thieves and petty criminals as well as lower-level 'yob culture' irritants such as graffiti, fly-tipping and abandoned vehicles.

As a local MP, Blair was actively involved in the implementation of these policies. In February 1999, the leading regional paper, the *Northern Echo*, even credited him with personally intervening to ensure that a fifteen-year-old 'local tearaway' was 'under lock and key at last'. 'There is a power to remand people in custody if they are a danger to the local community and obviously we want to make sure those powers are strengthened still further,' the prime minister told the *Echo*.

According to the local police, the strategy worked. By 2005, Chief Constable Paul Garvin was boasting that County Durham was one of the 'safest places to live' in Britain. For Blair it was vindication of his policies of tougher laws and punishments against those who violated the rights of the 'decent, hard-working majority'.

This approach may not have amounted to the creation of the 'paternalistic state' which Blair declared he wanted to avoid, but it was a paternalistic society in the sense that the behaviour of each of its members was expected to conform to the norms of the majority. Blair did not even subscribe to the pre-eminence of the state in such matters. When the state in the form of the judicial branch stood up for the rights of individuals, Blair was capable of being critical of it in the name of 'common sense'. Indeed as his old pupil master, Derry Irvine, was heard to remark on more than one occasion, for someone with legal training, Blair showed remarkable little respect for the law. Or, as another Labour critic expressed it, 'Tony is tone deaf on civil rights.' When it came to law and order, one of New Labour's slogans put it most succinctly: Blair was absolutely 'for the many, not the few' – the majority who abide by the law rather than the minority who break it.

When terrorism took a dominant place in the law and order agenda after September 2001, Blair saw it simply as a further vindication of his approach. ID cards, CCTV cameras and other security devices, prolonged detention without charge were simply curtailments of liberty that he believed ordinary citizens would be prepared to accept. 'If they've done nothing wrong they've got nothing to worry about.' The Guildford Four, the Birmingham Six and the other victims of appalling miscarriages of justice of the 1970s through to the 1990s seem to have made little impression on him, even though his government successfully reformed and improved the Criminal Cases Review Commission.

Blair and the home secretaries who were closest to him, David Blunkett and John Reid, continued to rail against clever lawyers who opposed their plans, even though they sat at the head of the judicial system. Opinion polls suggested Blunkett and Reid were justified in claiming the support of the majority of the people for their hard-line stance, although they failed to convince the majority of legislators, Labour and otherwise, in Parliament.

In the pomp of his early success, Prime Minister Blair attempted

to define what the political philosophy of 'Blairism' amounted to:
'If you really want to understand what I'm all about, you have to
take a look at a guy called John Macmurray – it's all there,' he
declared, referring to the leading proponent of 'communitarianism',
a Scottish communist turned Christian theologian, who died, aged
eighty-five, in 1976. Blair was introduced to Macmurray's works
during troubled times at Oxford University by Peter Thomson, the
Australian cleric who mentored him into practising Christianity. But
Blair also held private meetings with two other exponents of
communitarianism, both Americans, Amitai Etzioni and Robert
Putnam. An indication of the direction in which the Labour leader's
thinking was drifting was that both these philosophers were favourites
of President Clinton. They had also been cited by the religious right
in America and by Margaret Thatcher (another prime minister prone
to be out of sympathy with 'the state').

Etzioni argued that human beings are fundamentally social creatures
with obligations towards the community they are part of. He saw
an important place for non-governmental institutions as well, including
the church and voluntary groups. Above all, communitarianism was
heavy on the responsibility of the individual towards his community,
and the right of the community to curb his or her rights within it.
Etzioni even mused on whether it would be possible to revive the
use of the stocks. The Blair government was fond of 'naming and
shaming', or at least talked a lot about doing it, a stance which
resonated well with the tabloid press.

Ever the practical politician, Blair took from communitarianism
what he wanted – after all, as he said himself, 'I only know what I
believe.' The word 'community' was the most important part, a
guiding authority which was neither the state nor the government
(with their obligations to everyone) but cosily closer to real people.

In opposition, communitarian habits of thought had permeated
Blair's pronouncements. 'It's a bargain – we give opportunity, we
demand responsibility,' he wrote bluntly in the *Sun* in 1993. It provided
the intellectual spine for his defining rewrite of Clause IV of the
Labour Party constitution. In place of wholesale nationalisation, the
party now stood for 'the rights we enjoy that reflect the duties we

owe'. For a short period after he became prime minister, Blair's philosophy became known as 'the Third Way'. Communitarianism still underpinned this new concept. The four values outlined in a Third Way pamphlet Blair part authored in 1998 were equal worth, opportunity for all, responsibility and community.

After 1997, it wasn't always clear what the new prime minister stood for. On one side he presented himself as young and trendy; on the other he yearned to win over a silent majority which he took to be small 'c' conservative. 'Cool Britannia' often felt like half-baked Britannia and certainly not a 'young country'. Blair delivered a rabble-rousing, but largely incomprehensible, speech to the 1999 Labour Party conference attacking 'the forces of conservatism' (which seemed to be represented both by fox-hunters and the public service trade unions) and, of course, championed the pointless Millennium Dome – not necessarily pointless in conception but certainly pointless for what it contained. These sallies served to demonstrate how shallow the prime minister's cultural roots were.

I was the first journalist to interview Blair after his 'forces of conservatism' speech. The conference hall was still besieged by an enormous anti-bloodsport protest. I asked him if he didn't feel that fox-hunting had long been entwined with British culture, rather than being a reactionary affectation. He looked at me as if I were mad. A reference to literature, invoking the key hunting scenes in *Sir Gawain and the Green Knight*, had him searching for the nearest exit. So I pointed out that hunters and foxes feature on pub signs in most villages. It was clear there would be no meeting of minds on my concept. I checked the next time I was in his constituency – the Fox and Hounds is a short walk from Trimdon Labour Club. The local MP chose to overlook the proud hunting history boasted by Sedgefield. The thriving regional racecourse was one of the vestiges of a past when the area was even called 'the Melton of the North', and the county's hunting star, Ralph Lambton, was a friend of the sporting chronicler Robert Smith Surtees.

When Blair was running for election in 1997, he told me that he favoured a ban on hunting with hounds because it was a 'particularly vicious' form of cruelty. This was the standard New

Labour reply on a question about which many MPs seemed peculiarly exercised given its comparative lack of real importance. Blair was caught in an awkward straddle between the Middle England voters he wanted to entice into his fold, and Labour activists suspicious that he would ever deliver on his manifesto promise of 'a free vote in Parliament on whether hunting with hounds should be banned'. Blair's answer was to prevaricate; final decisions on a ban were delayed by Terry Burns's report and parliamentary procedure. Blair stood on the sidelines and avoided participating in free votes (once going to Bosnia to absent himself). But ultimately he used hunting as a gambling chip. Whenever he was under pressure within his party on unrelated matters, usually involving a move to the right, such as the breaking of the pensions–earnings link, he would put hunting back in play.

Blair had little instinctive sympathy for the rights of the minority to hunt, but many in the pro-hunting lobby believed he had given private assurances that there would never be a ban. Eventually, however, there could be no more procrastination and the massive Labour majority was able to exert its will, seemingly motivated more by class prejudice than animal rights, since many less ornate forms of hunting, including angling and shooting, were left unmolested. Lord Chancellor Charlie Falconer tried to appease the countryside voters with the remarkable assertion for a legislator that the new law was ineffective. The rather aptly named Falconer declared on the BBC's *Question Time* that 'everybody is happy' because hunting had been banned but hunting was still going on.

By 2000, New Labour was still saddled with the Dome, but the appeal of Cool Britannia had dissipated. Blair's heart may never have been in it. Instead, he turned back to communitarianism to help redefine his beliefs. This philosophy endorsed the market and private enterprise, so also appeared to support the mainstream values of modern Britain during the first term. It proved a useful instrument as Blair tried to entice as many people as possible, and especially erstwhile political opponents, into the fold. But the mantra that had worked so well for him with the constituents of Sedgefield, sharing 'traditional values in a modern setting', did not convert everyone, as he discovered in 2000 when addressing the national conference of Women's Institutes at Wembley Arena.

Blair had assumed that the values of the WI – community, self-help, volunteerism – would make the conference a pushover for his proselytising. Far from identifying common values, though, the assembled women detected a naked attempt first to patronise them, by boasting about the government's successes, and then to recruit them to the cause. The WI blew a loud raspberry at the prime minister. His speech was interrupted by heckling, slow handclapping and walkouts. Afterwards, members of the audience complained loudly that the prime minister's remarks had been 'too political'. It was a profoundly shocking moment for Blair and the aides who had been most closely involved in planning the charm offensive on the WI – Anji Hunter, speech-writer Peter Hyman and Alastair Campbell. When wooed by Mr Blair, Middle England would not always lie back and think of New Labour. It turned out not everyone felt loyal to the same imagined community.

Tony Blair did not abandon his central belief in rights and responsibilities expressed through communities, but having been rebuffed by the individualists of the WI, he refined his message for an audience which he thought likely to be more directly sympathetic towards it. In the run-up to the 2001 general election, he gave a keynote lecture to the Christian Socialist Movement in which he used the words 'community' and 'communities' more than twenty times. 'Equal worth, responsibility, community – these values are fundamental to my political creed,' he spelt out, linking his speech to the Third Way pamphlet.

In this speech, Blair acknowledged the rights of individuals: 'the equal worth of all citizens and their right to be treated with equal worth and consideration despite their differences are fundamental'. But the thrust of his argument was how individuality should be curbed by their responsibilities to the collective: 'a large part of individual responsibility concerns the obligations we owe one another . . .'. Ultimately, he reduced the individual to two collaborative functions – wealth creation and citizenship: 'The purpose of society is to empower the individual; to enable them to fulfil not just their economic potential but their potential as citizens.'

The stress on 'economic potential' betrays a New Labour obsession: its exponents frankly admired the very wealthy. Peter Mandelson had spelt out early on that the party was 'intensely relaxed about people getting filthy rich'. The belief was that the rich could be harnessed 'to put something back' into society. Few New Labour initiatives were launched without the leadership involvement of a wealthy figure such as Sir Richard Branson, but it was noticeable that these tended to donate their expertise rather than their cash to these endeavours. New Labour proudly proclaimed itself 'meritocratic', appropriating a philosophical concept. However, little attention was paid when the politician and sociologist Michael Young, who had first coined the term 'meritocracy', claimed that it had been both misunderstood and misused by Blair. Young's 1958 satirical novel *The Rise of the Meritocracy* warned that devotion to the concept would lead to a dystopia ruled by a self-perpetuating and selecting elite – a vision very different from the egalitarian cult of the successful proposed by New Labour.

'Ask when you last had to wait a year or more on a hospital waiting list.' Announcing his departure in Trimdon Labour Club, Tony Blair gave just half a sentence to the most important domestic initiative of his ten years. Just over a week before, the prime minister had told the King's Fund, the leading health think tank and trust, that his decision in 2000 to boost massively annual health spending had resulted in effect in a tripling of the government figure over the ten years to 'a budget of whatever it is, £90 billion or so'.

But in Sedgefield on 10 May, the prime minister wanted to speak as an international statesman laying down his burden – and to justify his involvement in the Iraq War. Something he may have wanted to do in his constituency to overwrite the lacerating attack made on the stage of Newton Aycliffe Leisure Centre the last time he had been elected MP. Reg Keys, a father who had lost his soldier son in Iraq and stood as the 'Truth and Justice' candidate, used his widely broadcast concession speech to accuse Blair of waging an illegal war before urging him to 'say sorry'.

In any case, Blair's methodically planned last few months had already ticked off his NHS achievements, paying due tribute to them.

On 30 April 2007, the King's Fund held a seminar to discuss the changes made to the health service under the decade of Blair's New Labour. It was a cosy affair, the sharpest moment being Blair's by now instinctive opening jibe at the media, when he recalled an encounter with a member of the public during a visit to a health centre: 'She said to me, "Why don't you make the media publish something positive about the health service?" It took me a long time and she said, "You're not saying anything" and I said, "I am trying to frame a polite reply."'

Blair took the opportunity to clarify 'my often mocked words of ten years ago' on the eve of polling that there were 'only 24 hours to save the NHS': 'What I was meaning was that ten years ago I think the question was does the health service as an institution have a future and today I think the question is how do we improve the quality of that future.' More doctors and nurses had indeed been one of New Labour's original pledges, but three years into government, Blair admitted that the NHS had not undergone the transformation he had promised. Speaking to the television cameras from Sir David Frost's sofa on 16 January 2000, in the midst of one NHS winter crisis, he announced that UK health spending would rise to the EU average – at that time a rise from about 6 per cent of GNP to 8 per cent. Chancellor Gordon Brown imposed his own control of the plans by commissioning a report from Sir Derek Wanless. Eventually, national insurance contributions were raised by 1 per cent to find the money.

On 27 June 2000, Tony Blair announced his health service plan to the Commons: 'to make the NHS once again the healthcare system that the world most envies'. The very next day he was up in the Northeast to lay the foundation stone for Bishop Auckland Hospital, the new private finance initiative project which would serve his constituents. In health as in education, he was a champion of public–private partnership, insisting that his constituents were interested only in the facilities and that 'to set up some dogmatic barrier to using it, is to let down the very people who most need our public services to improve'.

At Bishop Auckland Blair said, 'We have a real chance of rebuilding the health service in the way we all want.' However, the hospital and the community in which it stood soon experienced the teething troubles which characterised many of the new expensive NHS grand projects. Just as the hospital was about to open in 2002, a health authority report from Surgery Professor Ara Darzi (subsequently made a Lord and appointed health minister by Gordon Brown) forced a merger with the neighbouring hospital trust in Darlington – as it happened, the constituency of the then health secretary and widely tipped 'heir to Blair', Alan Milburn MP. Bishop Auckland's £67 million PFI debt was now combined with the PFI cost of the new £90 million Darlington facility. By 2003, there were accusations that the health secretary had intervened personally to ensure that his and Blair's local South Durham Health Care NHS Trust received the top '3 star' rating. This classification was worth an extra £1 million of government investment and it also freed the trust to run its own finances, including property sales and new borrowing.

Meanwhile, the health sector's Royal Colleges reported that the new Bishop Auckland hospital was a white elephant. Recruitment of medical staff was slow and wards operated at below capacity. The hospital was downgraded, and maternity and accident and emergency services were shut down. Locals now had to go to Durham for critical services and there were allegations that lives had been put at risk. However, in County Durham as elsewhere, sweeping government changes made it more difficult for local people to monitor what was going on. The South Durham and Weardale Health Care Council was abolished in 2004.

As Blair left office in the early summer of 2007, John Saxby, the County Durham and Darlington NHS Foundation Trust's chief executive, was also preparing to stand down, having presided over the area's hospitals in their various manifestations for fourteen years. He was jeered and jostled at a public meeting after warning that further bed cuts at Bishop Auckland were 'more than likely'. The chairman of the Save Our Hospital Action Group, David Fryer, said: 'We are shocked to hear of the possibility of more bed cuts. These planning discussions about what is needed at Bishop Auckland hospital should have been taking place five years ago.' But Saxby claimed

Bishop Auckland hospital had 'a vibrant future': 'I've seen many highs
– the delivery of private finance buildings at Bishop Auckland and
Durham for example. Building stock is much better now . . . We
also deliver much speedier services. In 1993 people were waiting
eighty-three weeks for an outpatient appointment, now 97 per cent
have an appointment within eight weeks.' Lower down the NHS
payscale, porters, cleaners and kitchen staff were threatening to strike
in a dispute brought on by the contracting out of services. Contract
staff at Bishop Auckland claimed to be earning 70p an hour less than
colleagues directly employed by the NHS in Darlington.

This then was the NHS legacy in Blair's back yard after ten years:
much more money being spent and some noticeable improvement
in access to healthcare. Nationally, the NHS net expenditure had
increased from £34.66 billion in 1997–8 to a planned £90.70 billion
in 2007–8 and fifty-five new hospital building projects with a value
of £30 million or above had been completed – the largest ever
hospital-building programme. At the same time there remained real
questions about value for money, bureaucratic upheaval and above
all long-term PFI debt. Public/private arguments remained unresolved
with the trade unions.

Over the ten years, people in the Northeast enjoyed an increase
in life expectancy, but it was still below the national average and
some two and a half years shorter than England's best-performing
region, the Southwest. Wide variations also persisted, favouring people
living in affluent areas over those less prosperous.

More people smoked in the Northeast. But during Blair's decade,
the number one health problem in the constituency had become
obesity – especially among children. The Northeast had the worst
record in the UK, with 18.3 per cent of children under eleven at risk.

On 10 May 2007 Blair's parting gesture to his old constituency
addressed the problem of children's health. Instead of selling Myrobella
for profit as many had predicted (excited newspaper reports valued
the property at £400,000, though £150,000 seems to have been closer
to the mark), the family turned it into the headquarters for a new
'Tony Blair Sports Foundation'. In his retirement, John Burton, who
was once a PE teacher, was appointed vice chairman to run the

foundation. Its stated aims were to get more young people playing sport by training more coaches and improving access to facilities. Locally, the foundation was part of a self-help initiative which would make any communitarian proud. A year before he left office, the prime minister opened the new Trimdon Colliery Community Centre, next door to Myrobella. It was a fun and fitness centre complete with an all-weather sports pitch meant for use by children. Barclay's Bank and the charity Groundwork East Durham helped fund the scheme.

Going in his own time

The Sedgefield speech marked the point of no return for Tony Blair as Britain's prime minister. He set the date for his resignation six weeks and six days hence; he said nothing about his intention to quit as an MP. John Burton had put it on record that it was Blair's intention to serve until the next general election, barring 'a big international job'. The impression was given, and taken, that there would be no early by-election. All other options remained open for the prime minister.

And so the race was on to become the next leader and deputy leader of the Labour Party. The following Monday, the parliamentary party opened for nominations, to be submitted until lunchtime on Thursday. A postal ballot would follow, with the result to be declared at a special party conference in Manchester on Sunday 24 June. Highly unusually, therefore, Blair would continue to be prime minister until Wednesday 27 June even though he had handed over the party leadership three days before.

Ever the reformer, Blair trampled on the conventions for the handover of political power in Britain. In the past, the end of a premiership came in a single twenty-four-hour period – or at best a lingering few days, as was the case with the transition from Thatcher to Major which had also been achieved while the incumbent party remained in office. Blair had first served notice of his eventual departure nearly three years earlier, in the autumn of 2004; in September 2006 he had set for himself a timetable of a year; now he named his own departure date and extended his long goodbye into an unprecedented six-week transition.

By force of will, and thanks to a position of political strength, Tony Blair transformed himself from 'a here today, gone tomorrow politician', as the late Robin Day once so memorably put it, into something akin to an American president, entitled to a dignified exit and handover. American presidents are elected on the first Tuesday in November but the new administration does not begin until the third week of the following January. Modern US presidents are also term-limited to eight years, representing two terms, in office.

On 30 September 2004, Tony Blair had become the first British prime minister to place a term limit on himself. Many, including he himself, have since suggested that it was a mistake for him even to discuss the possibility of stepping down because from that moment on he weakened his grip on office and hence his power. This view is an acceptance of the almost mythical lore of Britain's unwritten constitution: that to admit something which is inevitable – that a prime minister won't last for ever – is a mistake.

The 2004 announcement came at an odd time, though one which revealed what relations between Blair, his colleagues and his party were really like.

The Labour Party had just enjoyed (or endured) its annual party conference, complete with leader's speech and a week of focused media attention. The conference had not gone smoothly. For the second year running, and only the second year under Blair, the leadership had been defeated in a vote, this time the demand for renationalisation of the railways. And, in a sharp speech to conference on Africa, the rock star Bono had likened the relationship between Blair and Brown to the notoriously troubled, and ultimately destructive, collaboration between the two Beatles John Lennon and Paul McCartney.

Blair had much on his mind that week – political and family troubles, health worries, concern about his future – but far from consulting the annual forum of his party, he stayed in the background in Brighton and decided against making the most important statement yet about his leadership 'at Conference'. Instead, political editors from the main national television stations were contacted, barely before the ragged chorus of 'The Red Flag' (which still marked the end of the event, much to the annoyance of the New Labour reformers) had died away.

It was around lunchtime, during the drive back from Brighton, that I received the call instructing me to report to Downing Street for 8 p.m. in order to interview the prime minister. David Hill, Blair's director of communications, placed a total embargo on reporting or speculating about the appointment. However, the advance notice ensured that Sky News, BBC and ITN would all be ready to give the announcement, whatever it was, the full treatment when reporting restrictions were lifted at ten, in time for the main terrestrial news bulletins.

Television-only exclusives with the prime minister are comparatively rare, occurring on average usually just four or five times a year. Of these, perhaps only a couple are likely to contain major news. But the way this particular set of interviews had been arranged pointed to high drama. So as my colleagues Andrew Marr and Nick Robinson and I arrived at Downing Street there was a mood of some excitement.

The prime minister was not around but the camera crews were already setting up in one of the three interlinking drawing rooms on the first floor of Number 10, overlooking Horse Guards Parade. David Hill quickly took us into a small side room and sat us round a conference table. There was no need for pleasantries since we had just spent a week rubbing up against each other at the Bournemouth conference, so Hill got straight down to business: 'The prime minister is going into hospital tonight and he will tell you, when you speak to him, that it is not his intention to fight a fourth general election.' We then had a question-and-answer session lasting about twenty minutes on what these twin announcements meant.

The medical problem, we were told – backed up by documentation from Blair's doctors – was a recurrence of the irregular heartbeat, supraventricular tachycardia, which had led to his emergency stay at the Hammersmith Hospital, just under a year earlier. The condition was treatable, curable and not in any way debilitating. Professional journalistic curiosity wondered if there was more to it, but there seemed little further to say. The statement about not fighting a fourth general election was much more surprising. Hill explained what he thought it meant, but referred us to the prime minister himself, who would be arriving shortly.

For the past few years, visitors had not been allowed to use mobile phones in Number 10, but while I was waiting, I got a message to call Trevor Kavanagh, the political editor of the *Sun*, a friend and professional associate through News Limited. Trevor knew something was up but, most unusually, didn't know any details. Under embargo, I was able to fill him in. However, he added another piece to the puzzle – a rumour that the next edition of the *Independent* would report that the Blairs had bought a 'retirement home'. It turned out that they had indeed purchased a £3.6 million terraced house in Connaught Square, Marble Arch, but that evening neither Blair nor his aides would comment on that.

Blair arrived seeming tired but relaxed. The interview which followed blended the political and the personal in an unfamiliar way.

The stated intention to serve a full third term but not fight the subsequent general election was unprecedented. In the first place, Blair had set a term limit but potentially it could be as much as six years away. Maximum five-year second and third terms could delay that fourth election until 2011, permitting him fourteen unbroken years in office. In practice, four-year terms were more likely but that would still give him twelve years of power, thus narrowly beating Margaret Thatcher's record. Blair was only just coming to the end of his second term. And this from the man who said he didn't want to go on and on . . .

Secondly, by inference, Blair was saying on the record that he expected to win the upcoming third general election, due in the summer of 2005. Such presumption always risks a fall.

But thirdly, and most controversially, what did he mean by 'a full third term'? Given the general assumption that any new leader should be given time to 'bed in' – was it remotely acceptable to govern for three or even four years and leave the new leader just a few months to get ready for the voters? Once again, Blair seemed to be drawing on an American presidential precedent in which the selection of the next leader takes place while the incumbent remains in office. The other comparison to hand was with Spain, where the long-serving incumbent prime minister, José María Aznar, appropriately known as 'El Presidente', had handed over to the new party leader only in time for the election campaign. Unfortunately, the precedent for 'doing an Aznar' was not a happy one: Aznar's successor as leader of the right-of-centre People's Party lost the election to the Socialist José Luis Rodríguez Zapatero, thanks to a clumsy attempt to make political capital out of the Madrid train bombings carried out by an al-Qaeda cell in 2004.

The workings of British parliamentary democracy are volatile and Blair steadfastly declined to spell out what he meant by 'a full third term'. He stuck to the formula during the 2005 election campaign, often at events where he had Gordon Brown sitting next to him. But by then it had lost credibility. Blair's attempts to avoid one professional 'white lie' – that he would go on and on – had in practice led to another evasion. His view of how long he should stay in office had also shifted. Blair now rationalised his original intention to serve just two terms as serving ten years instead.

The Sedgefield speech was an admission of failure. The prime minister had not served a full third term. On 27 June 2007 he would have completed just over two years out of a maximum of five. Tony Blair was out of office having faced just two party conferences after Bournemouth 2004. And those who questioned the wisdom of his delayed departure announcement would appear to have been proved right. Of course they were, if it was taken at face value. There was also the possibility that Blair was executing a political manoeuvre to buy time for himself.

At the end of September 2004, Tony Blair was in a weak position: Gordon Brown and the Labour Party were restless, Iraq was festering, the prime minister's own health had failed and the new house was an intimation that the Blairs knew it would not go on for ever. At least since 2003, some of Blair's closest friends had been advising him to step down. The general election campaign was approaching and only a clear statement could prevent Blair's future becoming an issue.

The interviews that night may not have been quite as candid as they appeared, but they bought Blair nearly three more years of power.

4

WAR

17 MAY

I know there are many people that have suffered, that weight of responsibility stays with me and so it should.

Tony Blair, Sky News interview
with the author, 15 March 2007

Shoulder to shoulder

The public friendship between British Prime Minister Tony Blair and US President George W. Bush began in the snows of Camp David on 23 February 2001 and effectively ended on the lawn of the White House Rose Garden on 17 May 2007.

The two leaders would have a further round of meetings at the G8 summit in Germany, but with more than a dozen other prime ministers and presidents 'to brush by' or 'drop in on' there, as the parlance of summit diplomacy had it, that was hardly the moment for an intimate farewell. George Bush at home in the White House was. The warmth of that parting gesture was underlined by an invitation from George and Laura for Tony to stay overnight in the Queen's bedroom. (Unusually, particularly in the case of special hospitality being offered, Cherie Blair did not accompany her husband to Washington this time.)

Blair had been the first foreign leader from outside North America to visit the new president after his inauguration in January 2001, something that was to the forefront of Bush's mind as he opened their only public appearance together: 'Newly elected President, Tony Blair came over and he reached out, he was gracious – was able to converse in a way where our shared interests were the most important aspect of the relationship.'

In 2001, few would have predicted the friendship that was to be forged between the two men. Tony Blair and his team were very uncertain what sort of welcome they would meet from the new president. According to Campbell's diary, Cherie Blair muttered sarcastically, 'I bet they are looking forward to this as much as we are,' as their helicopter arrived at Camp David.

Blair had been the friend and protégé of the previous president, Bill Clinton. Their two parties, New Labour and Democrat, were aligned, and so were their positions within them. They liked to appear together on platforms extolling the merits of the new centre ground in politics. During the long American election campaign of 2000 Blair had entertained Bush's opponent, Clinton's Vice President Al Gore, in Downing Street. But memories were still fresh of the damage done to the relationship between the British Conservative Prime Minister John Major and the incoming Bill Clinton, because of assistance rendered to his Republican opponent, President George H. W. Bush, the current incumbent's father.

Bush junior was an unashamed Republican populist, who had underpinned his administration intellectually with neo-conservative ideologues. He had shown little interest in foreign affairs and had been to Britain only as a tourist, mainly to Scotland to stay with his friend Bill Gammell. (This was one of the great missed meetings of history. Gammell was also a friend of Blair's at Fettes but he never introduced his two pals. Gammell, who went on to play rugby for Scotland and to head Cairn Energy, got to know the Bushes through family connections in the oil business.) In the desperately close US election of 2000, Bush had been declared president only thanks to the ruling of the US Supreme Court on the disputed vote in Florida, the state under the governorship of his brother Jeb.

If the British were apprehensive, however, the Americans had already made up their minds. While the Blair party were still flying over the Atlantic, Bush's national security adviser Condoleezza Rice spelt it out in a briefing for the Washington media. The president admired Tony Blair, she said, and had no greater ally than the United Kingdom. Rice had become a tennis partner of Sir Christopher Meyer, newly appointed Britain's ambassador to the US, with, according to his memoirs, the instruction to 'get up the arse of the US government and stay there'.

A warm and intimate but entirely proper reception was immediately offered at Camp David. Although it was February, the snow lent a Christmassy feel and events took place in cabins with blazing log fires. There was an air of deliberate informality. The president wore jeans and his insignia-embossed bomber jacket and so did Blair since Bush had had a prime ministerially badged jacket specially made for him.

In 2001, the president's casual style caught the British unawares. Bush liked to josh with his audience, bantering unexpectedly with personal remarks about his guests or, just as likely, about the questioning reporters. It seems like fun, but there is an assertive undertone of 'It's my party and I'll do what I want to' to the humour. Bush's gentle mockery also actually puts the targets in their place. This is similar to the wit with which Eton, Britain's most socially elitist private school, typically equips its pupils. It was a reminder that behind the folksiness George W. too was born into the purple; the son of a president, grandson of a US senator, brother of a state governor and the educational product of an American prep school and Yale University where he was inducted into the elite and secretive Order of the Skull and Bones society.

Fettes is sometimes referred to as the Scottish Eton. But while Bush's style complemented his fratboy self-confidence, in social gatherings Blair underplayed his own status, deferring in a 'very British' way to his interlocutors. This accommodating approach was what gave so many who met him the impression that he was on their side. His jokes were generally self-deprecating.

At their first meeting Blair duly played along as Bush declared they had much in common. To Bush's rather disconcerting example that 'We both use Colgate toothpaste,' Blair parried back, 'They are going to wonder how you know that, George!' Later that evening the Blairs smiled politely as Bush laughed uproariously at the after-dinner movie, *Meet the Parents* – the comedy of manners in which a liberal suitor meets his right-wing CIA father-in-law for the first time.

The Americans had a strategy for that initial Blair encounter. They wanted to 'hug him tight', embracing the British prime minister in an unbreakable grizzly bear grip. The Bush administration succeeded with an overt strategy of compliments and kindnesses akin to the disorienting 'love bombing' rained on potential recruits by religious cults like the Moonies.

Blair later made two claims for his relationship with President Bush. Firstly, that he got on better with 'George' than he had with 'Bill' because George was more straightforward and meant what he said. Bush returned this compliment. Scarcely a public appearance passed without him telling anyone who would listen that Blair was a 'stand up kind of guy'. At that last joint appearance in Washington in 2007 he was blunter still: 'There's a lot of blowhards in the political process, you know, a lot of hot-air artists, people who have got something fancy to say. Tony Blair is somebody who actually follows through with his convictions, and therefore, is admired in the international community.'

Blair's second claim was that it was he, not Bush, who was the first to raise the problem of Iraq and the potential threat posed by Saddam Hussein. It's easy to believe that Blair would have read his advance briefings more thoroughly than the president, who had been tripped up with foreign policy questions during his election campaign a few months earlier. The 9/11 attacks had not yet taken place. Bush was a year away from delivering his first State of the Union Address in which he identified Iran, Iraq and North Korea as members of 'an axis of evil', stating specifically of Iraq:

Iraq continues to flaunt its hostility toward America and to support terror. The Iraqi regime has plotted to develop anthrax, and nerve gas, and nuclear weapons for over a decade. This is a regime that has already used poison gas to murder thousands of its own citizens – leaving the bodies of mothers huddled over their dead children. This is a regime that agreed to international inspections – then kicked out the inspectors. This is a regime that has something to hide from the civilized world. States like these, and their terrorist allies, constitute an axis of evil . . .

Blair wanted to show that he had not been led astray by Bush into war in Iraq, but his swiftness to find common belligerent ground with the president smacked of an eagerness to please. Any competent briefing paper would have shown that many of Bush's main foreign policy advisers believed that the ousting of Saddam could be the key to installing a democratic *pax Americana* across the Middle East.

This pattern of the rambunctious, outspoken president jollying along the British prime minister, often pushing him into places he hadn't quite been before, was to repeat itself over the next seventy-eight months with regular bilateral talks and, from the autumn of 2003, at least fortnightly and often weekly video teleconferences. Speculation about what had been agreed secretly behind closed doors frequently overlooked the real advances made by Bush towards his goals on the record.

Blair's first visit to Bush's Prairie Chapel Ranch in April 2002 was a classic example of George W.'s tactics. The invitation to the president's Texan home was presented as a mark of special favour, the more so since he turned it into an opportunity to meet the family. The talks coincided with the British school holidays and Cherie, the Blair children and their granny, Gale Booth, had taken the chance to visit Disneyworld – all were invited to supper at the ranch, although the Downing Street operation tried to keep this information from the British media.

Press opportunities at the ranch itself were rare; a media centre was usually set up at the high school in the nearby, one-street town of Crawford. There was no danger of Bush falling off the wagon here since Crawford was in a dry county. The town and the local congressional district had continued to elect Democrats, the Republican political consultant Karl Rove's Texan strategy having ironically failed in Bush's own backyard.

Bush and Blair appeared in the high school gym for their news conference, the White House's red, white and blue bunting blocking out most of the fan signs for the Pirates, the school's football team. At the time, the issue of the day was a heavy military incursion by Israel into Palestinian territories. Following the State of the Union Address, the US administration was also already agitating for action against Iraq.

After the usual badinage with the journalists ('We'll start with Ron Fournier – a fine man who works for AP, got a couple of kids, cares deeply about the future'), Bush expressed his Iraq policy in the same jokey manner: 'Maybe I should be a little less direct and be a little more nuanced, and say we support regime change.' He then enlisted Tony Blair on his side: 'History has called us into action. The thing I admire about this prime minister is that he doesn't need a poll or a focus group to convince him of the difference between right and wrong.' Accommodating as ever, Blair agreed 'doing nothing is not an option'. Morally, if not yet practically, Blair signed up to regime change in Iraq: 'I can say that any sensible person looking at the position of Saddam Hussein and asking the question, would the region, the world, and not least the ordinary Iraqi people be better off without the regime of Saddam Hussein? The only answer anyone could give to that question would be, yes.'

Asked about the widespread European view that there was no proven link between al-Qaeda and Iraq, both men argued that there was – Blair citing the danger of weapons of mass destruction falling into such hands and Bush noting Saddam's viciousness against his own people.

But Bush hadn't finished yet. He moved on to the Middle East, declining to call for an immediate halt to Israeli action: 'my words to Israel are the same today as they were a couple of days ago: withdraw without delay'. Then, so quickly you could hardly notice, he changed the terms for any peace negotiations by ruling out a role for Yasser Arafat, the elected president of the Palestinian Authority.

Bush already spoke of Arafat in the past tense: 'Chairman Arafat has failed in his leadership and he has let the people down. He had opportunity after opportunity to be a leader and he hasn't led. And I'm disappointed.' Less than six months earlier Blair had honoured Arafat with an official reception at Number 10, but now he stood by silently, ignoring an opportunity to differ with the president.

Two years later, this time at the White House, Blair was caught in another Middle East pincer movement.

In April 2004, the day before a scheduled Blair visit, the Israeli Prime Minister, Ariel Sharon, went to Washington and laid out his controversial plan for unilateral action, building the 'Security Fence' but withdrawing forces from some Palestinian territory. Bush immediately welcomed the Sharon plan. Only a public row – the last thing the polite British prime minister wanted – could have prevented Blair from being roped in when he was put on the spot, having been given no prior notice of the Sharon–Bush agreement, in the Rose Garden the next morning. Britain was duly committed: 'We welcome the Israeli proposal to disengage from Gaza and parts of the West Bank.'

And so the dance went on, with Bush feinting and joking, ready to admit problems over Guantánamo, Abu Ghraib, human rights and the UN in an 'Aw shucks' kind of way, but never really shifting from his course. Tony Blair followed in step. As he himself said, he never believed that a *Love, Actually* moment, publicly disassociating himself from a pushy American president as his fictional counterpart played by Hugh Grant does in the Richard Curtis film, would be in Britain's national interest.

So on 17 May 2007, there the two men were, back on the Rose Garden lawn for the last time. Sounds of a distant demonstration drifted with the pollen in the sunny air. Blair took it as his cue to say it once again as he had lived it:

BLAIR: . . . in any part of Europe today, if you want to get the easiest round of applause, get up and attack America, you can get a round of applause if you attack the president, you get a—
BUSH: Standing ovation. [Laughter.]

BLAIR: Yes. And that's – that's fine if everyone wants to do that, but when all of that is cleared away, you're left with something very, very simple, fundamental, and clear: that that battle for values is still going on. And you can debate about the mistakes and the issues and you can debate about Iraq, whether we should have done this or we should have done that. But, actually, what is happening in Iraq today is that our enemy is fighting us, and, therefore, if what happens when our enemy fights us is that we drift away from our friends, that we kind of make the little accommodations so that we don't escape some of the difficulty and the responsibility and occasionally an opprobrium of decision-making – if we do that, our enemy takes heart from that, they watch that. They watch what we're doing the whole time. They ask, are these guys standing up for what they believe, or if we carry on, is their will going to diminish and they're going to give up, because it's just too difficult, because the public opinion is too difficult, because the opinion polls tell them it's too difficult?

Now, that is the decision of leadership.

When I asked directly if he thought Tony Blair was leaving office because of their friendship, George Bush muttered, 'Could well be.' After a pause, his next slightly ominous, po-faced delivery to me, 'Nice to see you again', raised some nervous laughs from the assembled press pack before Bush himself chuckled at his own quip. Blair waded in, trying to defuse the atmosphere while also changing the subject: 'You'd kind of forgotten what the British media were like, hadn't you?' But true to form, Bush had the last word in the exchange: 'At least he looked up to ask the question.'

Whatever the consequences of their friendship had been, Bush was not going to disavow it now. Indeed the president did all he could to bolster Blair's insistence that in these final days it was not all over yet: 'You know, it's interesting, like trying to do a tap dance on his political grave, aren't you? [sic] I mean, this – you don't understand how effective Blair is, I guess, because when we're in a room with world leaders and he speaks, people listen. And they – they view his opinion as considered and his judgement as sound.'

But the next prime minister Bush would welcome to the US would be called Brown not Blair. A couple of weeks earlier the chancellor had been in Washington on economic business. While he was in the White House seeing officials, the president just happened to drop in for a forty-minute conversation. Bush didn't bother to deny it: 'I would hope I would provide the same opportunities for Gordon Brown. I met him, thought he was a good fellow.'

Iraq

On 17 May 2007 Tony Blair's jet flew directly from Andrews air force base to Kuwait (stopping only to refuel and change crew at Heathrow). In Washington the main business, such as it was, had been a video teleconference between the president and prime minister and British and American military commanders and advisers in Iraq. Now for the last time Prime Minister Blair was going to see the situation on the ground for himself. Since 148 British military lives had been lost thus far in the conflict Blair had opted the country into, and since so many were already predicting that he would have a single-word political epitaph, 'Iraq', there was an unavoidable sense that he had to make the country a stop on his farewell tour. But there was also an element of vanity about the visit – defiant vanity but still vanity. There was no real purpose for the journey, not least because Blair had been on his last swift Basra–Baghdad tour only five months before, in a pre-Christmas visit.

The prime minister had made similar trips at least once a year since American and British forces had taken over the country in the early summer of 2003. His first visit had been confined to the southern provinces around Basra under British command, but as the successive forms of Iraqi government were established, the standard pattern was set of a double visit to the governmental Green Zone in Baghdad and to Basra.

The travelling party usually comprised forty to fifty people. About half of them would be reporters, producers and media technicians. The other half was made up of the prime minister's advisers, security detail and support staff. Tom Kelly, Blair's official spokesman, always came, somewhat bafflingly joined by David Hill, the Labour Party's political director of communications, and usually at least three other press handlers. The chief foreign affairs adviser, Sir Nigel Sheinwald, would be accompanied by several other foreign affairs specialists from Number 10, and often at least one senior 'spook' from the intelligence services. Chief of Staff Jonathan Powell frequently accompanied the prime minister, but a rare sighting on this last Iraq tour was Ruth Turner, Blair's director of government relations. Turner was still under investigation by the Metropolitan Police's cash for peerages inquiry, and had habitually avoided direct contact with the press. However, on this occasion the attractive young woman had come along – somewhat surprisingly for this Muslim country, dressed in a sleeveless black tank top.

A news blackout was always imposed on these visits, including the prime minister's itinerary. Obviously the main reason was security, to prevent a warm welcome being prepared for Blair by insurgents. But there were also political considerations since the prime minister's commercial aircraft had to fly first to a nearby country which was ready to receive him, while preferring not to acknowledge doing so. Kuwait, Jordan and Israel were all used as bases. Then the party, including officials and accompanying journalists, would be taken on by military aircraft. RAF Hercules transport planes shuttled between Basra and Baghdad international airports or Balad airbase. Blair travelled in the cockpit, in civilian clothes and no body armour except for a communications helmet so he could speak to the crew. Everyone else went on to the slung seating in the dark body of the C-130.

Until Blair's last visit, the flights in were the tensest moments of his trips to the war zone. The Hercules planes landed and took off steeply, sometimes spiralling in a corkscrew pattern and releasing flak to divert ground attacks.

Roads out of the airbases were considered unsafe, so any further travel was by helicopter. The helicopters flew low and sometimes hedge-hopped, barrel-rolling over power lines with aircrew manning machine guns through the open doors on either side. In Baghdad, a British RAF Puma was usually mustered for the prime minister. His companions had to depend on the generosity of USAF Black Hawks to ferry them to the Green Zone's 'Washington' helipad – a gravelly former sports field. From there armoured vehicles, mostly 4x4s, run by teams of private security men drove the visitors to their meetings and negotiated the numerous checkpoints manned by other private security firms and members of coalition forces (seldom British or American and usually from the more obscure countries making a token commitment to the operation).

The precautions taken and the heavy protection provided to the travelling party hardly gave the impression of an improving situation or that some sort of normality was being restored to the daily lives of Iraqis. Worse still, security grew tighter and restrictions on movement greater with each successive visit by the prime minister. And it was only on his final visit that Blair came under hostile fire in both Basra and Baghdad.

On his first trip in 2003, the prime minister was able to move around quite readily by road. The British headquarters was in a palace in the centre of Basra, on the banks of the Tigris. Boats moved about freely on the river – it would be three years before a waterborne attack claimed the lives of four British troops. Tony Blair visited a primary school and, in a famous moment caught on camera, was kissed on the cheek by a small Iraqi boy. The next year it was still possible to drive around the south, although the atmosphere was changing – children by the side of the road had started to mime shooting at the military vehicles as they went by. As part of the handover process the occupying forces pulled back to the airport, taking over the main terminal. Although they occupied the building for several years, they made no effort to restore reliable electricity supplies or basic sanitation to it, using portaloos instead. The area commander expressed the view that getting such services going was 'up to the locals'.

After the destruction of the Golden Mosque in Samarra in February 2005 the insurgency turned into full civil war. As a result, tensions increased greatly even in the southern provinces. But locally operated civilian flights resumed from the terminal. For the final phase of their occupation, the British forces retreated across the tarmac to a makeshift barracks grouped round a modern German-designed hotel building which acted as headquarters. This military encampment was the only part of Basra seen by the prime minister on his final trip.

If anything, the security situation in the Green Zone in Baghdad was even grimmer. The area had a guarded periphery, but inside the walls it was not a single secure zone but rather a collection of armed compounds with roads in between them teeming with soldiers, private security and checkpoints. Even allies did not have right of access to each other's areas. In addition to the foreigners, several thousand Iraqis lived in the Green Zone; others queued to come through the checkpoints each day. A Blair visit would typically take in the Iraqi prime minister's compound, the president's compound, a British headquarters (most often the embassy) and the military (American) command post.

By the summer of 2007, Britain had handed over three of the four southern provinces to the Iraqi security forces and was on schedule to move to 'overwatch' duty only in Basra by the end of the year. (The full withdrawal to the airport and handover of the city base, as it turned out, actually took place earlier than expected on 3 September 2007, so serving as a key marker of Gordon Brown's new premiership.) UK troop numbers, which had peaked at 40,000 during the invasion, had fallen steadily and a further reduction from 5,500 to below 5,000 was underway. There was a heated dispute over what they had achieved. The lightly armed walkabout patrols had long been abandoned because of attacks and hostility. In Washington some senior military advisers were telling President Bush that the British had 'lost the war' in the south to the insurgents and faced a bloody withdrawal.

As with Basra, visits to Baghdad became progressively more difficult compared to the situation when the appointee Prime Minister Allawi was, at least nominally, in charge. His office had been a normally functioning building in a large well-maintained compound. On these earlier occasions, Blair had been able to drive up to the front door and walk in for his talks, as did the media for regular news conferences, with a podium for the principals and chairs for the press. Blair's return to Baghdad following the establishment of the Iraqi transitional government was delayed because of the long time it took to hold elections and then form a government, but he went to Iraq in May 2006 to endorse the new al-Maliki government, just a couple of days after its inauguration – the first Western leader to do so.

By that point the Green Zone was beleaguered: there were more barricades and body searches, including a full search of each member of the Iraqi guard of honour waiting at the presidential palace to greet the prime minister. It was noticeable that all visitors, except Blair and his closest officials, were kept out of the main buildings. Statements to the press now took place on the doorstep or just inside the main entry hall.

With each visit to al-Maliki a further security circle was added. First, eight-foot-high concrete barriers screened off the portico entrance area where news conferences were held. Next, the portico was bricked in on three sides. By the time of the last Blair reception, the area had been carpeted and filled with plush furniture, including a flat-screen TV, in the style of an Arabian antechamber. Most importantly, it had become accessible only through a glassed-in tunnel containing X-ray screening equipment.

In 2003 and 2004, the most vulnerable points of the Green Zone had been its entrances, where people lining up to clear security faced attacks. By 2007 there had been bombing and kidnappings within the Zone itself. Mortar attacks from outside were a daily occurrence, and they were being targeted with greater accuracy. On his inaugural visit in March that year, the new United Nations Secretary-General, Ban Ki-moon, had ducked instinctively during a news conference when a mortar exploded near the Parliament complex he was in. Al-Maliki, sitting at his side, had barely flinched.

One of the coalition's successes inadvertently helped hostile elements target visiting dignitaries. Most Western journalists had long ago ceased operations in Baghdad because of the dangers. TV news organisations still gathering pictures used only local crews, while even those outsiders who remained, such as the BBC's duty correspondent, complained that it was possible to make sorties on to the street only under guard and for no more than fifteen minutes at a time.

On the other hand, the Iraqi media were thriving.

Soon after the occupation, the British and Americans took action to stimulate the local press, television and radio, judging a multifarious media to be one of the essential ingredients of a successful democracy. Tony Ball, the former chief executive of BskyB, who had recently stepped down, spent some time *pro bono* in Iraq assessing what supplementary information sources should be provided from outside, such as a revived BBC Arabic service. This meant that there were now at least half a dozen local television crews waiting for the prime minister on his last trip, as well as radio reporters providing live coverage. As a result, it had become impossible to keep Blair's presence or his movements a secret (although the travelling media were asked to protect the identities of the local news teams and not to show pictures that could expose them to identification and reprisals). After fraught negotiations, journalists in Blair's party had been given their places by Number 10 only on condition that they observed a time-delay embargo in reporting his movements – but this, in effect, held only until the news was made public locally in Iraq.

Therefore, as Prime Minister Blair travelled about Iraq for the last time he had become a serious target. There were mortar attacks coinciding with his presence at three locations. The first was at his initial stop on the itinerary – the former Baghdad school complex now used as the British embassy. As his convoy drew up there was a burning 4x4 in the car park outside the front door. Photographers in the party were banned from taking pictures. However, two so-called 'legacy teams', Dan Chung and Martin Amis of *Guardian Weekend* and Nick Danziger and Robert Crampton of the *Sunday Times* Magazine, were travelling with the prime minister at the time and confounded Downing Street's attempts to deny that an incident had taken place. An hour or so later the same teams reported that the military headquarters had come under attack several times while Blair was receiving a briefing from the US Commander, General David Petraeus. Alarms were sounded, followed by loud bangs nearby. Staff working in the Green Zone commented to me that 'incoming' was now a daily hazard.

Between these attacks Tony Blair held his last, chaotic and tetchy news conference in Iraq. The chosen venue was a small room, deeper into the main Iraqi government building beyond the antechamber. It was so cramped that the ring of tripods and cameras at the front totally blocked out questioning reporters unless they clambered on top of furniture. Blair stood at one podium with Prime Minister al-Maliki and President Talabani alongside him.

Blair spoke of 'difficulties and challenges': 'Plainly the security situation remains very difficult but on the other hand there are real signs of change and progress also.' He admitted, '. . . there are more mortar attacks and terrorist attacks happening every day. That's the reality. The question is what are we going to do in the face of those attacks . . . the answer is we don't give in to them. The very purpose of the attacks . . . is so that you will carry nothing but that on your news and won't actually talk about the progress that's happening here. The fact is even with all the difficulties it's not the only story about what is happening in Iraq. And let's not forget one part of the progress which is here we are in the middle of Baghdad with a press conference with a free press able to ask its questions – of me and also of the Iraqi prime minister, huh?'

Al-Maliki said little. Reports persisted that the US and UK governments were disappointed by his Shi'a sectarianism and wanted him to 'get a grip'. The Kurd, Talabani, was optimistic in spite of his somewhat unnerving observation that 'car bombs can be done anywhere'. The Iraqi president rather optimistically claimed that 'the situation is improving' and that, while ten to fourteen of Iraq's eighteen provinces used to be subject to violence, now it was only two or three. Even some parts of Baghdad were 'totally liberated', he stressed.

During the brief question period that followed, Tony Blair lost his temper – the first time I had seen him do so at a news conference in the thirteen years since he became Labour leader. One of the gifts which drove Blair to the top of politics was that he was 'bomb-proof' under the fire of questions from journalists. No matter how rude, pointed or ignorant the questions might have been, they would usually be dealt with politely, with at worst a sigh, a smile or a hint of exasperation. Even when his answers were not wholly convincing, Blair's force of personality habitually turned any issue so that those listening to him at least saw it from his point of view.

But that day in Baghdad, Blair's subjective account of the progress being made was confronted by the objective reality all around the heavily and haphazardly fortified Green Zone. Reporters, both those from the travelling British party and those based in Iraq, cited the continuing violence and terrorism and wanted to know precisely what were 'the improvements' in the situation that Blair was referring to. He talked of how Iraq had been 'liberated from a terrible dictatorship' and was now facing 'an attempt to repress it in a different way fuelled by external forces'. But he became increasingly agitated when pressed to cite specific 'improvements'. He did not seem to be able to come up with any examples. Instead he kept exclaiming, 'Don't ask me, ask them,' gesticulating vigorously in the direction of his hosts. All diplomatic courtesies were set to one side and in the heat of that moment it seemed as though he had forgotten the names of the Iraqi politicians beside him. Neither al-Maliki nor Talabani rushed in to back up Blair.

The British visiting parties always left the Green Zone on time because the Americans were prepared to loan their helicopters only for a limited period – General Petraeus's flight back to his temporary home north of the city took priority at the end of the day. The mood did not lift on the Hercules flight to Basra or at British Command headquarters there. The prime minister worked through the usual programme of briefings from the brass and chats with the troops. That Saturday afternoon, several hundred men and women in fatigues were sitting and standing around the large open foyer of what had been intended to be the Basra airport hotel. There was no mood of excitement on either side. Blair worked the room, listening sympathetically to stories of operational life in Iraq and views of what was needed. Then he spoke at the microphone for a few minutes. He seemed as concerned by how this performance was being seen as by what was actually happening. 'This is my last chance to thank you for the work you've done here . . . the impression is given that everything is completely negative . . .' It all felt a bit bleak – a sense confirmed by Blair's answer to his embedded legacy reporter Robert Crampton's question, 'How long will it take for it not to be a mess?': 'I dunno. You can't tell. It will resolve itself, it just will. People will get sick of the killing.'

An hour or so remained for fraternisation, but as the prime minister continued his tour, the air-raid sirens sounded. The order came to take cover and don helmets and flak jackets. All duly scurried to the command, except for Blair who wore neither. Inside the building you could hear the loud 'crump' of a mortar landing and exploding not so far away. According to later reports, the missile struck the tarmac close to the Hercules transport plane that carried the prime minister back to Kuwait shortly afterwards. There the party transferred immediately during the darkness of early evening in the desert on to the private jet back to London. On this occasion British Airways had been unable to provide an aircraft. At such times, executive planes were chartered of the sort used by professional football teams and rock bands. For this journey to the Middle East, Number 10 had hired a plane from Royal Jet, a service owned by the Abu Dhabi royal family for its own purposes and rented out commercially.

The cabin crew were well used to deferring to hierarchy. Blair and his aides were ensconced in luxurious first class. The legacy profile journalists were in the next section, in large leather-upholstered lean-back seats. The regular UK reporters were crammed into cattle class economy seats at the back. Tired, fed up and parched, the hacks exchanged angry words with the cabin crew, who ignored their needs – instead shuttling past them from the galley at the rear with endless trays of canapés and champagne for the front of the plane. Eventually the reporters raided the galley, liberating food and drink for themselves. BA charter crews never made such a mistake and were usually waiting with refreshments when the hacks climbed aboard.

As had become Blair's habit during his latter years in office, there was no exchange of pleasantries with the accompanying journalists on the journey home; we did not see him again once he boarded at the front of the plane. If he chose to take it, the flight back to Britain would have provided him with ample time to ponder alone quite how the tragedy of Iraq had enveloped his premiership. The journalists in the stern debated rather less grimly how the invasion had precipitated the story they were now covering – the end of Blair.

Iraq was the pivot on which the Blair decade swung. His foreign policy in the four years prior to 2001 seemed almost a preparation for the excited, engaged 'liberal interventionism' which characterised his hyperactivity through 2002 and until the Iraq invasion in 2003. Blair's slow decline began almost as soon as Baghdad was liberated.

The taint of failure came from connected but separate factors which hit him over a long period, in two successive waves. Peculiar to Blair, given the case he had made for going to war, were the failure to find weapons of mass destruction, the presumed suicide of the British weapons inspector David Kelly and the argument over the government's use of intelligence. These became major issues first, almost simultaneously with the invasion. Subsequently, both Blair and Bush were assailed by greater issues of more general concern – the inability to stabilise Iraq and the ensuing sectarian and terrorist chaos inflicted on its people; and the American failure to live up to their own human rights standards in Abu Ghraib prison and elsewhere, especially in the Guantánamo Bay detention camp, established at the time of the Afghan invasion of 2001.

This meant that unlike George Bush Tony Blair underwent continuous political pressure, confronting major dissent over Iraq, both from within his own party and from the wider public. This held from 2002, when the first intimations of an attack on Saddam were crystallised by Bush's 'axis of evil' State of the Union Address, right up until the time Blair left office.

In the first half of 2004, a crisis of confidence meant Tony Blair seriously considered quitting; while at the same time in the United States, George Bush was cruising to re-election and a consolidation of his mandate thanks to 'Security Moms' and their ilk.

Blair overcame his internal doubts and soldiered on until 2007, but he was able to do so only by paying a significant price. Most obviously, he made the political concession not to 'go on and on', and because of his political weakness gave up any hope of moving against Brown. Much more significantly, the intractable issues thrown up by Iraq when the facts didn't match what Blair would have liked them to be, transformed his approach to politics. He fell to the politics of assertion, no longer interested in making arguments and fencing with the media. He became a 'conviction politician' who insisted he was right even if he couldn't prove it. As he put it to me himself during an extended interview on Iraq on 15 March 2007: 'You know, I'm not [pause] I've long since ceased in all this to pander to anyone's opinion on it. I mean I do not regret either the strength of our alliance with the United States or standing by the US president and the American people in the aftermath of 11 September and I'm never going to do that.'

9/11

Ironically, this transformational process began on the day when Blair's insight and his ability to articulate his argument reached their zenith – 11 September 2001 was the most impressive day of Blair's premiership. He got it right. The terrorist hijackings and attacks in the US could not be dealt with in a day. Instead, the immediate crisis required from a national leader just the qualities which Blair was able to display: a quick grasp of what had happened, some background knowledge, a plan of action, and the articulacy to express the mood and reassure the public.

Blair was fortunate that by chance he had his old team around him – Hunter, Campbell and Powell – as he absorbed the news of the attacks, as in the days of '96 and '97, when he had moved from hotel suite to hotel suite at the head of a small, tightly knit group of campaigners, before the burdens of office weighed him down.

The prime minister's task that day was to make the fraternal delegate's speech on behalf of the Labour Party to the Trades Union Congress, meeting that year in Brighton. Blair never warmed to the trade union culture, famously offering 'fairness not favours'. He had cut down his appearances at the TUC from annual to biennial, sending Brown or Prescott in his place in the off years. In 2001, he had decided to use the speech to discuss the European Union, one of the few enthusiasms he shared with most trade unions.

Anji Hunter, who was due to leave Number 10 for BP, elected to attend her last TUC, going ahead to prepare the ground in Brighton. Alastair Campbell was never one to cede face time with the boss, so he decided to accompany Blair as well. Campbell closeted himself in their suite in the Grand Hotel to help with the finishing touches to the speech and rather haughtily chose to brief the band of journalists who had travelled to Brighton over the phone, rather than in person.

The content of the speech to come was newsworthy – hinting at possible early entry for sterling into the euro – and I hurried back to Sky's live broadcast point in the Brighton Centre to do a preview piece at 2 p.m. My camera crew informed me that there had been an incident in New York City – on our live output I could see pictures of smoke coming from one of the World Trade Center's twin towers. They were watching Sky News in the Blair suite in the hotel next door as well. Campbell called me about the delay, making one of those jocular remarks we'd all regret later: 'I just knew you guys would set fire to some building in America when you've got an important speech by Tony to cover.' Then on the monitor we saw the second plane go into the undamaged tower. We all understood immediately what that meant. Even so, for a few minutes, as we absorbed the shock, there were several more phone calls from the suite – should the prime minister go ahead with his speech? Would anyone cover it?

The decision to cancel was the right one. Instead, Blair appeared briefly on the stage to address what had happened in explicitly moral terms and to announce that he was returning directly to London. He immediately blamed international terrorism, describing it as 'the greatest evil in our midst today . . . immune to the sanctity of human life'. 'I am afraid we can only imagine the terror and the carnage there and the many, many innocent people that have lost their lives. I know you would want to join with me in offering our deepest sympathies to President Bush and the American people and expressing our absolute shock and outrage.'

There were three elements to Blair's instant reaction, to which he would hold consistently for the next six years: unconditional support for the US, a desire to unite the widest possible coalition against terror, and the belief that Islamic fundamentalist grievances were connected to the need for 'justice to the Palestinians'. They would become the mantras for the globetrotting diplomatic tour of over twenty countries on which he shortly embarked.

For now though, the Blair party was left to make an unscheduled scramble out of Brighton. In such circumstances, that day of disaster was tinged with elements of farce and a 'Blitz spirit' of mutual co-operation. The prime ministerial entourage ended up sharing his railway carriage to Victoria with recalled journalists, who passed on phone updates from their newsdesks to the official party, which was largely devoid of communications. Typically, the train service was caught unprepared and its officials became preoccupied with their (routine) failure to provide first-class passengers, now including the prime minister, with the promised 'complimentary teas and coffees'. As the train pulled into the London suburbs, a large metal urn was carried triumphantly to the front, but when the tap was turned it only spluttered and hissed.

On 9/11 organisational chaos was understandable. But it was far from untypical, as those travelling with the prime minister would come to rue as they passed through more than twenty countries by Christmas. For all the media carping about 'Blair Force One' and extravagance, Number 10's resources were actually extremely stretched for foreign visits. Successful organisation of a trip depended on the efforts of a clerk, Gavin MacKay, and assistance from British diplomats and local officials in the host country, both usually a mixed and largely unknown quantity. Arrangements made for the accompanying journalists were even less satisfactory since these depended on the, at best, ambivalent attitude of an advance team consisting of a special adviser, aka Blair political aide, and a relatively junior Foreign Office secondee.

That autumn, Blair cemented his personal friendship with George W. Bush. In his party conference speech he told the American people: 'We were with you at the first and we will stay with you to the last.' On 20 September, Blair had flown to New York to attend the memorial service for the British victims of 9/11 at St Thomas's Church, going from there to Washington for talks with Bush. That evening the president placed Blair in the gallery as guest of honour for his speech to a special joint session of Congress, addressing him personally, 'Thank you for coming, friend . . . America has no truer friend than Great Britain.'

Although it was turning into a costly quagmire as Blair left office, the initial operation to oust the Taliban government from Afghanistan was uncontroversial and achieved at low military cost to British forces. (It was also uncompleted: Osama bin Laden was neither captured nor killed, and in 2005 a NATO force returned to confront resurgent Taliban fighters in Helmand province.)

But there was no similar consensus in Britain for an operation against Saddam Hussein's regime in Iraq. In public, for much of the year following 9/11, Blair insisted that it was premature even to discuss it. When questioned on the point during his monthly press conference on 25 July 2002 he responded: 'I think we are all getting a bit ahead of ourselves on the issue of Iraq. As I have said before, action is not imminent, we are not at the point of decision yet, and there are many issues to be considered before we are at the point of decision.' But, according to a Downing Street briefing paper drawn up four days before the July press conference and subsequently leaked in 2005, Blair had given Bush a qualified commitment at their summit in Crawford, Texas, in 2002 that 'the UK would support military action to bring about regime change, provided that certain conditions were met: efforts had been made to construct a coalition/shape public opinion, the Israel–Palestinian crisis is quiescent, and the options for action to eliminate Iraq's WMD through UN weapons inspectors had been exhausted'.

The July meeting two days later, on 23 July, appears to have shifted the British officials most closely involved towards accepting that war was inevitable and to start considering what case could be made in support of it (including early inklings of the dossiers). This is apparent in a Downing Street memo written immediately afterward by Matthew Rycroft, Blair's senior foreign affairs official. He gives an account of contacts with the Americans by Sir Richard Dearlove, aka 'C' – head of MI6:

C reported on his recent talks in Washington. There was a perceptible shift in attitude. Military action was now seen as inevitable. Bush wanted to remove Saddam through military action, justified by the conjunction of terror and WMD. But the intelligence and facts were being fixed around the policy. The NSC had no patience with the UN route, and no enthusiasm for publishing material on the Iraqi regime's record. There was little discussion in Washington of the aftermath of military action.

In September 2002, Blair crossed the Atlantic for an afternoon's summit with Bush at Camp David. The talks were held in much greater secrecy than usual. There was no press conference or media access to the compound.

In October, Downing Street produced its dossier, 'Iraq's Weapons of Mass Destruction', in which Blair's operatives under Jonathan Powell and Alastair Campbell collaborated with John Scarlett, the chairman of the Joint Intelligence Committee, to produce a gloss on information available through UK intelligence sources. Clearly the misgivings which C had detected in Washington about such a publication had been overcome.

This document included the headline-grabbing claims that Iraq 'would be able to use their chemical and biological weapons within 45 minutes of an order to do so . . . could deploy such weapons within 45 minutes . . . some weapons could be deployed within 45 minutes of an order'. These claims were relayed instantly by reporters, including myself, broadcasting live outside Number 10. (Journalists from regional newspapers were said to have told Lord Butler's committee that they received the dossier with the forty-five-minute claim highlighted in yellow pen.) Given that the claims turned out to be wholly false, some could argue that we were accomplices in a propaganda operation. I do not recall any attempts by government press officers to qualify the forty-five-minute claim as it appeared in the media. Indeed, it was only under subsequent questioning, at lobby meetings and elsewhere, that official spokesmen clarified that the British resources under threat could only be those in the immediate vicinity, such as forces based in Cyprus. The impression that only medium-range tactical targets were vulnerable was not the one given in the dossier, which talked about 'strategic missile systems' in a sentence immediately preceding one of the forty-five-minute claims.

In spite of the mounting evidence to the contrary, Tony Blair continued to be super-confident that Iraq possessed weapons of mass destruction, even when Iraq was under US and UK occupation. In the immediate aftermath of the war at the June 2003 St Petersburg tercentenary celebrations, Blair told me during an interview that there was 'stuff' we – the public and media – didn't know about. Questioned again at the end of July in Japan following Dr David Kelly's death, he repeated this claim: 'I don't want to set away something before they [weapons inspection teams] are actually ready to submit their findings but you asked me was I as confident now as I was in St Petersburg? The answer is yes.' In St Petersburg, Blair had told me that there was extra material evidence of WMD. This never materialised. But when I raised the question with him again in 2007, he demonstrated a lawyer's training to elide from the fact of extra evidence to the belief that it was there.

ADAM BOULTON: . . . at St Petersburg just after we had gone to war you told me that weapons of mass destruction, were, and I quote, 'were the basis in law for taking military action'. Given that there weren't any weapons of mass destruction, doesn't that mean that the war was illegal?

BLAIR: No, it doesn't mean that because the basis of the case was the UN resolution and whether it had been complied with or not and incidentally, just to repeat this, everybody at the time was convinced that there were WMD so history can but . . .

ADAM BOULTON: [interrupting] I would have thought you would have taken longer to check. I mean people like Hans Blix or President Chirac or whoever.

BLAIR: Yes, and I know you did the interview with Hans Blix but I had many conversations with Hans Blix at the time . . .

ADAM BOULTON: He said you used spin, you acted in bad faith, you were guilty of witchcraft.

BLAIR: Those weren't quite the conversations we were having at the time.

As it was, the British dossier provided a substantial part of the evidence cited to the UN by the then US secretary of state, Colin

Powell, to secure Resolution 1441. There are many who argue that Blair never got anything in exchange for his unstinting loyalty to the president. In fact, he got a good deal: time and support to pursue the UN track on Iraq including a second resolution after 1441.

As Defense Secretary Donald Rumsfeld made clear, the US was prepared to 'work around' the absence of British troops in the fighting force, an option which President Bush reiterated in March 2003 prior to the make-or-break vote in the Commons. But the preference, advocated not least by Blair himself, was to keep Britain on board. Bush never argued the case for deposing Saddam Hussein on specifics. He didn't need to. In the shock of 9/11 the American people gave Bush a licence to hit back against unspecified enemies. Saddam Hussein had already claimed a place high on America's 'most wanted' list. In spite of the imminence of war, Bush did not bother to equivocate about the absence of a link between Iraq and al-Qaeda at a brief 'press availability' with Blair in the White House on 31 January 2003:

ADAM BOULTON: One question for you both. Do you believe there is a link between Saddam Hussein, a direct link, and the men who attacked on September the 11th?
BUSH: [speaking faintly] I never made that claim . . .
BLAIR: [jumping in after an uncomfortable pause] That answers your question. Umm the one thing I would say, however, is that I've got absolutely no doubt at all that unless we deal with both these threats together they will come together in a deadly form.

Bush could also make the case for war centred on generalised unease about the potential threat of weapons of mass destruction falling into the hands of failed or rogue states. He could also make the case for taking a strategic opportunity to reorder the entire Middle East – as was explicitly advocated by Vice President Cheney, Deputy Defense Secretary Paul Wolfowitz and other neo-conservative supporters of the 'Project for the New American Century'.

Blair, however, felt the need for legal cover.

History may conclude that the space granted to the UK was

ultimately of little worth and that Britain would have been better to have deployed its diplomatic skills planning for the aftermath in Iraq, as Foreign Office worthies such as Sir Jeremy Greenstock have implied. Blair, however, relished the challenge of persuading the world. There was a certain amount of hubris involved, built up by the success of previous spin operations and over the Balkans in particular. Blair was not the only one to exaggerate his capabilities. 'Oh the Frogs always come round in the end,' Sir Christopher Meyer, Britain's ambassador to the US, informed me during Blair's fraught visit to Washington DC in January 2003, even though comment from Paris was already building towards President Chirac's explicit 'Non'. The feeling in London was that a second resolution could be a 'get out of jail free' card because it would guarantee the legitimacy of the war. Once it became clear that a second resolution could not be obtained, Blair had to reverse his arguments, using the cover of Attorney General Lord Goldsmith's unpublished advice to cabinet. He had produced arguments based on a belief in WMD rather than the legal conclusions of Goldsmith's report.

On 29 May 2003, Andrew Gilligan's infamous reports on Radio Four's *Today* programme coincided with a prime ministerial visit to Iraq, Blair's first since the liberation of the country from Saddam Hussein. Gilligan claimed in his first, unscripted delivery at 6:07 a.m. that a source had told him the government 'probably knew that the forty-five minute figure was wrong even before it decided to put it in' the dossier. In a later broadcast he reverted to the scripted line as approved by his night editor to state that the government viewed the forty-five-minute claim as 'questionable' rather than 'wrong'. Alastair Campbell, Jonathan Powell and others muttered to the travelling press party about a 'typical *Today* programme', but they seemed more concerned by a report that day in the *Guardian* of tensions between London and the US State Department.

Follow-up to Gilligan's allegations made at best a sidebar to the reports on Blair in Iraq. Most of the other media took the story for what it was – unsourced context in a continuing debate about the use of intelligence in the public case made for war, but two developments prompted Campbell to provoke a full-scale confrontation with the

BBC. On 1 June, Gilligan expanded on his claims in an article for the *Mail on Sunday*, for the first time naming Campbell as responsible for 'sexing up' the dossier. Susan Watts, BBC *Newsnight's* cerebral science correspondent, produced two reports drawing on conversations with a source, who it subsequently transpired was Dr David Kelly.

On 6 June, Campbell, Blair's director of communications and strategy, complained to the BBC about Gilligan's 'irresponsible reporting of what he claims to be information from intelligence sources'. On 12 June, Campbell demanded an internal BBC inquiry. All of this amounted to a one-sided escalation by Campbell of an issue which was not central to the national debate about Iraq. With the benefit of hindsight, energies at the top of government would have been better devoted to managing the post-war situation there.

Throughout June political life went on as usual. David Kelly went to Iraq for a five-day working trip. On his return, he informed Foreign Office and Ministry of Defence officials that he had spoken to Gilligan. Blair continued with his US-inspired practice of having 'editorial boards' of news organisations to lunch. He and Campbell entertained top BBC executives on 13 June. Conversation was banal and avoided the Gilligan issue. Blair suggested the BBC should concentrate more on what was going on in Britain.

The House of Commons Foreign Affairs Select Committee continued its inquiry into the use of intelligence. Simultaneously ineffectual and wrong-headed, the committee's conduct and conclusions seriously called into question the validity of these attempts by backbench MPs to scrutinise the actions of the executive. They were yet another example of an innovation parodied, rather than adapted from the US Congress. In its report published on 7 July, the committee cleared Campbell of 'sexing up' the dossier, while conceding that 'undue prominence' had been given to the claim that Saddam could have launched a WMD attack within forty-five minutes. Even after his name was in the public domain in July, the committee both publicly harried Dr Kelly and then mistakenly dismissed him as the source – memorably he was called 'chaff' to his face by one Labour committee member.

In June, the committee's function had provided Campbell with a platform from which to lambast the BBC. Nostrils flaring, eyes flashing, he banged the table during his appearance on the 25th, vowing not to let the matter rest. It was a performance he substantially repeated on live television three days later when he invited himself on to *Channel 4 News*, on the way home from a day spent at the Wimbledon tennis championships.

Campbell's behaviour was the apotheosis of the way Blair ran his inner office. He delegated relations with the media to Campbell to such a degree that he ceded control of them. Campbell was the match for Blair in physical stature and charisma and now he took licence to pursue his own vendetta – ultimately it was his integrity which was challenged directly by Gilligan, not the prime minister's. The records show that at points during the ensuing catastrophe, Blair intervened to ask if Campbell was sure he was proceeding wisely, but the prime minister never once countermanded his employee.

By the beginning of July, Kelly's voluntary approaches to officials meant that he had been identified within government as Gilligan's probable source. The expert, who was preparing for another weapons-hunting trip to Iraq, insisted, 'I most certainly have never attempted to undermine government policy in any way.' Technically, Kelly was a scientific expert rather than a member of the intelligence community. Downing Street also seems to have persuaded itself that Kelly was low level, even though he was being considered for a knighthood. Dr Kelly denied that he had directly accused Campbell of 'sexing up' the dossier. Taken together, this convinced Campbell that revelation of Kelly's identity as the source would 'fuck Gilligan', as he told Defence Secretary Geoff Hoon, according to his own diaries.

By 7 July, Kelly's likely role was known to all of Blair's closest advisers: Campbell, Jonathan Powell, Geoff Hoon, MoD Permanent Secretary Sir Kevin Tebbit, Chairman of the Defence Intelligence Committee Sir John Scarlett and Cabinet Office Intelligence Co-ordinator Sir David Omand. That day Blair met with his advisers to discuss Kelly and the government response to the Foreign Affairs Committee report. The prime minister wanted to know what Kelly would say about WMD if questioned publicly. He was told Kelly had supported the war but could be embarrassing on some specifics.

On 8 July, Blair held a further meeting on the matter. Government officials began the process which would lead to the rapid identification of Kelly as Gilligan's source. The Ministry of Defence announced that an unnamed official had come forward to say he had met Gilligan. (It subsequently transpired that Kelly had been authorised, even encouraged, to meet journalists to give them off-the-record background briefings on WMD.)

That afternoon, at the regular lobby briefing held in the House of Commons, the prime minister's official spokesman, Tom Kelly, volunteered information which could only make it easier for the media to identify the suspected source. Tom Kelly was habitually a somewhat constipated and grudging briefer, scrupulously and explicitly conscious of how far he should go as a member of the civil service. His normal practice was to veer too far on the side of caution for the taste of journalists working his beat, but that day, referring to notes, he narrowed down the categories from which the suspect came . . . not a naval man . . . not an intelligence officer . . . had been to Iraq, etc. Tom Kelly was caught in a storm whipped up by his *de facto*, but unaccountable and politicised boss, Campbell, and seemed uneasy. As we were leaving the briefing, he asked me privately what I thought. I replied that the man in question would be identified in a matter of days and that it would all end in tears. Government press officers continued their unusually helpful interactions. At the Ministry of Defence, the director of communications, Pam Teare, was happy to engage in a guessing game with reporters until the right name came up. On 9 July several newspapers identified Dr David Kelly as Gilligan's source.

On 17 July, Blair was once again on his travels, this time in the Far East, when news of David Kelly's death reached him. His trip had begun triumphantly in Washington with his address to both houses of the US Congress.

Satellite telephones on planes were a mixed blessing for reporters already struggling with an official schedule which seemed designed to deprive them of rest, but if they were there, you had to use them. As the plane approached Japan, check-calls to London disclosed first, that Dr Kelly was missing from his home and shortly afterwards, that a body had been found. Campbell had stayed on in the US on personal business, so eventually it fell to Godric Smith, the prime minister's other official spokesman, to give a holding brief as the plane went into its pre-landing descent. My first broadcast analysis was that there would have to be an official inquiry (right), that Campbell would go (right) and that Defence Secretary Hoon would go (wrong).

Downing Street announced that there would be an independent judicial inquiry and Blair ended up having to confront the media in unlikely settings in Japan and Korea.

The main Japanese summit took place in a gloomy mountain resort favoured by Prime Minister Koizumi: a place of pine forests and lakes lapping at the foothills of Mount Fuji. The water was so black you felt that a monster could rear up from it or that the deep would simply suck you in to drown. Blair and Koizumi gave a brief, heavily policed news conference that Saturday evening. At the end, Jonathan Oliver of the *Mail on Sunday*, under strict orders from his editor, stood up and shouted, 'Have you got blood on your hands prime minister? Are you going to resign over this?' For an instant Blair and Koizumi looked wearily into the cameras, before filing out without giving an answer.

The next morning, Blair honoured a commitment to do an extended television interview with me. There were no hitches — except the adamant refusal of the hotel management to let us place furniture on the tatami mats in the room set aside for the recording. The prime minister declined to recall Parliament, or to cut short his visit, parrying questions about Kelly's death with the fact that the judge's inquiry was now imminent. Nonetheless his words were shot through with shock, and the sense that things had got out of control.

BLAIR: . . . look first and foremost this is a terrible personal tragedy. What has happened is absolutely awful and whatever position anyone has taken in respect of this, and whatever the past few weeks, I don't think anybody in any quarter wanted or anticipated this happening . . .

ADAM BOULTON: Do you accept that whatever your officials did, whatever Alastair Campbell did, whatever is said about them, ultimately it is your responsibility because they worked for you?

BLAIR: Of course. In the end the government is my responsibility, and I can assure you that the judge will be able to get all the facts, and all the people, and all the papers that he wants to.

Blair's tour continued to be accident prone. The next day in Korea, Blair's meeting at the Blue House, the presidential residence, coincided with confirmation by the BBC that the late Dr Kelly had indeed been Gilligan's source. This caused a diplomatic incident at the subsequent news conference when the British reporter Nick Robinson chose to ask Blair about Kelly, rather than to pose a question to President Roh Moo-hyun, as he had been directed to by the Korean spokesman chairing the event. Before the British party could leave, Robinson was summoned to make an apology. He duly did this while pointing out that he had entered into no undertaking about which leader he would question. His explanation was listened to in silence by the Korean spokesman and then rejected with the words 'Apology: not accepted!'

En route from Korea to Hong Kong, Blair spoke to the travelling party of journalists informally for the first time since Kelly had gone missing. On foreign trips such gatherings usually took place with the prime minister standing up against the bulkhead at the front of the economy class cabin (which was often empty except for luggage on the governmental BA charters). It was usually difficult to hear what was being said as reporters clambered over the seats to get close. Even the official transcripts of the government recordings often had to include the explanation 'inaudible'.

On this occasion I was sitting in the front row next to Paul Eastham of the *Daily Mail*, inches from the prime minister. Eastham cut through Blair's briefing about Hong Kong, 'Why did you authorise the naming of David Kelly?'

Blair responded immediately, 'That is completely untrue, and why again, as I say, don't you wait for the inquiry . . . you should just wait for the inquiry to have a look at it. There is no point in trying to drag me into speculation about what the inquiry might find, or what it might not find, or might do.'

PAUL EASTHAM: But if you think you know the facts, why don't you tell us what they are?

BLAIR: Because Paul, what we have decided to, because of what has happened, is to have the inquiry, and I think we should just allow the inquiry to do its work. Now I know you will want to get me to answer these same type of questions in all sorts of different ways, I am not going to do it, we should let the inquiry find the facts.

There were then some exchanges about why ministers were still attacking the BBC if the best policy was not to comment. But I brought the discussion back to the key point:

ADAM BOULTON: Can I just ask the question that follows on from what Paul asked you, which is did you authorise anyone in Downing Street, or in the MoD, to release David Kelly's name?

BLAIR: As I just said a moment or two ago, emphatically not. I did not authorise the leaking of the name David Kelly.

ADAM BOULTON: That puts Alastair Campbell in a very awkward position because we know the Ministry of Defence did confirm the identity of David Kelly.

BLAIR: Look, that was a completely different matter once the name was out there.

(A day later Blair went home early after all because of a typhoon warning in Hong Kong.)

These exchanges are important because they were Blair's most explicit denial of any involvement in the sequence of events which led to Dr Kelly's death. Neither they, not their import, were examined by Lord Hutton's judicial inquiry which went along with the government's contention that how Kelly's name entered the public domain was a side issue. In the view of most journalists, public exposure infinitely increased the pressure on Kelly, making him the prey of the Foreign Affairs Committee and the media and directly triggering the MoD disciplinary procedures against him.

Blair had attended two high-level meetings immediately before the name became public, following which government officials, Tom Kelly and Teare, helped reporters tease out Dr Kelly's identity. Yet Blair 'emphatically' denied any involvement. Although, ever the lawyer, he did not extend the denial to the actions of his employees, while entering the qualifier that things were completely different 'once the name was out there', without specifying where 'there' was.

Blair's legal approach continued to the subsequent judicial inquiry, for which his close friend Charlie Falconer, who later became Lord Chancellor after a successful career at the bar, set the terms of reference and chose the presiding Law Lord, Brian Hutton.

It was customary during Hutton's proceedings in the Courts of Justice for witnesses to be asked a final, open question: had they anything else to say? Most, including BBC executives and civil servants, replied that the inquiry was about a human tragedy which they mourned and that they would learn any lessons necessary. Blair, Campbell and Hoon simply declined to say anything more. The government's argument, which Hutton accepted, was that what had happened was nothing to do with them – it had all been the fault of a bothersome BBC Radio report. Few in the court of public opinion felt reconciled to that verdict.

Prime Minister Tony Blair displayed a similar inclination to detach himself from responsibility for any other of the unpalatable consequences of the war on terror. He never publicly spoke out against any aspect of the detentions at Guantánamo Bay, until after specific changes were already underway. When pressed, he repeated the British government's principled opposition to the death penalty, but he argued that he was powerless to intervene in any of the cases in Iraq – that was a matter for the Iraqis, even though Saddam and his colleagues were kept under American guard until minutes before their executions. In the run-up to Saddam Hussein's sordid killing, Blair was reluctant to comment personally but I pressed him to do so during the monthly news conference:

ADAM BOULTON: Do you think he should get the death penalty?
BLAIR: Well as Margaret [Beckett] set out our position on the death penalty yesterday . . .

ADAM BOULTON: Well I want your position, you're the prime minister. You've been prime minister for ten years, she's been foreign secretary for five minutes. Do you think Saddam Hussein should be executed?

BLAIR: [irate] Hey Adam, excuse me thank you very much. I've just said she set out the position for the government yesterday. Yeah, and that's all I want to say on it [voice raised]. Right? Our position on the death penalty is well known, but actually . . .

ADAM BOULTON: So should he be executed?

BLAIR: I've just said, our position on the death penalty is well known. [*Pauses*]

We're opposed to it [*rapidly*] – as Margaret said yesterday. So that is . . .

ADAM BOULTON: And you oppose his execution then do you mean?

BLAIR: . . . so obviously we're opposed to the death penalty, we're in exactly the position that she described.

ADAM BOULTON: You oppose his execution?

BLAIR: Adam . . . [*extending palm and raising eyebrows*] . . . excuse me, that is just enough, thank you very much.

ADAM BOULTON: Why don't you say it?

BLAIR: Because I happen to want to express myself in my own way. If you don't mind [*shakes head and pauses*]. Thank you. Now, on identity cards [*chuckling*] . . . what did you have for breakfast then this morning?

The quip raised the couple of laughs needed to defuse the atmosphere. But it did not dispel my sense that Blair was sidestepping any moral responsibility.

The Blair doctrine

Tony Blair is famous for having sent British troops into more conflicts – Bosnia, Kosovo, Sierra Leone, Afghanistan and of course Iraq – than any other prime minister since Winston Churchill's tenure during the Second World War. This was an unforeseen aspect of his premiership. As a young man Blair had shown no enthusiasm for the military. He had avoided serving in the cadet force at school and, unlike Neil Kinnock, he had not been mad for toy soldiers and martial patriotism as a small boy. In his early days in power, Blair attended a conference in Paris where he spoke of belonging to a generation which might never be called upon to go to war:

> I was born in 1953, a child of the Cold War era, raised amid the constant fear of a conflict with the potential to destroy humanity. Whatever other dangers may exist, no such fear exists today. Mine is the first generation able to contemplate the possibility that we may live our entire lives without going to war or sending our children to war. That is a prize beyond value. (Speech at the signing of the NATO–Russia Founding Act, 27 May 1997)

Blair's entanglements in wars can be explained by his politics and his pragmatic temperament, rather than by passion. His belief was that Britain could be a force for good in the world if only 'hard choices are made'. In the case of war, this was a choice about paying a 'blood price' – with other people's lives.

Blair's willingness to use force fitted the mood of the times which saw the West engage in repeated small-scale wars. As Blair grew towards political maturity, Ronald Reagan and Margaret Thatcher (and later John Major and George Bush senior) were enjoying military successes in the Falklands, Grenada, Panama and the first Gulf War. On 16 June, Blair had to interrupt his farewell tour to attend the service held at the Falklands Islands Memorial Chapel in Pangbourne. The ceremony, with the congregation led by the Queen and including Margaret Thatcher, had even more poignancy that year as it commemorated the twenty-fifth anniversary of the conflict.

Under Blair, military coalitions overwhelmed resistance in the Balkans, Afghanistan and even Iraq during the 2003 invasion (at least in the campaign's initial execution, if not its aftermath). All these conflicts set and achieved limited objectives at a relatively low cost in lives on the intervening side.

The assumption of guaranteed military success with minimal

casualties has since been confounded in both Afghanistan and Iraq. It may have been military 'mission accomplished' when Saddam Hussein was deposed, but as Blair went, neither he nor Bush could claim victory. For the Americans in particular, the mounting death toll was heavy and painful. The war prompted the break-up of the Western coalition, with America and Britain on one side and France, Germany and much of the United Nations on the other. And in the form of al-Qaeda, a new and as yet unvanquished enemy had emerged, with guiding tenets that seemingly could not be reconciled with a 'new international order'.

As Blair preceded Bush from office, both hounded by the Iraq adventure, they left an uncertain world behind them. With their exit it seemed that a generation-long era in international politics was closing. This era could be taken as the twenty-five-year span from 1982 to 2007. For Britain it was a period of growing self-confidence as a nation. For the first time since Korea and Suez in the 1950s, British forces had been deployed abroad for 'constructive' political ends, rather than to cover post-colonial withdrawals. Britain had recovered economically. And successive governments developed a more muscular foreign policy, 'bridging Europe and America' as Blair saw it – although British prime ministers seemed to find the United States a more congenial partner than the European Union (in spite of winning many arguments there). Margaret Thatcher and Tony Blair were the two chief British protagonists of this era. The Falklands conflict and the Iraq invasion were its two battered bookends.

The Thatcher era

Mrs Thatcher's style and beliefs were bitterly controversial, but the way Britain changed during her eleven years in power undoubtedly restored national pride. John Major cemented this transformation by winning a fourth consecutive general election for the Conservatives. This meant that there were a clear six and half years after her departure from office for Thatcher's revolution to be consolidated.

In foreign policy terms, the Thatcher era was the period when

Britain stopped 'clinging to the wreckage', 'managing decline' or 'punching above its weight' to use the phrases beloved of both social-democratic apologists on the left and Tory 'Wets' to the right. But this change in perceived power was forged by experience rather than by rhetoric. The first Thatcher government had proceeded cautiously, feeling the way ahead. It was also responding reactively to unprovoked aggression against a British colony. The Argentine junta invaded Las Malvinas because the conventional wisdom was that Britain would do nothing much about it. The British government's unexpected decision to confront an offensive by outsiders in the Falklands, and the victory which followed, transformed thinking about what might be achieved in the late twentieth century through the limited use of force.

In the decade after the Falklands, Britain and America were increasingly willing to use force for interventions to right perceived wrongs. But in almost all cases, the definition of a threatened national interest was stretched to include indirect threats: unfriendly dictators in Latin America, supposedly linked to the narcotics trade for example. Even the ousting of Saddam Hussein from Kuwait was action in support of an ally and because of a perceived threat to oil security.

Military engagements were taken on with confidence in this period because there was little fear of escalation into a regional or global conflict, mainly due to the fact that the Cold War was coming to an end. Militarily, the Soviet Union was bogged down in Afghanistan; economically, its command economy was on the brink of collapse. The first President Bush, President George W. Bush's father, began to talk of a 'new international order'; and the academic and sometime US government adviser Francis Fukuyama developed the concept of the 'end of history'. Both men helped fuel the growing popular belief during this period that Western values – liberal free market democracy – would prevail globally because there was ultimately no other game in town.

By the time Tony Blair came to power, the Soviet Union had collapsed, and, along with it, the Cold War and the Warsaw Pact. The first leaders of the new Russia, Mikhail Gorbachev and Boris Yeltsin, had been identified as 'men we can do business with' by

Thatcher and Major. Rather more questionably, both Blair and George W. Bush took the same view of the new Russian president, the former KGB major, Vladimir Putin.

The rising powers of China, India and Latin America were believed to be aspiring to emulate rather than confront us. Militant Islamism was identified mainly with the Shiites in Iran and considered containable. Africa was simply a case for compassion.

The Balkans

In 1997 the Blair government swept into office promising to do something in many areas it alleged the Tories had 'shamefully neglected'. In truth, moving more decisively on a course already indicated by the previous government was perhaps a better description. A total ban on handguns (in response to the Dunblane school massacre in 1996) was one example of this. Another was Blair's determination to get a grip on the Balkans and the sectarian conflicts which had broken out there between the various nationalities and ethnic groups that had been contained in what was now known as FRY, or the Former Republic of Yugoslavia.

Mainly under the leadership of Josip Broz Tito, Yugoslavia had been an independent socialist republic since 1945. Tito kept the influence of the Soviet Union at bay, pursued noticeably more liberal policies at home and towards the West than the Soviet communists and founded the non-aligned movement.

Tito died in 1980. Through the ensuing decade an independent, centralised Yugoslavia became less sustainable. This was in part due to nationalist aspirations, provoked by the dominant Serbs (Russia's traditional allies), as well as the fact that the neighbouring Soviet Union had ceased to exist as a *de facto* guarantor of Yugoslavia's socialist totalitarian system, in spite of the smaller federation's declared independence.

The break-up of Yugoslavia resulted in a decade of conflict between 1991 and 2001 in what constituted a sizeable part of Eastern Europe. It was the first time since the Second World War that genocide took place on European soil and also the first time that the Western alliance, in the form of NATO, had entered an armed conflict – and one outside its own boundaries at that.

The first half of the 1990s was taken up with vicious wars of independence waged against the Serb-dominated central government by Croatia and Bosnia-Herzegovina. Slobodan Milosevic, the ethnic Serbian president of Yugoslavia, had stirred up the conflicts by agitating for the rights of ethnic Serbs, who made up the largest ethnic group within Yugoslavia, in every part of the republic.

Bold claims were made that this was 'the hour of Europe', the chance for the European Union to prove its foreign and security policy clout by sorting out a conflict in its own backyard. But the EU failed dismally – apparently more preoccupied with conceiving the euro single currency. Repeated EU crisis meetings throughout 1991 were unable to muster the political will, the manpower or the military might to act effectively. British Foreign Secretary Douglas Hurd repeatedly argued that it would take a deployment of 40,000 troops to contain the situation on the ground and that 'simply isn't going to happen'. (In fact at the height of its intervention NATO was to deploy some 50,000 troops.) Instead, historic ties and national interests came into play.

At a summit meeting outside Rome in November 1991, NATO encouraged the ambitions of every ethnic group in FRY by recognising the independence of Slovenia and Croatia, an inflammatory move advocated by Germany. Britain acquiesced not because of conviction but because it had secured a side-deal permitting an opt-out from Monetary Union at the approaching Maastricht negotiations. No one in the UK took much notice – the national media were preoccupied by the fatal disappearance from his yacht of the corrupt newspaper tycoon Robert Maxwell. In the conflicts that followed, over 100,000 people lost their lives and millions were displaced. The bloodiest atrocities occurred in Bosnia, where ethnic cleansing was carried out by both Muslims and Serbs. Notoriously, as in Srebrenica where 8,000 Muslim men were massacred, much of this took place while United Nations peacekeeping forces stood idly by.

Not for the first time in twentieth-century European history, bloodshed in this initial phase of the Balkan conflicts was halted only by the active engagement of the United States. Bill Clinton was very reluctant to entangle the US. However, he did agree to bombing raids from 15,000 feet. This combined operation was the first time that German forces had been permitted to take aggressive action since 1945. In 1995 President Clinton got the belligerent parties to sign up to the Dayton Accords, which established independent Bosnian and Serbian states, and protected the rights of Serbs in Bosnia within an autonomous enclave. The United Nations also set up an international court of justice in The Hague, intended to try alleged war criminals. Milosevic faced indictment for war crimes, but he also remained in power in Belgrade. At the end of 1997 he was promoted, becoming the president of the Federal Republic of Yugoslavia — as the rump Serbian-dominated nation was termed.

Blair became prime minister in Britain just as the second phase of the Balkan conflict was beginning. This was centred on the rights of ethnic Albanians in Kosovo, a semi-autonomous region of Serbia adjoining Albania and the Former Yugoslav Republic of Macedonia.

Under Milosevic, the Belgrade government had moved steadily to reduce the autonomous rights of ethnic Albanians during the 1980s and 1990s, claiming that the Serbian minority in the province of Kosovo was being persecuted. In 1990, ethnic Albanians largely boycotted a referendum of all of Serbia (in which ethnic Serbs had an inbuilt majority anyway) that was used to justify the shutting down of Kosovo's independent political institutions and the repression of the Albanian language. In 1991 and then 1992, the Kosovans organised unofficial referendums of their own, which voted overwhelmingly for an independent Republic of Kosovo and for Ibrahim Rugova as president.

Rugova advocated a policy of passive resistance, which kept Kosovo out of the conflicts in Croatia and Bosnia. By 1996, however, an insurgent Kosovan Liberation Army (KLA) had been formed. It was greatly strengthened in terms of weapons by the collapse of the authoritarian communist regime in Albania. KLA attacks on Serbs provoked harsh countermeasures by Serbian forces. In spite of shuttle diplomacy, the involvement of the Dayton 'contact group', and Kosovan appeals for a United Nations peacekeeping force, the cycle of KLA attacks and Serbian reprisals only escalated.

In January 1999, NATO agreed that it would be prepared to intervene with aerial bombardments against the Serbs in support of the Kosovans. Once again, Clinton refused to commit any 'boots on the ground'. In a statement to the House of Commons, Tony Blair used the somewhat weaker phrase, 'we do not plan to use ground troops'. The aerial attacks began on 24 March but they had little success in halting the ethnic cleansing. The raids were also a public relations disaster. On 16 April NATO planes, US F-16s, erroneously struck a Kosovan Albanian refugee convoy near Djakovica, killing more than sixty people. For five days NATO refused to comment in spite of persistent media pressure. The British government went quiet as well. It was a common practice of Alastair Campbell's news management at times of crisis to shut down, to emerge only for a single, intentionally definitive statement, timed if possible, just as the media heat of the incident was fading. (In the early days, Jon Snow's *Channel 4 News* encounter with Harriet Harman about sending her child to a grammar school was a classic example.)

After the Djakovica attack, my repeated requests for an interview were finally granted. Alastair Campbell had chosen the Cabinet Room as the location and we decided to interview Blair with the arc of the cabinet table stretching out behind him – this visually effective shot was to be used many times since. Naturally, the prime minister's tone was one of regret – of course this was a tragic event which he would much rather had not taken place. There was also a hint of exasperation, as if to say, what can you expect – sometimes things go wrong. But characteristically, there was not a flicker of doubt from the prime minister that the policy he was pursuing was right. Mistakes did not push him into questioning his basic attitudes. This remained his stance in spite of some sneering from British diplomats and military commanders when US planes 'accidentally' hit the Chinese embassy in Belgrade (out-of-date CIA intelligence was blamed).

In the meantime, Blair's intimate advisers were tasked with overhauling the NATO public relations operation. Anji Hunter, Alastair

Campbell and Julian Braithwaite (an up-and-coming Foreign Office secondee to the Downing Street press office) were dispatched to Brussels. Walls were knocked down to create a 'war room' and daily briefings by NATO spokesman Jamie Shea became a fixture on all international news networks. The success at NATO became one of Campbell's proudest boasts and emboldened him to establish similar spin controls for the Afghan and Iraq conflicts.

This was the context against which Tony Blair gave the most important foreign affairs speech of his premiership. Almost inevitably, given his acceptance of the pre-eminence of American power, he chose to make it during a trip to the US in April 1999. The timing was important too. Tony Blair was in the United States for the fiftieth anniversary celebrations and summit of NATO, to be held in Washington DC. While there he, Gerhard Schröder and Bill Clinton would also hold one of their 'Third Way' events, musing in public at the Democratic Leadership Council.

The main item on the NATO agenda was a redrafting of its articles to permit out-of-area interventions. This was considered more appropriate to the coming century than the original terms of the organisation as established in 1949 – an essentially defensive pact to ensure prompt action should Russian tanks or planes advance from the East.

The idea of a broader interventionist mandate was becoming widely acceptable. In 1998, Kofi Annan, Secretary-General of the United nations, used his Ditchley Foundation Lecture 'Intervention' to suggest a re-examination of UN articles to permit more intervention in an interdependent world. But, as so often the case, putting it into practice would be quite another matter. Blair's real mission in Washington was to persuade an extremely reluctant President Clinton to commit ground troops – 'American boys and girls' as Clinton had emotionally put it when explaining his caution – to saving the Kosovans.

Blair therefore went to the US not only with a new doctrine but with an immediate first test for its application. To help write it, the Downing Street chief of staff called in Professor Lawrence Freedman of the Department of War Studies at King's College London. Freedman was an expert in limited war and was already engaged in writing the official history of the Falklands conflict. Blair would later recommend him for a knighthood, and he was among the guests at one of Blair's last personal receptions held in the final few days at Number 10. In 1999, though, Freedman was by no means an intimate of New Labour. The approach to him came 'at short notice, out of the blue' and he was surprised that far from just contributing to a draft, his words were virtually unchanged in the speech as delivered. Freedman's contribution gave Blair a certain intellectual swagger. He even felt bold enough to contradict an Iron Chancellor (though not Gordon Brown), citing Bismarck's contention that the Balkans were not worth the bones of one Pomeranian Grenadier.

What subsequently became known as 'the Chicago speech' was delivered in the late afternoon of 22 April 1999 to the Chicago Economic Club in a rather dingy 'ballroom' at a downtown hotel. Appropriate to his audience, the prime minister talked about globalisation, changing international financial institutions and how Chicago had inspired Selfridges, Oxford Street's main department store. But Blair moved on very quickly from the economic to the geopolitical and the potentially military: 'We are all internationalists now, whether we like it or not. We cannot refuse to participate in global markets if we want to prosper. We cannot ignore new political ideas in other countries if we want to innovate. We cannot turn our backs on conflicts and the violation of human rights within other countries if we want still to be secure.'

While paying tribute to the principle of non-interference, he also buried it: 'the principle of non-interference must be qualified in important respects'. In its place, Blair proposed a new system of relations which accepted the post-Cold War pre-eminence of Western nations, and went beyond realpolitik to embrace action based on 'values': 'a new framework. No longer is our existence as states under threat. Now our actions are guided by a more subtle blend of mutual self-interest and moral purpose in defending the values we cherish. In the end, values and interests merge.'

The prime minister referred pointedly to the situation unfolding in the Balkans: 'Unspeakable things are happening in Europe . . . awful things we thought we'd never see again . . . ethnic cleansing, systematic rape, mass murder.' He noted almost with satisfaction that 'Our armed forces have been busier than ever – delivering humanitarian aid, deterring attacks on defenceless people, backing up UN resolutions and occasionally engaging in major wars as we did in the Gulf in 1991 and are currently doing in the Balkans.' This displayed Blair's essentially utilitarian approach – if you've got armies you might as well use them. And his comparatively casual acceptance of the consequences, i.e. 'occasionally engaging in major wars'.

And while his main intent was to call for further action in the Balkans, there was also something prophetic in the global troublemakers he identified: 'Many of our problems have been caused by two dangerous and ruthless men – Saddam Hussein and Slobodan Milosevic.' The Chicago speech was a very frank exposition of Blair's international preoccupations in 1999. Saddam Hussein, against whom Britain and America had carried out the 'Operation Desert Fox' bomb and missile attacks and were still imposing no-fly zones and UN sanctions, was very much present in his mind. The prime minister also made reference to Israel and Palestine, but Islamic fundamentalism was absent (climate change was taken up in passing).

Officially, the ideas outlined in Chicago were called 'the doctrine of international community', but subsequently they became known as 'the doctrine of humanitarian intervention'. Blair himself later took to using this phrase. Whatever it was labelled, the doctrine had emerged from the prime minister and his personal advisers, including David Miliband, then head of the Downing Street Policy Unit.

The mandarins at the Foreign Office had not been consulted and were dismayed. On the other hand, Blair was developing a strong working relationship with 'the generals', as Number 10 took to referring to them. 'CDS', Chief of Defence Staff Sir Charles Guthrie, and Sir Michael 'Whacko Jacko' Jackson, who commanded the Kosovo operation, became close advisers. Both military men noted later how Blair could see things from their point of view. The prime minister asked about potential casualties in a Balkans campaign and was given some troubling estimates of the 'Butcher's bill', in Jackson's phrase. He listened soberly but 'he didn't flinch', Jackson recorded.

The Washington summit that followed the Chicago speech turned out to be perhaps the most difficult few days in the Blair–Clinton relationship. The British briefed that the US would come on board; the Americans' counter-briefed against Blair. The outcome was inconclusive. For the time being, the bombing raids continued and the refugee crisis deepened. In total, more than a million Kosovans were displaced that summer.

Blair took to megaphone diplomacy through the media for his calls to action and gave top priority to powerful television images, backdrops and strong soundbites. After General Guthrie and Anji Hunter had recce'd the situation on the ground, he made two highly emotional trips in May 1999 to the huge, sordid refugee camps that were mushrooming across the Kosovan borders in Macedonia and Albania. There were around 200,000 people crowded into the Stankovic 1 camp at Blace, the no-man's land bordering Macedonia. After visiting a family in their tent, Blair took the moral high ground: 'This is a battle for humanity, it is a just cause.' He went further at Elbasan in Albania, dressing in the national colours of red and black. Hailed by chanting crowds, he declared: 'It is a battle between good and evil, between civilisation and barbarity. Our promise to you, all of you is that you should return in peace to the land that is yours.'

As with Thatcher in the Falklands, Blair was justifying the use of force in the moral terms of right and wrong, without in his case any direct national interest. She, as a child of the war years, instinctively saw foreign affairs with the mindset of that time, having witnessed the failure of appeasement. Now the much younger Blair was doing the same thing. In Chicago, on his Balkan visits and in the British media, Blair repeatedly drew parallels between the treatment meted out to the Kosovans and the Holocaust.

As international diplomatic efforts became more purposeful, Blair and the French President, Jacques Chirac, told Clinton that they could be successful only if backed up by the threat of force. Furthermore, they implied, the threat itself might be enough to do the trick without the need for actual fighting. Neither Britain nor France, however, was central to the main diplomatic negotiations. These involved Russia, the Serbs' old ally, represented by President

Yeltsin's fixer Viktor Chernomyrdin, United States Deputy Secretary of State Strobe Talbott and EU/UN envoy Martti Ahtisaari of Finland.

At the beginning of June Russia added its weight to the calls for a total, verifiable withdrawal of Serb forces from Kosovo as a precondition for an end to the bombing. In spite of being strong-armed by Yeltsin, Milosevic believed that Russian troops would still look after Serbian vital interests and so the Serbs agreed to the withdrawal on 9 June. The bombardment stopped the next day. The UN Security Council passed a resolution deploying NATO forces to oversee the return of refugees.

So eventually that summer, just as Blair had wanted, ground forces – including British troops – did indeed move into Kosovo to protect the ethnic Albanians. It was a triumphant example of the 'risk averse' use of force. The only casualties on the Western side were two helicopter pilots killed in a training accident. No British troops lost their lives in the advance. Serbian resistance proved much weaker than had been feared. And General Jackson ignored orders from NATO's (American) supreme commander, Wesley Clark, by refusing to get drawn into a potentially dangerous confrontation with Russian forces over who should occupy Pristina airport (shades perhaps of Berlin 1944). The Serbian side claimed to have lost fewer than 3,000 military and civilian lives, in spite of 36,000 NATO bombing sorties. The number of Kosovans killed between 1996 and 1999 remains the subject of debate but has been estimated at some 10,000.

On this first test of 'humanitarian intervention', Blair's luck had held. As he told the adoring crowds who were chanting 'Tony, Tony' when he visited Pristina, he believed his moral imperative had been justified. Even so, the adventure had not been perfect either militarily or diplomatically.

Intensive bombing from high altitude (even if British pilots went in lower than the Americans were prepared to) proved remarkably ineffective. Milosevic had managed to preserve almost all the Serbian forces' best equipment, partly by using shelters and setting out decoy targets. The bombing certainly didn't halt the activities of the Serbs. Faultlines in the chain of command for NATO operations had also been exposed in the political tensions between the member states' national political leaders and on the ground between Jackson and Clark as SACEUR (Supreme Allied Commander Europe).

The most important feature of the conflict from a diplomatic perspective was that NATO's military intervention – out of area, in a non-defensive action – had not had the support of a UN Security Council resolution. This was the chief charge from some on the left who opposed the operation, including Tariq Ali, Noam Chomsky and Edward Said. At the time, such criticisms were little more than an irritation to Blair – above all because he stood shoulder to shoulder on Kosovo with President Chirac and Chancellor Schröder.

Politically, retreat from Kosovo did not immediately bring down Milosevic. He was ousted sixteen months later as a result of domestic developments in Belgrade rather than foreign pressure. Nonetheless, Blair would claim credit – as during his 2002 speech at the George Bush Senior Presidential Library – for removing Milosevic and undertaking 'regime change' in the former Yugoslavia. Milosevic became the first head of state to be put on trial for war crimes in an international court, but he died before justice was done. A refugee problem persisted in Kosovo for many years. And even as Blair left office, the final status of Kosovo remained unresolved. (The country finally declared its independence from Serbia on 17 February 2008.) Russia was still the key and awkward powerbroker, with President Putin far less amenable to Western aspirations than Boris Yeltsin had been.

In Chicago, Tony Blair had outlined 'five major considerations' before intervention: '1. Are we sure of our case? 2. Have we exhausted all diplomatic options? 3. Are there military operations we can sensibly and prudently undertake? 4. Are we prepared for the long term? 5. Do we have national interests at stake?' On Kosovo in 1999 he could answer an unconditional 'yes' to the first three questions. On the fourth point, he firmly stated his commitment to help the Kosovans in the future. As to the fifth, the 'doctrine of international community' predicated that national interests could be threatened by instability and repression in foreign countries.

In 1999, Blair's fortitude and judgement were applauded on the world stage. Kosovo became an inspiration and model for 'humanitarian intervention' based on moral principles. In Chicago he had already yoked Milosevic and Saddam Hussein together; in 2002 and 2003, and after the invasion of Iraq, he would draw similar parallels between Saddam and Hitler, and 'the way he treats his own people', along with the alleged presence of WMDs as the other justification for war. Kosovo may have encouraged Blair to think he was right in Iraq, but there his Chicago 'considerations' would dog both him and Bush. Military supremacy was proved but the four other key considerations remained wide open to question: just cause, diplomacy, long-term commitment and national interest.

Blair and Thatcher – a dual legacy?

Tony Blair never denied that he was Thatcher's child in two senses: she had been an inspirational leader during his formative years as a politician, and the relatively confident and prosperous nation which he took over in 1997 could be seen as her legacy. Certainly there would not have been a prevailing national mood of geopolitical optimism, an assumption that Britain once again counted for something in the world, had it not been for the victories in the Falklands and the 1991 Gulf War.

Blair was the first of Thatcher's successors who was inclined to celebrate her. John Major was chosen to take over by the same Conservative Party which ejected her from office. Major constantly had to define himself against her, promising a more collegiate style of government, even though he never really recovered from her suggestion that he was her favoured candidate because she could be a 'very good back seat driver'.

Thatcher was the chief political enemy of Neil Kinnock, the flawed but heroic Labour leader, throughout the 1980s. She beat him soundly in the general election of 1987. He in turn believed her to be the enemy of the vulnerable whose policies 'killed people'. Once they had both stood down from leading their parties, the only retrospective compliment Kinnock would give his old opponent was that she had been the first woman prime minister.

From 1992 to 1994 John Smith opposed John Major. As a frontbencher, Smith had come closer than his leader Neil Kinnock to discomforting Thatcher in the House of Commons during the resignation of Michael Heseltine brought on by the Westland helicopter affair. But Thatcher was not his main target and she was in any way antithetical to him. The paternalistic Scot who believed in the power of community had little in common with the leader who had famously declared 'there is no such thing as society'.

Blair was much more generous. Obviously, as a Labour politician, he considered his ideology to be very different from hers, but Mrs Thatcher had achieved two things Blair very much wanted to emulate: she had transformed her party and she had been a success, winning three successive general elections. Unlike Kinnock, Smith or Major, Blair was happy to be seen consorting with Thatcher. He considered that she had useful things to tell him, and it can only have been a bonus if his links reassured the Conservatively inclined voters he was wooing for Labour. Tony Blair consulted Margaret Thatcher both before and after his 1997 election victory. He even employed the services of her foreign affairs adviser Sir Charles Powell, whom he later recommended for a peerage.

The Powell family came to symbolise continuity in British politics from Thatcher to Blair and even beyond. The sons of a career RAF officer, Charles, Jonathan and Chris came from the non-partisan side of public service but showed a strong grasp of politics.

Charles Powell was a Foreign Office diplomat sent to Number 10 who became perhaps Margaret Thatcher's closest aide. He and his charming wife, Carla, provided private as much as public support to the prime minister, putting her in touch with well-connected admirers. Charles Powell stayed with John Major to help smooth the transition during the first year of his premiership, before leaving Downing Street to accumulate a string of lucrative directorships. Carla, meanwhile, had struck up friendships with New Labour figures, including Peter Mandelson and Anji Hunter, and the couple came to perform a similar informal service to Blair as they had to Thatcher.

Charles's younger brother Jonathan was another career diplomat.

As an official at the British embassy in Washington, he looked after Blair and Brown during a US visit when they were in opposition and subsequently accepted Blair's offer to become his chief of staff.

A third brother, Chris, held Labour's advertising account for a period. In 1995 he hosted a New Labour weekend retreat near his manor house in the New Forest which became notorious because John Prescott made a big fuss about not being invited. In the succeeding generation, one of Charles's sons, Hugh, had connections across the political divide like his father. Hugh Powell was both in charge of security policy in David Miliband's Foreign Office and a personal friend and think tank adviser to David Cameron, his Eton and Oxford contemporary.

In July 2007 Blair made his first post-prime ministerial appearance amongst his friends at the reception for the wedding of Jonathan Powell and Sarah Helm, held at the New Forest manor. With a sense of the baton being passed down the generations, this provided the first opportunity for Hugh Powell to meet his new boss, David Miliband. In 2008 Powell was given ambassador status as an envoy to Helmand province.

Prime Minister Blair's first official meeting with Margaret Thatcher was an off-the-record chat about the statecraft of the job. He was an open admirer of her style and copied much of it in government. Thatcher had declared that she wouldn't want to waste a lot of time with arguments in cabinet; Blair likewise stressed his confidence that he had been elected on a personal mandate and that it was his responsibility to deliver. Intriguingly, Margaret Thatcher exerted the same fatal attraction on Gordon Brown shortly after he became prime minister, when he too invited her back for tea at Number 10.

As her relationship with Charles Powell demonstrated, Thatcher had an unhierarchical approach to colleagues: she was more interested in what they had to say than in the status they happened to enjoy. Blair took this approach a stage further, often circumventing the established structures of government decision-making. If anything, he cut back formal cabinets further than Thatcher, reducing them to weekly sessions typically of less than an hour. Instead, he took important decisions at *ad hoc* meetings of officials, advisers and ministers.

Thatcher was often accused of being imperious. 'The Lady's not for turning,' as her speechwriter Ronnie Millar studiedly put it, but she never tried to enshrine her approach by restructuring government. Blair did. He oversaw changes which took power out of the hands of elected politicians and career civil servants by making them share it with others. He multiplied vastly the number of special advisers with a role in policy-making, and in the case of his two most senior aides – Alastair Campbell and Jonathan Powell – formally instigated an Order in Council delivering them the power to give orders to civil servants. In Parliament, Blair imported outsiders by the use of the peerage. He made a record number of appointments to the Lords and many of the new barons and baronesses were then given posts in his government, among them Derry Irvine, Charlie Falconer, Sally Morgan, Andrew Adonis and Paul Drayson.

In the latter years of the Blair government and especially following the Hutton and Butler inquiries into Iraq, Blair's informal style of decision-making was criticised for its lack of rigour. Robin Butler had had an awkward relationship with Blair when he was the first cabinet secretary to serve the new prime minister, and in his report he led those critics who suspected that decisions taken on sofas in the den could be a useful way of evading accountability.

The changes Blair made were not just casual or haphazard, though. He may have believed that he had managed to execute what Margaret Thatcher would like to have done but never succeeded in achieving. Blair installed an executive style of government in which control rested with individuals who were directly loyal to him – 'one of us', as she might have put it. He compounded this presidential approach with appointees at its core by failing to honour the Labour Party rule that the members of the last (elected) shadow cabinet in opposition should make up the first cabinet in office. He agreed to carry over some fairly unlikely, and short-lived, secretaries of state into government – including Gavin Strang, David Clark and Tom Clarke – but there were no places at the cabinet table for Michael Meacher and Derek Foster.

So, from the very beginning of Blair's first term, some ministers and officials complained that they were not properly in the loop. Blair's mantra was always 'what matters is what works'; what works did not include observing conventions. Complaints about Thatcher's high-handedness became critical only in her final years, 'when she stopped listening', as one of her last cabinet ministers put it. Before then, the status-conscious sometimes moaned that she concentrated too hard and was too willing to countenance advice, even when it came from a comparatively junior figure.

The second time Blair consulted Thatcher was over his decision to commit Britain militarily in the Balkans. He often echoed her, saying that sending troops into conflict is the most difficult decision a head of government has to take – a point repeatedly stressed during interviews I conducted with him over the years.

It therefore seemed particularly ungracious and uncharacteristically cowardly that Blair failed to attend the unveiling of a seven-foot statue of Margaret Thatcher in the Members' Lobby of the House of Commons in February 2007. Major and Cameron were there, as was the ever attentive Lord Powell. By common agreement, the most gracious tribute came, somewhat surprisingly, from Mr Speaker, 'Gorbals Mick', the former Labour MP Michael Martin. While Thatcher joked that she would rather her statue had been cast in iron than bronze, Blair's absence was perhaps an indication that he wished his own legacy would not be seen as a continuation of hers.

5

WORLD STAGE

29 MAY – 1 JUNE

*What is important is that . . . we step up to the plate, both in terms
of aid, in terms of help, in terms of fighting the killer diseases and in
issues like conflict resolution and peacekeeping.*

Tony Blair, Johannesburg, 1 June 2007

Africa

After Northern Ireland, Tony Blair's work on Africa is the top
exhibit for exponents of his achievements.

Blair had a clearly established record of concern for Africa. He
had ordered the buccaneering but successful UK military intervention
in Sierra Leone in May 2000, a country in which he had an unusual
personal interest because his father had been a law lecturer at Freetown
University for several years in the 1960s. After 9/11 he had placed
the continent at the centre of global concerns in his famous visionary
Brighton party conference speech: 'The state of Africa is a scar on
the conscience of the world. But if the world as a community focused
on it, we could heal it. And if we don't, it will become deeper and
angrier.'

In spite of the terrorist attacks on the US, he followed his speech with an international meeting on Africa held at Chequers in the autumn of 2001. Then in February 2002 he visited Mozambique, Senegal and Sierra Leone to launch NEPAD, the New Economic Partnership for African Development. Next he established the Commission for Africa which drafted a 'coherent package for Africa' that fed into the 2005 G8 summit, hosted by Blair at Gleneagles in Scotland. Helped in part by the mood of solidarity brought on by the London terror bombings of 7 July 2005, Blair secured significant commitments at Gleneagles both on climate change and on a $50 billion boost in foreign aid.

In the meantime, he made close friendships with African leaders including Nelson Mandela and his third wife, Graça Machel, and General Obasanjo of Nigeria. He championed the idea of extending G8 meetings to G8 + 13, or rather G8 + 5 emerging economies + 8 of the most influential aid recipient nations.

Blair also saw improved relations with African Muslims as a key to his post-9/11 bridge building with the Islamic world. Here his most notable success was with the mercurial Colonel Gaddafi of Libya. The previous Conservative government had placed Libya on the 'most wanted' list in 1984 following the shooting dead of WPC Yvonne Fletcher by someone at the Libyan People's Bureau in St James's Square, London. In 1986 Britain had actively supported the US bombing raid on Tripoli. And relations further deteriorated after the 1988 bombing of Pan Am flight 103 above the Scottish Borders town of Lockerbie.

In the early years of his premiership, the Blair government became involved in bringing Gaddafi in from the cold. In 1999 Britain secured the surrender to justice of the two suspects in the Lockerbie bombing: Abdelbaset Ali Mohmed al-Megrahi, a former Libyan security services officer, and Al Amin Khalifa Fhimah, a baggage handler in Malta, where the bomb was allegedly placed on the plane. This required some unique innovations in Scottish criminal law: the two men were tried in Holland but by a Scottish court. Only al-Megrahi was convicted. He was sentenced to life in Greenock Prison but was in 2007 granted leave to make his second appeal against conviction.

The rise of al-Qaeda led Gaddafi to suggest that he and the West shared a common enemy. George W. Bush's 'either you are with us or against us' global warning after 9/11 hastened the *rapprochement*. At the United Nations in 2003 Britain and Bulgaria sponsored the final lifting of sanctions against Libya, which had already been suspended in 1999 in response to the handing over of the bombing suspects. At the same time Gaddafi formally accepted 'moral responsibility' for the Lockerbie bombing and laid out a $2.7 billion compensation package for the families of the victims. That year Gaddafi also confessed that Libya had its own weapons of mass destruction programme and invited a United Nations team into his country to dismantle it. Libya remains, along with South Africa, a model of successfully managed disarmament and non-proliferation.

In March 2004 Blair visited Gaddafi in Libya, at 'the Tent' which he used as his headquarters as he led the life of a nomad. Blair was the first British prime minister to set foot in the country since Winston Churchill in 1943, and one of the first Western leaders to pay an official visit following the rise of Gaddafi.

So a tour of Africa was always seen as an essential leg of Tony Blair's long goodbye. He wanted to make the trip and so did two of his closest advisers: Liz Lloyd, then deputy chief of staff but formerly African aide, and Justin Forsyth, a former anti-globalisation protester and now international development adviser to Blair. (Dressed in a turtle costume, Forsyth had taken part in a demonstration during the G8 summit in Seattle in 2000 in support of an import ban on shrimp caught in nets without escape hatches for turtles, something the WTO refused to sanction under its trade rules.)

The choice of countries was pretty obvious too, spanning the spectrum of Blair's interests: Libya, Sierra Leone and South Africa. Although Libya was in fact added only at the last moment at the direct request of the oil giant BP – or rather BP's new CEO, Tony Hayward, and the company's director of communications, Anji Hunter, in her post-Downing Street role. The visit provided an opportunity for both BP and Blair to bask in the glow of a new exploration deal, marking the company's return to Libya three decades after having been thrown out following Gaddafi's nationalisation of the country's oil reserves.

Blair's 2004 visit to Libya had been a hurried and chaotic affair. An away-day flight to Tripoli followed by a dash by road 'to the Tent'. Wherever it was pitched became the centre of government. That spring it was set up on a smart new stud farm outside the capital, but nobody seemed quite clear exactly where this was. Blair's official motorcade overshot the turning and had to execute a U-turn on the four-lane motorway.

The grass was green and large mimosa trees were in bloom around Gaddafi's small, flat-sided tent – about ten metres square and made up of his own specially printed canvas emblazoned with silhouettes of palm trees and camels. Next to it stood a gleaming, modern Winnebago mobile home. A small herd of ragged camels added a more authentic touch as they wandered at will around the encampment, even sticking their heads into the tent. The herd was not there by chance. The Downing Street advance team had expressed an interest as to whether there would be camels around. Sure enough, as if to order, the straggly beasts appeared.

At this first meeting the numbers were kept down. Blair and 'the brotherly leader and guide of the Revolution' met one-on-one, apart from translators and an aide apiece. Their entourages were permitted to look on but not, in most cases, to enter the tent. Gaddafi said little but obligingly strode around for the cameras in his dark brown robe, small hat and dark glasses. Blair confirmed that he could now do business with Libya and its leader, whom he described as a potential ally in the battle against Islamist terrorism.

Blair's second meeting with Gaddafi, which was the first stop of his farewell tour of Africa, was more businesslike and therefore perhaps less exciting than his first. The location was the same, the tent, but also different because its site had moved to Gaddafi's native heath around Sirte on the edge of the Sahara desert; the area the Libyan leader aspired to make the national capital.

The British Airways charter had been given permission (and flight information) to fly only into Tripoli, so the Blair party was decanted into a Libyan Airways special flight. The Afriqiyah Airbus 340 was startlingly decorated on the outside with brightly coloured, swirling figure nines – a reference to 9/9/99 the foundation day of the African Union. The interior was more startling still: over-stuffed Moroccan leather sofas and swivel armchairs laid out for conversation rather than in rows, with a Jacuzzi at the front adjoining the cabin taken by the prime minister. Further back, the occupants of the press section dubbed it 'the pimp plane'.

After landing at Sirte, Blair's motorcade – largely consisting of black Mercedes 4x4s – made slow progress through the red sand. For a scrubby desert, the area is fairly densely populated with concrete homes and military/radar installations. Once again the encampment stretched out along one side of an otherwise insignificant, straight rural road. The Winnebagos were still there but only a token pair of camels. The tent had grown much larger – and was now a vast oblong about twenty metres by thirty, much like an English wedding marquee, but still draped with the same camel and palm tree fabric.

Dressed formally in a blue suit, white shirt and red tie, Blair told the travelling media party: 'Our relationship has absolutely transformed in the past few years.' And since this time there was room, everybody – prime minister, officials and press – piled into the huge main tent. After some minutes of confusion, during which only the cameramen got anything done, everyone except the principals was suddenly ordered out. Taking the wise advice of their man on the ground, BP's chairman Sir Peter Sutherland and CEO Tony Hayward shrank into a dark corner under the canvas. They remained there, unnoticed, as the diplomatic talks got underway – spotted and brought forward by the prime minister only when a security guard tried to sling them out.

The new BP concession was officially signed with due pomp later that evening – a large and tangible fruit of improved relations. The oil and gas field, the size of Belgium, was expected to yield some $28 billion dollars over the next forty years. A Shell concession and defence co-operation deals were additionally said to be in the offing. With potential profit comes competition.

The prime minister was also 'grateful' to meet the 'Ben-ghazi families' of 400 Libyan children allegedly infected with HIV because of the incompetence of Bulgarian and Palestinian medical staff. He expressed the hope that relations between the EU and Libya might soon be restored. The nurses and doctor remained under Libyan sentence of death until later in the summer of 2007 when they were released, seemingly following the personal intervention of Cécilia Sarkozy, then wife of the newly elected French president.

Only a few hours flying time above Africa took the prime minister from the gritty aridity of Sirte, to the muddy fecundity around Lunghi airport, Sierra Leone. Blair had made a day trip of a few hours there as part of his four-nation West Africa tour five years previously. This had yielded some striking pictures of dancers diving through flaming hoops as the prime minister looked on, but the impact of the visit had been largely lost because it coincided with the death of the Queen's sister, Princess Margaret. Showing how impressively well organised the small Downing Street team can be when it's a question of protocol, the prime minister had stepped off the plane wearing a black tie and dark suit. But some time was wasted while we in the press pack located a suitably neutral backdrop against which Mr Blair could record a fitting tribute to a senior member of the royal family – whom, it turned out somewhat surprisingly, he claimed he had never met. (An assertion contradicted by his wife Cherie in her memoir.)

In 2007, the same small airport terminal was packed out with people. African issues dominated as Blair made his first public appearance with two local presidents – his host Alhaji Ahmad Tejan Kabbah of Sierra Leone and, from neighbouring Liberia, Ellen Johnson-Sirleaf, Africa's first elected female head of state. Angered when I put it to him that critics in Britain were describing this as a 'vanity' tour, Blair launched into a passionate defence of his commitment to Africa explicitly contrasting it to 'the principle of non-intervention' twenty years ago. 'What I have done I have done for the future because that is the only thing that matters. People want pretty much the same things everywhere.' He told 'the cynics' that they should compare the improved situation in countries such as Sierra Leone and Liberia with what it was like five years earlier, and reiterated his demand for international intervention to protect the inhabitants of Darfur in Sudan.

A few days later, he made the same points in a valedictory essay titled 'What I've Learnt', written for the *Economist* magazine. The first of five 'reflections' was 'Be a player not a spectator':

> Earlier this week I visited the people of Sierra Leone, still struggling, but at least able to contemplate a better future. But as important is the next-door state of Liberia, now properly democratic. It might never have been so had Sierra Leone fallen into the hands of the gangsters. Similarly, as a result of Kosovo, the Balkans changed . . . So when we come to Darfur, do we really believe that if we do not act to change this situation, the violence will stop at the borders of Sudan?

Blair's personal determination to be a player in Sierra Leone resulted in it receiving one of the largest British cross-departmental foreign aid efforts. In all, more than 260 staff from the Foreign Office, the Ministry of Defence and the Department for International Development were deployed in the country. In his speech Blair pointed to dramatic improvements in healthcare, education and the economy. He was treated to an aggressive display demonstrating the impact of British military and police trainers.

Carefully avoiding wearing any 'silly hats', and donning his robes for only a few seconds, Blair was invested as an honorary 'Paramount Chief' in the village of Mahera, a few kilometres from the airport. He was berated for not visiting the capital, Freetown, but it would have taken hours to get there by road (the promised aid-funded road-building project had not yet materialised). It would have been a journey of just a few minutes by helicopter over the wetlands but one not without risks. A helicopter from the only commercial service covering the route crashed less than a week after Blair's visit, killing twenty-two people and triggering an air-safety corruption scandal.

From the moment Peter Mandelson took over the Labour Party press office in 1985, political messages were backed up whenever possible with striking images for the camera. Children were perhaps most frequently chosen as the backdrop, and no major announcement ever passed without a school visit. Tony Blair even launched his 2001 election campaign in front of a bewildered assembly of schoolgirls.

In 2007, though, it was not just another cynical photo-opportunity. The children of Sierra Leone were different. The sight of them that afternoon must have made the prime minister feel it had all been worthwhile. In the past five years two primary schools had been established around Lunghi and a new secondary school was being built. Blair's aide Liz Lloyd said she was most struck by the uniforms. Boys and girls who barely had schools five years earlier were now smartly decked out in blue or green uniforms, according to their school. They lined the roads singing, 'Hello Mr Blair. How are you? We are glad that you have come and we hope you come again, and bring us rain.' This last phrase was hardly necessary as the afternoon monsoon had already begun, soaking their smart new uniforms.

Southern Africa has tested British prime ministers ever since Harold Macmillan sensed the 'wind of change'. The search for a peaceful political settlement in Rhodesia preoccupied the Wilson, Callaghan and Thatcher governments; the issue of sanctions against apartheid South Africa divided Margaret Thatcher from the rest of the Commonwealth and most of the European Union; in contrast, John Major's relationship with Nelson Mandela and the Harare Declaration were some of the rare bright spots of his premiership.

Despite Major's success, however, in Britain the anti-apartheid, anti-colonial movement had been dominated, though not exclusively, by the socialist and Christian left. A visit to South Africa was an essential rite of passage during Blair's period as opposition leader. On a walkabout of the shanty town of Soweto he famously got more experience than he was bargaining for when he stuck his head into the home of a woman as she was giving birth. Once Blair became prime minister, President Mandela was an automatic ally. Mandela was the star visitor at the European Council Britain hosted in Cardiff in 1998. And once he left office in South Africa, he returned to Britain in 2000 to be the external guest at the Labour Party conference, where he thanked the party for its 'solidarity'.

Mandela shared Blair's ability to turn news events into memorable occasions and to recruit allies from unlikely places. In 1995 he had boosted John Major during the Commonwealth Conference in Zimbabwe, praising the Harare Declaration – and talking cricket. But he could also share Blair's suspicion of the press. On his first visit to Britain following his release from prison, he rebuked me at length when I asked about his relationship with his then wife, Winnie Mandela. And at his last appearance with Blair, my attempt to shout a question was taken as a shocking breach of decorum by Mandela's tough Boer spokeswoman.

For the bulk of Blair's premiership, however, Mandela was an *éminence grise*, as his increasingly popular soubriquet 'Madiba' or 'tribal elder and leader' underlined. In practice, Blair had to deal mostly with the current president, Thabo Mbeki – a far more prickly character than Mandela, whom he had served as vice president. Mbeki was born into the 'aristocracy' of the ANC black resistance in South Africa. He suffered under apartheid and many of his family, including a son and a brother, were assassinated, but he spent twenty-eight years of his adult life in exile, based in Britain, operating mainly as an ANC ambassador. According to his critics, this enforced absence from the struggle at home made Mbeki all the more determined to assert his radical credentials once elected president.

Mbeki's views on Zimbabwe and on AIDS were major bones of contention with the Blair government. As Zimbabwe spiralled into economic chaos, Mbeki refused to engage in 'megaphone diplomacy' against Robert Mugabe, his sometime 'brother in liberation', even though the collapse of Zimbabwe resulted in chronic migration across the border into South Africa. Instead, Mbeki suggested that land reform was unfinished business in his own country. On AIDS, he championed the dissident minority of scientists who proposed that the disease was not linked to the HIV virus. Mbeki argued that AIDS was a disease of poverty. He sometimes gave the impression that he resented the high profile interventions by Western governments on AIDS, which he believed implied that Africans were promiscuous germ-carriers. His personal views earned him criticism from Nelson Mandela though, and Mbeki eventually stated publicly that they did not represent the views of the South African government.

It was a mark of Blair's optimistic, 'can do' disposition and his pragmatism that he remained on good terms with Mbeki throughout the ten years, whatever the private misgivings expressed by officials. Talks with the president at Union Buildings in Pretoria provided the climax to the South African visit. But from the long and warm embraces between Tony and Cherie and Nelson and Graça, and the glowing tributes exchanged, the Mandela photo opportunity clearly meant much more than a courtesy call. Now frail, Mandela spoke from notes and did not take any questions but – ever the astute and constructive politician – he even managed some words of praise for Gordon Brown.

The Blairs' other engagements in Johannesburg were also informal. The prime minister touched on another theme of his ten years by inaugurating a new university chair in Genocide and Holocaust Studies. And, having carefully ensured that most of the travelling journalists were being entertained by the High Commission across town, the Blairs slipped out for a stroll through the luxury shopping arcade attached to the swanky hotel the party was staying in.

Blair presented this final African tour as an attempt to promote the Gleneagles issues of Africa and climate change up the agenda for the last G8 summit he would attend in Germany the following week. Almost alone of foreign leaders, he gave a welcome to George W. Bush's environment statement in which the US president proposed an American-hosted track of talks involving the world's thirteen worst greenhouse gas polluters to run in parallel with the UN intergovernmental efforts.

Perhaps appropriately, maybe ironically, Union Buildings, high on its hilltop, provided a magnificent backdrop for Prime Minister Blair's African farewell. The city of Pretoria was said to have been founded at the end of the Boers' 'Long Trek'. The executive Capitol was built on Boer farmland called Arcadia and designed by Sir Herbert Baker in the English monumental style he also deployed in New Delhi, for South Africa and India Houses in London and for Rhodes House in Oxford. As Mbeki waited under a pergola overlooked by a large statue of Hermes, his guard of honour greeted Blair in the same semicircular open courtyard where Mandela had been sworn in as president in 1994.

After private talks, the two men strolled along a red carpet which ran through the impressive terraced gardens, stocked only with indigenous South African flora. Mbeki himself was effusive, if slightly patronising towards Blair, expressing himself 'very glad indeed to see him here as he is about to leave office'. Africa's most important politician was 'very pleased with the role he [Blair] has played and of course inspired by his very strong and bold positions on Africa'. 'It has really helped a great deal. Now, I feel that there is not anyone in the world that would not want to put the African issue on the agenda and for this I say thank you for your positions that have helped to raise the profile.' The president also offered 'congratulations' for 'what has been achieved in Northern Ireland'. Characteristically, Blair didn't bridle. He conceded immediately that 'people either say nothing has happened or everything has happened. The truth is since Gleneagles a lot has happened.' Then he plunged into his 'to-do' list for 'next week's G8'. He re-emphasised his concerns on climate change and the aid promises made at Gleneagles, while hailing the commitments which had been agreed on 'AIDS, debt relief, primary education, killer diseases'. On Zimbabwe, the most sensitive issue between the two men, Blair did not openly challenge Mbeki, who insisted once again that 'quiet diplomacy . . . not what I say [will bring a] solution in this region of Africa'.

Blair had already ensured that his involvement with Africa would continue after he left office. On 24 April 2007 he had travelled to Berlin for the launch of the Africa Progress Panel. The group was chaired by the former UN Secretary-General, Kofi Annan, who made it clear at this inaugural meeting that Tony Blair would become a member. Blair was deliberately constructing a rod, or rather a yardstick, for his own back because one of his main reasons for staying on into the summer was to attend the G8 in Germany to reaffirm and secure the Gleneagles commitments on Africa.

International celebrity

Once again, Blair had attempted to increase pressure on political leaders by cranking up public interest. That was one reason for his

Africa visit – along with personal vanity. The same pair of motives came together on 5 May in an interview he recorded with Bob Geldof for the Number 10 website. Geldof started off by setting the scene, 'At this sort of an end of an era sort of moment', and laying on the compliments, 'Here is where I am brown nosey, a clear success of your administration [which] was things African.' As Geldof pointed out during their exchanges, his own campaigning for Africa stretched back twenty-five years, long before the Blair era, but the prime minister had in a sense made the cause official by appointing 'Sir Bob' as a member of the Commission for Africa in 2004.

Casual listeners to the podcast would have been bewildered as Geldof's restless intelligence took the conversation off at tangents, such as China's involvement in Africa, whether democratic values were universal values and the 'celebritisation of politics' versus the 'politicisation of celebrities'. Blair gave a demonstration of why he was the politician rather than the celebrity, gathering his thoughts more precisely, while continually flattering Bob. The prime minister made his signature, constructive argument, stressing that there was a 'false difference between the politics of self-interest and the politics of values', and that in Africa China would realise 'it has a real interest in stability, in the growth of greater democratic accountability, better governance, the exploitation of natural resources and assets not in a way that in the end leads to either conflict or economies that are distorted'. Blair offset this boy scoutish approach by recognising that to attract attention you had to point to 'real horrors', but that this persuaded some that it was 'hopeless then'. Citing Darfur, he suggested that 'the Europeans haven't really thought through the consequences', such as the migration which will follow unless countries on the doorstep were 'sorted out'.

The son of a journalist, and a one-time rock writer, Geldof then turned the conversation adroitly from Africa to celebrity: 'In a couple of months you will be a celebrity rather than the prime minister, won't you? . . . Are you a celebrity?' Blair engaged with the question rather than deflecting it:

I think you kind of, the fact that you are so well known and people feel that they know you because they have seen you so much, I mean I am under no illusions that when I go to a place and everyone is kind of pleased to see you, it may be nothing to do with that they agree with your politics at all, in fact they may totally disagree with them, but you are a kind of well-known person. And I think it is just the way it is and you know people expect to know an awful lot more about people than ever they used to.

Coming at the end of his prime ministership, these remarks echo Blair's public warning to his children in the early days that people didn't offer them treats because they liked them but because of who they were. Now he seemed wearily to accept that some intrusion went with the job. Geldof responded intuitively, by being both relentlessly intrusive and complimentary, as he jumped from point to point: 'I know you enough to know you are not the sort of person who can just do the celeb circuit. I mean you will make a wedge I hope, but beyond that you are quite, I have met a lot of people in your position and you are very comfortable with power which is just as well if you are a leader. You know, don't you, you need a job where you can exercise that?'

Blair's reply was moving, or perhaps just schmaltzy: 'I think you need a life purpose.'

Many critics have decried Tony and Cherie Blair's obvious fondness for celebrity activists such as Bono and Bob Geldof. Yet, as this exchange with Geldof showed, Blair was both knowing and unrepentant about his 'celeb' friendships.

For the most part, not being fools themselves, the celebrities could be quite insightful about the Blairs. Which, as Geldof might have said, was just as well, since the job of prime minister nowadays tended to thrust politicians and celebrities together. One function of being prime minister was to represent the nation and this included meetings with those at the top of their fields whether artistic, sporting or intellectual. Celebrities were likely to recur as prime ministers dealt with diverse issues or causes because the organisations behind them invariably seek out celebrities as their advocates. As Blair said to

Geldof, people were pleased to see you just because you were well known and this could be very effective in getting a foot in the door.

Most controversially, and thanks in part to contemporary security concerns, prime ministers and celebrities had become more like each other in their lifestyles in spite of vast differences between them in personal fortunes – and whether they liked it or not. Both were protected by round-the-clock security details. Both had personal staffs available to help them. Both travelled almost exclusively by chauffeured car, private planes and helicopters. Both had townhouses at fashionable addresses and country estates. Neither could go out in public without attracting attention. Both, and their families as well, were the constant target of paparazzi and professional gossipmongers.

On taking office, Blair gave up the prospect of making any new 'real friends'. As he himself put it: 'Everyone I see wants something from me.' The only people the Blairs could be certain liked them for themselves rather than for who they had become were old friends from 'before'. But gates, doormen and appointment secretaries kept old friends at bay and it was seldom possible to share prime ministerial life experiences with them. Some old friends simply got left behind.

Tony and Cherie Blair turned for companionship to the celebrities they encountered in the course of their prime ministerial duties, in part because it was easier. They found they confronted the same kinds of daily challenges, such as the total loss of privacy, how to protect the children, how to get most quickly from A to B, or what to think of So-and-So, a new face they were bound to meet on their circuit. As much human warmth could be expended in welcoming a rock star's newborn baby as used to be the case with a neighbour in Islington.

Tony Blair was as much at ease with celebrity friends as his wife. On the day in December 2005 that civil partnerships came into force there was a monthly news conference. I asked him about the many new marriages taking place that day including Elton John's. 'We send Elton and David our warmest congratulations,' he replied. The familiarity of that first-name reference to David Furnish made it clear that this was a personal greeting.

But where there was a celebrity there was an ego. Bob Geldof got through his podcast with Blair without naming his frequent partner in campaigning, Bono, except for a passing reference to 'my shorter friend'. In practice, the Irishmen formed a two-man pressure group during the Blair decade – sometimes in alliance with Richard Curtis, the well-connected Brit-flick screenwriter, Make Poverty History organiser, founder of Comic Relief and husband of Emma Freud.

Geldof and Bono lobbied Blair, and he opened the door to other world leaders. To begin with Geldof had the experience, accrued since his organisation of Band Aid, and Bono was the truly international celebrity, thanks to U2. As Bono put it in his 2004 speech to the Labour Party conference, Geldof had opened his eyes to African campaigning:

> I'm here as part of a journey that began in 1984–85, with Band Aid and Live Aid. Another very tall, grizzled rock star, my friend Sir Bob Geldof, issued a challenge to 'feed the world'. It was a great moment. It changed my life. That summer, my wife Ali and I went to Ethiopia on the quiet, to see for ourselves what was going on. We lived there for a month, working at an orphanage. The locals knew me as 'Dr Good Morning'. The children called me 'The Girl With the Beard'. Don't ask!

Geldof seemed to be the boss when it came to campaigning in the early days. At the G8 meeting in Cologne in 1999, I interviewed Bono about the Jubilee Debt Forgiveness Campaign. Bono told me that he was fed up with politicians and wasn't going to do any more lobbying. His next appointment was with Blair, which I was due to cover. When Bono didn't turn up, Geldof asked me if I had seen him. I replied that he had told me he wasn't coming. Immediately Geldof left the hotel, but returned a few minutes later accompanied by 'his shorter friend' who was wearing his trademark wraparound orange shades.

In the years which followed, their campaigning roles came into equilibrium. Bono was the driving force behind their NGO, DATA

(Debt, AIDS, Trade, Africa), and as the bigger international star was much more effective than Geldof in lobbying Americans such as George W. Bush and his first Treasury secretary, Paul O'Neill, whom he managed to inveigle on to a fact-finding mission to Africa.

During his star turn at the Labour conference in Brighton, Bono produced one of the wittiest takes on the Blair–Brown relationship, shot through with his own particular brand of ironic rock star self-deprecation.

> I want to say a few words about two remarkable men. Like a lot of great partners, they didn't always get along as the years passed. They didn't always agree. They drifted apart. They did incredible things on their own, as individuals. But they did their best work as a pair. I love them both: John Lennon . . . and Paul McCartney. I'm also fond of Tony Blair and Gordon Brown. They are kind of the John and Paul of the global development stage, in my opinion. But the point is, Lennon and McCartney changed my interior world – Blair and Brown can change the Real World.

This was a graceful tribute, well calculated given Blair's other-life fantasy of staying in the music business after getting a taste for the stage with his college band Ugly Rumours. Bono gave him an electric guitar as a consolation present.

Bono's speech was also remarkably well timed. The prime minister and the chancellor had just endured a torrid summer during which John Prescott had had to intervene as peacemaker. Blair later claimed he had come close to quitting. But not the least of Bono and Geldof's skills was their ability to be on good terms with both men. It was a talent they managed to pass on to others in the field. The development specialist and former 'turtle protestor' Justin Forsyth worked for DATA. He had become Blair's adviser on climate change and international development in Number 10 and was one of two officials (the other was financial adviser Geoffrey Norris) to keep his place in the summer of 2007 when Brown took over as prime minister.

Before that, though, Blair faced his eleventh and last G8 meeting.

This time it took place at Heiligendamm, a staid resort on the Baltic coast in the former East German province of Mecklenburg-Vorpommern.

6–8 JUNE

G8, Putin and 'Yo Blair!'

The annual meetings of the world's richest democratic nations have been red-letter days in the British prime minister's summer diary since 1975, when the French president, Valéry Giscard D'Estaing, proposed and hosted the first leaders' fireside chat at the Château de Rambouillet, south of Paris. The US, Japan, UK, France, Italy and West Germany were the founder members (Canada being invited to join in 1976), entertaining each other on a yearly rotating cycle. As in the European Community, though with less resistance here from continental allies, Britain's policy was one of widening membership and discussion rather than deepening internal cohesion. G7 commenced the move to becoming G8 after John Major invited Russia's Mikhail Gorbachev to attend the end of the London summit in 1991; the first official meeting of the G8 was held in Birmingham in 1998.

During his tenure, Tony Blair pressed for greater outreach as the agenda converged on climate change and African development, effectively turning the G8 into G13 by including the G5 of emerging industrial powers in many sessions: Brazil, China, India, Mexico and South Africa. At Evian in 2003 and Gleneagles in 2005, President Chirac and Blair took this a step further inviting a G20+ by including a number of other developing countries. At Sea Island in 2004 and St Petersburg in 2006, neither George W. Bush nor Vladimir Putin were so keen to replicate this welcome as hosts. Indeed, Putin wanted to include an alternative additional delegation from the former Soviet Commonwealth of Independent States, which he argued was also in need of international aid.

Over the years, the scale of G meetings has waxed and waned. At one stage foreign and finance ministers turned up as well, but by the time Blair was elected they had been confined to mini-summits of their own. The leaders habitually insisted that they wanted to have intimate, unstructured encounters, but this conflicted with their urge to announce achievements to their electorates at home. The media were deemed to be 'intruding' and were usually corralled in their own 'village' some distance away, only to be summoned in pools to be handed the soundbites from on high.

Heiligendamm provided a resonant and melancholy location for Blair's last stand. Even in the June sun, it was a seaside town harking back to the decorum of a late-nineteenth-century health spa rather than the glitz and bikinis of the Mediterranean. In deference to the chilly winds, large hooded two-seater deckchairs faced inland on 'the white sand by the sea', as the beaches are known. The place evoked modern German history. The country's oldest seaside resort founded in 1793, it survived as a playground for the communist nomenklatura after the Second World War, and by 2007 had been modernised by Western capital. The leaders stayed in the white clapperboard Kempinski Grand Hotel, a conversion of a former sanatorium. Even 'Molli', the innocent narrow-gauge railway maintained by local enthusiasts, seemed an unspoken shadow of the Nazi past, clanking, hissing and steaming as its carriages disgorged journalists at the gates of the main compound.

The back-slapping club of leaders in power would cheerfully overlook ideological differences but it shunned a wounded member of the pack. So, with the exception of the ever-loyal Bush, none of the others found time for fond farewells to Blair. He was not the only leader attending his last G8; Vladimir Putin stood down as president – in title at least – at the end of his second term in May 2008; and Japan's Shinzo Abe was to resign unexpectedly in September 2007. The chief excitement was the debut of the newly elected French president, Nicolas Sarkozy. Seemingly never without a mobile phone to his ear, he didn't disappoint the gossips: his soon-to-be-divorced wife flew home after the opening-night dinner, and he gave a breathless news conference, much played on YouTube, which led to false accusations of drunkenness.

Blair was left to pursue his goals for the summit on his own. These were twofold. First, securing confirmation, and perhaps even delivery, on the commitments he had gained on climate change and Africa at the Gleneagles summit two years previously. Second, restoring some kind of cordiality to Britain's strained relations with the Russian president.

Putin had been one of the big disappointments of Blair's ten years. Blair clearly hankered after a close relationship with the emerging Russian democracy to match Thatcher's with Gorbachev and Major's with Yeltsin. He was almost indecently quick to hail Putin as another 'man we can do business with' and caused controversy in March 2000 by going on an official visit to meet the then 'acting president' just *before* he had actually been officially elected president. Rather than meeting in Moscow, Putin insisted that Blair came to St Petersburg, his home town and political powerbase.

It was a visit full of reminders of changing political balances. As we drove out of town through the suburbs, Alastair Campbell proved remarkably familiar with the local geography. It turned out he and Fiona Millar had visited Leningrad – as it was then called – a number of times during the Soviet era on organised youth visitor programmes. The glories of the Tsarist past, however, seemed more Putin's preoccupation. The main meeting took place at a wintry Peterhof, Peter the Great's palace. The candidate held court in one of the grander picture galleries, expounding at length as Russian leaders tend to do. His theme was imperial too – he argued that Britain and Russia were twin bookends, one at either end of Europe, looking inward but also outward: Britain west to the US, Russia, more warily, towards China.

Meetings with Putin became regular features of Blair's international programme, but the relationship palled over Iraq. The Russian president's decision to make common cause with France against a second UN resolution finally blocked Britain's efforts. Putin didn't bother to curb his sardonic temperament after the invasion during a kiss-and-make-up visit by Blair to his dacha, smirking to the assembled press: 'For all I know Saddam Hussein is out there in a cellar somewhere sitting on a pile of weapons of mass destruction.'

There was no evidence of any special relationship when Blair joined other world leaders for the two summits Putin contrived to hold in St Petersburg – the first coinciding with the 300th anniversary of the city's foundation in 2003, followed by the actual G8 meeting in 2006. Both took place in the highly secure conference park which Putin had had built specially, with each delegation accommodated in its own mansion within the gated compound.

Putin was particularly irritated by the haven given by Britain to dissident oligarchs such as Boris Berezovsky and what he saw as the unjustified self-righteousness of Western criticisms of his democratic performance. The British ambassador in Moscow had become a target of officially sponsored harassment for voicing such opinions. At the 2006 St Petersburg summit, being host didn't stop Putin exercising his acid tongue at his critics' expense. Challenged on democracy, he first remarked, 'We certainly don't want democracy like they have in Iraq.' Then in an aside to British reporters at his main news conference, he took a swipe at Tony Blair with a random reference to the cash for peerages investigation by the Metropolitan Police. 'We carefully hear out all our partners,' he said. 'We take into consideration their views on such issues but we take our decisions ourselves . . . There are also other questions, questions, let's say, about the fight against corruption. We'd be interested in hearing your experience, including how it applies to Lord Levy.' The official translation of proceedings did not record these comments.

St Petersburg 2006 was an uncomfortable summit for Tony Blair and not just because Putin paid little attention to the Gleneagles agenda. War had broken out in Lebanon a few days before between Hezbollah, based in the south of the country, and Israel. Once again, lines were being drawn between Blair and Bush and the other leaders, as the US and UK governments refused to condemn the Israel Defense Force's response to the rocket attacks and kidnapping of soldiers on Israeli territory.

This argument provided the background for perhaps the most damaging incident of Tony Blair's final year in power – the overheard conversation between the prime minister and the US president that became known simply as 'Yo Blair'. Some have suggested that the

FSB (as Yeltsin had rebranded the KGB) may have been behind the open microphones. But accidents do happen. On this occasion Sky News and I were well placed to exploit the incident.

Summit meetings take place in a looking-glass world. On one side of the security cordon the leaders meet. The world's media look on from the other side, largely thanks to live feeds of television pictures, pooled to all the broadcasters present and available on local CCTV screens to other journalists. This material is mostly ignored because it typically consists of boring scenes of arrivals and departures, 'grip and grin' encounters, and 'roundtable' shots of leaders milling around and preparing for their meetings. Both the G8 and the European Union cut the feed when it gets interesting, as soon as the talking begins.

However, such material is what television journalists have to use to 'wallpaper' the gaps in video in their reports. On the morning of 17 July 2006, we were looking through the images coming out from the last session of the summit for something which would distinguish it – on such occasions even an overheard greeting between leaders can work as a focal point in the soundtrack. Naturally we highlighted the casual encounter between Blair and Bush, in which Blair ambles up behind the seated president and starts a conversation while standing at his shoulder. Bush replies but he barely turns his head to Blair and continues eating his lunch.

When we played the footage back, we were immediately aware that the private conservation between the prime minister and president had been recorded. It dealt with Blair's two main anxieties of the summit – that an adequate agreement might not be reached for developing countries, and Lebanon. It also showed for once how the two men talked to each other in private – deferentially on the prime minister's part and almost dismissively on Bush's.

There was no doubt that the exchange was of great public interest and we decided to report it. But the sound quality was poor. To be easily understood by viewers it needed to be boosted and to have subtitles put up. This would have to be done at the main studio back in London. In the meantime James Rubin, then Sky News foreign affairs commentator, and I discussed the conversation on live television broadcasts from the summit. But by far the quickest way to distribute the story was online. That year I had started a blog on the Sky News website. Less than an hour after Bush and Blair had been chatting we posted a full transcript of what we had heard ('as best we could make it out') under the headline 'Blair & Bush Raw & Uncut':

BUSH: Yo Blair! How are you doing?

BLAIR: I'm just . . .

BUSH: You're leaving?

BLAIR: No, no, no, not yet. On this trade thingy . . . [*inaudible*]

BUSH: Yeah I told that to the man.

BLAIR: Are you planning to say that here or not?

BUSH: If you want me to.

BLAIR: Well, it's just that if the discussion arises . . .

BUSH: I just want some movement.

BLAIR: Yeah.

BUSH: Yesterday we didn't see much movement.

BLAIR: No, no, it may be that it's not, it may be that it's impossible.

BUSH: I am prepared to say it.

BLAIR: But it's just I think what we need to be an opposition.

BUSH: Who is introducing the trade?

BLAIR: Angela.

BUSH: Tell her to call 'em.

BLAIR: Yes.

BUSH: Tell her to put him on, them on the spot. Thanks for the sweater, it's awfully thoughtful of you.

BLAIR: It's a pleasure.

BUSH: I know you picked it out yourself.

BLAIR: Oh, absolutely, in fact I knitted it myself!

BUSH: Right . . . What about Kofi? That seems odd. I don't like the sequence of it. His attitude is basically ceasefire and everything else happens.

BLAIR: I think the thing that is really difficult is you can't stop this unless you get this international presence agreed . . .

BUSH: Yeah.

BLAIR: I don't know what you guys have talked about but as I say

I am perfectly happy to try and see what the lie of the land is but you need that done quickly because otherwise it will spiral.

BUSH: I think Condi is going to go pretty soon.

BLAIR: But that's, that's, that's, all that matters. But if you, you see it will take some time to get that together.

BUSH: Yeah, yeah.

BLAIR: But at least it gives people . . .

BUSH: It's process, I agree. I told her your offer to . . .

BLAIR: Well . . . it's only if I mean . . . you know. If she's got a . . . or if she needs the ground prepared as it were . . . Because obviously if she goes out, she's got to succeed, if it were, whereas I can go out and just talk.

BUSH: You see, the . . . thing is what they need to do is to get Syria, to get Hezbollah to stop doing this shit and it's over.

BLAIR: [inaudible]

BUSH: [inaudible]

BLAIR: Syria.

BUSH: Why?

BLAIR: Because I think this is all part of the same thing.

BUSH: Yeah.

BLAIR: What does he think? He thinks if Lebanon turns out fine, if we get a solution in Israel and Palestine, Iraq goes in the right way . . .

BUSH: Yeah, yeah, he is sweet.

BLAIR: He is honey. And that's what the whole thing is about. It's the same with Iraq.

BUSH: I felt like telling Kofi to call, to get on the phone to Bashad [Bashir Assad] and make something happen.

BLAIR: Yeah.

BUSH: [inaudible]

BLAIR: [inaudible]

BUSH: We are not blaming the Lebanese government.

BLAIR: Is this . . . ? [At this point Blair taps the microphone in front of him and the sound is cut.]

Of course, other journalists had heard the exchange. (The White

House Press Office had already asked the American TV networks not to use the overheard material.) But there is no doubt that the Sky News blog diffused the story around the world. Other websites referenced us with hyperlinks; we had more than 400 posted comments that day. And the transcripts printed in the newspapers the next day all used our punctuation and stage direction. On the plane home, the prime minister's official spokesman was working from a printout of our blog story. As an ex-journalist, Tom Kelly took the report as a fair cop: 'I've told him I would have done exactly the same,' he said to me, gesturing with his head up the plane to where the prime minister was sitting. Number 10 even helped by filling in some of the inaudible interludes on the transcripts.

Blair's critics in the media seized on the 'Yo Blair' incident as proof that the prime minister had indeed become Bush's poodle. The freethinking Tory author Geoffrey Wheatcroft even produced a short polemical book with that title. It has been suggested since that the president had not in fact casually greeted the prime minister using the American street lingo term and that rather he had said 'Yeah Blair.' But that was not how it sounded on the tape and 'Yo, Blair!' certainly makes sense as the salutation at the beginning of the conversation that followed. It was difficult not to wince a little when comparing the demeanour of the two men. Standing, Blair was accommodating almost to the point of toadying – even prepared to sacrifice his own credibility in the Middle East to save the US Secretary of State Condoleezza Rice. Seated, Bush took all this as nothing more than due tribute, munching on, casual almost to the point of rudeness with the prime minister.

The exchange looks less damning, however, if the two leaders' temperaments are taken into account. Albeit caught in a more compromising circumstance, Blair behaved the way he always tended to behave, and familiar George W. Bush traits were displayed as well. Blair's public schoolboy good manners were naturally diffident but he often appeared able to give a lot of ground socially without seeming to lose his authority. Many observers have noted how brusquely he allowed himself to be treated by Anji Hunter, Jonathan Powell and especially Alastair Campbell. Even with the general public, he developed 'the masochism strategy' and would absorb outspoken attacks in a way no previous prime minister had done. 'I hear what you say' or 'I know there are strong feelings about this' were his stock rejoinders, often delivered with a smile and one hand raised on the end of an almost straight arm, in a modest gesture of fending off. Conversely, Bush had the swagger of a swell from one of America's exclusive prep schools (he was the head cheerleader at Phillips Academy, Andover, before going up to Yale), coarsened by deliberate Texan folksiness. If allowances are made for their personalities, Blair probably hadn't been sucking up quite so much and Bush probably wasn't quite as offensive as it perhaps seemed.

Blair was always willing to take hits for causes in which he believed when caught at the centre of the action. He took his punishment at the Heiligendamm summit too, though perhaps not in the way that he had hoped. In Germany the NGOs united to express disappointment that, by their calculation, the rich nations had only closed the $30 billion gap between promises and paid aid by just $3 billion. Most excepted Britain from their criticisms, including Bono, who gave a bad-tempered press briefing while insisting that he didn't blame Blair. A statement from Max Lawson of Oxfam summarised the mood: 'We must not be distracted by big numbers . . . This means the G8 will still fall far short of the Gleneagles pledges. The millions of people in Africa need the concrete annual increases they were promised – nothing less. Too much is at stake . . . the new money announced today is important in the fight against HIV/AIDS and to provide education for all, but it should be seen for what it is – a small step when we need giant leaps.'

The Blair team produced its own more optimistic account of key elements in the Heiligendamm Africa Communiqué, but the language, in Blair's characteristic near-verbless shorthand, does not bother to boast: 'Heiligendamm has very helpfully spurred different countries to increase their aid . . . good language on trade for Africa . . . strong commitment . . . strong support . . . will take Africa Agenda forward.' The sun that set on Blair's G8 summiteering in Germany seemed also to be going down on the priority Africa had enjoyed on the agenda during his administration. There was only one more meeting left too for President Bush, who had matched Blair in practical commitment, if not rhetoric. Gordon Brown vowed to carry forward the cause but there was little sign that the new generation of rich-country leaders would become so personally involved. They were less interested in meeting Bono and Sir Bob and more directly concerned about climate change and economic stability.

There are many debates to be had about the efficacy of aid. In some quarters, even specific medical intervention against disease is accused of stunting the development of proper local medical services. But within the terms which he set himself – goals which were shared and reinforced by the international community – Blair's Africa policy represents one of the undoubted successes of the ten years. Under him, as also under Thatcher and Major, Britain was one of the few nations to honour its foreign aid pledges (remarkably, the US is the other deliverer). As Blair left office, it was the only laggard on course to hit the UN giving target of 0.7 per cent of GNP. Blair's pragmatic, inclusive style suited dealings with Africa. He recognised that most African leaders were far from perfect, yet he engaged with them without condescending in pursuit of positive ends. His influence was almost immediate. Without Blair (and Bono) it is unlikely that either Bill Clinton's or Bill Gates's foundations would have applied themselves so rapidly and effectively to some of Africa's problems.

Prime Minister Tony Blair did not just advocate Western intervention in the economic and development spheres. He also championed military intervention to prevent suffering. He left office unashamedly expressing the wish that he had been able to use force more widely in Africa. During his final months in power Blair repeatedly raised the unfolding crisis in Darfur. 'I would like to see troops going in now,' he told me in April 2007 during an interview on Iraq. But his strong words were also an admission of his practical impotence. He conceded that Iraq had made further 'liberal intervention' less likely, and impossible for him personally to implement in his remaining months. Away from the Iraq controversy, he also cited Zimbabwe as a failure. The country had deteriorated drastically during his ten years but he had failed to find a way to intervene effectively. He doubted that there had ever been such a way.

Tony Blair and his advisers left office with the knowledge that they had done what they could. In a speech in November 2007, Jonathan Powell, Blair's chief of staff, expressed particular pride in what had been achieved in Sierra Leone. Like Blair, he compared this favourably to the way the international community had turned away during the genocides in Burundi and Rwanda before 1997. As Blair himself might put it, he didn't solve everything in Africa but he did something. He had been a player. He had stepped up to the plate.

Blair's last task at his last G8 summit cannot have been one of his personal highlights – a bilateral meeting with President Putin. This had been promised since the beginning of the summit but had been repeatedly put off, largely because of a series of calculated snubs by the Kremlin. In case anyone had failed to register the hostile signals, the Russian delegation broke their normal practice and pointedly refused to refer to the Blair meeting before or after it took place. Putin also pushed back its timing until after the close of the summit, seeing Blair for less than half an hour. As they sat, motorcades streamed past outside, heading to the airport where the official planes had already started to take off.

Diplomatic relations had cooled even further in the year since the St Petersburg summit, largely because of the murder in London in November 2006 of the Russian citizen Alexander Litvinenko. A former FSB operative, he defected to Britain in 2000 and was a known associate of Boris Berezovsky. Litvinenko had died slowly and painfully at University College Hospital of radiation poisoning. Traces of an unstable and highly toxic isotope, Polonium-210, were found along the route taken by another ex-FSB agent, Andrei Lugovoi, who had close ties to the Putin camp and had travelled from Moscow to Britain to meet Litvinenko. The British prosecuting authorities had requested the extradition of Lugovoi to face murder charges. Russia had claimed such an extradition could not take place because it would violate the constitution. Both sides had summoned the other's ambassador for an official carpeting.

Blair gave his account of the meeting in a brief news conference on the airport tarmac. Bizarrely, David Hill refused to let the official plane stand as a television backdrop because of the environmental themes at the G8. So the cameras pointed in the opposite direction for Blair to describe the meeting as 'very frank. We went through all the issues.' The prime minister stipulated that 'actions rather than words' were now required from the Russian president.

Then, since this was his last foreign trip as prime minister accompanied by the press pack, he posed with the journalists for an official picture, taken by the Press Association photographer Stephan Rousseau. He had done this before only with the travelling press corps accompanying his election battle bus. This time, his BA charter plane, Blair Force One, was in the background.

6

'FERAL MEDIA'

12 JUNE

I am going to say something that few people in public life will say,
but most know is absolutely true: a vast aspect of our jobs today –
outside of the really major decisions, as big as anything else – is coping
with the media, its sheer scale, weight and constant hyperactivity.
Tony Blair, speech on Public Life, Reuters, 12 June 2007

On 12 June, with just a fortnight to go as prime minister, Tony
Blair made one of the less predictable detours on his path to
resignation by delivering a speech on the media. He insisted that he
was neither 'whingeing' nor responding to his 'latest whacking'.
Nevertheless he allowed himself a faint gloat at his tormentors: 'As
I always say, it's an immense privilege to do this job and if the worst
that happens is harsh media coverage, it's a small price to pay. And
anyway, like it or not, I have won three elections and am still standing
as I leave office.'

The speech was billed as 'A Lecture by the Prime Minister on
Public Life', but since it was delivered at the Reuters News Agency's
new headquarters in Canary Wharf, there was never any doubt what
it was really about. Indeed, Tony Blair repeatedly yoked the two
together as he argued 'at present we are all being dragged down by
the way media and public life interact'.

Although the speech picked up on themes and even phrases used by Alastair Campbell in his numerous exculpatory articles and utterances, it was authentically in the voice of Blair, drafted by the prime minister himself in longhand. More temperate and less angry than Campbell, Tony Blair was also more thoughtful and ultimately conciliatory.

Displaying the disarming self-awareness that he so often deployed in his last years in office (beginning with his 'I've not got a reverse gear' party conference speech in 2003), he started with a concession: 'I first acknowledge my own complicity. We paid inordinate attention in the early days of New Labour to courting, assuaging and persuading the media.' Less self-consciously he then revealed that this obsession still prevailed with the observation that 'you can't let speculation stay out there for longer than an instant'.

In a classic demonstration of triangulation, Blair expressed sympathy for contemporary journalists, who shared the present 'difficulties' with those in public life. He argued that both were having to adapt to new pressures, such as a multiplicity of media outlets resulting in fragmented audiences; diverse technology, notably the internet, where broadcasters and print journalists were becoming the same; and above all 'a news cycle twenty-four hours a day, seven days a week'.

Blair's argument drew on what he had picked up during the many hours he spent dining with media proprietors, columnists and editorial boards. In a further gesture of sympathy he even parodied one of his own most famous remarks. On taking power in 1997 he had told his new parliamentary party, 'The people are the masters now. We are the servants of the people.' This was itself an echo of Labour's landslide victory in 1945 since Blair was reworking and inverting Hartley Shawcross's somewhat boastful statement to Parliament: 'We are the masters at the moment and shall be for some considerable time to come . . .' Blair's new version for the media was now: 'They are not the masters of this change but its victims.'

However, this was where common cause ended as Blair contrasted the efforts he had made to counter the media's problems, with the vicious way the media had responded. 'I introduced: first, lobby briefings on the record; then published the minutes; then gave monthly press conferences; then Freedom of Information; then became the first prime minister to go to the Select Committee's chairman's session; and so on. None of it to any avail.' He claimed that the media had reacted with cynicism: under-reporting Parliament and concentrating not on 'honest mistakes' but on 'allegations of misconduct'. Coining a new technical term he went on to claim that '"impact" is what matters'.

His central section was argued with real emotion to the point of tautology:

> Broadsheets today face the same pressures as tabloids, broadcasters increasingly the same pressures as broadsheets. The audience needs to be arrested, held and their emotions engaged. Something that is interesting is less powerful than something that makes you angry or shocked. The consequences of this are acute. First, scandal or controversy beats ordinary reporting hands down.
>
> News is rarely news unless it generates heat as much as or more than light. Second, attacking motive is far more potent than attacking judgement. It is not enough for someone to make an error. It has to be venal. Conspiratorial.
>
> Watergate was a great piece of journalism but there is a PhD thesis all on its own to examine the consequences for journalism of standing one conspiracy up. What creates cynicism is not mistakes; it is allegations of misconduct.
>
> But misconduct is what has impact. Third, the fear of missing out means today's media, more than ever before, hunts in a pack. In these modes it is like a feral beast, just tearing people and reputations to bits. But no one dares miss out. Fourth, rather than just report news, even if sensational or controversial, the new technique is commentary on the news being as, if not more, important than the news itself.

After this, as any hack reporter could have told him, came the 'We name the guilty men' section. Here the prime minister put his credibility at risk by choosing to single out for attack Britain's weakest and lowest-circulation 'quality paper', the *Independent*. He conceded that 'it is a well-edited lively paper and is absolutely entitled to print what it wants, how it wants, on the Middle East or anything else'. But clearly all those lengthy polemics against the Iraq War from Robert Fisk and Patrick Cockburn had left their scars. The prime minister seized the glib slogan of the editor, Simon Kelner, that he produced 'a viewspaper not a newspaper', as the main exhibit in his charge that the media now 'confuse news and comment'.

When the speech was announced, there had been a pretty consistent private reaction from the prime minister's friends: 'Good, it's about time he took on the *Mail*.' This was in general recognition of the fact that the powerful Associated Newspapers group had been outstandingly unforgiving in its assault on the policies and personalities of the Blair era. Alastair Campbell had repeatedly expressed his 'hate' for the *Mail* papers. But on this occasion, as early in his premiership when he attended the funerals of Associated's editor-in-chief, Sir David English, and proprietor, Vere Harmsworth, Blair ducked it. There was no mention of the *Daily Mail*, *Mail on Sunday* or *Evening Standard* in his Reuters speech – nor of Rupert Murdoch, News International, *The Times* and the *Sun* either, which had so buoyed New Labour by endorsing the party prior to the 1997 election. Instead, Tony Blair referred only to the puny *Independent* and, in passing, to the BBC, Britain's biggest media organisation and a general-purpose punchbag.

Out of office, Blair conceded that it was a mistake to single out the *Independent*. His real target had been the *Daily Mail* but he feared what the paper would do to him and his family should he have targeted it. Blair said that he had thought long and hard about whether it had been wise to be so friendly in the early days with senior executives at Associated Newspapers, but he argued that the tone of the group had grown much worse with the rise of Paul Dacre.

The conclusions of Blair's media speech were unsurprisingly sketchy and anti-climactic, although, ever the politician, he fell back on unspecified changes in regulation as a solution. Given that the Press Complaints Commission regulating newspapers was 'traditional' and his questionable belief that Ofcom would soon be able to regulate all television content on the internet, Blair suggested: 'As the technology blurs the distinction between papers and television, it becomes increasingly irrational to have different systems of accountability based on technology that no longer can be differentiated in the old way.' (The Blairs had sought recourse through the Press Complaints Commission – particularly in the early years – but had not always been happy with the outcome.)

However, the outgoing leader modestly declined to offer a blueprint of how this might be done: 'I am not in a position to determine this one way or another.' Instead he set out a blood-chilling survey of the consequences if no action was taken:

> this relationship between public life and media is now damaged in a manner that requires repair. The damage saps the country's confidence and self-belief; it undermines its assessment of itself, its institutions; and above all, it reduces our capacity to take the right decisions, in the right spirit for our future. I've made this speech after much hesitation. I know it will be rubbished in certain quarters. But I also know this has needed to be said.

More in sorrow than in anger for sure, this was still a bitter valediction from a prime minister who had taken greater interest than any other in the media (except perhaps the stricken John Major). The speech had less impact than he might have hoped for. It was hailed by Blair's established allies within the 'commentariat', such as John Lloyd and Roy Greenslade, who had expressed similar views themselves and may even have provided the intellectual underpinning for Blair's analysis. While recognising some of his insights, though, most media commentators judged him to be too compromised a figure, too implicated, too intimately embroiled in media relations for too many years to be a valid censor.

The speech had also ducked a second vital question along with that of the *Daily Mail*: Iraq. Blair referred to the Hutton Inquiry in passing, but few journalists could agree that it had established 'the facts' which they 'refused to accept'. He did not deal with the dossiers of evidence produced on Iraq's weapons of mass destruction threat, which subsequently turned out to be wrong. And most considered that the prime minister had overreached himself at Canary Wharf when he argued: 'I would only point out that the Hutton Inquiry (along with three other inquiries) was a six-month investigation in which I as prime minister and other senior ministers and officials faced unprecedented public questioning and scrutiny. The verdict was disparaged because it was not the one the critics wanted. But it was an example of being held to account, not avoiding it. But leave that to one side.'

As Blair recognised, his departing righteous indignation with the media was a little hard to take given the efforts which he and his underlings had expended trying to court and manipulate it during his hegemony. Attempts to win over, or neutralise, the hostility of the media had begun long before either Blair or Campbell became key figures. The change started with the election of Neil Kinnock as Labour Party leader and the appointment of Peter Mandelson as its director of communications. During this period David Hill – ultimately Campbell's successor at Number 10 – and his then employer, Roy Hattersley, the deputy leader, were also highly active in reaching out to what they generally regarded as 'the Tory press'.

Mandelson began his quest to win over, or at least neutralise, the media for New Labour as soon as he became head of the Labour Party Press Office under Neil Kinnock. Ultimately, they were rebuffed in the 1992 general election when the *Sun* treated Kinnock with exceptional harshness.

While the media had previously been viewed as suspect and kept at arm's length, Mandelson instead instigated personal contacts at the highest possible level between the Labour leadership and journalists. For example, he took Neil Kinnock to lunch with the *Sun*. Mandelson and Campbell also cultivated personal relationships with journalists on the political beat. They regularised the flow of routine information and began to use the distribution of exclusives as a means to reward or punish correspondents. They persuaded, cultivated and co-opted those they could and attempted to bully or undermine those who were judged to be hostile.

Individuals and organisations that proved susceptible to pressure would be revisited again and again. The BBC offered particularly fertile ground. In opposition, Mandelson himself, as an old friend of the Director General, John Birt, knew which buttons to press (he was even employed as a BBC consultant prior to becoming an MP). Once Campbell took over he seemed to employ deputies to deal with the Corporation. Both Tim Allan and Lance Price had worked for the BBC and could identify where to exert influence on the Corporation bureaucracy.

Only the BBC, and to a much lesser extent other regulated broadcast news outlets, could be influenced so directly. British newspapers and the journalists they employed were unruly and partisan. When a politician or party was deemed to be powerful, as New Labour was during its rise, print journalists and their proprietors could easily be curbed by threats and blandishments. Once Blair became leader, Mandelson was determined not to repeat any mistakes. This time they found they were pushing at an open door. Even the *Sun* endorsed Blair in 1996. New Labour's leaders were astonished at the ease with which they could influence the media during the 1990s, and this sowed the seeds of the contempt which Blair would subsequently feel for journalists in general. As opposition leader, Blair dined enthusiastically with proprietors and publishers such as Lord (Vere) Harmsworth, Sir David English and Rupert Murdoch – and the *Daily Mail*, the *Sun* and *The Times* all backed him in 1997.

It was perfectly possible not to get pressured by either arm of this pincer movement and to still maintain a professional distance, but most print journalists did not resist, either rolling over to be tickled or cowering at the power of New Labour. It was certainly not comfortable for those who were judged to be against 'the project'. Mandelson had a habit of denouncing in front of their colleagues journalists who had displeased him. The highly respected and hard-working George Jones of the *Daily Telegraph* was subjected to a particularly nasty public attack before one election news conference when he was accused of working for Conservative Central Office.

Mandelson managed to make life-long enemies in particular of some of the most influential political correspondents, who bided their time and then showed no mercy when his political career ran into trouble; some of them helped it get into difficulties in the first place. This was Mandelson's tragedy, and played a significant part in both of his departures from cabinet office, but it also confounded the common impression that he was a profoundly untrustworthy and dishonest individual. He was not – with the one fateful, personal mistake of failing to make full disclosure of the personal loan from Geoffrey Robinson MP on his Britannia Building Society mortgage form.

Mandelson never lied or dissimulated to me, in contrast to Campbell and Blair and many of their underlings. His fault was rather that he was too brazen in supporting his cause. Unlike Campbell, he was central in developing the intellectual arguments on which New Labour was built, and had a sense of ownership of them, as is very clear in the book *The Blair Revolution* which he wrote with Roger Liddle. He could go too far in over-promoting what he so passionately believed in. His personal loyalty to Blair survived twice being sacked by him and he remained – with Campbell and Anji Hunter – one of the trio of intimates who continued to be close advisers to the prime minister long after they left his service on paper.

Alastair Campbell

I'm just an extension of Tony. That's what I am. And I did a job for him and I think while I was there I did a good job. But there were times I didn't do such a good job. But I said on the day I left that the good memories outweighed the bad . . . Now fuck off.

Alastair Campbell, interviewed
in the *Guardian*, 8 March 2004

A handful of journalists required no pressure at all: by his own admission Alastair Campbell was 'a part-time propagandist' for Labour during his time as a journalist on the *Daily Mirror* and the now defunct *Today* newspaper.

I first noticed Campbell during the party conference season in Brighton at the Grand Hotel shortly after it had reopened following the 1984 IRA bomb attack. For a comparatively young journalist,

Campbell was remarkably self-assured. He appeared late at night playing the bagpipes in the hotel foyer. An altercation followed between him and his long-time friend and client, the late Tony Bevins, and two hostile Scottish journalists, Alan Cochrane and Bruce Anderson, whose career highlights already included stints with Mandelson at LWT's *Weekend World* and in the Conservative research department. The pipe-playing soon stopped.

At around this time I got a measure of how Labour regarded the journalist Campbell. Kinnock was doing some end of conference interviews but got delayed. I was asked to wait in the backstage office. After a while, Campbell wandered in and began to chat with Jan Royall, Kinnock's loyal secretary, who later became Baroness Royall and a Labour whip in the Lords. After about half an hour's wait I was thrown out on the grounds that no journalists were allowed in the office. There was no suggestion that Campbell should leave as well.

Campbell was an obsessive personality who had a habit of forming addictions and dependencies on individuals. In the 1980s he was slavishly loyal to Neil Kinnock and to Robert Maxwell, proprietor of the Mirror Group, who died mysteriously in 1991 having plundered his own companies' pension funds. Campbell also confronted alcoholism with the support of Fiona Millar, his highly assertive partner.

Although he has sometimes been placed, erroneously, at the centre of the New Labour project and even been described as one of its architects, he was not an automatic choice as press secretary when Blair became party leader in 1994. Two other journalists were shortlisted for the post: Andy Grice, who ironically was the political editor of the *Independent* at the time of Blair's Reuters speech, and Philip Bassett, an industrial correspondent of the *Financial Times* and *The Times*. Bassett eventually joined the government to work as an aide in Downing Street before moving on to act as special adviser to Lord Falconer and Baroness Ashton. In 2001 he married his long-term partner, the Labour minister and peer Baroness Symons.

Campbell was an intimate of Neil and Glenys Kinnock during the 1980s and was supportive of Kinnock's reforms, but he was not in the nucleus of what became the New Labour project. His personal politics were somewhat to the left of Blair, as was shown in some of his articles during this period. Even well into the early 1990s, Campbell was using his *Today* column to rail against the 'barmy' idea of tuition fees and to state that education funding would instead be 'best addressed by increases in general taxation'. The authors of the project were Blair, Gordon Brown, Mandelson and Philip Gould, supported by Roger Liddle and Anji Hunter. Campbell knew them well, however. By the late eighties he was a regular visitor to Blair's office, kicking around ideas for his newspaper columns.

Blair had tasked Anji Hunter, who had run his MP's office since 1986, with finding a press secretary. Grice turned the offer down for family reasons and Bassett was judged to be less of a 'people person', so Campbell got the job. Blair was obviously impressed with his new hired gun. The week of Campbell's appointment I had to interview Blair in the sepulchral rooms of the leader of the opposition. Making small talk while we waited for the cameras to roll, I mentioned Campbell's new job. Blair reacted with that mixture of naivety and detached indifference which marked him out for the very top: 'Oh, do you know Ali?' he exclaimed. 'I think he's absolutely fantastic!'

Campbell did do a fantastic job for Blair in the first six or so years that he worked for him, but from 2000 (and particularly 2001) on, he turned progressively from an asset to at best a liability and at worst a seriously destructive force.

At the beginning he was indeed a breath of fresh air. Unlike Mandelson, whose high-handed manner had alienated many, Campbell could be one of the lads when required. But he was also shrewd, gauging what each journalist was after, and which were trustworthy and which not. He knew what journalists wanted and did not hesitate to satisfy them, sometimes unscrupulously. During the 1997 party conference negative headlines were building up because of a string of mishaps. Campbell blotted them out of the *Sun* the next day by informing Britain's top-selling daily that a well-known but mentally ill actress, Nicola Pagett, had been sending him explicit love letters. The *Sun*'s front-page headline blazed: 'EXCLUSIVE: TV STAR'S TWISTED LOVE FOR BLAIR'S TOP MAN', while the opening sentence helpfully clarified that 'the Premier's trusted Chief Press Secretary was the innocent victim of the actress's deluded passion'.

Campbell was a much better public relations man than he had ever been a journalist. Good journalism requires detachment; PR thrives on commitment and conviction. Campbell brought the total and blinkered dedication of a football fan into office with him. Perhaps because of the convergence of party political ideologies on to the centre ground, his petulant partisanship typified the way in which New Labour conducted its media operation.

In opposition and then in government, New Labour set up a media-monitoring unit which published printed bulletins several times a day containing précis and quotations from national and regional newspapers and magazines, and reports on the contents of major radio and television news bulletins. These documents were the creation of a young Australian, Andrew Sholl, who had cut his teeth with the Australian Labour Party. For politicians, they obviated the need to keep up with the media at first hand because they were so detailed. Live '2-ways' with television reporters and commentators were also closely monitored, though the finer points of equivocation were not always picked up.

When mixed in with a computer database of politicians' previous remarks, these bulletins provided the raw material for another New Labour innovation – rebuttal. No statement which might disadvantage the party, or mis-statement by the opposition which might indirectly help the cause, was allowed to stand alone. The press office would intervene, either demanding retractions or drawing attention to what it considered to be its opponents' errors.

On media management, Campbell's relationship with Blair was similar to that which Margaret Thatcher had enjoyed with her press secretary, Bernard Ingham. Both prime ministers trusted their press secretaries, not only to manage their relationships with the media – to decide who got access and who didn't – but also to read and watch the news for them. But Campbell was much more intimate with Blair than Ingham ever was with Thatcher. He behaved as an equal in Blair's company; Ingham never aspired to be more than a civil servant.

Campbell thought nothing of contradicting Blair in front of other people, albeit usually in a slightly self-mocking tone. He would decide whether the prime minister was stopping or going, talking or shutting up, and Blair would usually meekly follow his orders (to be fair, it was usually convenient for him to do so). Early in the administration, before the myths were fixed, Blair shot a party political broadcast with a crew not used to working at Westminster. One crew member's abiding memory was of 'those two people, a man and a woman, who were so rude to the prime minister'. They could be identified easily as Campbell and Hunter.

Campbell extended his control much further than Ingham. He managed to stop Blair doing doorstep interviews. With previous prime ministers, doorstep interviews were the routine way to get their on-the-hoof reactions to developments. But no matter how loudly the reporters shouted, Blair was told to walk past the cameras. Usually, press officers would be sent ahead to scout the terrain and check if any reporters lay in wait. They would ask what you wanted to talk to Blair about, but this was usually for their own information. Blair never paused to talk, although on one or two rather farcical occasions he re-emerged from his destination, having been briefed and allowed to collect his thoughts, to then give his 'spontaneous reaction' to the camera teams who had been asked to wait.

Alastair Campbell went further. He controlled what Blair knew about what the media were saying. Blair has since said that he didn't even read the daily news briefs, except on Wednesdays before PMQs. So Campbell's own words, usually deeply critical of journalists' work, were all Blair had to rely on. Anji Hunter thought even this was going too far and often tried to prevent Campbell from relaying media criticism. Towards the end, the two men were in agreement: Blair said he didn't read the papers and Campbell couldn't be bothered to either.

Campbell also set Blair to work as a journalist. In one year so many publications were given articles with his byline that he was sarcastically honoured with a 'Freelance of the Year' press award. It was an open secret that 'Tony Blair' pieces were ghosted for him by Campbell and a growing team of writers made up of Fleet Street veterans including Phil Bassett and David Bradshaw.

Years before he even became prime minister, Tony Blair had already established the most professional and extensive political press operation ever seen in Britain in peacetime. Once he was elected in 1997, the operation effectively moved from Labour Party headquarters into Downing Street. The difference was that there were now more resources available to fund it, thanks to the public purse. Blair stressed the importance he attached to his press secretary by giving him authority over civil servants.

Campbell subsequently marked out his territory by moving the press operations into Number 12 Downing Street, until then the traditional domain of the government chief whip. The large ground-floor suite of Georgian rooms was transformed into an approximation of a newsroom with a central row of facing computer desks. Campbell himself abandoned Ingham's bow-windowed office overlooking the street, for a corner office at the back of the building, commanding the garden, Horse Guards Parade and St James's Park.

For the first couple of years of Blair's Downing Street tenure, the press office and the media seemed to have an almost symbiotic relationship. The Conservatives were in disarray and – after such a massive Labour landslide – minority parties were largely irrelevant. There was little public concern for close scrutiny of the government; instead the media often merely relayed what New Labour was saying and doing. Blair has since described his first term as a wasted opportunity; it is certainly true that he took a non-confrontational approach which avoided controversy.

The prime minister's director of communications continued to fulfil the press secretary's functions by briefing meetings of lobby journalists twice daily when Parliament was sitting. He was a much more powerful source than Westminster journalists had ever had before. Ingham, for example, never attended cabinet; he waited outside to debrief a cabinet secretary before then passing on to reporters what he had learned. Ingham's successors under Major – Gus O'Donnell, Christopher Meyer and Jonathan Haslam – also stayed at arm's length, or 'out of the loop', as at least two of them complained. By contrast, Campbell sat in on cabinet as a matter of course, along with Jonathan Powell, Anji Hunter and Sally Morgan, the prime minister's political secretary. With Blair, this group made up the core which became known as the 'sofa government', taking important and un-minuted decisions informally in Blair's den, just off the Cabinet Room.

Campbell was more than 'his master's voice', he was often 'the horse's mouth'. His closeness to Blair meant that he could articulate what the leader was thinking, sometimes before Blair had actually thought it. Even once Blair became prime minister, it was not uncommon for phrases which Campbell had first used spontaneously in discussion to crop up again as set passages in Blair's speeches or Commons contributions.

This creative process worked in a mutually reinforcing circle, provided the prime minister and his director of communications were in harmony. In briefings and articles Campbell was able to flesh out and test ideas, but once the lobby correspondents identified the unusually authoritative nature of Campbell's pronouncements, they increased the pressure on him to say something newsworthy. With his journalist's ear for quotes and headlines, Campbell could not resist temptation. Nor could the hacks. At the daily lobby briefings the pursuit of information was often abandoned for the game of trying to push him into a juicy gaffe.

Sometimes the consequences could be trivial, if embarrassing and a little unfair on Campbell. He made headlines when he used the phrase 'bog standard comprehensives' during lively exchanges over schools policy. The government was accused of disparaging the existing educational system. This was not Campbell's intent, and everyone in the briefing room knew it; he was simply deploying colourful language to dramatise the change and choice which Blair hoped to introduce into secondary schools – the tone of his voice had placed the words 'bog standard' in quotation marks but the quote was too good to miss. (Had cameras and sound recorded the briefing, the story would never have 'got legs' because the context was clear.)

Campbell was generally aware of the authority of his words and relished the power he wielded. He was widely considered to be more powerful than a cabinet minister and wasn't shy to flex his muscles. Social Security Secretary Harriet Harman was just one senior minister who was publicly contradicted and forced by Campbell to retract a statement. Harman's joint sacking along with her feuding deputy Frank Field was preceded by Campbell making them both figures of fun; at a social gathering, Campbell had demonstrated his superiority by goading the then ambitious junior minister Charlie Falconer into praising the job Harman and Field were doing. Both social security ministers were out of the government within weeks.

Campbell was far from embarrassed in 2000 when two television programmes captured his seeming supremacy. The veteran BBC documentary reporter Michael Cockerell made a film of life in Downing Street centred on the press secretary. On it Blair was caught coming into Campbell's office and deferring to him. The impressionist Rory Bremner picked up on this aspect of the relationship on his Channel 4 television show: a series of sketches showed a thuggish Campbell brusquely dictating orders and policies to a feeble Blair. It was a venomous modern version of the Jeeves and Wooster, master and servant paradox which dates back at least to the Roman dramatist Plautus.

By the second half of the first term, relations between the media and Campbell had curdled. Contempt and hostility manifested themselves on both sides. Campbell delighted in mocking the mannerisms of individual journalists (Robert Peston, then political editor of the *Financial Times*, was a favourite target) and would on occasion hand out 'Garbage Awards' for stories which he judged to be particularly inaccurate. The problem was Campbell's slave-like devotion to his cause. He believed that the ends of a successful New Labour government justified any means of treating the press. For example, in 1998 with great fanfare Labour introduced an 'annual report' which checked what progress was being made in delivering the promises stated in the election manifesto. It listed hundreds of individual pledges and rated them as done, in progress, or yet to be acted upon. The second year a slimmed down annual report was produced without the checklist (the then leader of the opposition, William Hague, likened this new version to 'a Harry Potter'). From the third year on, the annual report was dropped altogether without apology or explanation from Number 10.

For Campbell, truth itself took a back seat to the cause – another big difference from Sir Bernard Ingham, who regarded lying as the worst possible charge that could be laid against him. On one occasion, the fact of whether a reshuffle was taking place or not depended on whether Blair was in London or Chequers. Campbell confidently told me that the prime minister was enjoying a country weekend. He wasn't. He and Campbell were closeted in Number 10 working out the reshuffle, which was announced the next morning. 'Sorry, Adam, you know why I had to tell you that,' Campbell apologised later that day. A simple refusal to answer my question would have been preferable.

Campbell's over-confidence was further boosted by the UK government-led overhaul of the NATO press operation during the Balkans conflict. The full arsenal of news war rooms, rebuttals, daily briefings and partisan press spokesmen was introduced at NATO's sleepy Brussels headquarters. In fact, a team of half a dozen officials from Number 10 was sent to Belgium, but Campbell was not slow to claim the credit personally. This operation marked the introduction of a 'coalition information service' which purported to produce dossiers of factual information relevant to the conflict and became a hallmark of Campbell's international media operations. In the immediate aftermath of 9/11, a new coalition information service produced files on Islamism to coincide with Blair's alliance-building trip to India and Pakistan. But the practice reached its apotheosis with the two dossiers – infamously known as the '45-minute dossier' and the 'dodgy dossier' – which inadvertently did so much damage to the British and American cause in the Iraq conflict.

By 1999, Campbell was often referred to as 'the real deputy prime minister' or 'the second most powerful man in Britain'. Blair was blasé, presumably because he had a strong aide performing what was judged to be an excellent job, and taking the media burden off his shoulders. But as Campbell became to most intents and purposes a political figure in his own right, tensions within New Labour were inevitable – especially once Fiona Millar, Campbell's partner and mother of his three children, herself became a powerful figure within Number 10 as Cherie Blair's chief aide.

Campbell's growing stature exacerbated two crises within the New Labour 'family' on either side of the 2001 general election: Peter Mandelson's second resignation on 24 January 2001 and 'Cheriegate' in late 2002.

Peter Mandelson's career as a Westminster politician effectively came to an end when he was forced to resign from the cabinet for a second time. He had first quit as trade secretary in December 1998, along with Treasury minister Geoffrey Robinson, following revelations that Robinson had privately loaned him £373,000 for a house purchase. However, within a year Blair had brought him back into the government fold as Northern Ireland secretary. Now there were murky suggestions that Mandelson had intervened to assist with UK passport applications on behalf of the billionaire Hinduja brothers. A subsequent official inquiry failed to substantiate these charges against Mandelson, but by the time the report's findings were published it was too late. With hindsight, Mandelson believes he may have been the victim of a turf war with Jack Straw at the Home Office, which was then seized on by Campbell.

After some days of lurid headlines about the Hinduja affair, Campbell decided that Mandelson had to go and he prevailed upon Derry Irvine, the Lord Chancellor and another long-time Blair counsellor, to support him. Mandelson was summoned to a meeting at Number 10. While this discussion was going on, Campbell ensured that Mandelson was finished by briefing the lobby that he was on the way out. He did not do so explicitly but anyone of any experience gathered in the Number 10 basement, which then served as a briefing room, knew exactly what Campbell meant when he said, 'Peter Mandelson is at this moment upstairs discussing his future with the prime minister.' I immediately walked across the street to the television cameras and reported that Mandelson was out. Some minutes later, he himself emerged to confirm it. Metaphorically, Campbell had kicked the chair out from under Mandelson's feet and left him dangling.

This was a decisive moment of rupture within New Labour that was never fully healed. It brought Campbell closer to the Brownites and expedient men of business such as Jack Straw and Robin Cook, but he was never again fully trusted by those such as Anji Hunter, Cherie Blair and Ben Wegg-Prosser who had invested emotionally in the project. Typically, Tony Blair managed to stay aloof and to retain both Campbell and Mandelson as friends and advisers.

The immediate impact of Mandelson's fall was muffled, partly because he had a very small personal following, partly because those sections of the media that had long targeted him had got their scalp. More importantly, the general election was due – though it had to be delayed by a month because of the added complication of an outbreak of foot and mouth disease. Mandelson was re-elected as MP for Hartlepool with a resounding majority, but he left the House of Commons in 2004, nominated by Blair as Britain's EU commissioner for trade.

2001 general election: John Prescott's punch

John is John and I'm lucky to have him as my deputy.
        Tony Blair reacts to the 'punch incident', 16 May 2001

As I was to experience at first hand, the notorious Prescott 'punch incident' displayed the strength of the New Labour media management operation and its ruthlessness, and showed how pervasive and dominant media managers had become within the party. 'Cutting out the cancer' was never even considered an option since the tumour and the organism amounted to the same thing.

The Labour Party were nervous throughout the 2001 general election campaign – even though another Blair victory looked a foregone conclusion. Ultimately, nobody was very surprised when the 1997 landslide was all but repeated in the vote on 7 June with a Labour majority of 167. The only day that a lengthy and largely comatose campaign lit up was Wednesday, 16 May, when three senior ministers were attacked by the voting public.

Jack Straw, the outgoing home secretary, was heckled and slow hand-clapped by the Police Federation during a speech to their conference in Blackpool.

On a visit to Gisela Stuart's marginal constituency in Birmingham, the prime minister was berated by Sharon Storer, a local postmistress, about the NHS in full view of the television cameras. Ms Storer's 48-year-old partner, Keith Sedgewick, was receiving treatment for Hodgkinson's lymphoma at Queen Elizabeth Hospital. One of her complaints was that he had been accommodated overnight on an improvised bed when hospitalised for a bone marrow transplant. Rejecting Blair's plea, Storer refused to go inside away from the cameras to discuss the matter privately, telling him instead: 'All you do is walk around and make yourself known but you don't do anything to help anybody.'

Both these incidents occurred mid-afternoon on the day that the Labour Party had transported the national media to Birmingham for the launch of the party manifesto. The apparatchiks in Millbank Tower had not expected to be jumpy and in full 'rebuttal mode', as they now were. And this was before the early evening when John Prescott's fists swung into action in the decaying North Wales seaside town of Rhyl – as it happened, just down the coast from Prestatyn where Prescott had been born on 31 May 1938.

Prickly, pugnacious and pompous, John Prescott had nonetheless been a loyal and useful sidekick to Tony Blair. He had stood against Blair for the leadership in 1994 and then settled for election to the post of deputy leader; Blair appointed him deputy prime minister after the victory of 1997.

Unlike Blair, Prescott had authentic working-class and trade union roots. Before Parliament and a mature degree at Ruskin College, Oxford, Prescott had been a steward on cruise ships and an activist in the National Union of Seamen, but he was also an early Labour moderniser – remarkable given the trajectory which had led him to become MP for Hull East.

Perhaps the finest moment of his career came during John Smith's leadership, when Prescott's passionate speech to the party conference was decisive in persuading the trade unions not to object to the watering down of the block vote as the Labour Party moved closer to 'OMOV' – one member one vote.

In government, Prescott insisted on a grandiose and sprawling department, overseeing transport, local government and the environment, which quickly became regarded as dysfunctional. His main use, though, was as a fixer for Blair. He chaired cabinet committees and sometimes acted as a go-between in Blair's fraught relationship with Gordon Brown, on occasion hosting peacemaking dinners in the neutral territory of his Admiralty Arch flat.

Prescott also acted as the rallier of the party faithful. Half comic, half bullying, he was a highly effective motivational speaker. At general elections, Prescott toured the regions in his battle bus. This cheered the party workers and conveniently kept him away from the national media, who were given only the patchiest outline of his schedule. Typically, Prescott's contribution to the day of Labour's 2001 election launch was to appear by satellite link from a highly marginal target seat in Dorset. There were sound problems: first the audience couldn't hear Prescott, then Blair couldn't cut him off: 'Do you need any more?' Prescott asked. They all laughed.

But the mood when Prescott arrived in Rhyl was ugly rather than amused.

Countryside protesters were a recurrent feature of Blair's first and second terms. Their essential grievance was Labour's pledge to outlaw fox-hunting with dogs, but they bore other grudges as well. There were frequent complaints that rural life was comparatively poorer, less well serviced and not understood by the predominantly urban and suburban Labour Party. Activist farmers, including some in North Wales, were ringleaders in the 2000 fuel protests which successfully forced the government to back down on planned duty increases.

The outbreak of foot and mouth disease in 2001 was a further potential provocation to rural communities. The first case was diagnosed in February but it was some weeks before Labour announced its plans to postpone holding the general election scheduled for May. Even though there were movement restrictions and closed rights of way in much of the countryside, some senior activists still wanted to stick to their plans. Alastair Campbell, for example, repeatedly told journalists that he had recently been to the country and it was still perfectly possible to have a decent walk (on roads) after a pub lunch. Blair's instinct to delay was decisively backed by Anji Hunter, herself from farming stock, and the soundings she took in the wider community.

Foot and mouth lasted from February to September and cost an estimated £8.5 billion and the destruction of 6 million sheep and cattle. Inevitably, there were complaints about some aspects of the official response to the outbreak, but Blair refused to set up a public inquiry. (Before the news conference for the manifesto launch, Downing Street officials asked me what question I was going to ask. In a rare fit of good humour I confessed I was considering the countryside and foot and mouth. National television correspondents usually get to ask the first few questions; this time I was called only about forty minutes into the news conference, the only time I can remember that happening to me. Circumspection rather than honesty is sometimes the best policy.)

Prescott had deliberately set himself up as a hate figure for countryside campaigners. For him, hunt supporters fitted into a glib class stereotype – hunters equal toffs – so he mocked them at any opportunity. At the party conference in Brighton in 2000, the deputy prime minister had publicly referred to the 'contorted faces' of the Countryside Alliance protesters outside the hall.

Videotapes of the incident in Rhyl show several hundred demonstrators under police supervision in front of the hall where the deputy prime minister was to deliver his rallying speech. Prescott clambered out of his battle bus, made eye contact with the protesters and gestured at them by raising his arms from his side and leaning back as if to say 'bring it on'. They jeered back. To the bafflement of his escorts, Prescott then decided to walk to the hall door on a path through the middle of the crowd, rather than by the pre-planned route which would have taken him around the edges of the protest.

Fatefully, this brought him within arm's reach of some of the demonstrators. One of these, Craig Evans, a farm labourer from nearby Llandyrnog, was there to protest against what he called an 'erosion of rural life'. 'We in the countryside feel excluded and alienated from the process of democracy and politics,' he explained later.

Evans threw an egg at John Prescott as he passed and scored a bullseye. Prescott instantaneously lashed back with a rather nifty left jab and, as they say, 'a struggle ensued' between the two men. In a subsequent newspaper interview, Evans claimed that he saw a 'mad glint' in the deputy prime minister's eye: 'He was boiling with rage . . . He didn't hit me in self-defence, or because he was scared. He hit me because he was angry. It was pure anger. I saw it coming and rode the punch – but it connected and it hurt.' Evans had a bloody nose and a bruised face, but it was he who was detained by the police after the incident. Both combatants were eventually interviewed by the North Wales constabulary but the Crown Prosecution Service did not bring charges against them.

Evans said he regretted throwing the egg; Prescott never apologised. He called the whole incident 'frightening and regrettable', but reference to it became part of his patter to sympathetic audiences: 'I wish I had ducked a bit quicker at Rhyl. Mind you, I think the other guy thinks that as well.' Five years later, slow-motion footage of the punch was even included in the video montage celebrating Prescott's career which followed what was to be his last speech as deputy prime minister to the Labour conference. Prescott's memoirs, published in spring 2008, were titled *Prezza: Pulling No Punches*.

Until the fight took place, Prescott's visit was just another item on Sky News' crowded election diary. However, along with other news organisations, we had sent a camera and reporter team to Rhyl, firstly because this was a relatively rare chance to see the DPM in action and secondly, in Sky News' case, because Shirley Lewis, our excellent north west bureau chief at the time, had found out that a sizeable protest was planned.

We had no live broadcast facilities on site because coverage of the event was 'a watching brief'. Then Shirley telephoned me directly because I was the political editor to ask what we should do as she had just witnessed Prescott punch someone. We went over what had happened in detail and Shirley gave me an account, which subsequently proved to be entirely accurate. She also told me that we would soon have pictures of the incident: still photographs first, followed by moving pictures from several camera angles (she was party to local negotiations which meant that some news organisations agreed to share their individual material that evening).

I had no hesitation believing Shirley – she was at least as experienced a reporter as I was and we had worked together a number of times. I went on air from our Westminster studio and reported that Prescott had punched a protester in Rhyl and expressed the view that this was a serious matter and potentially a resignation issue for him.

When I came out of the studio, a Labour press officer was already waiting on the phone. He told me that party officials travelling with Prescott confirmed the incident had not happened; that Labour was demanding an immediate retraction and an apology and that I had just ruined my career. I replied that I would wait to see the pictures and continued to report live on what was by now becoming a major story.

Labour's tactics may have had some success elsewhere – wire services were reporting only that Prescott had been involved in an incident outside an election rally. So it was a relief, but not a surprise to me, when the photographs and then the television pictures clearly showed Prescott's fist connecting with another man's face. (Even then, the BBC's main evening news did not lead with the story.) I continued to broadcast and the Labour Party continued to phone. Most interestingly, Lord Falconer – a junior minister but operating as counsel to the campaign – rang to warn me that I was making a grave personal mistake and was laying myself open to legal action by Prescott and the Labour Party.

I was unconvinced by any of this pressure; rightly as it turned out. One of the regular highlights of subsequent *An Evening with Alastair Campbell* stage shows was the former spin doctor telling how he got a phone call earlier that evening from 'JP' asking. 'Ali, I've just punched a bloke, what shall I do?' Campbell's diaries give a slightly muted version of this but the facts stand. At the very time that Labour was officially denying the story and issuing naked threats, Campbell and co. knew exactly what had happened and were consulting their lawyers, Falconer and (according to Campbell) Lord Chancellor Derry Irvine. I do not like to think what the consequences might have been for Craig Evans had no cameras been present.

Labour's response to the incident was to assess public opinion: if the party and Prescott could get away with it, then they would. (In another context, the former prime minister, John Major, once told me that this is the attitude which must be taken by all serious politicians in pursuit of votes.) Blair didn't want a bigger crisis in the middle of his election campaign and he certainly didn't want to lose the shield which Prescott had become for him. At the morning press conference Blair joked and wriggled: 'John is John,' he declared. Nick Robinson of the BBC told the prime minister that he sounded like a mum making excuses for her yobbish son on the steps of a magistrates' court. Immediately after the press conference I was berated for my coverage of the story by both Campbell and David Hill, the man who was to succeed him at number 10. Campbell warned me I was in danger of being 'sanctimonious'.

My job at Sky News was to give a live commentary of political events as they were happening. I had felt able to comment on the Prescott punch because it was a matter of personal conduct rather than party politics, on which I was professionally bound to stay impartial. Personally, I was disgusted by Prescott's behaviour. I hate violence and don't think that politicians should assault members of their electorate and I believed the deputy prime minister had belied his own government's moralising on yob culture and anti-social behaviour. I considered that his own behaviour should, and could in other circumstances, have cost Prescott his job. Some close to Blair thought the same.

However, as I freely and repeatedly acknowledged at the time and have reported since, that was not the verdict of public opinion. Perhaps because Prescott was a well-loved 'character', perhaps because he had at least injected some life into a dull election campaign, opinion polls backed him. Blair claimed subsequently that in his constituency shortly afterwards several people he canvassed expressed regret that he'd never do something like that himself.

It was for Labour to judge whether Prescott made a worthwhile contribution in his remaining six years as deputy prime minister. His record as an administrator was not strong. In 1997 he set his only target on transport: 'I will have failed . . . if in five years time there are not many more people using public transport and far fewer journeys by car.' In fact, by 2007 car journeys had increased by more than 10 per cent. Prescott wanted to match devolution for Scotland and Wales with regional devolution in England, but the plan for elected regional assemblies was abandoned after 78 per cent voted against the idea in the first referendum held in the Northeast. Improvements in Britain's rail services were not a feature of Prescott's tenure.

Then there were the scandals. The transport secretary using a car for a journey of a couple of hundred yards at the 1999 Labour conference. He blamed security and his wife Pauline's desire to protect her hairdo. The 'V signs' he variously flicked in the Commons chamber and on the doorstep of Number 10. He became even more of a target of ridicule in his final years because of a number of newspaper exposés. The *Daily Mirror* revealed that the deputy prime minister had had an affair with his diary secretary, Tracey Temple. There were stories too about the hospitality Prescott had received from an American billionaire interested in turning the Millennium Dome into a supercasino. Prescott had enjoyed a stay at Philip Anschutz's ranch and had been presented with a cowboy suit. Perhaps most damaging of all were the photographs published in the *Mail on Sunday* of him playing croquet with his staff on a Thursday afternoon at Dorneywood, his official country residence. Croquet, with its associations of privileged gentility, did not fit with either the public's view of him or Prescott's own self-image.

Prescott had little alternative but to go with Blair. He acknowledged this in his speech to the 2006 Labour conference in which he admitted to delegates: 'I know that in the last year I let myself down. I let you down. I just want to say sorry.' But he continued in office, albeit shorn of departmental responsibilities, until June 2007. In one of his most effective appointments, David Cameron had asked William Hague to shadow Prescott in the Commons chamber, pitting Parliament's most able debater against Prescott who often had difficulty getting his words out correctly. This trait was in evidence in his final appearance at the dispatch box on 20 June, when he mangled Hague's compliment that he was 'a cross between Ernie

Bevan and Demosthenes' into a reference to 'Dame Osthenes'. Hague picked this up, predicting that the dame would be 'very flattered that the deputy prime minister has singled her out for praise today'. But the Conservatives mainly satisfied themselves at this farewell performance with gentle teasing about the £2.5-million cost of Prescott's non-department. He retorted with boasts about the regeneration of Britain's cities over the ten years and digs at the Tories over the poll tax and Michael Heseltine visiting Liverpool 'with a bus load of bankers'.

For me, as a working journalist, the consequences of the Prescott punch were twofold: bad mouthing and a boycott by the deputy prime minister. Prescott has claimed publicly – though usually in interviews for non-national media outlets and audiences – that what happened in Rhyl was 'set up by Sky'. This is untrue and libellous. No evidence has ever been produced by Prescott; we have simply decided that the best course is to ignore his blustering.

Prescott avoided speaking to me on principle whenever he could since that day and became less available to Sky News, although we continued to treat him like any other politician. Not having access to the deputy prime minister was less trouble to me as a television political editor than might have been thought. In fact, Prescott spoke to me on three occasions after May 2001. Once, during the firefighters strike I went to conduct a news interview since there was no other Sky News reporter available. Prescott disappeared into another room as soon as he had completed the interviews with our rival news channels. I heard a lot of shouting through the door and then, after perhaps half an hour's delay, we conducted our business. He spoke to me twice more on the phone, to deny things which I wasn't saying after Labour officials reported back an inaccurate and inflammatory version of a report, or, in one case, a question which I had asked at an off-the-record lobby briefing.

I regretted none of the commentary I had given on the deputy prime minister. My words never departed from the impartial and balanced stance which we must observe under British law. I had, however, previously got on well with both Prescott and his wife and missed his numerous amusing contributions to our programmes:

Prescott swearing loudly and repeatedly during a taped interview because he was being put off by 'that fucking taff speaking fucking taff' – Labour spokesman Denzil Davies giving an interview in Welsh nearby. Prescott leaning forward into the camera and saying 'sorry viewers' when I told him it was impossible to start a live interview again. Prescott telling me on air 'the prime minister is in Number 10 drawing up his list', when Alastair Campbell had just lied to me that he was at Chequers and that no reshuffle was imminent. As he and Blair stepped down from government, we asked Prescott to give us his reaction to the new prime minister: he declined colourfully, expressing his hatred for me.

If a further lesson was needed, the Prescott incident was it. New Labour and its media handlers acted out of expediency, not out of their obligation to tell the truth. Bullying was, I suppose, one of their habitual tactics – although it was largely ineffective, but it made a lot of enemies, including senior correspondents from the institutions whose proprietors Blair was courting. Most news organisations resisted pressure. But one, the BBC, seemed almost deliberately to make itself susceptible to it. Campbell appointed two ex-BBC men in a row as his deputy – among their talents, perhaps most prized was that they knew which BBC managers and producers to court or threaten. Regrettable though it may have been, neither the BBC nor the Labour Party emerged with much credit when an official Corporation edict banned reference to Mandelson's sexuality, even after Matthew Parris had mentioned it during a BBC *Newsnight* discussion of Ron Davies' 'moment of madness' on Clapham Common.

Withholding access to interviews is a more effective sanction but fortunately it is also transparent. A boycott soon becomes obvious. On one early occasion in December 1998, Alastair Campbell excluded Sky News from interviews with Peter Mandelson when he left the cabinet for the first time. This was because I had reported on air that I had been told to 'fuck off' when I asked whether the prime minister would do an interview on camera to repeat the expression of full confidence in Mandelson that Campbell had just informed us of in his briefing. It was quite usual for journalists to take up individual enquiries with officials as soon as a briefing proper had ended. This was what I had done. Campbell believed that we were having a private chat and that I was wrong to report it. I felt that our conversation could hardly have been off the record since there were still about half a dozen colleagues with in easy earshot and Campbell had made no secret of what he was saying. I had to explain to my boss, Nick Pollard, why we did not have any Mandelson footage. Kindly and honourably supporting a rival under pressure, the BBC let us have access to their interview. Only after a lengthy phone conversation later that evening did Campbell re-instate my access. Both of us knew and liked Peter Mandelson, and we were well acquainted with each other if not quite friends. It had been a fraught day on the brink of Christmas.

Post 2001: Nemesis

Is it becoming worse? Again, I would say, yes. In my ten years, I've noticed all these elements evolve with ever greater momentum.
Tony Blair, speech on Public Life, Reuters, 12 June 2007

As the second term began, there was a general recognition that the relationship between the media and the government was in a dire state. Campbell was already talking privately to Blair, as well as some journalists (including myself), about wanting to leave his post. Some desultory feelers had even been put out around Westminster in search of a possible replacement. But nobody really believed that Campbell would go and there was little surprise when Blair managed to prevail upon him to stay – although he was less successful with Anji Hunter, an even longer-standing member of the old firm, who quit in late 2001.

Far from stepping down, Alastair Campbell was now more powerful than ever and he and Blair introduced reforms in the way they interacted with the media. As Blair pointed out in his Reuters speech, these included two innovations which improved open government: monthly news conferences by the prime minister and twice-yearly appearances by him in front of the Liaison Committee of senior backbench MPs who chaired the departmental select committees. However, the media greeted these initiatives with less enthusiasm than they perhaps deserved because they were part of a concerted effort to bypass political journalists and instead appeal to the public directly. Campbell himself stepped back from giving briefings, while remaining director of government strategy and communications. Instead, he appointed two civil servants as the prime minister's official spokesmen: Godric Smith, a veteran of the Number 10 Press Office; and Tom Kelly, an ex-journalist who had been chief spokesman for the Northern Ireland Office. As was to become apparent during the second internal New Labour crisis of 'Cheriegate', the crucial attraction of these new appointments for Campbell was 'deniability'. Unlike Campbell, both Kelly and Smith could credibly tell journalists that they could not answer their questions because they were out of the loop.

In case anybody missed the message that political journalists were being sidelined, Campbell symbolically moved the morning briefing, which Number 10 hosted, out of Downing Street – and indeed out of Whitehall altogether. Giving the excuse that there were no government premises large enough to host the meetings, Number 10 rented space in the Foreign Press Association off Pall Mall and invited UK-based foreign journalists to attend the briefings as well. An intention of this change was to inconvenience political correspondents who mainly operated from the press gallery in Parliament by adding at least twenty minutes travel time to and from the briefings. However, the lobby journalists refused to be discouraged.

Campbell seemed to have a fondness for the FPA, a former home of Gladstone in Nash's Carlton House Terrace. In January 2004 he chose it as the location for his own news conference following publication of the Hutton Report. Standing at the foot of the ornate staircase, he accused BBC executives, including Chairman Gavyn Davies and the director general, Greg Dyke, of lying, while claiming that he himself had always told the truth. Davies and Dyke resigned shortly afterwards.

Another attempt by Campbell to transform the briefings also

failed. He announced that in future they would often be given by ministers rather than officials. However, this strategy blew up in its very first week of implementation when David Blunkett proved understandably reluctant to answer questions outside his departmental brief and when, during a joint briefing, Chief of Defence Staff Admiral Boyce contradicted Defence Secretary Geoff Hoon on Britain's readiness for war. In a rare gesture of cross-media solidarity, television news outlets also declined to broadcast anything other than the monthly news conferences, so Campbell was unable to divide and rule.

Although his hostility towards the media and contempt for his former trade of journalism were matters of record, Campbell would always deny that he had any malicious intent towards the domestic media in making these changes. So it is significant that the Gordon Brown government immediately made reversing most of them a central feature of its 'restoration of trust' agenda following the prime ministerial handover. The chief whip moved back into Number 12 Downing Street, displacing the news war room. A career civil servant, Michael Ellam, was installed as the senior media official in Downing Street and the morning lobby briefings were moved back close to Parliament and Downing Street in an annex of the Treasury on Horse Guards Parade. Brown pledged to continue with Liaison Committee appearances, but reflecting different abilities, 'monthly' prime ministerial news conferences were initially cut back to 'regular' engagements. In this, Brown could claim to have taken a lead from Blair, who failed to hold a news conference during May and June 2007, his last two months in office. Although once he had bedded in, Brown's briefing became at least as frequent as Blair's.

The 'Cheriegate' affair of late 2002 cruelly exposed the weaknesses in Campbell's new official-led briefing system. The prime minister's wife had bought two flats in Bristol, the city where her eldest son, Euan, was going to university. There were allegations that she was helped in the transactions by Peter Foster, a well-known fraudster from Australia who had been imprisoned on two continents. Foster had become the boyfriend of Carole Caplin, Mrs Blair's personal trainer and friend. Godric Smith, the prime minister's widely liked and trusted official spokesman, denied on the record that Foster had been involved. Emails between Foster and Cherie, subsequently obtained by the *Daily Mail*, proved that he had been. In the British media, the furore even overshadowed the European Council in Copenhagen where Tony Blair was agreeing to admit twelve, mainly, Eastern European nations into the Union. Alastair Campbell and Fiona Millar – then serving as Cherie's aide – eventually prevailed on Mrs Blair to make a tearful apology live to the television cameras in which she declared, 'I am not superwoman,' and talked about the pressures of her first child leaving home.

Few blamed Smith. He had simply relayed what he had been told by Campbell, while Campbell claimed he had been misled by Mrs Blair. But this crisis further damaged relationships within Downing Street. Fiona Millar and Alastair Campbell had both warned against Cherie's relationship with Carole, largely because they feared Caplin might someday publish her account of it. As the crisis unfolded, they didn't bother to hide their opinion from journalists. Fiona's fiercely held views on education had also divided her from her employer. As a couple, Millar and Campbell were outspokenly opposed to any sort of selection in education. Friends were dropped if they chose to educate their children privately. The couple even disagreed with the Blairs use of the London Oratory for their children. The tangential association of this crisis with Euan's higher education raised these hackles all over again. Fiona Millar left her job soon afterwards and increased her pressure on Campbell to resign as well. She continued in her roles as governor of a number of state schools and as a campaigner on education. In January 2006 she organised a rally at Westminster against Blair's city academy proposals, which was attended by both Campbell and former party leader Neil Kinnock.

Godric Smith accepted he was compromised, through no fault of his own. He came to the decision to step down as PMOS. After a period of drift, he was appointed director of communications at the Olympic Delivery Authority. Tom Kelly remained Blair's sole official spokesman to the end. However, Blair left him in a similar predicament to Smith when in 2007 Kelly insisted to the lobby that, 'as far as I know', the prime minister had not been re-interviewed by the Yates inquiry into cash for peerages. It eventually transpired that the prime minister had been re-interviewed a week or so previously, but the explanation that Kelly had not been told was accepted. There was no further explanation as to why the prime minister had allowed his spokesman to continue inadvertently misleading the media and public. In November 2007, Tom Kelly took up a post outside the civil service as director of communications for the British Airports Authority. Alastair Campbell published his diaries in July 2007, just days after Blair left office. During his time with Blair, Campbell openly admitted that he was writing diaries for publication. To me and others he jokingly referred to them as 'his pension fund' and on more than one occasion when asked to do something by a colleague from the prime minister down, he would reply: 'Fuck off, I'm writing my diary.' Historians, journalists and other outside commentators – including me – have always written books about British politics, while memoirs by politicians are a staple of the higher-quality publishing trade. However, the publication of diaries by an insider such as Campbell, so soon after the events described, was a flagrant breach of precedent in Britain – and it was a process in which Blair acquiesced.

Campbell's diary-writing had consequences for the Blair administration. Firstly, it emboldened others to 'kiss and tell' and in practice made it impossible for cabinet secretaries to force others to abide by embargoes. By their own admission, neither the press officer, Lance Price, nor the British ambassador to Washington, Sir Christopher Meyer, would have gone ahead with their instant memoirs had 'Alastair' not been intending to do it. Blair's chief of staff, the former diplomat Jonathan Powell, publicly deprecated 'kiss and tell' books such as Campbell's, yet he published his own account of the Northern Ireland negotiations which passed on gossip and shattered the thirty-year rule on the publication of official papers. By contrast, after his retirement from government, the senior diplomat Sir Jeremy Greenstock wrote a book about the Iraq invasion drawing on his involvement at the United Nations, Whitehall and Iraq but bowed to official pressure and stopped its publication.

There is a powerful argument that disclosure to the general public is a good thing. However, a number of Downing Street insiders and others who had dealings with the administration told me that they were inhibited in their interactions and did not trust colleagues because they knew that their private conversations would soon be published.

The second consequence of the Campbell's diaries culture is that the Blair administration, more than any other, has been perceived in terms of its personalities rather than its politics *and* its personalities. Powell and Blair both read advance proofs of Campbell's book, afterwards Blair commented dryly that he was surprised that 'At least it has two heroes, Ali and me.'

Finally, the publication of Campbell's diaries lays him and the Blairs open to charges of hypocrisy. Tony and Cherie Blair resorted to legal means and extreme vilification to avoid disclosures of matters which they considered private by those with whom they came into contact. For example, their first nanny faced an injunction, and all subsequent ones had to agree to privacy clauses in their contracts. Campbell himself was equally harsh with people whom he considered potential or actual 'blabbers'. He and Fiona even fell out with Mrs Blair because of what they considered to be her unwise friendship with Carole Caplin. When Campbell's diaries appeared Ms Caplin had some justification in pointing out that, as it turned out, it was he not she who had blabbed.

The year of the Iraq invasion, 2003, was the pivot for the Blair administration. Some could never forgive the decision to take military action in the absence of direct provocation. But the manner in which Downing Street made the case for war also contributed significantly to the damage done to Blair's government as it stood accused of over-enthusiastic and ultimately untrustworthy spin. These failings were in turn exacerbated by the bad blood which had already accumulated between the media and the government and within New Labour itself because of Campbell's power. When I first heard that Dr David Kelly's body had been found, I knew Campbell would have to go. His resignation on 29 August 2003, the day after Blair gave evidence to the Hutton Inquiry, was inevitable and an outcome he had himself long foretold.

For his remaining four years in power, Blair continued with the media relations structure which Campbell had left in place: Tom Kelly now as the lone official spokesman, while a party political director of communications, David Hill, remained in the background but in charge. Hill suited the behind-the-scenes role better than the man who designed it ever had. After a typically wild and long-haired sixties studenthood, Hill was taken on as an assistant to the Birmingham MP Roy Hattersley. His parents were worthies in the local constituency Labour Party. The long-suffering Hill stayed with Roy through the turbulent seventies and eighties. And so without moving he became the chief aide to the deputy Labour leader.

Kinnock and Hattersley worked closely together, perhaps because Hattersley was never a credible rival to the leader, and Hill continued to play a steadying role behind the scenes. In opposition, he worked as a press spokesman for the Labour Party under John Smith and Tony Blair. This continued into government. It was Hill who, in November 1997, took the decision to go public with the correspondence relating to Bernie Ecclestone's controversial million-pound donation to the party. This precipitated the biggest test so far for Blair's young government, but Hill was resolutely straightforward. When he phoned to alert me of the key unscheduled briefing, I lazily suggested that it would probably be boring and I might not go. I am very grateful that he immediately told me it wouldn't be and urged me to be there. Hill worked on the 2001 election campaign but he also spent some years working in the private sector for one of the Tory Lord (Tim) Bell's PR companies.

Unlike Campbell, David Hill had no issues either with ego or honesty. His particular skill was as a crisis manager, especially in shutting stories down. As I suggested to him over the summer of 2003 while negotiations were going on to fill Campbell's position, the Blair government undoubtedly needed him more than he needed them – even if his appointment was unlikely to be a boon for journalists. So it turned out. For Tony Blair's last four years in office, what had once been the most celebrated and 'proactive' media management operation in modern politics became one of the most defensive. Blair continued to lunch with editors and dine with proprietors but 'don't say anything off the record that you wouldn't say on the record' became the governing code. David Hill's partner, Hilary Coffman, another long-term party servant, dealt almost exclusively with gossip eruptions relating to the private lives of the Blair family, while the dour civil servant Tom Kelly briefed cautiously, costively and with deniability.

Meanwhile, having driven hostility in relations between the government and the media to a new low level before resigning, Campbell continued afterwards to be a private adviser to Blair. He helped to broker the *rapprochement* with Brown which led to them fighting the 2005 election as a co-presidency, even sharing ice-cream cones together. Campbell carried on enjoying a friendship with Blair beyond his retirement as prime minister, but many of those who stayed loyal to Blair were shocked and alienated by the speed with which Campbell cashed in through the publication of his diaries within days of Blair stepping down.

For most of the ten years, Tony Blair affected to rise above day-to-day conflict with the media. Even when the row over Andrew Gilligan's *Today* broadcast on Iraq was at its hottest, important decisions were delegated to Campbell. It was he, not Blair, who decided 'to go to war with the BBC', to try 'to fuck Gilligan', and who made intemperate appearances before a Commons Select Committee and on *Channel 4 News*. For all Campbell's feints towards leaving, it was Tony Blair who in the end took the decision that it was time to dispense with his services as director of communications. For these reasons, the Reuters speech and its attack on the 'feral media' came as a surprise – not least because the prime minister at last exhibited a thin skin which he had kept well covered during his years in power.

There may indeed have been things which needed to be said in the Reuters speech; Tony Blair certainly seems to have found it cathartic. But his argument was half-baked in that it addressed only one side of the problem. The Blair administration had not just been at fault for courting the media; over the decade it had also taught many journalists tricks when it came to misrepresenting, dissembling, stonewalling, cultivating and bullying.

7

EUROPE

21–23 JUNE

My position throughout the course of my time as prime minister has been to get out of this endless and destructive negativity, and realise that Britain has a lot to offer Europe. And Europe has a lot to offer Britain.

Tony Blair, Brussels, 23 June 2007

Tony Blair held his very last news conference as prime minister in Brussels, starting at 5.48 a.m. local time on the Saturday morning of 23 June 2007. It was either the forty-second or the forty-seventh European Union summit he had attended, depending on whether you counted the five 'extraordinary' non-scheduled gatherings he'd been to.

There was a sense of closure for the prime minister because this last 'all-nighter' meeting had reached an agreement on the constitutional treaty which had preoccupied EU politics for most of his ten years in power. After the single currency came enlargement and the new member states. They in turn led to the operational changes in the Nice Treaty. From there it had been on to the proposed new constitution, drawn up by Valéry Giscard d'Estaing and rejected in the French and Dutch referendums of 2005, which had resulted in the drafting of this alternative, simplified 'amending treaty'.

In the early hours of that morning the national politicians had completed their work together and reached agreement between themselves. Now each country had to ratify the deal but that was almost certain to happen because – this time with the exception of Ireland – all countries, including the UK, were going to avoid holding referendums. (Ireland's eventual no vote stymied those hopes.)

Blair had always regarded the constitutional discussions as a distraction from what really mattered to people. He never quite realised that this common sense view was less likely to placate Europhobes than to inflame them because of its dismissive approach towards matters they claimed were of fundamental importance. The agreement put Blair back on track; whatever its merits, he was relieved that Europe could now stop navel-gazing, 'put the constitution to one side' and address concerns of more direct interest to the public, such as 'the economy, defence and climate change'. His message that morning was one of liberation. The agreement was 'a chance to move on . . . to get out of this bind'.

Blair believed there really had been a great deal at stake. A less engaged negotiator could have allowed everything that had been gained by Britain over the decade to be rolled back. In this, he meant not just the systemic shift replacing a new European constitution with just another set of technical reforms. His view was that, with everything up for grabs, there would have been an attempt to push a weaker British prime minister off the concessions he had previously won. Blair had impregnably preserved Britain's privileged position.

By staying on to conclude this last international engagement, Blair considered he had done Gordon Brown a favour – giving him the chance of a fresh start on Europe. After ten years, Blair was probably the leader at the table with the greatest technical expertise, especially since Chirac was not there, having left office in May. Now he could claim a technical victory because Britain's 'red lines' had not been violated.

The red line strategy had become Britain's habitual tactic for European negotiations, allowing it to state in advance key areas which were non-negotiable. European partners were antagonised but the lines saved time. Blair knew what the sceptical press and public were prepared to tolerate and would seek the widest possible endorsement of his negotiating position before leaving home. This meant he could turn away pressure from other governments to give ground by stating bluntly that he had no mandate to do so. Overnight, Blair had had to say as much to Chancellor Angela Merkel. Even so, the deal was not likely to be popular at home – but that burden could be slung around the departing leader's neck. It would always be 'Blair's deal', although Gordon Brown had been consulted throughout, including on a speakerphone for conference calls with the British team in those final hours.

The government could only try to sell the treaty to the British electorate by negatives: its whole argument was that this new treaty was 'not a constitution' and the red lines were actually a series of boasts about what the treaty did not do. The red lines gave Britain 'opt outs', permitting the UK 'not to sign up' to central agreements on foreign and security policy, social security legislation and common law.

Tony Blair had been helped to power by the deep divisions in the Conservative Party as it turned its back on the EU following the ousting of Margaret Thatcher. As prime minister, he had promised that Britain would play a constructive role in the European Union, but one of the failures of his premiership was that Britain remained unreconciled to Europe, still debating whether the UK should or should not be a member of the Union.

So even as the prime minister celebrated the completion of this latest piece of important business, he could still only express hope about Britain's European future. There was an inevitable weariness as he argued again that 'Britain's interest is to be at the centre of Europe'; now it had a chance 'to get out of this endless and destructive negativity that we've seen'. Finally, Blair looked back twenty years, before his own administration, and cited all the developments since then – the Single European Act, Maastricht, Amsterdam, Nice, Lisbon and the latest agreement: 'I make this plea to my own country – Europe has changed.' Blair claimed he had been able to 'always promote our interests without trampling on other people . . . We have a Commission president today who is a reformer. We have got an enlarged EU with real allies for Britain today.' Commission President José Manuel Barroso, a former Portuguese prime minister who owed his job to Blair's support, led the polite return of compliments: 'Tony Blair has taken Britain from the fringes to the mainstream of the European Union. He has done this by engagement not vetoes . . .' But Barroso also conceded, 'I have to say . . . that in Britain, honestly, the debate for Europe is not yet won.'

The European Union lends itself to the 'Great Man' theory of history because its procedures flatter national politicians' sense of their own importance. The Union progresses its business through a succession of private roundtable discussions between heads of government (prime ministers and presidents). At EU Councils, no officials are allowed to be present in the chamber, except for one note-taking 'Antici' per country (named after the Italian who decided all EU ambassadors needed an assistant), who carry their reports to the delegation offices outside. At plenary sessions a prime minister might also be joined by his foreign secretary, finance secretary or Europe minister but officials are still excluded. To get round this, John Major concealed his European adviser, Stephen Wall, under his desk for the Maastricht negotiations; and Jack Straw became famous for his texting skills. (Gordon Brown took longer to come to terms with technology. Shortly after becoming prime minister he was shown a document draft on the way into the Commons chamber on a BlackBerry screen. 'This is really good,' the prime minister barked. 'Thank you, Prime Minister,' the surprised official purred. 'No, no I mean this telephone thing!' Brown corrected him.)

This concentration on the leader suited Blair's temperament. In the EU, a prime minister really can take big decisions sitting round a table and cutting deals with his peers. In Blair's time, the treaties of Amsterdam, Nice, Rome and Lisbon were decided in this way – so was the admission of twelve new member states, and the launching of the euro currency.

This process meant that Blair's European diplomacy was shaped by his personal relationships with other national leaders. He encountered them at Councils at least three times a year – and then buddied up again with the French, German, Italian and EU leaders at the annual G7/G8 summit. British prime ministers tended to enjoy the clubby G7/G8s more than EU Councils. The rich nation summits were mutual backslapping sessions for masters of the universe, generally without hard decisions to consider or make (Gleneagles in 2005 was an exception), but at EU Council meetings the prime minister had to deal with his equals, who could corner him uncomfortably. The French president, whether Mitterrand or Chirac, notoriously insisted that protocol made him first among equals because he was both a head of government and a head of state.

Geographically, Tony Blair's alliances with the smaller member states followed the usual pattern for British leaders: constructive, pragmatic working relations with the Scandinavians, the Dutch, the East Europeans and the Portuguese; and mutual incomprehension with the Belgians and Luxembourgeois. Such contacts were essential to building alliances, but it was relations between the big-country leaders that really set the direction of the Union. In the EU the big countries were: France and Britain, both permanent members of the G7 and the UN Security Council; Germany, G7 member and largest European economy; and, a pace behind, Spain and Italy (another G7 member) by dint of size and history.

Over his ten years, Blair's leadership of Britain was man-marked by four other strong and comparatively long-serving European heads of government, each of whom significantly influenced the dynamic of his foreign policy: Jacques Chirac, president of France, May 1995 – May 2007; José María Aznar, prime minister of Spain, May 1996 – April 2004; Gerhard Schröder, chancellor of Germany, October 1998 – November 2005; and Silvio Berlusconi, prime minister of Italy, June 2001 – May 2006 (also April 1994 – January 1995 and April 2008 –).

Chirac

Encounters between Blair and Jacques Chirac punctuated the decade, with Blair never quite getting the better of the French president. The rift between them over the Iraq War had the gravest consequences, as well as being profoundly damaging to Blair. For all his eagerness to build a strong relationship with Chirac, the two men had completely different temperaments and never quite understood or trusted each other. Blair was positive and informal, but also self-controlled and, increasingly through his decade in power, a conviction politician. Chirac was deeply sceptical about what politicians could achieve, but he had a profound respect for the institution of the presidency which he was happy to exploit. He could be emotional and outspoken and lose his temper in public. Whereas Blair believed in the positive benefits of the use of force, Chirac had a deep-seated distaste for war. As a rising young Enarque (graduate of the exclusive École Nationale d'Administration), Chirac had volunteered to do military service in the Algerian War. He became a captain, but was scarred by what he experienced. In March 2003, during the run-up to the Iraq War, one of the symbolic gestures missed by Blair and Bush was Chirac's state visit to Algeria.

Over their decade of diplomatic fencing, each man came to pretty much the same conclusion: each thought the other arrogant, with too high an opinion of himself and untrustworthy. Although Blair was later to claim that his personal differences with Chirac had been exaggerated.

To begin with, Blair's team tried hard to impress Chirac, and his socialist prime minister, Lionel Jospin. This approach was typified by the arrangements for their first Anglo-French summit in November 1997. They staged a Cool Britannia event, bringing in Sir Terence Conran and the florist Paula Pryke to deck out the vacant, thirty-eighth floor of Canary Wharf Tower. Chirac, or *mon ami, Jacques*', got into the spirit of the event, even referring to Blair as 'Tony' and saying through his interpreter: 'I see a young, dynamic, modern England. I like it.' British onlookers were a little bemused by the event, which seemed to have been inspired by the liking of Chirac's predecessor, François Mitterrand, for meetings surrounded by the modern architecture of *grands projets* he had commissioned. Chirac simply looked quizzical. The press conference at the end of the meeting, held at the foot of the tower, was cut short; partly because the 'News Bunny' – a reporter in a rabbit suit from a failing cable television company – was trying to get into the shot, but mainly because the Blair government had been hit by its first sleaze crisis.

The public health minister, Tessa Jowell, was seeking an exemption from the EU ban on tobacco advertising for Formula One motor racing. Jowell's husband, David Mills, a lawyer, had had the Benetton Formula One team as a client. The boss of Formula One then revealed he'd given a £1 million donation to the Labour Party. Labour eventually returned the money.

For all the talk of a new start, Blair's early European policy conformed to classic Foreign Office norms. He tried to forge close relations with both the French and the Germans, in an attempt to counterbalance the Franco–German axis, which was often referred to as 'the motor' of the European Union. An opportunity to do this presented itself following the end of the tight alliance between Helmut Kohl and François Mitterrand after the French president's retirement and subsequent death in 1996. Chancellor Kohl wept openly during the president's funeral.

So in 1998, Blair took forward an initiative inherited from John Major. He and Chirac signed the St Malo Agreement at the French naval base there, committing their two countries to defence co-operation only loosely linked to NATO. But when Schröder was elected later that year, Blair hailed him as a kindred spirit. The German chancellor came to Millbank Tower, New Labour's fabled HQ, in June 1999 for the publication of a pamphlet he had jointly produced with the prime minister, 'Europe: The Third Way/ *Die Neue Mitte*'.

During Blair's first term the tactic worked. In 1999, France did not obstruct the Lisbon agenda – a British-led push for economic liberalisation. The British press were so short of stories they had to write about how Blair, Chancellor Brown and Foreign Secretary Cook had travelled to Portugal by three separate planes. Both France and Britain participated in the air strikes against Serbia over Kosovo.

By 2000, Jacques Chirac was one of the first visitors to see the newly born Leo Blair, in whom he would subsequently take a, not altogether, helpful interest. That December, in spite of Britain's failure to join the euro, the country was not isolated for once at an EU treaty negotiation, or 'intergovernmental conference' as the jargon had it. During the protracted '5-shirt' dealings in Nice, Blair was able to act as peacemaker when Schröder shot back at Chirac: 'Why do you always assume Germany will do what you want?'

Even by EU standards, Nice reached a messy conclusion only in the small hours of the Monday morning, having drastically overrun its allotted time of the previous Thursday and Friday. Quite unexpectedly, I became an icon of the tedious process after an unflattering photograph of me lying, fully clothed but flat on my back, waiting for the outcome appeared in newspapers around the world. Whether you were a journalist or a politician there was nothing to do but wait for a conclusion at these events. The EU moved forward by consensus – 'Nothing is agreed until everything is agreed' – which meant that a single country holding out could delay proceedings by hours. It may have looked like it but I was not sleeping; I was still reporting on the hour through the night. I had only myself to blame for the picture. The photographer from Deutsche Presse Agentur showed it to me on his screen and asked if I minded him diffusing it. In the spirit of journalistic openness and confident that it would never get used, I agreed and forgot about it – only to see it prominently displayed in the *Evening Standard* handed to me when I boarded the plane back to London the following evening. Sky News kindly procured for me a copy of the picture signed by the prime minister and his spokesman. In his message Campbell speculates what the man and woman in the back of the shot, who were also lying down, are getting up to, while Blair's comment is more direct: 'Surely it wasn't that boring.'

The outcome at Nice weakened Chirac's authority. He was judged to have performed poorly as chairman and to have cut side deals to buy off individual countries without informing the conference. This was partly explained by a stomach complaint which kept him always within a few yards of his private bathroom; others wondered if he was getting past it.

The Blair–Chirac relationship fractured irreparably after the events of 11 September 2001. *Le Monde* declared 'NOUS SOMMES TOUS AMÉRICAINS', and France cautiously backed the invasion of Afghanistan, but Chirac was developing a worldview to counterbalance the George W. Bush administration. The French president advocated a 'multi-polar' global power structure at a time when Blair maintained that there was only one superpower, the United States.

As the Americans' attention turned towards Saddam Hussein, Anglo-French summits and EU Councils provided the stage for the two European leaders to argue it out. Complicating matters further, the EU agenda had now shifted on to the most contentious area of all – the budget. This always pitted France and Britain against each other, each seeking destruction of the other's most cherished policy: the British rebate for the UK and the Common Agricultural Policy for France. Blair tried to keep Iraq and Europe separate, but Chirac never failed to pursue his war diplomacy by other means. Council meetings became opportunities for him to throw rhetorical hand grenades at Blair and his perceived allies, and it was never quite clear whether he would attack the European or the Iraq flank. Or indeed both – as he did at a routine Council chaired by Germany's Chancellor Schröder in the autumn of 2002.

Unlike Blair, who liked to keep his contacts with the press at such meetings as limited as possible, Chirac always enjoyed giving a lengthy press conference at the end of the proceedings, ostentatiously brandishing his fountain pen to write down the detail of every question. In the meantime, his officials kept the world up to date with his words of wisdom. Chirac was in bullish form, having been re-elected for a second term in May. Avuncularly or patronisingly, he brought up Blair's youngest son in an exchange over Iraq: 'How would you be able to look little Leo in the eye in twenty years' time if you are the leader who helped start a war?' Downing Street brushed aside questions on this. Blair was more concerned to discover that Schröder and Chirac had privately agreed a deal to take the Common Agricultural Policy out of the budget negotiations until 2013 – effectively preventing the radical reform which Britain was seeking. It was a major setback (which Blair was unable to roll back completely three years later when he secured a budget agreement under his EU presidency at the end of 2005). As Schröder looked on amazed, Blair confronted Chirac in the corridor, 'or margins' as they are referred to in the EU. It was an angry, standing, face-to-face encounter which ended with a magisterial rebuke aimed by Chirac at Blair. 'You have been very rude and I have never been spoken to like this before.'

Chirac did not brief on 'le row' and it was not mentioned in the usual 'upsums' or summaries of the meetings usually given to the media. However, senior members of Blair's staff, including Jonathan Powell, uncharacteristically briefed journalists about it, in the belief that it built up a plucky Blair and damaged Chirac, who looked pompous and out of touch. The Élysée retaliated by postponing the annual Anglo-French summit which had been due to take place in November.

Over the next few months, British and French officials competed with each other aggressively over Iraq and the efforts to secure a second UN resolution endorsing an attack. The French made an official protest against Britain for briefing that Chirac was 'playing a selfish and dangerous game'. Meanwhile, the Franco–German axis was being recommissioned. Chancellor Schröder was re-elected in October 2002 on an anti-war platform, and there was no political option which would lead Germany to support the invasion. Germany and France started to feed joint papers into EU deliberations again. And on 22 January 2003 Chirac and Schröder celebrated forty years of the Franco-German alliance.

Just over a week later, the French president at last entertained Blair and five other British ministers in Le Touquet. The hospitality was lavish, as it usually was when France played host. But in spite of his gallantry – Chirac claimed the differences with Blair were 'minor, much less than what might appear' – he hardened his stance against imminent military action on Iraq, telling the joint news conference: 'Firstly, I feel that war is always the worst possible solution; and would add that in that region, above all others, we don't need any more wars. Having said that, I repeat, I feel that we need to wait. We have adopted a strategy of using inspectors.'

He gave a lengthy disquisition on the imperatives facing the two European nations, somehow managing not to mention the United States while rejecting US Secretary of Defense Donald Rumsfeld's recent public musings about Old Europe (France and Germany) and New Europe (Britain and the more recent European democracies in Iberia and the East). Where Britain and France were concerned, Chirac recognised no division between old and new:

We represent two ancient civilisations, two old nations, two old cultures. For centuries now we have been side by side and sometimes we have been fighting each other. But we have forged also links and had interests that were not always the same. There is no surprise in this. And now today in the European context we have to have the will, the determination and the imagination to pare down all our differences and strengthen what unites us. But of course there is no magic bullet . . .

In contrast, Blair spoke briefly and briefest of all about Iraq – pinning his hopes on the evidence which was to be presented to the UN Security Council on 5 February by US Secretary of State Colin Powell. Evidence which, to Powell's embarrassment, would later turn out to have been drawn heavily from the much disputed British intelligence sources. Instead, not bothering to make the arguments or to challenge Chirac's analysis, Blair ran quickly through other areas where there was some degree of collaboration between the two countries: 'there are far more things that unite us than that divide us'.

The Franco-British diplomatic hostilities intensified. Blair sent Baroness Amos to Africa to try to win over swing votes on the UN Security Council; while Chirac sent his prime minister, Dominique de Villepin. But Blair's attempts to turn a familiar Franco–German ploy, the signed open letter, against Chirac, pushed the French president to a new level of fury.

Blair and his friends, Aznar of Spain and Berlusconi of Italy, organised a letter to be published around the world as a newspaper article which supported the American position on Iraq. The signatories to the so-called 'letter of eight' were five current EU members – Britain, Spain, Italy, Denmark and Portugal – together with three Eastern European countries which were waiting to join – Poland, Hungary and the Czech Republic.

France had never been as keen as Britain on the enlargement of the EU. British governments of every political hue had favoured widening the Union, even if – or perhaps especially if – that meant loosening its ties towards a trading block. France, on the other hand, had always championed deepening the Union by increasing the obligations of member states to the centre.

In an interview with a Polish newspaper ahead of a Polish diplomatic visit to France, President Chirac let fly: 'These countries have been not very well behaved and rather reckless of the danger of aligning themselves too rapidly with the American position.' With affronted dignity, he addressed his complaints mainly at the applicant countries, branding them 'infantile' and 'dangerous', dismissing them like children who should be seen but not heard. 'It is not really responsible behaviour. It is not well-brought-up behaviour. They missed a good opportunity to keep quiet . . . I felt they acted frivolously because entry into the European Union implies a minimum of understanding for the others,' Chirac said.

He was even more furious with ten further Eastern European countries which had put their names to a similar letter, eight already with entry dates to the EU and two – Romania and Bulgaria – which were still in membership discussions. 'Romania and Bulgaria were particularly irresponsible. If they wanted to diminish their chances of joining Europe they could not have found a better way,' Chirac fumed, arguing that he was right not to direct similar anger at nations which were already EU members. 'When you are in the family . . . you have more rights than when you are asking to join and knocking on the door.'

On 10 March 2003, Chirac declared in an interview on French television that France would not accept the draft of a second Security Council resolution authorising war. Diplomatic historians will always argue whether this meant 'no never', but given the timescale in which US and UK forces were by then locked, it amounted to a veto.

Six days later, Blair's alliance building paid off. He and President Bush were not lonely figures at the final meeting before full conflict when prime ministers Barroso of Portugal and Aznar of Spain flanked them at the last-ditch Azores Summit.

The invasion of Iraq began on the same day the European leaders gathered for their spring Council summit in Brussels. Chirac and Blair barely spoke. The next day there was a media outcry when it was claimed that Chirac had not joined in the condolences around the conference table following the overnight news of the first British casualties. The French president sent the prime minister a private handwritten note later in the day.

From then on the Blair–Chirac relationship struggled even more. In the aftermath of the war, Blair hosted an Anglo-French summit in November in London – the second that year because of the delayed invitation to Le Touquet. This time, there was no Cool Britannia flash; Chirac was entertained in Lancaster House, the conventional location for government receptions. The two men announced plans to celebrate the centenary of the *entente cordiale* in 2004 – but any *entente* was contrasted with, rather than reflected in, their own understanding. Once again, Chirac violated Blair's unwritten rule of never talking about his family by mentioning his pleasure at having been given a photograph of young Leo. It was an unmissable opening. I asked Chirac what Blair should say to Leo when he looked him in the eye, now that he had been one of those starting a war. Chirac was eloquently insouciant, speaking with a weary Gallic shrug of the shoulders and a pursing of the lips: 'I can't, of course, predict what the prime minister will say to his son when he wants to tell him these things.' Then he shifted the emphasis in his voice: 'But I can say of course that these things are not easy.' Everyone in the room caught his drift. Tony Blair did not smile. His press office rang round asking the British media not to use pictures of the president holding the framed photo of Leo.

The *entente cordiale* celebrations passed without note. Chirac made some gestures to rekindle a relationship with Blair. In February 2004, at Chirac's suggestion, Schröder held a tripartite summit in his new Berlin Kanzleramt – the spectacular concrete and glass chancellery with more than a passing resemblance to a giant washing machine – but this jarred with Chirac's other ambition, that Germany and France should be a pioneer group at the core of the EU. The tripartite meeting also led to accusations from those not present that the big countries were trying to form a *Directoire* for the Union. An angry Silvio Berlusconi proclaimed that the meeting had created a '*pasticcio*' – a hotchpotch of a mess.

There were no follow-up meetings. Blair tried a couple of times to have joint briefings with the German chancellor and French president, but after complaints from friends such as Berlusconi, such gatherings ended up being opened up to others. In May 2004, Chirac sent Blair a costly case of 1989 Château Mouton Rothschild; costly for both of them since cabinet rules were that ministers must pay for expensive (over £140) presents from foreign politicians if they wished to keep them. Meanwhile, a Blair gift to Chirac, on display in the presidential museum in the Limousin, became a source of amusement to visitors. The museum cataloguist could find no better description than 'a dish with two legs'.

The Iraq War continued to divide the two leaders. Chirac blocked the establishment of a NATO training mission to Iraq. The president told British journalists that the relationship between France and Britain was '*un amour violent*' – a tempestuous affair. Around the same time a French ambassador put it to me perhaps even less diplomatically: 'We fall out with you because in the end we trust you and know we are, in the end, on the same side. We hug the Germans tightly because we don't trust them.' In May 2005, Chirac's authority suffered a huge blow when the French people voted '*non*' to the new EU Constitution. Chirac did the best to preserve his dignity, praising the democratic process, but there was now no chance that he could run again for the presidency. The end of the ratification process was a big boost for Blair – he no longer had to deal with the nightmare of holding a UK referendum, a small irony since his decision to hold one in Britain had forced Chirac's hand to do the same. However, when the minister who had first pushed him into a plebiscite called to gloat, Blair was in no mood for congratulations. He put down the phone, remarking 'The thing you should always remember about Jack Straw is that he is a tart' at the way his cunning scheme had worked. Nonetheless, Blair believed that the French rebuff made it easier to prevail over Chirac in the end, if not to deal with him.

In Blair's view, the decisive rupture with Chirac – and even more decisively with Schröder – came over the appointment that year of the next president of the European Commission. Chirac and Schröder had decided on the Belgian prime minister, Guy Verhofstadt, and made their choice public by parading him around the summit. Blair was the first outsider called in to endorse the choice. Instead, he turned to Verhofstadt and said, 'I'm sorry, Guy, Britain cannot support you – it's nothing personal.' According to Blair, Schröder was stunned and simply could not accept that the Franco–German axis could be defied in this way. However, other countries had reservations about the Belgian as well. Blair eventually prevailed with the safe choice of the pragmatic José Manuel Barroso, one of the leaders who had been closest to him in the preceding years.

In the summer of 2005, the Blair–Chirac relationship took a further plunge as haggling continued over the EU budget. Chirac urged Britain to make a *communautaire* gesture, describing the refusal to surrender the £3 billion-a-year rebate first secured by Thatcher as 'pathetic'. By now, Blair was angry and frustrated and willing to hit back with his alternative vision of Europe. 'I'm not prepared to have someone tell me there is only one view of what Europe is, and that is the view expressed by certain people at certain points in time. Europe isn't owned by anybody; Europe is owned by all of us . . . Let's not try to characterise this as a debate about who's most in favour of Europe. That's not what the argument is about and I'm not having anyone call me out on that basis.' The issue was not resolved at that meeting, and not just because the prime minister of tiny Luxembourg was in the chair. The UK took over the rotating EU presidency in July for the remainder of the year. The general assumption was that only a big country would be able to secure a deal.

In the meantime, Anglo-French sparring took a comical twist. The conflicting bids of London and Paris to host the Olympic Games in 2012 were the latest bone of contention. Both Blair and Chirac had decided to fly to Singapore to lobby in the final hours before the Olympic Committee voted. In the run-up to the decision, Chirac went on yet another alliance-building visit, this time to a tripartite summit with Chancellor Schröder and President Putin. Unfortunately for Chirac, some of his amusing opinions on international cuisine were caught on an open microphone as he chatted to the German and Russian leaders in a Russian café. 'The only thing [the British] have ever given European farming is mad cow. You can't trust people who cook as badly as that,' he said. 'After Finland, it's the country with the worst food.' 'But what about hamburgers?' Vladimir Putin chipped in, referring to America. 'Oh no, hamburgers are nothing in comparison,' Chirac said. Vladimir and Gerhard laughed. Chirac then recalled how George Robertson, the former NATO secretary general and previously a defence secretary in Blair's cabinet, had once made him try an 'unappetising' Scottish dish, apparently meaning haggis. 'That's where our problems with NATO come from,' he smirked.

Chirac's tasting menu of politically incorrect prejudices could not have been better designed to alienate the Olympic spirit of the panellists deciding the Olympic venue. It must at the very least have lost the Finnish vote. Some in France blamed the president for Paris losing to London.

Schröder

Blair's relationship with Gerhard Schröder was as tortured but never as rich or complex as his interactions with Chirac. Schröder's English was rudimentary when he came into office; Blair spoke French not German and had never evinced any particular interest in the country. When Schröder was elected, he was hailed as 'the German Blair' ('Herr Blair' to the tabloids), and Blair saluted the 'tremendous result' in Germany at the 1998 conference in Blackpool. Schröder made his first foreign visit as chancellor to Downing Street, and the two leaders went on to share a platform with Bill Clinton in Washington to debate the new politics of the 'Third Way'.

But Schröder had little chance to be a Blair-style moderniser, even if that were his intention. The SDP's great reforms away from socialism had already been set at Bad Godesberg in 1959; Labour had abandoned Clause IV only in 1995. Blair's reforming zeal was far greater than Schröder's, while Germany's Social Contract gave far greater importance to unions and state corporatism. Germany had not yet had its Thatcher. There should have been common cause since Schröder, like Blair, battled against resistance from the left as he tried to reform a social democratic party and his national economy, but after 2001, the putative friendship between Gerhard and Tony had turned to mutual antipathy. Torn apart by Iraq and EU rows, about the only thing they had in common was a liking for going around in shirtsleeves.

This breakdown in relations led to bad behaviour on both sides when Blair paid his final visit to Chancellor Schröder in 2005 during the run-up to the German federal election. On landing in Berlin, Blair broke protocol by heading first to a lengthy private meeting with Angela Merkel, the candidate of the centre-right CDU–CSU (Christian Democratic Union–Christian Social Union) and effectively leader of the opposition. Gerhard Schröder had his revenge once Blair arrived at the Kanzleramt. While the photographers were taking their pictures, Schröder muttered to Blair, 'This is our last meeting, let's not fall out.' But moments later he opened their news conference with caustic observations on British government policy. Demob happy, Schröder spoke in English for the first time. A few minutes into the news conference he dismissed the interpreters announcing, 'We all speak English now.'

The bad blood continued to flow. Following his narrow electoral defeat and during the transition period to Merkel's government, Schröder represented Germany but pointedly turned down Blair's invitation to dinner at the last EU summit he would attend, at Hampton Court. Sally Morgan, one of Blair's inner team, described it as the end of 'a long and dysfunctional relationship'. But Schröder hadn't finished. Making his resignation speech to the German Parliament that November, Schröder allowed himself an oblique dig at Blair and Iraq: 'I can think of a recent disaster that shows what happens when a country neglects its duties of state towards its people. My post as chancellor, which I still hold, does not allow me to name that country. But you all know I'm talking about America,' Mr Schröder said to laughter. 'People do not want the state in their faces, but they want it at their side.'

Schröder went on to use his memoirs, published less than a year after he had stepped down, to settle old scores. In the book he observed that, while Bush took political decisions as if they were the 'result of a dialogue with God', and Blair was the 'sorcerer's apprentice', unable to control what he had started in Iraq.

Schröder soon had to face incoming insults in his political afterlife.

A leading US legislator called him a 'political prostitute' for accepting a job – within a month of the handover of power to Merkel – from the Russian giant Gazprom on the board of Nord Stream, a $1 billion gas pipeline which Schröder had underwritten with German taxpayers' money while still in office. No surprise perhaps then that his otherwise vitriolic memoirs described President Putin as a modest and disciplined leader with 'one of the hardest jobs on earth'.

Blair ultimately failed to get on with the centre-right President Chirac and the centre-left Chancellor Schröder. He took to cutting the regular summits of European socialist leaders which preceded European Councils. He had got off to a poor start when France elected a socialist prime minister shortly after his own victory in 1997. Lionel Jospin complained that Blair had failed to support him during his campaign; and very deliberately sketched out an alternative map for socialism at their first joint left-wing conference in Malmö. Blair and Brown were soon locked in a bitter battle with France over attempts to extend European taxation laws to savings and auctions; the UK won.

Things began warmly with Romano Prodi in Italy, but the intensity of the professor's intellectual interest in reform was not matched by his actions. Both men suffered from the inconvenient disclosure that Blair had telephoned Prodi to discuss some of Rupert Murdoch's proposed media ventures in Italy – a story which Downing Street attempted at first to deny.

Ironically, Britain's Labour prime minister forged his two closest friendships in Europe with Conservatives – Aznar of Spain and Berlusconi of Italy.

Berlusconi

Most European commentators held their nose when Silvio Berlusconi was returned to power in June 2001. The usually circumspect *Economist* magazine pronounced him unfit to govern. His earlier brief stint in power had been remarkable only for his good luck in playing host at the G7 Naples summit. He was Italy's richest man, a media billionaire who brazenly used his own television networks and newspapers to support his political cause. He planned to dismember the state-owned RAI radio and television empire. His business and political career had been built on strong ties to Bettino Craxi, Italy's corrupt former socialist prime minister, who in turn was believed to have close links to the Mafia. Inevitably, Berlusconi was under investigation by Italy's highly politicised magistracy, but he had already expressed the intention of fighting back by exploiting parliamentary immunity and changing the law in his favour. His party was going to govern in coalition with some neo-fascist factions.

The conventional advice, in short, was to give the new Italian prime minister a wide berth. Blair, however, was on the hunt for new allies in Europe and he was the first foreign leader to hold talks with Berlusconi after his return to power. The Blair team were still high from Labour's second election landslide and tacked a stopover with 'Il Cavaliere' on to a swing out to the Middle East. Berlusconi deployed his over-the-top-charm, praising the women in the party almost to the point of becoming a parody, smarmy Italian Romeo. Over dinner he recounted the story of his life, bursting into song to dramatise it and dwelling on how he had become a crooner onboard a cruise ship because he had fallen in love with one of the dancers. Some might have run a mile, but Blair and his party were won over.

Blair decided that Berlusconi was a man who did what he said and was a pro-American ally within Europe. In the aftermath of 9/11, he included Berlusconi with Chirac and Schröder at a Downing Street brainstorming session on how to deal with Islamic fundamentalism. Berlusconi responded by staunchly supporting the wars in Iraq and Afghanistan, in spite of overwhelming public opposition in Italy. Italian civilian airline schedules were disrupted to serve the war effort; Italian forces took casualties; and Italian citizens were taken hostage (in one case, Berlusconi appeared to use his own funds to secure a release).

The Blair family had a liking for holidays in the sun. Italy and France were favourite summer destinations until the prime minister's last years in office when he took to Cliff Richard's villa in the Caribbean. His first Tuscan retreat was near San Gimignano in a house owned by Geoffrey Robinson, the Labour MP. But the generous

Robinson was closer to Gordon Brown, a controversial businessman
and, in any case, lost his government job along with Peter Mandelson
in 1998. The Blairs moved on to the grander house of Prince Girolamo
Guicciardini Strozzi, and then in 2002 upgraded even further to a
former Italian royal estate near Pisa as a guest of the regional
government. Locals were unimpressed when a public beach was closed
for the family's benefit. Meanwhile, Chancellor Schröder rather showed
the prime minister up by holidaying with his family at his own
expense in a comparatively modest hotel nearby. In 2004 Blair was
back at the Strozzis. But he took a break from his break which
became his most controversial holiday yet.

Tony, Cherie, Kathryn and Leo were invited for a short stay on
Berlusconi's Villa Certosa estate in Sardinia. It boasted among its
attractions five swimming pools, an artificial lake and a James Bond-
style secret tunnel. Berlusconi had hosted Putin there the previous
year. His hospitality was excessive even by his own standards. The
Italian prime minister took the chance to show off his twenty-metre
Magnum powerboat and the yacht he had recently bought from
Rupert Murdoch. He also serenaded his guests whenever the moment
seized him, clicking his fingers to summon his personal wandering
minstrel from the shadows. The Blairs' first evening ended with a
firework display reflected in the lake, blazing out the words 'VIVA TONY'.
It was not a private visit; there were plenty of photographers and
television cameras to film the Blairs strolling round the Costa Smeralda
in casual clothes. Berlusconi's decision to wear a bandana throughout
made the pictures especially memorable. It later emerged that he was
protecting a recent hair transplant. Blair liked to joke about the visit,
telling how he gestured to his head, suggesting Berlusconi remove his
bandana since their boat was approaching a harbour teaming with
cameras. 'Oh yes,' Berlusconi replied going below. He came back on
deck looking exactly the same: 'I put on clean one.'

The worst Berlusconi got out of the visit was a hack on the left
knee when playing football with Blair. 'I had some trouble with the
left,' he obligingly told the local A&E, before hammering the quip
with a grin: 'You know, I've always had problems with the left.' But
Blair's reputation was lastingly tarnished. The leading Italian newspaper

dubbed the Blairs 'The Sultans of Bling', itemising the gifts of watches and jewellery the family had received from Berlusconi. The Marxist journalist Martin Jacques might have been expected to attack Blair for fraternising with 'the most dangerous political phenomenon in Europe', but close allies were furious as well. The very mild and very loyal leader of the TUC, John Monks, called Blair 'bloody stupid for his friendship'. The reformist former cabinet minister Charles Clarke judged the relationship to be one of the biggest mistakes of the ten years.

On his friendships and holiday destinations Blair paid no attention to the views of his advisers. He would continue to do what was right for himself and his family. Remarkable in Italian politics, Berlusconi managed to stay in office for a full five years while still finding the time to write the lyrics for a CD of Neapolitan love songs. Throughout that period, Blair considered him a close friend and ally in Europe, their biggest disagreement confined to Blair's refusal to call an emergency G7 following the tsunami in Indonesia as Berlusconi had suggested.

In 2006, the British government's entanglements with Berlusconi nearly cost the battered prime minister one of his most loyal cabinet ministers, amidst further damaging allegations of sleaze. As with the Formula One imbroglio at the beginning of Blair's first term, the focus fell once again on the business dealings of Tessa Jowell's lawyer husband, David Mills. Mills had worked for Berlusconi and his companies, setting up tax shelters. Italian magistrates had been investigating the Italian prime minister and Mills on corruption charges throughout Berlusconi's years in power. As his likely exit from office approached, they became emboldened – the statute of limitations for prosecution was also running out. In March 2006 it emerged that in 1999 Mills had received a $650,000 gift from what he called the 'B people', which the Italian authorities claimed was a bribe from Berlusconi. Mills denied that Berlusconi was the 'B' in question or that he had been bribed.

Jowell was embroiled because she had signed mortgage papers secured by the money in 2004, the same year in which Mills told his accountant about the money; the accountant then reported the gift to the UK tax authorities. A media frenzy ensued, during which Mills claimed he was the victim of Italian political machinations. Blair was forced to order an inquiry by the cabinet secretary, Sir Gus O'Donnell, who ruled that Tessa Jowell should have reported the gift earlier but was unable to do so because her husband had not told her about it. Therefore she had not broken the ministerial code. Blair exonerated her: 'Tessa Jowell is an excellent minister who is widely respected. I have full confidence in her.' Jowell announced her official separation from her husband and kept her job.

Blair expressed personal regret when Berlusconi lost the election in May 2006. Some aspects of the case against Mills and the Italian prime minister remained unresolved as Blair left office. Berlusconi was the first to offer the ex-prime minister a job, representing the international university he hoped to set up in Florence. But, following the fall of Romano Prodi's government, *Il Cavaliere* was already plotting a political comeback at the head of a new political party, armed with a 'Tony Blair-style' ten-point plan. He succeeded in regaining office in April 2008 when his conservative bloc achieved victories in both houses of the Italian Parliament.

Aznar

José Aznar was less flamboyant than Silvio Berlusconi, but personally closer to Blair and perhaps more influential on him. A scion of a Francoist political family – both his father and grandfather were members of the fascist government – Aznar was personally dependable where Berlusconi was unpredictable. He also had warm hospitality to offer. The Blairs spent the Easter following the 1998 Good Friday Agreement in a Spanish wildlife reserve as guests of the Aznars. For further visits, Aznar invited his friend Paco Peña, who coached Blair on the guitar. In 2002 Blair, Berlusconi and Rupert Murdoch (and John Major) were all guests at the wedding of Aznar's daughter.

Blair and Aznar shared a political agenda. Both wanted much quicker liberal economic reform in Europe and both were casting around for allies to counter the Franco–German axis and the 'chocolate four' – France, Germany, Luxembourg and Belgium. Both were acclimatised to terrorism – the IRA in Britain, ETA in Spain. Both believed, incorrectly, that an accommodation could be reached on Gibraltar (the Gibraltarians managed to stymie the deal between London and Madrid, organising their own referendum in 2002 in which 98.97 per cent voted against joint sovereignty). Both had an Atlanticist perspective and continued to back Bush after the immediate global solidarity brought on by 9/11 had worn off.

Aznar's most profound influence on Blair was personal. He provided the model of a leader voluntarily limiting his own term in office. Infuriated by the longevity of his predecessor, socialist Prime Minister Felipe González, Aznar ran for office on a clear pledge not to serve more than two terms. He stuck to it. He served until the end of his second term, then left office in April 2004 aged just fifty-one, having handed over the party leadership to Mariano Rajoy. Blair was greedier for his period in power and less specific than Aznar. Yet, later in the year that Aznar went, Blair, clearly influenced by his friend, unveiled his intentions not to seek a fourth term.

Neither exit was entirely smooth. The Madrid bombings on 11 March 2004 upset political calculations, and the socialist José Luis Rodríguez Zapatero unexpectedly became prime minister, helped by a clumsy attempt by the Partido Popular to link the attack to Basque separatists. Zapatero soon gave a flavour of his likely relations with Blair by describing his fellow socialist as 'a dickhead' over Iraq. In contrast, at his last press conference in Brussels in 2004, Aznar bluntly singled out Blair for praise: 'besides being a great friend, he is among the leaders who are worth it in Europe'. When Blair quit Number 10, the *Sunday Times* asked Aznar, who had become a director of News Corporation, for some advice for the outgoing prime minister. 'I don't give advice to Tony. He is a very close friend and I appreciate him very much. We did a lot of things together. But in my experience – and this is not advice – it's necessary to establish a difference in your life . . . he should never forget the wisdom of Winston Churchill, who said that all great nations are ungrateful.'

★

Blair's last few years in Europe were his most successful. He had real achievements to boast of after the UK's presidency of the EU in the second half of 2005. The Hampton Court summit in October persuasively argued that the post-treaty agenda for the EU needed to be further economic reform. It established a common purpose which permitted Blair to secure a budget deal in Brussels in December. This was a remarkable feat of skilful negotiation by the prime minister and a constructive compromise – Britain agreed to a reduction in its projected rebate, but gained in return the unfreezing of budget discussions on the Common Agricultural Policy, long before the 2013 deadline which Chirac and Schröder had stitched up in the deal which provoked 'le row'.

Gordon Brown's Treasury rubbished the budget deal, even though its officials had been party to it throughout. But Blair owed a considerable share of his success to Angela Merkel whose opening gambit had been to tell both Blair and Chirac, in a reference to Germany's net contributions to the EU, 'I'm paying and I want a deal.'

As Prime Minister Blair left the stage, his frustrating relations with Chirac and Schröder had been replaced by the promise of partnerships with Merkel of Germany and Sarkozy of France, on a shared agenda for economic reform – until the next divisive crisis at least. And yet Blair had ended up following his predecessors. He had been a pragmatic and competent manager of Britain's membership of the Union without ever committing himself fully to it and – as Barroso pointed out – without winning, or even entertaining, the argument in favour of membership with his own electorate.

With hindsight, two of his closest advisers, Jonathan Powell and Alastair Campbell, both speculated that one of Blair's biggest regrets was that he hadn't 'done the euro'. Back in 1997, there had been a once-in-a-generation opportunity to transform Britain's European stance for ever by becoming a founding member of the euro single currency. In opposition, both Blair and Brown had spoken warmly about the idea. Plans were drawn up for entry shortly after the 1997 general election, as Robert Peston reported in the *Financial Times*. In the intense glow of Blair's first electoral honeymoon it is likely that he could have taken the pound into the eurozone, albeit by expending a large amount of his political capital, but the new government didn't make that choice. Both Blair and his chancellor dithered, and then took the easy option – retreating to other priorities.

There were strong arguments for and against British adoption of the euro – both economic and political. Britain had been spooked by Black Wednesday. Had Blair gone in, Labour would have been weaker and the Conservative Party would have regenerated more quickly. Blair would have lost much of his hard-won press backing. He might not even have won a third term at all.

The euro was of course primarily a political project, a leap of faith which Blair and Brown decided not to make. All the considerations had weighed heavily on Blair, who recalled that he had been rather more hesitant than Brown about the euro in 1997. Eventually, the two men agreed that the matter should be judged on its economic merits alone. This amounted to the kiss of death because there would always be major economic uncertainties once political idealism was set aside. There was no prospect that Brown's first shelf full of reports would result in entry and, sure enough, it didn't.

Blair denied that he had left Europe as unfinished business for Britain, claiming he had moved the country from the margins into the centre. Shortly after he left office, there were suggestions that he might be asked to deal with it, not for Britain but as the first president of the Council. Such a new job would come into being once the treaty Blair had just agreed was ratified. It meant a potential return to the Council headquarters – the pink-stone Justus Lipsius building where Blair was speaking early that morning on the second floor (or '20th' according to the EU lift buttons). Mr Blair might have felt some affinity for the sixteenth-century Flemish philosopher who gave his name to the edifice. Lipsius had vacillated over which branch of Christianity to follow. He had also been one of the first to try to define the respective rights and responsibilities of citizens and the state. But that was for another time.

That Saturday, Blair still had far to go: his journey to Rome to see the Pope lay ahead. 'Let's get some sleep,' the prime minister said and turned on his heels.

8

THE PRIVATE MAN

23 JUNE

Goodbye — I don't think we'll miss you!
Cherie Blair bids farewell to the press,
Downing Street, 27 June 2007

Chequers

Most prime ministers fall in love with Chequers, the country house nestling in the Chiltern Hills in Buckinghamshire, which is for the use of the incumbent prime minister and family.

Margaret Thatcher found it one of the bitterest losses on her fall from power. Norma Major cherished the place so much that she wrote a book about it. So if they were still with us, its donors, Ruth and Arthur Lee, could claim to have fulfilled their purpose as spelt out in the stained glass window they built into the property:

This house of peace and ancient memories was given to England as a thank-offering for her deliverance in the great war of 1914–1918 as a place of rest and recreation for her Prime Ministers for ever.

Chequers has a venerable history dating back to 1100, with connections

to Oliver Cromwell, Nelson and Lady Mary Grey, the younger sister
of the Elizabethan pretender, who was kept prisoner there. David
Lloyd George acquired it from the Lees for the use of prime ministers,
in what could be viewed as a house for peerages deal. Ultimately,
there was some bitterness between him and the childless Lees, but
they did at least leave Chequers as Lord and Lady Fareham.

Patronage inevitably became an issue during Tony Blair's tenure.
Access to Tony and Cherie's guest lists for lunches, dinners and parties
was hotly contested under the Freedom of Information Act – even
though the terms of the Chequers Trust firmly insist that they had
to pay out of their own pockets for the food and drink consumed.

Blair's guests sometimes didn't do him any favours. After a dinner
in the early years, the chattering classes were titillated to learn that
Derry Irvine, the Lord Chancellor, referred to the prime minister
who had recently appointed him as 'the Boy Blair' and ordered him
out of the room to replenish his glass. Irvine apparently saw little
reason to change his manner from the days when he was Blair's pupil
master in their barristers' chambers. On another occasion, the pop
star Mick Hucknall was embarrassed when it was revealed that the
female companion who had been his escort to dinner was just that
– a former escort girl. (The woman later recalled to the *Mail on
Sunday* how Cherie Blair had welcomed her: 'She took my hand
and my arm and said, "We've heard so much about you. It's wonderful
to meet you at long last. I've been telling him [Hucknall] to bring
you over for a while now. Mick's told us so much about you."')

Chequers formed the backdrop for some key moments in the
Blair years.

In November 1997, Alastair Campbell had to argue with the
trustees to get the television cameras in for the prime minister's *On
the Record* interview to rebut the row over Bernie Ecclestone's million-
pound donation to the Labour Party. Campbell argued that it was
indeed in the interests of Blair's 'peace and recreation' that he should
be allowed to give his side of the story. John Humphrys and the
BBC cameras filmed an interview which is remembered for two
things: an over-enthusiastic make-up job which left the prime minister
with bright yellow flesh and pink cheeks, looking not unlike a

Pinocchio puppet and his rejection of wrong-doing with the ringing assurance: 'I hope that people know me well enough and realise that I would never do anything to harm the country or anything improper. I never have. I think that most people who have dealt with me think that I am a pretty straight sort of guy.'

Since the trustees generally kept the media at the gates or in a nearby pub, Chequers was a favoured location for more intimate and extended talks. As with the US president's Camp David retreat, an invitation to Chequers was meant to be taken as a compliment. President Clinton stayed at the house, and George W. Bush was welcomed there on his first visit to the UK as president. (President Bush went one better than Camp David with even more highly prized invitations to his Prairie Chapel Ranch in Austin, Texas. In presidential mode, Blair tried this a couple of times with Myrobella, his constituency home. Bush and Jospin were amongst those invited to Sedgefield for pubs and fish and chips, but County Durham never became a firm fixture for prime ministerial events, perhaps because Blair himself visited for only about one day a month.)

During the first term, the Blairs used Chequers like any other middle-class second home, though on a rather grander scale. The children enjoyed the swimming pool and Princes William and Harry played football on the lawns with Euan and Nicky. Chequers was also the habitual venue for family get-togethers. Cherie Blair celebrated her fiftieth birthday there with a marquee party, and the Blairs usually spent Christmas on the estate before their New Year dash abroad for some winter sun.

As Euan, Nicky and Kathryn grew up, the demands of teenage life more often kept them and their mother away from Buckinghamshire. Blair frequently found himself alone at Chequers from Friday to Saturday, except for his youngest son Leo and staff. He especially enjoyed teaching Leo music and singing. Blair spent the time on his reading, writing and telephoning. He read more for work than pleasure. In spite of his elite education, he displayed little interest in the arts: not for him, Macmillan's rereading of Jane Austen, Ted Heath's musical virtuosity, or even John Major's enthusiasm for Trollope. On *Desert Island Discs*, Blair's book choice was *Ivanhoe*, but this was at the suggestion of Derry Irvine during a preparatory brainstorming session and, conveniently, the programme's broadcast happened to coincide with a BBC television adaptation of Sir Walter Scott's classic. He also regularly played tennis with the coach at the nearby RAF Halton base and sat in the sunshine if there was any.

On Sunday evenings, Blair's advisers and political friends got used to receiving handwritten faxes, and subsequently retyped emails, from the prime minister outlining action plans developed from his weekend cogitations.

During one of his last weekends, on Sunday 6 May, Blair confounded his technophobe reputation by recording a YouTube message to the French people, congratulating them on the election that day of their new president, Nicolas Sarkozy. Dressed in an open-necked blue shirt against a soft background of wood panelling, the prime minister spoke in French for nearly four minutes, passing on '*mes félicitations*' and warning the French of the consequences of electing a reformer in the Blair mould: '*Le changement n'est jamais chose facile.*' (Over the next year the clip received nearly half a million 'hits' but the website – usually an open forum for comment and the exchange of opinion – stopped anyone 'answering back'.)

Chequers also provided a base for some solo socialising by the prime minister. Friends would drop by or he could nip out to the houses of other weekenders in the area, including Sir Jackie Stewart, the world champion motor racing driver, and, a bit further away in Woodstock, Rebekah Wade, and Matthew Freud and Elisabeth Murdoch.

Big-house hospitality is not the easiest thing to pull off. However born to the role the hosts may be, in my view anyone invited for 'a weekend' should have their escape routes well planned in advance.

I went to Chequers once as a guest during Blair's ten years, one chilly Eastertide early in the premiership. The invitation had come unexpectedly to four journalists: Elinor Goodman of Channel 4, Andrew Marr of the BBC, John Sergeant from ITN and myself. None of us knew why we were there and we weren't any clearer after we'd been greeted warmly by the prime minister, open-necked, at his front door. Alastair Campbell was the only other guest present.

Our small talk over drinks in the drawing room was pretty stilted, grasping gratefully for the English landscape paintings on the walls. A quick check of the labels on the way into lunch showed Mr Blair to be a bit shaky on his attributions between Turner and Constable.

The dining room was solid and dingy, the atmosphere that you'd expect on an infrequent visit to distant but affluent elderly relatives. The occasion was not a glittering soireé. Neither a convivial social occasion nor a regular media encounter, it can best be described as an awkward working lunch with political editors from television news on one side and Blair and Campbell on the other. Things didn't get any easier when the prime minister broke the ice with 'Well, how am I doing?' Television reporters broadcast live opinions for a living, but it's much more difficult to opine straight into the face of your subject while you are eating his food. Far from lecturing us, Blair's instinctive approach was to try to assimilate us into his big tent, all sitting together swapping views as like-minded adults.

The government was then in its 'post-euphoria, pre-delivery phase' and we babbled unhappily about the public services and public indifference to the changes being made. As always on schools, health and delivery to the public, Blair showed himself the master of statistics and the latest think tank policy. Campbell looked on silently from the end of the table. After lunch came the tour of the house. He must have done it hundreds of times, but Blair was an enthusiastic guide, stocked with anecdotes about the books, and the old master Churchill had 'improved' with his own paintbrush.

I was still wondering what that had been about as we bade our farewells. While the ever-obliging Blair posed for a picture with Danny, my mini-cab driver, Campbell engaged us in some banter about some of our colleagues in the parliamentary lobby. None of us was particularly kind about the minority of political journalists, almost all working for newspapers, whose main interests were gossip and scandal rather than reporting Westminster. Even such mildly disobliging remarks about colleagues were a mistake. Campbell would soon teach us that there was indeed no such thing as a free lunch at Chequers.

What we had said could be used as cover, passed off as informal consultation with senior reporters on a plan Campbell was determined to execute. When the Easter recess ended he moved immediately to distance Number 10 from the lobby. Campbell stopped giving briefings himself – given his intimacy with Blair, he had always been a highly informative and valuable official source. Now he shut himself off and created a new civil service post of PMOS, prime minister's official spokesman. Crucially, unlike Campbell, the civil servant spokesmen could credibly plead ignorance about what was going on and give out less and lower-quality information. At Chequers, Blair and Campbell had drawn us into sympathising with some of their complaints against some journalists without telling us what their plans were. Now, in their view, our comments had provided at least some of the justification for changes in the briefing system, which disadvantaged the media as a whole.

The Blairs took full advantage of Chequers to throw farewell parties. On Saturday 26 May, Tony and Cherie invited several hundred of those and their partners who had worked with them to a Saturday-night party. Given the numbers involved, this mostly took place in tents pitched on the lawns.

A week later, on the night of Saturday 2 June, Blair hosted a dinner which was very much a 'no partners' event. Cherie was not present. This was Blair's private celebration for the team of '97 – those who had been closest to him, and most involved in political evangelism on his behalf, during his time in power. His original plan had been to have a dinner for Peter Mandelson and those of Mandelson's friends who had stuck by him, notably Roger Liddle and Patrick Diamond, who had worked on policy for both Mandelson and the prime minister – a remarkable gesture of friendship on a par with the invitation Blair had issued immediately after sacking Mandelson from the cabinet for the first time, to stay at Chequers with his partner Reinaldo Avila da Silva. But Campbell and Sally Morgan got to hear of the plan and invited themselves along to the Mandelson tribute. Blair gave in and converted the event into a 'last supper' – although there were rather more than twelve disciples. Gathered round the table were those who saw themselves as Blair's loyal team from the days of opposition onward: Jonathan Powell, Anji Hunter, Sally Morgan, Kate Garvey, Alastair Campbell, Tim

Allan, Philip Gould, Peter Mandelson, James Purnell, Geoffrey Norris, Liz Lloyd, Pat McFadden, Peter Hyman, David Miliband, Sarah Hunter and Ben Wegg-Prosser, plus Mandelson's friends Diamond and Liddle.

As an ice-breaker, Kate Garvey – who had left the events team at Number 10 after the 2005 election for Freud Communications – organised a short video. This was entitled *Guide to the Real World for Tony, 'the Prime Minister'*. Based on the premise that a 'severely damaged' man had been kept away from ordinary living for a decade, this featured a series of 'how to' introductions: Kate Garvey on checking-in at airports and using the telephone (dialling, and finding numbers rather than always having the Downing Street 'switch' on the other end); Sarah Hunter on walking around in public; Anji Hunter on using money and driving (opening the door yourself, sitting in the front seat, stopping at red lights, etc.); Philip Gould on using a credit card ('as you can see mine's gold – yours won't be because you haven't got enough money, but you will in time'). Verisimilitude was provided by links from Jon Sopel in the BBC News studio, and a location stand-up by me, recorded while the Blairs and Mandelas were posing for the cameras in Johannesburg. Intriguingly, Alastair Campbell was the only one to take on another persona, wearing glasses and assuming a cod Viennese accent, to give his diagnosis as 'an expert in psychological flaws'. (Perhaps private recognition that despite his denials he had been the source of the notorious quote about Brown.)

Then came the speeches. Anji Hunter burst into tears and said, 'Didn't my old friend do well?' Jonathan Powell and Alastair Campbell competed to be the dominant male after Blair, but the prime minister had the final say. Looking around the table, he lavished praise on his followers: 'If these people were working for anyone they could win any election, anywhere around the world. Without you guys we'd never have achieved what we've done . . .' Then he gave more than a hint that, in his view, they had signed on for a life of service: 'We have achieved a great deal but I also know that we have still got a great deal to do togther.'

Immediately after they left Downing Street, Gordon Brown allowed the Blairs to enjoy a final stay at Chequers, which lasted into the following week, not least because the builders were still in their new London home at Connaught Square.

Initially, Brown's declared intention was to use Chequers only for official work but he quickly succumbed to the lure to recreation and leisure in the Buckinghamshire countryside. Tony Blair, meanwhile, suffered withdrawal symptoms. He expressed an interest in buying Winslow Hall, twenty miles away. Built between 1698 and 1701, it was a Grade I listed building designed by Sir Christopher Wren, with a Catholic chapel in its grounds. But in 2008 it was confirmed that the Blairs had purchased the South Pavilion of Wotton House – another Grade I listed building in the area and onetime home of the actor Sir John Gielgud. The price tag of £4 million left the media wondering even more at their mounting mortgage bill.

Tony Blair had treated Chequers more as a home and less as an official residence than his two predecessors. John Major preferred to weekend at his own more modest constituency home outside Huntingdon and was guilelessly proud of the improvements he had made to the grounds. He used Chequers for entertaining Boris Yeltsin, including the abandoned country stroll which provided one of his favourite anecdotes. (After barely 300 yards, Yeltsin requested to be driven to the nearest pub for some refreshment, only to find it shut on arrival. His aides banged on the door shouting that the president of Russia was outside. 'Oh yes,' replied a voice from within, 'and I'm the Kaiser!') Mrs Thatcher went to Chequers regularly, and entertained there officially, but she was always ready to break off for business. On a Sunday morning she was usually willing to offer a quick word to the television cameras on the news of the day while standing outside what she always referred to as 'Chequers Church', even though it was several miles away in the next village.

Religion

Blair hated to be filmed going to church. His enforcers actively impeded efforts by the media to do so, and complained vigorously if pictures were snatched. As an active Christian since his university days, for Blair religious observation was more than simply going through the motions and doing the proper thing – it meant much more than that. His faith was a highly personal matter which, while prime minister, he was prepared to protect even to the point of not telling the truth about it.

Tony Blair's wife, Cherie, was a 'cradle Catholic'; his four children were all brought up in the faith and had attended Catholic schools. In his early years as prime minister, Blair was blunt about his family's habits of worship: 'My wife is Catholic, my kids were brought up as Catholics, I have gone to Mass with them for years because I believe it is important for a family to worship together. I would not want to go to an Anglican or Protestant church when my wife or kids go to a Catholic one.'

As leader of the opposition he had been a regular attender at St Joan of Arc church, Highbury, near his Islington home. Some, including Cardinal Basil Hume and Ann Widdecombe, a Conservative MP and Catholic convert, criticised him for breaking canon law, but he was popular with fellow parishioners, who sent a petition of support to *The Universe* Catholic newspaper praising his 'modest and unobtrusive' contribution. It was the same in his Sedgefield constituency. The Blairs attended St John Fisher church, whose minister in the 1990s, Father John Caden, became a close family friend, christening young Leo Blair.

As early as 1996, Cardinal Hume, the leader of the Catholic Church in Britain, wrote to Blair, who was already seen as 'prime minister in waiting', and asked him to desist from taking communion. Blair said he would comply but commented, 'I wonder what Jesus would have made of it' and 'I find many of the angry debates between Catholic and Protestant completely baffling.' In fact, he continued to take communion on several subsequent occasions before joining the Church, including, controversially, on a prime ministerial trip to Denver.

At Chequers, Blair hardly ever attended the nearby Church of England services favoured by Thatcher (herself born a Methodist). Instead, he and his family started going to the nearest Catholic church, the Immaculate Heart of Mary at Great Missenden. But as his religious observances began to draw attention, he switched first to attending Westminster Cathedral on his return to London on Saturday or Sunday evenings and then to private masses held at Chequers, usually on a Saturday evening, by the Great Missenden priest Canon Timothy Russ. Sometimes the family attended; sometimes Blair was on his own.

John Rentoul, his biographer, quotes Blair as saying: 'As a private individual I find prayer a source of solace and I read the gospels. They are compelling texts, and a most extraordinary expression of sensitive human values.' His religious practice went well beyond taking part in worship with his family, but he continued to be reluctant to discuss it, claiming on one occasion that he was alone in Westminster Cathedral because his family were late.

In fact, even before Alastair Campbell's famous injunction 'We don't do God', Downing Street and the prime minister resolutely and consistently denied any suggestion that Blair was considering conversion to Catholicism. Denials which, with hindsight, must be set against his conversion, or acceptance into the Roman Catholic communion, which took place six months after he left office on 21 December 2007. In 1997 his office said: 'He's not Catholic. He's an Anglican'; in 1998 Alastair Campbell declared: 'End of story. He is not converting'; the same year Blair himself told the then Archbishop of Canterbury, Dr George Carey, that he had no intention of converting; in 2004 the prime minister said, 'I am saying no. Don't they run this once a year? I think they do.'

Blair kept this up, even though his dealings with the Catholic Church were elevated to the highest level during his latter years in office as his direct personal lines of communication with the Vatican were dramatically improved by one remarkable young man called Francis Campbell.

Campbell was an Ulster Catholic born in Newry in 1970. He had a distinguished school career, followed by studies in politics and philosophy at Queen's University, Belfast, the Catholic University at Leuven and the University of Pennsylvania. He worked for the European Commission before transferring to the British Foreign and Commonwealth Office in 1998. Within a year, Campbell was on secondment to Blair in Number 10, rising over the next four years from policy adviser to private secretary. In 2003 he was promoted to the British embassy in Rome as first secretary for external affairs. In 2005 he took a sabbatical from government service to become senior policy director for Amnesty International, but in December that year he was appointed Britain's ambassador to the Holy See – 'our man with the Pope'. This appointment was significant in two ways: it was the first time the ambassador had been chosen by open competition – the post was advertised and applied for – and it was also the first time a Roman Catholic had been appointed to represent Britain at the Holy See since the Reformation under Henry VIII.

Unlike his predecessors, Campbell, as a co-religionist, could associate freely with members of the power structure around the Pope – many of them priests, bishops and cardinals. Campbell's hospitality for parties and dinners – so British in its somewhat chaotic, home-cooked style – was a hot ticket with the Curia. Once he became ambassador, Campbell refused to let his style be cramped, continuing to entertain in his new apartment when FCO bean counters forced the disposal of the *palazzo* historically occupied by the British ambassador. From the moment Francis Campbell first started to work for Blair, relations between the British government and the Vatican acquired an intimacy that they had not enjoyed since the sixteenth century.

Often also on hand to help out with social affairs was the celebrated hostess Carla Powell, the glamorous Italian-born wife of Lord (Charles) Powell, the career diplomat and close adviser to prime ministers from Thatcher to Blair. While her husband pursued a frenetic private international business career, Lady Powell retired to a villa in the Sabine Hills not far from Rome, expanding her network of friends to include 'the Cardinals'.

In February 2003, the Blair family and their entourage went to the Vatican for an audience with Pope John Paul II, shortly after the Pope had held talks there with Tariq Aziz, Saddam Hussein's Christian deputy prime minister. True to form, Downing Street spokesmen first denied that the meeting was going to take place (Blair was ostensibly in Rome for talks with Prime Minister Silvio Berlusconi), then they refused to comment, before finally insisting that there would be no pictures available. It proved much easier to get truthful information out of the Vatican and Dr Joaquín Navarro-Valls, the formidable director of the Holy See Press Office. Vatican press releases confirmed that the meeting was to take place and that it would provide television coverage afterwards. Later, again in the face of Downing Street denials, the Vatican confirmed that the imminent war in Iraq had been discussed. In the build-up to the conflict, Dr Navarro-Valls had already expressed the pontiff's view that President Bush would have to answer to God for his actions.

The Holy See did not, however, provide a full picture of the meeting. Television images show Blair's motorcade drawing up in the courtyard and the prime minister alone meeting and greeting the pontiff. Mrs Blair, her mother, and some of her children also took part in the audience as did Catholics travelling in the party, including Cherie's hairdresser Andre Suard and Downing Street official Kate Garvey.

Return visits to the Vatican multiplied from then on. The general election campaign was put on hold in 2005 by the death of Pope John Paul II. Blair attended the funeral and so did the main opposition leaders: Conservative Michael Howard, who was Jewish, and Liberal Democrat Charles Kennedy, a Catholic from birth. Even allowing for John Paul's exceptional accomplishments as the Polish Pope who may have helped speed the collapse of Soviet communism, it was a remarkable guest list. No previous papal obsequies had been honoured by such a senior roll call of British politicians.

Blair held talks with Cardinal Joseph Ratzinger, who was then effectively John Paul's number two as Prefect of the Congregation for the Doctrine of the Faith, at the time of the funeral. As prime minister, Blair had two further audiences with him following his elevation to the papacy, on 3 June 2006 and 23 June 2007. Blair flew on to this last audience – his final official foreign engagement as prime minister – directly from the final European Council he attended as prime minister. Coming just days before Blair's resignation, this last Vatican visit seemed almost a deliberate public assertion of the importance of his religion to Blair – and of his new freedom to do as he pleased and associate with whomever he wanted.

The eight-strong party of friends and advisers included Carla Powell and her brother-in-law Jonathan, Blair's outgoing chief of staff, as well as some high-rolling family friends, Bernard and Helene Arnault, who headed the LVMH (Louis Vuitton, Moët, Hennessy) luxury goods conglomerate. They were given the red carpet treatment at the Apostolic Palace. Blair seemed moved as he said to the Pope, 'Thank you so much for receiving me,' which was almost a pun given Blair's impending reception into the Church.

Themes of conversion shot through this visit to the Vatican. Against normal protocol, the Archbishop of Westminster, Cardinal Cormac Murphy O'Connor, who would soon become ultimately responsible for Blair's religious indoctrination, joined the papal audience. The Pope gave the prime minister a standard gold medallion but Blair's gift was much more personal – a signed portrait of the nineteenth-century convert and leader of the Oxford Movement, Cardinal John Henry Newman. 'Holy Father, that is his signature,' Blair pointed out to Benedict. After a meeting with the Vatican's *de facto* prime minister, Secretary of State Cardinal Bertone, the Blair party had lunch at the Venerable English College, the seminary for Englishmen training for the priesthood.

Blair bowed to requests from the accompanying archbishop not to announce his conversion during this visit, but after a period of 'reflection'. He did not publicise his decision until the end of December 2007 after being received into the Church by Cardinal Cormac Murphy O'Connor in the chapel of Archbishop's House, Westminster.

There are many, including some who regard religious faith as a delusion, who will argue that Blair was entitled to be disingenuous since his faith was essentially a private matter. He could have just refused to comment, as he did with family matters, but here he and his officials gave an impression contrary to what turned out to be the truth. Of course, this is one area where Blair's prevarications were convenient to him.

It was expedient for Prime Minister Blair to remain an Anglican and it would undoubtedly have been awkward had he become a Catholic while still in office. Since the reign of George IV and Catholic emancipation there has been no bar to a Catholic becoming prime minister; indeed most of Britain's high political offices have been held by non-members of the Church of England, though not the premiership. The prime minister remained the most senior adviser to the monarch, who was Defender of the Faith. Number 10 also made the nominations for ecclesiastical appointments, including the Archbishop of Canterbury. Although it was claimed that the Blair administration merely acted as a forwarding address for the nominations which emerged from the Church hierarchy, this was not the case. Blair never actually acted on hints from his officials that it was time for the government to stand aside on Church matters. He rejected several shortlists which were presented to him on bishops and he took an active role in securing the Archbishopric of Canterbury for Dr Rowan Williams – an exercise in patronage whose dubious wisdom is matched only by his choice of Andrew Motion as poet laureate (on that occasion, Number 10 decided they didn't want the controversy of appointing the more deserving poet, U. A. Fanthorpe, as both the first woman and the first lesbian in the post). Had the prime minister already quit the Church of England, it would have been far more difficult for him to exercise power in this way. By delaying his conversion he also prevented a concentration of public interest on such matters.

A conversion in office might also have complicated negotiations on Northern Ireland, given that the crux of the Troubles was a sectarian divide in which the Irish government was the ultimate guarantor for Catholics and the British government the guarantor for Protestants. Although in practice, Blair's passionate interest in the Bible and his ecumenical instincts seem to have served him well in his dealings, at least with the Protestant clergyman Ian Paisley (the man who once heckled Pope John Paul II while brandishing a placard calling him the Antichrist).

Blair's own explanation for his conversion and its timing was problematic. He denied that he had become a Roman Catholic for doctrinal reasons, although that may dismay some of his new spiritual guardians. He seemed entirely at ease in either Church. His main reason for making the change he said was so he could worship with his kids. As to the delay in making the crossing, once again the main inhibitor appears to have been the media rather than high politics. He conceded that conversion while in office 'would have been tricky' but mainly for the fuss the 'feral beasts' would have kicked up.

To what extent did Blair's faith affect his actions as prime minister? Certainly he never voted or advocated the Catholic agenda on social policy such as abortion (although he habitually avoided casting his own vote on such 'conscience' questions). His government's introduction of statutory recognition of civil partnership for homosexual couples alienated religious traditionalists across the spectrum. His promotion of stem cell research in Britain was a direct rebuff and challenge to the prohibition in the US advocated by President Bush. Amongst British Catholics, reaction to Blair's professed religious beliefs depended not on their faith but on where they stood politically. The convert Ann Widdecombe accused Blair of hypocrisy, but the liberal Tory grandee Lord (Chris) Patten merely let it be known that he was relieved Blair had not used 'Father Seed' for his conversion, a reference to the oleaginous Westminster Cathedral canon, Father Michael Seed, who specialised in celebrity conversions and near-conversions of such famous names as Princess Diana, Alan Clark and Widdecombe herself. In public comments, Seed had linked himself to Blair's spiritual journey. Blair also had extensive discussions about his developing faith with three prominent women – Baroness Shirley Williams, a former Labour cabinet minister and SDP founder, herself a Catholic; Baroness Patricia Scotland, a minister promoted by Blair; and Ruth Turner, his last director of government relations, the daughter of a theology professor and designated chief executive of his new interfaith foundation set up in the spring of 2008.

Blair's religious observance set him apart from most of his colleagues. Some, including Tessa Jowell, who was confirmed in the Church of England while a minister, sympathised with his spiritual quest. Most were merely bemused by a personal journey which seemed to be going in the opposite direction from their common 'progressive' agenda. Blair rejected such charges, arguing that the Christianity he had discovered at Oxford University had also led him away from the self-interest of Thatcherism. Thatcher believed that her Methodist-based Christianity supported her political beliefs. While the two prime ministers disagreed on the outcome, they had in common the exceptional conviction for British politicians that religion should inform their daily work. Others, including the militant atheist Alastair Campbell, were angered and unsettled by it with unpredictable consequences.

In the summer of 2000, Blair agreed to travel to Tübingen University to give a speech on ethics as part of a religious seminar. Campbell was so perturbed by this that, on the plane over, he persuaded Blair to insert into his speech the half-baked proposal that yobs causing trouble on the streets should be marched to cashpoints to pay on-the-spot fines. This achieved Campbell's purpose of taking the headlines away from God, at the price of leaving the prime minister with a policy which he was forced to recant in public. The timing was particularly unfortunate given that, just days later, Blair's son Euan was arrested in Leicester Square for being drunk and incapable after celebrating the end of his GCSE exams.

Media interest in Blair's faith was piqued by the arrival in the White House of George W. Bush, an avowed born-again Christian. Shades of Nixon and Kissinger dropping to their knees in the Oval Office on the eve of the president's resignation were conjured in television interviews when Blair was asked, first by Sir David Frost and then by Jeremy Paxman, whether he had prayed together with the president over Iraq. The prime minister was visibly narked, but politics took precedence as he gave emphatic denials. Blair seems to have had little difficulty compartmentalising his work and his religion. During the 2005 general election campaign he stated that it would be 'unhealthy' if religion moved to centre stage as it had done in the US and that he did not want a system in which politicians went around 'beating our chests about our faith'.

However, the suspicion lingered that the prime minister's faith gave him a different perspective from that of most of his colleagues, a view which was crystallised in Private Eye's regular satire of Blair as the self-righteous and hypocritical 'Vicar of St Albion's', who propagated his prejudices in pages which parodied a parish magazine. The frames which Private Eye choose to fix prime ministers often contribute importantly to a wider public perception of their characters.

Margaret Thatcher was well served by the cosy 'Dear Bill' letters allegedly written by her husband to golfing chums, but John Major was further belittled by the Adrian Mole spoof 'The Diary of John Major aged 47 and ¾s'. The Vicar of St Albion's was replaced by Gordon Brown's depiction as the Stalinist 'Supreme Leader' with his numbered 'Prime Ministerial Decrees'.

In truth, Blair did have some of the smugness of the caricature. Unlike Major, his predecessor, or Brown, his successor, he had little difficulty taking decisions or committing himself. This decisiveness may have been informed in complementary ways by his faith. Firstly, religious people are used to dealing in absolutes, and may act on their beliefs rather than evidence. Secondly, to a believer, judgement on any action taken is always subject to an appeal – in the afterlife. Blair had expressed these views explicitly in his comments on Iraq – that he did what he believed was right and that history and God would be the ultimate judges.

God took up a lot of Blair's spare time; correspondingly, following St Paul's injunction to 'put away childish things', he devoted less of his leisure than is usual to such pursuits as sport and culture. Blair was neither aesthetically sensitive nor was he what is generally known as well-read – except when it came to religious works. He claimed familiarity with the Koran as well as the Bible, and he knew his way around contemporary interdenominational texts. An annotated, holiday reading list he suggested to a colleague included, *The New Jerome Biblical Commentary*; four volumes from the *Penguin History of the Church: The Early Church, Western Society and the Church in the Middle Ages; The Church and the Age of Reason; The Church in an Age of Revolution; Honest to God* by John Robinson; *The Moral Universe*, a Demos pamphlet; *Memory and Reconciliation*, produced by the Catholic Truth Society; and *Towards a Theology for Inter-Faith Dialogue*, the Report of the Lambeth Conference of 1988. As soon as he left office, he took up these genuine preoccupations not just in his own conversion to Roman Catholicism but also in his plans to set up a foundation dealing with interfaith issues.

Visitors to the Blairs' private quarters were surprised to find fewer examples of general reading material – books, magazines and newspapers – strewn around than is more typically usual in metropolitan upper-middle-class homes. As president, Bill Clinton still managed to read three general interest books a week, often inviting authors and academics in for a discussion of them. Tony Blair was accompanied on holiday in his final year by a copy of *Three Men in a Boat* by Jerome K. Jerome, a favourite from his youth which he was rereading.

The British novelist Ian McEwan has described, both in reportage and fictionalised in his book *Saturday*, an encounter with Blair at the opening party for the Tate Modern gallery in 2000: Blair confuses him for an artist and claims to have several of his paintings at home, adding that one of his children was named after him. The reader is left to conclude that the prime minister is both a fake and a philistine. In fact, Blair's confusion may in part be explained by his wife's friendship with the painter Euan Uglow, a name not so very different from Ian McEwan – and certainly one that tallies with the first name of Blair's eldest son. Although Downing Street had frequently denied it, it emerged after Uglow's death in 2000 that Tony Blair and Cherie Booth had been introduced to the artist by his friend Derry Irvine when they were pupils in his chambers. Uglow could take years on a painting and Cherie had been a £5-an-hour life model for the artist at his Clapham studio in 1978–80 while she and Tony were courting. Uglow had executed a painting of her, *Striding Nude, Blue Dress*, but at his request and, it was alleged, Tony Blair's intervention, his agents, the Browse and Darby Gallery, had not shown it during his lifetime. The painting was finally displayed in a retrospective in London in the summer of 2007. Even so, the Tate encounter still suggests that Blair had not heard of Ian McEwan, one of Britain's most prominent contemporary novelists, and that he could not accurately remember the name of Euan Uglow, a significant figure in his wife's life. (But Tony Blair was, at least, remembering another Euan in the name of his eldest son: Euan MacDonald, one of Blair's closest friends at Fettes and, like Blair, one of the public school's rebels. MacDonald committed suicide in 1973 while Blair was at Oxford University. Along with the fatal cancer of his mother, Hazel, the death of his friend was instrumental in driving Blair towards religion.)

Rather than books or pictures, Blair's leisure preferences were his family and strumming on his guitar. He enjoyed working on piles of official papers, preferably in the sunshine. His love of sunning himself at Chequers led during the 2005 election campaign to accusations that he was wearing make-up at a morning news conference. The prime minister's face was orange. Asked about his colour he explained that he had been out in the garden over the long weekend. His lack of literary or cultural curiosity also extended to history, including pertinent modern history. When it was suggested to him that the US found it difficult to reconcile with Iran because of the hostage crisis, he replied, 'What hostage crisis?', apparently ignorant of the US embassy occupation which contributed heavily to Jimmy Carter's 1980 election defeat. Similarly, senior civil servants were surprised to draw a blank with their references to John Major's Hillsborough Agreement and the Balfour Declaration.

As a leader, Blair compensated for his ignorance in two ways. Firstly, he was an assiduous reader of briefs, with the lawyer's knack of absorbing a great deal of information quickly. Although little of it would be lodged for good, for concentrated periods he could pose as the master of the subject under discussion. Secondly, he made a virtue of substituting intelligence for knowledge. Blair was never afraid 'to ask the stupid question' during meetings.

Combined with the professionalism of the British civil service, these skills made Blair a successful negotiator. He seldom left a summit – EU, NATO, Northern Irish or otherwise – without having achieved his objectives. However, short-term successes were not necessarily a guarantee of the wisdom of Her Majesty's government. Events often turned out to be moving in a different direction from that which Blair thought he had captured on paper. This was proved by the decade of frustration following the Good Friday Agreement, the refusal of the EU Constitution to die, and above all over Iraq, when nuanced positions both failed to achieve a legitimising nod from the UN and proved completely ill equipped to manage the tides of international opinion. Over time, Blair's concentrated periods of intense, but essentially detached, concentration were unlikely to overrule the passions of those living a conflict, or passionately engaged by it.

Blair's attributes of being a quick studier and asking the obvious questions are also those of most journalists. This helps explain his growing antagonism towards the media: the same magnetic poles do not attract each other. And there were further twists to this mutual repulsion. Blair would argue that, for journalists, merely exercising these analytical talents was the end as they were then expressed in reports; whereas, for him, it was merely the beginning of a process which resulted in 'doing' something. Journalists would respond by questioning what had been achieved and pointing out that for politicians, as much as journalists, identifying an issue and proposing a course of action are not necessarily the same as accomplishing it.

Family

Tony Blair's hostility to the media seems to have grown with the volume of journalistic criticism of his administration, but the biggest single cause of friction over the ten years centred on his family. From the very begining, Tony and Cherie demanded a news blackout on their children, but they were sometimes prepared to break it themselves, often for what seemed like political advantage. As with Blair's religion, the family demanded privacy but were not above exploiting both the cloak of privacy and the issue it was drawn over. By and large, television and news organisations complied: there was a natural consensus, as with the royal family, that children still in full-time education should be off limits – but it was a relationship that was under strain from the outset. Blair was applauded when he revealed that he had explained to his offspring that they enjoyed treats such as a VIP trip to the British Grand Prix, not because people liked them but because of who he was. That rationale was strained when the Blair children did something because their father was prime minister, such as attending a Harry Potter film première, while Number 10 still insisted this was a private family matter which should not be covered.

When Tony Blair ran for the Labour Party leadership in 1994, the news media were notified in writing that there would be no pictures or access to the three children – Euan, Nicky and Kathryn – then all still at primary school. In exchange, the media were provided officially with a few formal family pictures. As his career progressed, photocalls at election time were introduced – the Blair family going to the polls in Sedgefield and then subsequently on the doorstep of Number 10 – official glimpses of the children which had to last for the next four years. Number 10 fiercely enforced a policy whereby no pictures were allowed by photographers or television cameramen as the children went about their lives coming and going from Number 10. (Bewilderingly, the Blairs also sometimes broke their own injunction by including the children in the portrait on their annual Christmas card. This always ended up in the papers, sometimes accompanied by 'Glenda Slag-style' comments on their appearance.)

In 1994, the BBC, Sky and Channel 4 obediently complied with the blackout on the children as they compiled television portraits of the man who would be Labour leader. However, rival channels were somewhat put out when the ITN profile contained footage of Blair playing football with 'the kids'. His office apologised, claiming there had been a mistake and insisted that the ban remained in force. In fact, as Michael Brunson, the former political editor of ITN, explained in his autobiography, a trade-off had been brokered by Peter Mandelson. ITN got the pictures in exchange for not running an interview clip in which Cherie presumptuously said 'when' rather than 'if' about the family's arrival in Downing Street.

And so it went on. Ros, the Blair family nanny, was legally blocked from publishing her friendly memoirs of the children, while Tony and Cherie would talk about the kids when it suited them in feature interviews. Or Leo would be produced to sing 'I Tawt I Taw a Puddy Tat', as his father had taught him, to the French president. Cherie's health trainer, Carole Caplin, was intimidated and marginalised as a blabber and liability by Alastair Campbell even as Campbell himself compiled his own 'pension fund' memoirs of the Blair years.

In 2000, while covering the prime minister abroad, I received an angry phone call from Number 10 demanding that Sky News stop showing pictures of baby Leo. What had happened was that Cherie had been campaigning for Labour's David Lammy in the Tottenham by-election and our cameraman had taken pictures of her getting out of her car. In the corner of the frame, we had caught Leo's feet as he lay in a cot in the back seat. The child was not identifiable and not really visible. Yet a year later, Blair wandered out into St James's Park to have a look at the finishing line of the London Marathon. The next day's *Daily Mail* carried a front-page picture of Blair with baby Leo in his arms. The 2001 general election was just weeks away.

In 2000, the Number 10 team reversed their own strategy and outed one of the children themselves after the incident in which a drunk Euan Blair had been picked up by the police in Leicester Square. The prime minister had been minding the rest of the family while Cherie was on a short break with Leo and her mother, staying with the British ambassador in Portugal. Given that the government was already embarked on its campaign against anti-social behaviour in general and underage binge drinking in particular, the news potential of the story was obvious. The involvement of the police made it all the more sensitive, firstly because it could be used to justify reporting the story and secondly because, as usual, unofficial police sources had ensured that their contacts in the media knew all about this juicy titbit.

It was a tabloid news story which would have been right up Campbell's street when he was a journalist, although by now he had turned against his own profession, as he confessed in his diary that year: 'Is it sensible to be at war with them? I wanted to undermine them, divide and rule.' On this occasion, he short-circuited competitive journalism, innuendo and exclusives by summoning all the main political correspondents, briefing them on the facts of the case and sanctioning the full reporting of the story immediately. I was now able to break the story on Sky News, which I duly did – commenting, when asked, that it was the sort of mishap many parents and children go through, that it had no political significance and was a matter for the family, likely to be a chastening experience for the boy concerned. Soon afterwards I learned that an anxious Mrs Blair had been watching the coverage in Lisbon, and that she thanked me for what I had said. Though it was clearly well intentioned, I tended to find such messages rather uncomfortable.

For Blair, 2004 was probably his most difficult year; certainly it was the only time he considered stepping down in his second term. The situation in Iraq was bloody; he had fallen out in Europe with Chirac and Schröder; Gordon Brown was restless and John Prescott had had to step in to referee. The reform agenda was going much more slowly than he had anticipated. And the pressure of seven years in the Downing Street 'goldfish bowl' was adding to the normal strain of growing up for his adolescent children. That spring, there was another crisis involving one of the Blairs' three teenagers. Once again the emergency services were involved, but this time there was none of the comic potential of Euan's earlier escapade.

As is sometimes the case, the press who already had the story leaked it to television and radio, in the hope that we would place it into the public domain, but on this occasion Downing Street, mainly represented by Hilary Coffman, was adamant and threatening that there should be no coverage. The Press Complaints Commission brokered an agreement of restraint on the grounds that the private life of a child is of paramount concern under the Editors' Code of Practice. There was a chance that family members could be damaged further by the revelation, so once again news organisations honoured their side of the bargain and did not report it. However, full details of what had happened were easily obtainable at the time and continued to be well known and discussed in media and political circles.

Cherie Blair was prompted to write a letter of thanks to some editors, but the media's behaviour ultimately earned them scant thanks and no respect from Tony and Cherie.

A few months later in September, informed speculation was rife that Blair had recently considered standing down as prime minister, and there was once again the risk that the suppressed story would come to light thanks to some unguarded comments, supposedly made in support of Blair by the TV star and Labour peer Melvyn Bragg. At the time, Bragg's wife, Cate Haste, was co-authoring a book with Cherie Blair titled *The Goldfish Bowl* about life at Number 10, so his comments were taken to be well informed. Bragg told Alastair Stewart on the ITV News channel (since defunct): 'The real stress was personal and family. My guess is that the considerations of his family became very pressing and that was what made him think things over very carefully. He was under colossal strain, you could see it. Another guess is that it was domestic rather than anything else, but not in any sense about him and Cherie.'

This prompted a fresh wave of press interest about the 'spring wobble'. In Ireland, the *Sunday Independent* named the child concerned and gave a partial account of what had happened, but the British press continued to hold back. Cherie Blair, however, went on the publicity circuit for her book, and some conspiracy theorists even alleged that Bragg's comments could have been designed to boost interest in it. When asked about Bragg on the *Richard and Judy* television show, she said: 'There never was a moment when Tony was going to resign, and, to be honest, I think he [Lord Bragg] is mortified that he said it . . . We can't always tell what goes on in men's minds; I wish we could.'

Blair was the first prime minister in more than a hundred years to bring up children in 10 Downing Street. (Chancellor Nigel Lawson had a young family at Number 11 during his six years as Chancellor of the Exchequer.) But far from making the Blairs exceptional, family life brought them closer to the experiences of the British electorate. Cherie Blair drew widespread sympathy when she talked about juggling competing demands, and her children leaving home, in her 'I Am Not Superwoman' speech at the end of 2002, following the involvement of Carole Caplin's conman boyfriend in her family's affairs. Even the Blairs' manipulation of the state education system to secure the best option for their children was no different from the behaviour of many other parents. If anything, exam and entrance criteria were probably more rigorously enforced for fear of showing favouritism to the prime minister's children. Certainly, the family felt this when Euan very narrowly missed his place at Oxford.

Difficulties over family life occurred because of Tony and Cherie Blair's ambivalent attitudes to the various 'understandings' governing their lives. Blair never accepted that he had entered into any deals on whose hospitality he should accept for holidays or what he should do with 'the kids' – they were his children and he would do and say what he wanted with them 'like any other parent'. At the same time, he resented any comments which this conduct gave rise to.

Cherie Blair was a more unpredictable and chimerical figure. Those she had dealings with never knew what she was going to do or say – and that applied as much to those who regarded her as a close friend as to journalists. Sometimes she could be gushing and obliging; at other times she would blank those she knew well or be downright rude to them. Without any publicity, she worked much harder for good causes that any other recent prime ministerial spouse, entertaining several times a week at Downing Street and making private visits. Yet one of those who knew her very well through just such unsung work also complained that with her private social engagements 'Cherie became very "Oh, can't we get someone to give us a private plane for that" as soon as she entered Downing Street.' This unpredictability extended to journalists with whom she would socialise and then tease or abuse (as she did in her final words to the press pack on leaving Number 10: 'I don't think we'll miss you'). When my first marriage ended, Cherie both rebuked me, and less than twenty-four hours later embraced me in public in front of a line of television cameras. She earned respect as the first truly working mother in Downing Street – and a brilliant barrister at that. Yet she allowed her career to take second place to her 'First Lady' activities. Cherie's politics were to the left of her husband's, and yet she seemed to aspire more to the trophies of success. She was a mass of contradictions – with the one cold certainty that there would be no way back for those who fell out with her. And in the end most people did.

Cherie's basic insecurity manifested itself in her troubled relationships with the women who worked for her and her husband, in particular Carole Caplin and Anji Hunter. Cherie Booth achieved great things in her own right, moving from a broken home in working-class Liverpool to the London School of Economics, the top of the class in the Bar exams and then success as a barrister. She had her own political ambitions too, unsuccessfully contesting Thanet North for Labour in the same 1983 election in which Blair became MP for Sedgefield. Since both could have ended up in Parliament at the same time, the couple's claim that they had a pact that there would be only one professional politician in the family and that the other would fall in behind the first to get elected sounds like a *post hoc* rationalisation.

It is fair to assume that Cherie, who was a post-1960s feminist, envisaged her adult life as a private career woman in her own right and not as a public wife, an appendage to someone else. She was unprepared for the attention attracted by her husband's political rise. As Tony Blair ventured out confidently on to the social circuit, she had just three sections to her wardrobe: casual clothes, black clothes for court and a single green frock for 'best'. It wasn't long before the Glenda Slaggs of the media started to contrast the dishy young MP with his dowdy wife. Carole Caplin came to the rescue. She offered to act not just as personal trainer but as a clothes stylist as well. Cherie's appearance started to provoke some favourable comments, and a friendship was born between the two women. Carole caused embarrassment to the Blairs because of her brief career as a topless model, her relationship with Peter Foster, a convicted conman, and because of her New Age beliefs. Campbell and Millar eventually succeeded in forcing her out of the inner circle, but she remained a more loyal and more discreet friend of the family than they did.

Anji Hunter had always been Tony Blair's friend. They first met as private school teenagers at a weekend party outside Edinburgh. Blair asked her to introduce him to another girl he had 'the hots for'. Their friendship continued once Blair went to Oxford University, Hunter was expelled from St Leonards in St Andrews for being 'agin the system'. So she completed her A-levels at the rather more liberal St Clare's in North Oxford, staying on in the city for some time afterwards. Blair's fellow Ugly Rumours band mate Mark Ellen was Hunter's long-term boyfriend. She was a guest at Tony and Cherie's marriage in 1980, held at his old college, St John's. In 1986 she joined Blair as his only parliamentary aide soon after his election and stayed working for him until late 2001, except for maternity leave and stints working for the Labour Party and Margaret Beckett MP.

Blair referred to Anji as 'my first defeat' in his private Labour leadership victory speech in 1994 and there has been much speculation about romantic ties between them, but in spite of a deep personal friendship both denied this absolutely and nobody has ever produced any evidence to contradict them.

Hunter, who was based in East Sussex, would often stay at the Blairs' home in Islington, sometimes sharing a bedroom with their young daughter Kathryn, until well into the 1990s. However, soon after Tony Blair became party leader, the pressure told, as tongues began to wag that Anji, unlike Cherie, was always polite, confident and well turned-out – the perfect 'office wife'. There was a showdown in a party conference hotel suite and Cherie made it clear to Anji that she was no longer welcome. Except when his wife was around, Blair totally ignored her injunction, but typically he did not openly challenge it.

Alastair Campbell and Anji Hunter were the two closest aides to Blair in his victorious 1997 general election campaign. Unlike Campbell, though, Hunter found she did not have a defined role in the new government. Cherie Blair did not invite her to the victory lunch she held in Number 10 Downing Street on 2 May 1997. Shortly afterwards she evicted Hunter from the office she was occupying with some secretaries, taking it over for her own purposes. Tony Blair left the matter to others to mediate and Michael Levy was involved in drawing up an unofficial contract circumscribing Hunter's activities.

On one occasion Cherie and her sidekicks Roz Preston and Fiona Millar summoned Anji Hunter to appear before them at a 'kangaroo court' to answer for her behaviour. The meeting took place at the Inns of Court and neither side told the prime minister about this emotional confrontation. Hunter's strategy was to put up with the cattiness which she regarded as a mere distraction from the political project she was engaged in. Contrary to the impression which both Levy and Cherie appeared to have formed, there was no question of her giving up and leaving in the early years in government. Instead, her role steadily built up as she acted as Blair's gatekeeper and office manager, and his eyes, ears and personal ambassador to cabinet ministers, Labour MPs, the party, the opposition, business, media proprietors and senior journalists.

Anji Hunter's family background was in business and she decided voluntarily to leave for the private sector towards the end of the first term. Blair successfully obstructed a move to British Airways and

also persuaded her to back out on a planned move to BP, with a
direct appeal, 'Are you in or out?' on the day he won his second
term. She regretted her decision not to move on almost immediately
and was due to announce her agreed departure in September 2001
– but then al-Qaeda intervened. Hunter did not finally leave Blair's
service until November of that year, becoming director of
communications for John Browne's BP.

The first time Anji and I remember talking to each other in
anything more than passing was during the Littleborough and
Saddleworth by-election campaign in the summer of 1995, brought
about by the death of the irrepressible Tory MP Geoffrey Dickens.
However, our relationship remained solely professional – contact to
contact – until 2001. We both agree that it would not have been
possible for our relationship to have developed in the way it did had
we each remained in our jobs as political correspondent and senior
government official. As it was, we married in July 2006, with both
our families and our five children in attendance. For all the pain
which the break-ups of our first marriages caused, I am profoundly
grateful that Anji made our marriage happen by having already
decided to leave Number 10.

By the time the Blairs left Number 10, Anji's relationship with
Cherie was back on a polite footing. Cherie and Millar, meanwhile,
had fallen out.

Tony Blair was a red-blooded heterosexual. If the trip in opposition
to News International's conference at Hayman Island was a highlight
of his career, this was partly because he and Campbell enjoyed ogling
the behind of the sexy air stewardess who tended to them in their
small private plane. Blair, however, was also a loving husband. Unlike
his predecessor, John Major, who had conducted a clandestine affair
whilst a minister with Edwina Currie, he never lived in the shadow
of an impending scandal. But for all the warmth of his marriage
and his family life, he had the ability to set it all to one side to talk
to his friends as if quite unattached or to retreat into himself, his
work, his religion – often by himself at Chequers.

9

BROWN

24 JUNE

I'm absolutely delighted to give my full support to Gordon as the next leader of the Labour Party and as prime minister and to endorse him fully. He has shown, as perhaps the most successful chancellor in our history, that he has the strength and the judgement to make a great prime minister.

Tony Blair, 11 May 2007

For an outgoing prime minister now openly counting his remaining days in office, 11 May 2007 had been a comparatively quiet and low-profile day. Blair held talks at Downing Street with President Talabani of Iraq and at last gave his full endorsement to Brown as party leader and prime minister. He then left the country, flying to Paris for meetings with two presidents: the departing Jacques Chirac and his incoming successor, the newly elected President Sarkozy. Tony and Nicolas were firm friends by now, and Blair was neither surprised nor dismayed that the president spent much of their private time together discussing his sex life. Sarkozy confided to the monogamous prime minister that he was unwilling to stop philandering, even though his second marriage to Cécilia was now under threat. Cécilia Sarkozy was already reluctant to become France's first lady. And within months of entering the Élysée, at the beginning of 2008, Sarkozy had divorced Cécilia and married the Franco-Italian singer and model Carla Bruni. Chirac cut a more dignified figure and graciously made a point of lingering over his goodbyes far longer than was usual, embracing the prime minister until they had to part.

But nobody paid much attention to Tony Blair that Friday; this was Gordon Brown's day. At last, thirteen years after the death of John Smith, the Brownites believed a wrinkle in history was being ironed out as Gordon Brown declared his candidacy for the leadership of the Labour Party (and by default the prime ministership).

For veterans of the Kinnock years and the rise of New Labour, Gordon Brown's campaign launch was an unwelcome blast from the past. The style and delivery of the event, both good and bad, demonstrated that control freakery would not die with Tony Blair.

The Brown campaign had had difficulty organising itself before his official declaration because of scrutiny of the activities of paid staff by the new media. In particular, the blogger Guido Fawkes had set up a 'Spadwatch' to ensure that 'spads' ('special advisers' being paid by the state as civil servants) were not moonlighting for any political campaign at the taxpayers' expense.

In a defensive move, Brown had declared that some of his staff would temporarily resign from the civil service to run his campaign, but it would have looked presumptuous for them to do so before he even became a candidate. Nobody wanted to 'do a Portillo' and install telephone lines for a campaign headquarters prematurely.

In his decade as chancellor, Brown had been particularly prone to relying on political staff, among whose ranks at one time or another were Ed Balls, Ian Austin and Ed Miliband, who all went on to become MPs and Labour ministers. His media relations were at first handled by Charlie Whelan, an ebullient former union press officer, but Whelan was forced out in the early years of government because neither Blair nor Campbell would tolerate his partisan, 'pro-Gordon' approach. Their opportunity arose in the autumn of 1997. Brown won the argument to keep the pound from joining the new euro currency, but Whelan paid the price after being overheard on

the phone in the Red Lion pub, opposite the Treasury, loudly briefing
against the prime minister.

Latterly, Brown had found an equally zealous media handler in
Damian McBride, who switched from the civil service to a political
job to better serve his master. Many of McBride's differences from
Whelan were superficial: he supported Arsenal rather than Spurs and
had modernised from phones and pagers to texts and email as his
chosen medium to abuse those insufficiently useful to the cause.
However, McBride remained on the Treasury's books as a special
adviser and a member of the official salariat and carefully refused to
brief on behalf of *Candidate* Brown.

The advance work for the launch therefore fell to Sue Nye,
Brown's chief assistant, and to younger volunteers. Nye escaped
scrutiny because she did not take a salary. She was married to the
economist Gavyn Davies, who had been placed 700th in the 2007
Sunday Times Rich List with an estimated fortune of £100 million.
The couple met in the 1970s when they were both working for
Prime Minister James Callaghan. Davies went on to make his fortune
in the Goldman Sachs flotation. During the Blair years he was attacked
as a 'Tony crony' when he was appointed chairman of the Board of
Governors of the BBC. He resigned following the Hutton Inquiry,
making no secret of his disillusionment with the Blair government.
Like Greg Dyke, the sacked BBC director general, his political
affections are believed to have strayed subsequently – at least as far
as the Liberal Democrats. None of this, however, affected Sue Nye's
relationship with Brown. Indeed, at the height of the David Kelly
imbroglio she was naturally placed to be an informal conduit between
the government and the Corporation.

Nye's style was modernistic and she chose a typical, glossy, New
Labour venue as her office. The Imagination Gallery off Tottenham
Court Road would have been an appropriate backdrop for any of
Labour's recent well-turned-out leaders: Neil Kinnock, John Smith
and Tony Blair (Nye worked for them all). It is a large, reconditioned
Victorian block now filled with showrooms and executive offices.

On Friday 11 May 2007, the building's forecourt was protected
by police and crash barriers; satellite broadcast vans ran down the

street opposite and the small, dedicated crowd gathered on the pavement were there to wait until Brown left that day (they also applauded the Channel 4 News anchor Jon Snow as he donned his bicycle helmet). Young men in sharp suits and ties and young women in black two-pieces guarded the entrances to the gallery. Journalists were firmly guided into a cramped holding pen, just off the main atrium, to wait and wait. The event started an hour late, partly so as not to clash with live television news coverage of the disappearance in Portugal of three-year-old Madeleine McCann.

Of course, a reconditioned building such as the Imagination Gallery had an atrium. Gordon Brown's refurbished new Treasury on Horse Guards Parade had one too. Once, these spaces had been dingy lighting-wells open to the elements; now they were roofed over and their brick walls refaced. Such atriums sat well with Gordon Brown's ethos: nineteenth-century functionality put to a practical contemporary use. In the Treasury, brightly coloured abstract art of no obvious merit stretched down three floors of brick wall. In the atrium of the Imagination Gallery a massive banner hung over the banisters. GORDON BROWN FOR BRITAIN it declared, above a Union Jack superimposed on near-silhouettes of unidentifiable, multi-racial children.

The precise venue for the launch was another converted space, this time at the top of the building: a long, narrow gallery with plate-glass walls and a ceiling of stretched plastic sheeting held taught by steel wires – Dome-style. The event was neither a press conference nor a rally but an uneasy hybrid of the two. With the enthusiastic, clapping supporters at the front, the phalanx of dispassionate reporters was forced to sit some rows back, below the raised platform for the television cameras.

Brown wasted no time. In the opening sentences of his speech he paid his dues to Blair and, as was only proper, welcomed the idea of a contest (two left-wing MPs, Michael Meacher and John McDonnell, were still trying to muster sufficient nominations): 'Today I announce that I am a candidate to lead the Labour Party and to lead a new government. Tony Blair has led our country for ten years with distinction – with courage, passion and insight . . . My task is to show that I have the vision and the experience to earn the trust of the British people . . . let me say I welcome any other candidate who wishes to stand . . .'

But as Brown himself said, he needed to show he had 'new ideas', effectively to differentiate himself from Blair. He went on to lay out the themes particular to him – most of which were familiar by now. First he opined on Britishness, the inclusive Brownite anti-venom for the Scottish questions: 'Britain is a great country . . . The Britain I believe in is a Britain of fairness and opportunity for all . . .'

Then came the comparisons with Blair, how Prime Minister Brown would be different and also how he would be the same. 'For me, being New Labour means that as challenges change we must change too.' The use of the term 'New Labour' was significant. Sometimes, notably in his 2003 conference speech, Brown had been shy of using it as he courted favour widely within the party, almost as if to face down the reality that, in practice and ideology, he had been one of the main instigators of the rebranding. Now throughout his leadership bid, Brown was to say 'New Labour' again and again, reclaiming from Blair the foundations by which he intended to govern and declining to leave any election blandishments hostage to New Labour's enemies. He pledged to continue with Blair's programmes on education, health, climate change and 'with the challenge of terrorism . . . strong in defence and security'.

He promised new practical policy reforms, including a draft Queen's speech, and increased parliamentary accountability – especially on going to war. But he avoided dramatic new ideas or promises to divert from Blair's policy agenda. Instead the man's style, it seemed, was the point – the justifier of change. Brown suggested that his style of governing would be very different: ' When you fall short, you listen . . . As a politician I have never sought the public eye for its own sake. I have never believed presentation should be the substitute for policy. I do not believe politics is about style.' Without mentioning Blair, this was still pointed stuff, the more so as he talked of his father, 'a minister of the church' and the moral 'compass which has guided me through each stage of my life'. Blair had liked to keep his beliefs private and usually skirted around detailed exposition of what motivated him in politics.

By accident, the clumsy execution of Brown's launch mirrored the change of style he was hinting at. The event was not slick. As a teenager, Gordon Brown permanently lost the sight in one eye as a result of a rugby injury. He found it hard to read speeches. Even when they were printed for him in extra large type, he had to look down. Audiences typically saw more of the top of his head than his face. For the launch, a clear glass autocue reflector screen was attached to the podium so that he could read from it and keep his head up. Unfortunately, the screen had to be placed so centrally that it obscured most of his face for most of the time. It was not possible to shoot round the screen because the room was so narrow and the cameras were placed so far back. The television professionals had pointed out the problem to the organisers beforehand but, with typical New Labour bossiness, they were told no changes were allowed.

After his statement, Brown took questions exhaustively for more than half an hour. The very first questioner expressed ennui at the prospect of 'the same old faces in different jobs', but Brown was excited not bored; nor was he drawing back from his partnership with Blair. He cited the words that 'Tony, who is my friend' had been prompted to say about his chancellor that morning during his photo-op with President Talabani and equated them to 'nomination'. He suggested that in Iraq the need was more to 'win hearts and minds' through 'political reconciliation and economic development' than to change strategy. Most intriguingly, he declined to explain what he meant by 'reaching outside' to form a 'government of all the talents'.

The first task of a candidate for the Labour leadership is to secure the requisite number of nominations from MPs (15 per cent of the parliamentary party) to allow his or her name to go forward to a postal ballot of an electoral college made up of party members, party representatives in Parliament and affiliated trade unionists. Brown's message to his MPs was direct (and notably similar to Blair's appeal in 1994) – under his leadership Labour stood the best chance of winning the next general election, which meant he was their best chance of being re-elected. To underline this point, Gordon Brown spent the rest of the day touring marginal constituencies around

London, using public transport when he could. So the Brown campaign wagon rolled through Stevenage and Watford – two seats captured in the 1997 landslide by women, Barbara Follett and Claire Ward, who were prominent Brown supporters – before moving on to Enfield Southgate, the totemic constituency lost to Labour by the Conservative cabinet minister Michael Portillo in 1997 but which had been regained from the Labour minister Stephen Twigg by the Tory David Burrowes in 2005.

Thus, for all the printer's ink spilt and the evident angst of the two protagonists, the partnership between Gordon Brown and Tony Blair ultimately delivered what had been its original main objective: a peaceful transition from one man to the other with both getting their chance to be prime minister. Undoubtedly, there had been moments of near homicidal rage between the two men; times when Brown wanted to drive Blair out of office and times when Blair probably, and Cherie certainly, wondered whether there was an alternative to Brown following on. But as their working relationship ended, it was evident that these negative feelings had never come to a head; neither Brown nor Blair had ever gone nuclear. Blair had not sacked Brown or even moved him from his powerful position as chancellor (not least because he relied on Brown and could not think of anyone who would have been a better finance minister). Brown had not resigned from the government and openly challenged Blair (a marked contrast to the way in which the interactions between Margaret Thatcher, Geoffrey Howe and Nigel Lawson eventually undid her government). In many ways, it could be said that the Blair–Brown relationship provided the creative tension which helped drive New Labour.

The (non) deal

Gordon Brown was the first to give way by deciding not to contest the leadership against Tony Blair following John Smith's death on 12 May 1994. Ever since, journalists, biographers and even film-makers have speculated on the nature of 'the deal' which led to Tony

Blair having a clear run for the leadership (though not an uncontested one, as Brown was to enjoy in 2007. In 1994 Margaret Beckett and John Prescott were nominated and ran as candidates for the leadership). Most of this speculation was redundant because, ever since the days when they shared the same small office as freshmen MPs, almost all of Blair and Brown's conversations had been conducted in private, one-on-one, and no written record had been kept. Their advisers most often likened their working relationship to a political marriage. Behind closed doors much was said, and most probably left unsaid, between Blair and Brown, but the two men disclosed little about their understandings to outsiders – and what they did say was usually self-serving and sometimes contradictory.

In any case, since Prime Minister Blair was eventually followed by Prime Minister Brown, it could be argued that the deal, such as it might have been, was eventually delivered. As Tony Blair had often suggested, all Gordon had to do was wait – even if he had to wait much longer than he had expected.

It was not difficult to predict that Tony Blair was going to become the leader in May 1994. The day of Smith's death, I and many of my colleagues were at a Conservative Party conference in Inverness. When I finally arrived back at our Westminster studio in the early afternoon, I found Michael White of the *Guardian* waiting to be interviewed: 'Well?' he said. 'It's got to be Blair–Prescott,' I replied. 'Just wanted to check,' Michael said. What struck us as stunningly obvious, however, was not how it felt to those intimately involved.

There was no deal – no explicit undertaking by Blair to give way to Brown at an agreed time – but the understandings and misunderstandings of the leadership contest were entirely consistent with the psychological natures of the two men.

Blair was in Scotland when he heard the news of John Smith's fatal heart attack. The call came through while Blair was being driven from Aberdeen's Dyce airport into the city to deliver a speech at the outset of Labour's European election campaign. The television cameras caught up with him on his way back to London. He paid tribute to Smith: 'I think the whole country will feel the loss, and our thoughts and prayers go out to Elizabeth and the family. It's simply devastating.'

Nobody doubted that Blair mourned Smith and felt deeply for his wife and their three daughters, but, compared to the outpouring of emotion and tears from many who spoke that day, Blair was remarkably controlled and dry-eyed, almost clipped. The television pictures showed a determined man moving towards his destiny.

Appropriately, for two Scots-born men, Blair and Brown largely reached their understanding about the leadership in Edinburgh rather than at their famous Granita dinner in Islington, Blair's adopted London home. Edinburgh was a frequent location for their most intimate meetings during the 1990s. Brown's home base in Queensferry was nearby but they usually met on neutral territory provided by friends.

Decency dictated that open planning for leadership campaigns could not begin until John Smith had been buried and mourned. Officially, the campaigns were not launched until 10 June, almost a full month after the leader's death, but the leadership was effectively decided in the fraught run-up to Smith's funeral, in a series of talks at a range of venues, including the London home of Blair's brother Bill. (The limelight-avoiding barrister was appointed a High Court judge in early 2008. He and his Chinese wife, Katy, provided strong support behind the scenes. Cherie Blair agreed to become patron of the Chinese for Labour society. The prime minister also had a sister Sarah who stayed out of the public gaze from first to last.) It is a measure of the closeness between the two men at the time that many of those who helped them had gone from being Blair's friends to being friends of them both. Their hosts included acquaintances of Anji Hunter and two of Blair's closest friends from Fettes, Amanda Mackenzie-Stuart and Nick Ryden.

Mackenzie-Stuart had been the first girl admitted to Fettes and is recorded as Blair's 'first girlfriend'; during his last 'Oxbridge' term, Blair's new school housemaster, Eric Anderson, allowed him to stay at the home of her father, Lord Mackenzie-Stuart, a judge. By 1994, he had been appointed president of the European Court of Justice in Luxembourg. Amanda made her father's vacant flat by Dean Bridge in central Edinburgh available to Blair and Brown to continue their tortuous discussions in complete privacy.

Ryden was a lifelong friend of Blair and godfather to his youngest son, Leo. Both had been in Arniston House at Fettes, and over the years, Ryden was reliably trotted out to reminisce about the future prime minister's schooldays. After one colourful account of corporal punishment back then, Ryden was amused to receive an official inquiry from Strathclyde Police who were contemplating launching a child abuse investigation. Ryden had remained in Scotland, choosing to go to Aberdeen University. His family were the founders of Ryden's the Edinburgh estate agents, but he himself had chosen to be a partner in Shepherd and Wedderburn solicitors, although his field was property. Ryden also liked to recount how, at the height of his difficult talks with Blair, Brown went to the bathroom, only to have to phone Blair for help because he had locked himself in.

The nub of the understanding which emerged was actually born out of the absence of a deal.

The two rising politicians had always agreed that they would never stand against each other. There would be no point in a potentially destructive competition because of their friendship and because of the similarity of their political aspirations.

For nearly ten years after they met in 1983, their common assumption was that the leading figure in the relationship would be Brown. Indeed, the first inclination of a shift in the power balance came in 1992, when Brown rejected Blair's suggestion that he should stand for the vacancy left when Neil Kinnock resigned as leader following Labour's defeat in the general election. However, once again displaying the absence of a killer instinct which had prolonged his efforts to get into Parliament, Gordon Brown chose to defer loyally to John Smith, backing him for the leadership. Tony Blair followed suit, calculating that he was not yet politically strong enough to mount his own challenge, although one measure of his ambition was that he very nearly launched a campaign for the deputy leadership.

The 1992 campaign had damaged Brown in another way as well. Two reasons are generally given for Labour's failure to overcome John Major's divided and failing Conservative government: the unelectability of Neil Kinnock and the shadow Budget. As Smith's *de facto* number two, Brown was deeply implicated in this latter controversy. The pair had trooped over to a suitably parliamentary-style panelled room in the Institute of Mechanical Engineers where Smith had delivered his speech as if he were already chancellor. It was a piece of theatrical presentation dreamed up by Peter Mandelson. The problem lay in the substance of what Smith had to say, which amounted to significant increases in taxes for middle-income families and upward – in return for no particular promised improvements in public services. (Even the much maligned Kinnock realised this was an error and attempted to soften the tax implications over dinner with journalists at Luigi's, an Italian restaurant in Covent Garden. An incandescent Smith then forced Kinnock to recant publicly the qualifications he had given. A fictionalised version of this supplied the action of David Hare's play *Absence of War*. Hare was given privileged access to the Labour campaign in 1992. Kinnock and Smith were pretty easily identifiable as the hero 'George Jones' and the anti-hero 'Malcolm Pryce'. The play did not feature Blair or Brown surrogates.)

Brown remained absolutely loyal to Smith although he may have had private doubts about the shadow Budget package. Perhaps conveniently for him, reports began to circulate that Brown had muttered, 'You have just lost us the fucking election' to the shadow chancellor as they left their presentation. And it is remarkable that he and Blair did almost precisely the opposite in the campaign they led five years later, when they guaranteed both public service improvements and no income tax increases. However, at the time Brown had little alternative but to champion the policy.

Smith succeeded Kinnock in 1992, supported by both Brown and Blair. Brown became shadow chancellor and Blair shadow home secretary, but over the next couple of years Blair shone more brightly as a political star. The Major government was effectively finished off within months of its re-election by the Black Wednesday economic crisis of 16 September 1992. But neither Brown nor Smith was able to exploit this to his personal advantage because both had been strong supporters of Britain's membership of the European Exchange Rate Mechanism. Brown cut a slightly tarnished, or at any rate shop-soiled, figure.

By contrast, the charismatic Blair found himself up against Michael Howard, a clever but manipulative home secretary. The two men had already shadowed each other at energy and would go on to do so again when Blair was prime minister and Howard became leader of the opposition. They were both barristers and respected each other; they even formed a polite friendship which led to dinners at each other's homes. Such cross-party socialising would have been unthinkable for Brown. For all their camaraderie, though, Blair often got the better of Howard with the direct populist appeal of his 'tough on crime, tough on the causes of crime' initiatives.

There was also a suggestion that Blair had begun to doubt Brown – not for his beliefs but for his lack of resolve. Tony Blair's father-in-law, the reliably indiscreet actor Tony Booth, has since offered his version of this: 'Tony thinks Brown's a blinker. Someone who gives way in a stand-off. Tony never blinks, no matter who he meets,' Booth told the *Mail on Sunday* as he linked this opinion directly to Blair's decision to run for the leadership. 'The truth is that both Brown and Smith treated Tony like a junior partner and contemptuously called him "the boy" as they prepared for power. Even at John Smith's funeral Brown tried to humiliate Tony. When Tony arrived he found himself in a pew behind a big pillar while Brown and the rest had prime positions in full view of the TV cameras and so on.' This is an analysis of Brown which chimes with those others who have portrayed him as a 'ditherer' and a 'bottler'. In spite of these mounting doubts, it would not have been in Blair's nature to bring about unpleasantness by mentioning them to his friend Gordon.

By May 1994, many in the media had already elected Blair as Labour leader-in-waiting. He was well aware of this because of the frequent requests for access which came in from journalists. At his meetings with Brown in Scotland, Blair was explicit – as far as he was concerned their pact not to stand against each other still remained but he, Blair, was going to stand for the leadership. Effectively, he told Brown that he was the stronger candidate of the two and as such demanded a clear run.

There was no deal because Brown left without accepting what

Blair had said. Unlike his rival, Brown had been in two minds about standing, even though he seems initially to have assumed that Blair would support him. Brown had consulted with his friends and allies but he had not found the level of explicit support which he had anticipated, especially from the cross-section of friends he had in common with Blair.

Blair's determination to stand turned the tables on Brown. The younger man had got in first, which meant that if Brown now stood he ran the risk of being seen as disloyal or a splitter. Or worse even than that perhaps, there was the real chance that he could be defeated by Blair. Blair's decisiveness had left Brown in the weaker position of being a potential challenger. At some point in the second half of May, acceptance of Blair's argument dawned on Brown and he made the lonely decision that he was not going to stand. He was bowing to the better part of valour since a Gallup poll of Labour Party members for the BBC's *On the Record* programme on 30 May showed Blair's strength: Blair 47 per cent, Prescott 15 per cent, Brown 11 per cent, Beckett 5 per cent, Cook 3 per cent, Don't know 19 per cent. (Ever since, Brownites have argued that this is irrelevant because Brown would have had most of Blair's 47 per cent had Blair done the decent thing and not put his name forward. But that is to ignore the overwhelming evidence that Blair was a much more popular choice than Brown.)

The next day, 31 May 1994, Blair and Brown had their infamous dinner at Granita restaurant in Islington. Stephen Frears made an excellent television film of *The Deal* with the same writer, Peter Morgan, and the same actor as Blair, Michael Sheen, who would go on to make the Oscar-winning movie *The Queen*. Vikki Leffman, the restaurant owner who served Blair and Brown that Tuesday evening, has subsequently disputed just about every detail in the film: the table layout, the menu, the tablecloths, what they ate and drank, how many courses they had, etc.

More substantively the deal was not done at Granita. Brown had already accepted that he would not stand, although he had not officially stated it yet. The Granita meeting was about how Blair could placate Brown and get him on board for the campaign to come. Blair was instinctively inclined to conciliate (once he had got his own way) and he still had high regard for Brown's talents, readily accepting that he needed him at the heart of his team. However, in placating Brown, Blair made two strategic mistakes. Firstly, he ceded too much power to his future chancellor, allowing him unprecedented authority over domestic policy. Secondly, he did not stand against Brown and beat him. Had he done so, it is difficult to see how the senses of entitlement and grievance could have taken such poisonous hold in the breasts of Brown and his supporters. But did Blair expressly state that the job could be Brown's after a set period of time? That seems most unlikely given Blair's instinctive precision with words. That same verbal facility, however, may well have left Brown with the impression that he had been given some kind of assurance.

For sure, during his period as opposition leader, Blair made no secret of his view that the eight years, two successive four-year terms, served by an American president was 'about right' as the period of time he would want to be prime minister. He sympathised with the difficulty that had faced Margaret Thatcher, arguing that it had been a mistake to say she would go on and on, but that she had been forced into it for fear of seeming weak. He was determined not to repeat her mistake, even if that meant admitting that he was mortal. At the same time, Blair also pointed out to Brown that they were both still relatively young men in their forties. There should be plenty of time for both of them.

But unlike American presidents, British prime ministers are not legally term-limited. Had there been no attacks on 11 September 2001, would Blair have left at the end of his second term? He certainly believed so and still considered going in the 'wobbly year' of 2004. He also admitted that his big projects were only kicking in at the end of his second term and he wanted to see them through. But perhaps it is more likely that he would have been beset by the delusion of indispensability which seems to take over most politicians in office.

At Granita terms of some kind were understood, if not quite explicitly agreed. The following afternoon, Peter Mandelson rang me to say that Gordon Brown was putting out a statement that he would not be a candidate for the leadership and that he was backing Tony Blair for the job. That evening, Blair and Brown staged one of the most awkward picture opportunities ever witnessed in British politics. They came out into New Palace Yard, apparently walking and talking together. The great advantage of this location was that it is within the precincts of the Palace of Westminster, where cars drive in by Big Ben and where no television cameras are allowed. We were forced to stay on long lenses the other side of the fence in Parliament Square – out of earshot or even question-shouting distance.

I had heard the news of Brown's withdrawal while covering a campaign poster unveiling by Robin Cook. No friend of Brown, Cook, who ended up running Blair's campaign, was immediately at me to know just who it was who had called. He was especially eager to find out if it was Peter Mandelson. The manoeuvrings around Blair and Brown in the summer of 1994 have subsequently acquired an almost mythic reputation as the model of treachery and double-dealing, especially among supporters of Gordon Brown. It did not feel like that at the time. From the beginning, Blair was the obvious candidate. But many of the prominent New Labour figures, those who would eventually support him, were genuinely in conflict with themselves because of their sympathy and admiration for Brown. At the time, Mandelson considered himself to be working for Brown. I remember a conversation with Mandelson in which I teased him about his divided loyalties; he claimed that he had not yet worked out who he would support. There is no doubt that Brown expected Mandelson to support him but that is not the same as Mandelson having broken his word. The opinion researcher Philip Gould faced exactly the same choices as Mandelson and went the same way, to Blair. Gould's friendship with Brown certainly suffered as a result, yet he never faced the same opprobrium as Mandelson.

During the first term, Blair's supporters took a relaxed view on Brown, sometimes depicting him as a tragically deluded figure complete with 'psychological flaws'. But 9/11 renewed Blair's sense of purpose. It was from then on that Gordon Brown's impatience mounted.

In his valedictory speech to the Labour Party conference in 2006, Blair went out of his way to praise his chancellor: 'I know that New Labour would never have happened, and three election victories would never have been secured, without Gordon Brown. He is a remarkable man. A remarkable servant to this country. And that is the truth.' (A day earlier Brown's attempts to compliment Blair in his speech, prompted Mrs Blair to remark, 'Well, that's a lie,' according to one report taken up by the media.) But Tony Blair also expressed deep frustration with his own time in power: 'Every time I've ever introduced a reform in government, I wish in retrospect I had gone further.' These two remarks encapsulate the two sides of his working partnership with Gordon Brown. Throughout the ten years, most in Downing Street regarded Brown as an obstacle to the policies with which they wished to transform Britain.

Brown successfully derailed proper discussion of whether Britain should join the launch of the euro currency. He imposed the straitjacket of his interpretation of the Wanless Report on Tony Blair's spending pledges on the NHS. He gave speeches which seemed to question expanding the involvement of the private sector in public services while enthusiastically backing private finance initiatives, which took public sector debt off the government's books.

At the annual party conference, Brown's slot was always just before lunch on Monday. The prime minister spoke after the lunch break the next day. The chancellor's speeches became performance art, live barometers of how his rivalry with Blair was faring.

He came closest to open insurrection at Bournemouth in 2003.

The platform was already set for a turbulent week. It faced two difficult votes on health and housing which it could lose because of trade union unrest. Brown was in no mood to help Blair out. The chancellor's speech was an overt appeal to the sympathies of dissident Labour activists. As his refrain, he chose: 'Best when we are Labour'. There was no mention this time of New Labour. Instead, his slogan could be taken only as a calculated rebuff to Blair's conference speech of the previous year when he had defended New Labour reforms with the catchphrase 'At our best when at our boldest'. In Bournemouth, Blair had no alternative but to retaliate. His leader's speech the following day was one of his more melodramatic performances. He spoke surrounded by a live backdrop of supporters, earning a standing ovation shortly after he began by declaring: 'I can only go one way. I've not got a reverse gear.'

In January 2004, Brown quite literally held the government to ransom over the introduction of top-up tuition fees. When the government attempted to introduce these in direct contradiction of a 2001 Labour manifesto pledge, it faced the biggest backbench rebellion since 1945. Eventually it won by just five votes. Brown made no secret of the fact that the government had been saved only by the delivery of his personal vote. As a reporter, that day I had the surreal experience of dealing with two government whipping operations, one loyal to Number 10 Downing Street, the other to Number 11. The official camp knew that they would survive only when the Brownites stated that their tally pointed to a government victory.

Yet Brown's simmering discontent never quite became white hot. As Alexander Pope put it in another context, he appeared 'willing to wound, and yet afraid to strike'. He came to the rescue of Blair and Labour in 2005 by campaigning jointly with his rival in the run-up to the general election. It cannot have been too hard for Brown to make this decision in his own self-interest. Blair had by now already indicated that there would be a handover of power during the third term, but there would be no power to hand over unless Labour won the election.

The renewed partnership in 2005 resulted in some painfully stilted public performances by the two men, including Blair pursuing an unwilling Brown with an ice-cream cone he had just bought for him. A party political broadcast, directed by the Oscar-winning director Anthony Minghella, was designed to show that the two could talk naturally to each other, but it had obviously taken so long to make that there was no attempt at continuity of clothes or location. Yet Brown came through for Blair on the crucial question that was costing Labour votes: Iraq.

Labour held its business manifesto launch at the data service company Bloomberg's London headquarters. The event was overshadowed by the release the previous evening of Attorney General Goldsmith's advice on the legality of the war. Brown had never put himself forward to defend the Iraq adventure, although he had voted for it as a member of the government and had made the right noises when he had little alternative. But now as Blair and Brown were sitting side by side, there could be no escape. The inevitable question was asked: in the same circumstances would Brown have taken the country to war? The chancellor didn't flinch. 'Yes,' he replied simply, much to the distress of the reporter who had asked the question. Blair was clearly much relieved as Brown then continued: 'I not only trust Tony Blair but I respect Tony Blair for the way he went about that decision.' Precious little wriggle room there.

If Brown never struck against Blair fatally, though, Blair never quite eliminated Brown either. He would complain about Gordon and even sometimes wind him up, teasing him to his face in front of Number 10 officials. Blair had at least as good a sense for what Philip Gould called 'eye-catching initiatives', even if he hadn't thought of them himself, but after the election in 2001 when he most probably had the political strength, and after 2005 when he almost certainly didn't, Blair declined to move against Brown. Plans may have been drawn up, but he made no serious attempt either to remove Brown as chancellor or to curb the power of the Treasury. Instead, to the deep frustration of many departmental ministers, Blair allowed Brown to keep his independent powerbase while trying to work around it by building alternative structures of his own.

The coup

When it came, the final push against Tony Blair was not orchestrated by Gordon Brown. He was, however, consulted about it once it was underway and sought to benefit from it. The instigators of the attempted coup to force Blair to set a date for departure were all strong supporters of Gordon Brown. And, as one Blairite in Brown's first cabinet remarked to me afterwards, 'attempted coup' was probably a misnomer because the coup worked: Blair named his time of departure within days of 'surviving' the attack against him.

After the event some – including David Miliband, who said as much during a BBC Radio interview at the height of the crisis – claimed Blair always intended that the 2006 conference should be his last. That may have been so. But floating the idea to confidants was very different from making a declaration of intent, as Blair was forced to do in September 2006.

Blair's authority was already being sapped by the Metropolitan Police inquiry into cash for peerages, but the summer of 2006 was made unusually difficult for Labour by the war over Lebanon between Israel and Hezbollah. The United Nations, and most European governments, agreed that the Israeli response to the rocket attacks, incursions and kidnappings originating from across the Lebanese border was 'disproportionate'. Supportive as ever of the US government, Blair refused to join in the condemnation, calling instead for restraint by both sides. This was not how public opinion, let alone progressive opinion, saw it. But Blair was by now convinced that he was right, regardless of political sensitivities. He took the same attitude into a back-to-work interview with *The Times* for publication on 1 September. Asked about his plans for standing down, he suggested resignation was far from his current thoughts: 'I have said I will leave ample time for my successor. Now at some point I think people have got to accept that as a reasonable proposition and let me get on with the job.'

These comments were the final straw for a group of malcontented Midlands MPs loosely linked to the West Bromich East MP and junior minister Tommy Watson. Many of them had come under pressure from Muslim constituents and felt their own seats were in danger. Over the summer they had talked about sending a letter to Blair demanding clarity on his future. As it happened, they had already scheduled for that Friday a meeting/end-of-holiday pub-crawl/balti-house blowout to discuss their grievances. The group agreed a plan whereby members from the 2001 intake (MPs first elected at the 2001 general election), led by Watson and Siôn Simon, a disillusioned Blairite loyalist, would send a letter to Blair asking for his departure. The hope was that further letters would be sent by other MPs from the 1997 and 2005 intakes. If after all this there was still no satisfactory response, waves of ministerial resignations would follow. Simon drafted the letter and it began to circulate via a dead-letter email address that he had set up. It stated: 'Sadly it is clear to us – as it is to almost the entire party and the country – that without an urgent change in the leadership of the party it becomes less likely that we will win the next election . . . This is the brutal truth . . . We therefore ask you to stand aside.'

Over the weekend, some MPs who had been approached tipped off Number 10 about the plot and the contents of the letter. Watson, meanwhile, suddenly decided that he needed a break in Scotland and cast around amongst his contacts for a decent hotel. Conveniently, the Midlands Mafia could oblige and Watson was found a room at a golfing hotel, the Fairmont St Andrews, run by Steven Carter, a former manager of the Birmingham Holiday Inn (not to be confused with the strategy chief Stephen Carter appointed by Gordon Brown in January 2008). While in Scotland, Tommy Watson paid a visit to Gordon Brown's home in Queensferry – a purely social call, he insisted, to present Fraser, Brown's recently born younger son, with a *Postman Pat* video.

Blair was out of town – first at his annual Balmoral weekend with the Queen and then at a speaking engagement in Leeds – but his officials, headed by Ben Wegg-Prosser and Ruth Turner, proposed a fight back with a counter letter to be signed by loyalists. Blair's parliamentary private secretary, Keith Hill, took charge of this, backed up by the chief whip, Jacqui Smith. Karen Buck, MP for Regents Park and Kensington North, one of the 'Blair Babes' who had won her seat in the 1997 landslide, agreed to be the chief signatory. Wegg-Prosser and David Hill both briefed journalists that Brown was believed to be behind the plot, pointing out that Brown's most prominent henchman, Ed Balls MP, had spent the whole of Monday 4 September working from his room in the House of Commons even though Parliament was in recess and he had his own ministerial office in his department. Ian Austin MP, another Brown acolyte, had also been highly active.

The crisis peaked on the Wednesday when Blair and Brown had two lengthy meetings in Downing Street. During the initial breakfast-time encounter Brown was sullen and threatening. Shortly after the meeting ended Tommy Watson told the media that he was resigning from his post in the government. Blair managed to get his retaliation in first by releasing a statement that declared, 'I had been intending to dismiss him' for being 'disloyal, discourteous and wrong'. Khalid Mahmood, a parliamentary private secretary who had long expressed his disquiet, then quit, followed by a further five junior ranking ministers.

By the time the chancellor and the prime minister met again in the afternoon, both were pulling back from the brink. They agreed on the terms of public statements to be issued the next day. Brown said that he would support Blair to go in his own time, but the prime minister made the bigger concession, agreeing to announce that he would stand down within the next twelve months. Brown was caught on camera driving away from the second meeting with a broad grin on his face. He later claimed his jollity was due to thinking 'about my new baby' rather than the conversation he had just had with the prime minister.

The following day both men were true to their word, making apparently spontaneous statements to the television cameras even though no reporters were allowed near to ask questions. Brown delivered his part of the bargain in Glasgow, Blair his at Quinton Kynaston School in St John's Wood, London. The prime minister began by apologising for the behaviour of the Labour Party, saying the conduct of the past week 'has not been our finest hour to be frank'. He insisted, 'I'm not going to set a precise date now,' but confirmed what was already an open secret – the coming 2006 party conference would be his last. Tony Blair's successor would be in place by September 2007 at the latest.

To his admirers, Blair's third term, his final two years in office, were his best. With little left to lose, he acquired a ruthless edge which enabled him to drive through decisions he believed in and to dragoon Gordon Brown into supporting them. These included Adair Turner's report on the reform of the pensions system, which had been bitterly resented by the Treasury; the commitment to renew the nuclear deterrent, which was actually announced by Gordon Brown during a CBI dinner (Rosyth dockyard being a big employer for his constituency); and approval in principle for a new generation of nuclear power stations. John Reid and Brown reached agreement on a budget for the Home Office and on the major decision to split the department in two. Blair brokered a budget settlement for the EU and Blair and Brown claimed victory over the red lines they had defended for Britain in the new EU Reform Treaty. Finally, Brown committed himself to the highly contentious military deployments in Iraq and Afghanistan.

All this was achieved while the ritual of the orderly transfer of the Labour leadership from Blair to Brown proceeded without a hitch. It almost seemed as though the establishment of the takeover as fact liberated the two men to rediscover the political ideology they shared, now that personal rivalries were irrelevant.

Gordon Brown soon had all the security he could have asked for. His period as an official candidate lasted less than a week after he put his name forward – just time to record a humble interview with the BBC presenter Andrew Marr, a Scot and former editor of the liberal-left *Independent* newspaper with whom Brown felt comfortable. By the following Wednesday, almost the entire Labour contingent in the Commons had bowed to the inevitability of Brown's election. On 16 May, just as Blair was arriving at the White House for his last visit to the Bushes, Brown secured his 313th MP nomination. Since there were only 352 MPs available and since they could nominate only one candidate, this meant that there was no longer a sufficient quorum available to nominate anyone else. John McDonnell, the left-wing MP for Hayes and Harlington, and the only other contender still in the race, admitted defeat. Tony Blair would not step down until the last week of June, but there would be no contest. Gordon Brown was now Labour leader elect and, thanks to Labour's unshakeable majority in Parliament, prime minister elect.

In a statement, Brown told the voters (who would now not get the chance to be consulted on his elevation): 'I am truly humbled.

I will strive to earn your trust.' He promised 'a new government with new priorities', saying, 'I will work hard for you. This is who I am. And I will do my best for the people of Britain.'

There were some demands that Blair should step aside immediately for the new prime minister, but he made it clear that he intended to stick to his timetable of a 27 June departure. In this he got the support of President Bush, who told their joint White House press conference: 'He's got a lot to do 'til he finishes. He's going to sprint to the finish.' Much more significantly – but entirely in character with their long and tortured relationship – Brown also declined to try to push Blair out when presented with a chance to do so. 'I've always said that Tony Blair should have the right because of the service he's given to this country to make his announcement and do things in the time he wants to do. I'm very happy to honour his wishes in this matter.'

Although certain of victory, Brown continued to campaign for the job – a task which coincided with the promotional tour for his book, *Courage*. Aided by his old university friend Colin Currie and a researcher, Brown had been inspired to write the eight short pen portraits of personal heroes and heroines following the death of his first child, Jennifer Jane, who had lived for just ten days following her premature birth in December 2001. On 26 May 2007, while Blair was giving his farewell party for staff at Chequers, Brown was on the stage at the Hay Festival of Literature in the Welsh Borders. He cut a somewhat uneasy figure in blazer, open-necked shirt, chinos and black socks and shoes but managed to smile and joke with his interviewer, Mariella Frostrup, and dealt politely with a predictable volley of questions about the Iraq War. The event was judged a triumph and Ms Frostrup was booked to host another Q&A later in the year, this time with the new prime minister at the Labour Party conference.

Before then Labour had to call yet another conference to crown the new leader. For a second party conference running, Labour assembled in Manchester on Sunday 24 June. As they had the previous October, delegates marvelled at the regenerated city centre around them, rebuilt under Blair's administration. The last time they had been in Manchester their task had been to bury Blair; this time the conference was to announce the outcome of the elections for the new leader and deputy leader. Gordon Brown and Tony Blair shook hands in front of a giant back-projected Union Jack as Blair relinquished the party leadership but not, for a few days yet, the premiership.

The excitement at the leadership conference was provided by the election of Harriet Harman as deputy leader in place of John Prescott. Harman beat Alan Johnson, Peter Hain, Hilary Benn, Jon Cruddas and Hazel Blears in a contest which would leave a nasty aftertaste for Labour because of the inability of some of the candidates, notably Hain and Harman, to manage their campaign finances in accordance with electoral law. Harman owed her success to backing from prominent Brownite supporters headed by the Ed Balls–Yvette Cooper political power couple. Had just three MPs switched away from her, she would have lost to Alan Johnson.

There was also a hint of payback. The loud protests of Harman's husband, Jack Dromey, a trade unionist and the Labour Party treasurer, had helped to launch the cash for peerages inquiry which in turn helped to force Blair from office. Harman had long aligned herself with Brown and had written an unhelpful article in the *Sunday Times* at the height of the September 2006 coup, in which she stated acidly that Blair's foreign policy had become a 'symbol of mistrust and division' and a sign that the government did not listen. Indeed, one of the reasons that Blair always supported John Prescott to remain as deputy leader was the fear that Brown's faction might replace him with either Clare Short (pre-2003) or Harman (subsequently).

Harman was a totemic figure within the Labour Party – though probably more admired from afar than close to. She was actually older than either Blair or Brown and had been in Parliament longer than either, having won a by-election in Peckham in 1982. But for the next quarter century she had managed to remain the progressive, feminist, modernising icon of the Labour Party.

Harman had been inevitably included in Blair's first cabinet, as social security secretary. But the prime minister perhaps indicated a lack of confidence in her abilities by teaming Harman with the rather more cerebral Frank Field. Field himself was disappointed not to have been given the cabinet seat. Relations between the two soured quickly with each spending more time thinking conspiratorially about the other rather than about welfare reform. Both were sacked from the government in Blair's first big reshuffle of 1998 although Harman subsequently returned in legal jobs below cabinet level. Frank Field remained an enthusiastic, if disappointed, supporter of Tony Blair. Following her fall from the cabinet, Harman was identified as a Brownite.

Harman had a sizeable following at the grassroots of the Labour electorate, and Gordon Brown's supporters believed she would complement him well as a Home Counties, middle-class woman. The new political 'marriage' was thus paraded before the cameras, and Brown immediately loaded Harman down with titles to keep her busy, announcing that she would become chair of the Labour Party, leader of the House of Commons and minister for women. He did not make her deputy prime minister.

When Prime Minister Gordon Brown at last got the chance to form a government on 28 June 2007, he promoted the coup plotters. Seven of the ten Labour MPs who had publicly supported the coup got government jobs. Tommy Watson was appointed a government whip along with Mark Tami and Wayne David. Iain Wright, MP for Hartlepool since Mandelson's departure to Brussels, became a local government minister. At the top table, Ed Balls became secretary of state for education (or rather 'Children, Schools and Families' as his department was cosily renamed); Douglas Alexander became international development secretary and general election planner; Ian Austin and Yvette Cooper were made ministers with the special right to attend cabinet.

However, Brown had also promised to listen and to be inclusive. The cadre of rising young 'Blairites-for-Brown', whose significance had been their refusal to organise an alternative candidate against him, were all rewarded: David Miliband, foreign secretary; James Purnell, culture secretary; Andy Burnham, Treasury chief secretary.

Brown's task was made easier by the mass departure of Blair loyalists from his own generation. Most of them stepped aside voluntarily before Brown had to decide whether to sack them, in the process sparing themselves the question of whether they could stomach serving under Brown. This group included John Reid, Patricia Hewitt, Hilary Armstrong, Peter Goldsmith and Valerie Amos (who had long been canvassing for a role outside the cabinet).

Blair was sorry that no job could be found for Charlie Falconer but he had been doomed by the very reforms he had so long championed. The decision to split the Home Office and to insist that the new Lord Chancellor and justice secretary should sit in the Commons, left Lord Falconer without a seat at the cabinet table. His chances were not helped by the early release of convicts forced by prison overcrowding: Falconer first publicly denied thousands of prisoners were going to be released each month and then had to announce that they would be after all. He and Brown had always been on friendly terms but his intimate relationship with the Blairs must have counted against him. As did his ready wit. One of Falconer's last engagements as Lord Chancellor was to address the Association of Chief Police Officers' conference in Manchester. He startled his audience by telling them that if they were getting a bit bored and wanted 'early release, then I'm your man'. He went on to say that his best chance of staying in government was to 'join the Liberal Democrats', a jibe at Gordon Brown's plan to assemble a 'government of all the talents'.

The most tearful departure was that of the foreign secretary. Margaret Beckett had been the grande dame of Blair's government, having occupied cabinet seats throughout the ten years; before that she had been *pro tem* leader of the party on John Smith's death. She was one of the safest pairs of hands in Blair's team. Although there was an echo of Jim Callaghan's bluff 'Barbara, I need your job' dismissal of Barbara Castle in 1976, Beckett (unlike Castle) had been an enthusiastic supporter of the incoming leader. Aged sixty-four, she had not had time to establish herself in just a year as foreign secretary – and, in a sense, her departure was Blair's fault. He had never planned to send Beckett to the Foreign Office, even though he had long wanted to move Jack Straw.

Blair did not trust Straw, who had taken to developing independent policy (statements on the EU referendum and Iran were just two of Jack's pre-emptive strikes). Straw had also made himself expendable with an embarrassing pair of home-town trysts – first in South Carolina and then in his Blackburn constituency – with US Secretary of State Condi Rice.

Blair's plan had been to make Charles Clarke foreign secretary. He had given him a near promise to that effect when Clarke reluctantly accepted 'the worst job in government' as home secretary. Unfortunately, errors by the Home Office had done for Clarke, as for so many of his predecessors. He had no excuses about the release of foreign convicts back into British society. He had to go. But Blair could not promote a beleaguered minister to the FCO. Clarke turned down offers to be secretary of either defence or trade, so he was sacked instead. There was a vacancy and Margaret Beckett got it – to her surprise as much as anybody else's. 'Fuck me!' was her reaction when Blair made the offer.

Like Gordon Brown, Blair said he would have gone for 'a generational switch' at his next reshuffle. That is not how it was when he was in power. 'Big Beasts' stalked all his cabinets: politicians who were at least his contemporaries, who had made their own contributions to the return of Labour to power and who had their own cadres of personal support in the party. Brown had none to keep him sharp. Straw, Peter Hain and Alistair Darling were far too accommodating to challenge him. Others who might have done were left in the cold – including Beckett, Clarke, Reid, Byers and Milburn.

Tessa Jowell, perhaps the most active Blair loyalist of all, had several meetings with Gordon Brown in the days before the handover. Her devotion to the 2012 Olympic Games, which she helped secure for London, was second only to her love for Blair. She accepted demotion to minister for the Olympics but retained her right to attend cabinet. She also became the minister responsible for the 2008 London local elections and for maintaining links to Ken Livingstone, her fellow Olympicophile.

Brown could present his new government as a fresh team. Telling statistics were produced to contrast it with Blair's cabinet, reinforced by the order in which the new ministers paraded up Downing Street. The first woman home secretary, Jacqui Smith; the first brothers, David and Ed Miliband; the first married couple, Yvette Cooper and

Ed Balls; average age forty-nine, to the Blair cabinet's fifty-four; number of ministers under forty, five, compared to Blair's two.

Brown had fewer women in his cabinet – down from eight to six – but the prime minister's new spokesmen pointed out with satisfaction that Brown had just four Scottish ministers in his cabinet compared to Blair's six (if places were allocated by population share there would be just two Scots). The generation shift had a telling consequence. A dozen members of Blair's last cabinet had been older than him, but Brown had just one senior, the new justice secretary, Jack Straw, who had seamlessly accommodated himself to the new settlement of power. Brown did not make Straw, or anyone else, deputy prime minister; he insisted that he would be running the country at all times and wherever he happened to be in the world. For all his talk of consensual government, curbed by cabinet and Parliament, under Brown there would be only one boss. This was markedly different from the Blair–Brown rivalry which had provided the creative tension to drive the Blair administration.

That Friday, Prime Minister Brown seemed to get off to a good start as he took command in the aftermath of an attempted bombing by terrorists of the Tiger Tiger nightclub in the West End of London.

The two men

During his ascent to power, Brown was often compared unfavourably to Blair: Blair was normal; Brown was somehow 'odd', obsessive. There was no doubting Brown's single-mindedness, which could lead him to be brusque and uncaring of his companions or his surroundings. This was certainly the character I saw when he made the single speech of his, never to be officially declared, 1994 leadership campaign. (This preceded his decision to pull out in favour of Blair and took place at a Labour Party conference in Swansea which was effectively a beauty contest for hopefuls before the race began.) He and his aide, Charlie Whelan, arrived late in a battered taxi, and Brown marched to the podium to bellow, without looking up, a speech shot through with revivalist socialist jargon. I kept the transcript handed out to journalists. It was all written in bold capital letters, presumably so Brown could read it more easily. The font size got bigger towards the end with some letters on later pages being half an inch high.

Brown began by claiming the legacy of John Smith. He reminded his audience that (unlike Blair) he had stayed with the family until the end: 'Yesterday on the little Island of Iona, we buried a great man. Today, we must begin to do justice to that man's great legacy.' There was no ambiguity about the passing of the socialist torch: 'The flame still burns, the work continues, the passion for justice endures, and the vision will never fade – the vision of Labour in power, Labour using that power for – as John said in his last public words – the only worthwhile endeavour: a life lived in the service of others.'

The text was a portrait of Brown's driven passion. The themes which would characterise his agenda when at last he became prime minister were already present. There was much talk of 'Labour in the service of others . . . Labour in the service of the young and their education . . . Labour in the service of women's rights . . . Labour in the service of the millions in poverty at work . . . Labour in the service of millions deprived of work . . . Labour in the service of the poor of the world.' Intriguingly there was already a hint of Brown's interest in Britishness and his desire to honour veterans as he looked ahead to the fiftieth anniversary of D-Day: 'Let us commemorate the contribution of this generation whose sacrifice delivered victory at El Alamein, in Normandy, in Burma, at sea and over Berlin itself, with a right – not to jamborees and spam fritter competitions [the dig here was at John Major's own plans] – but a right to a Health Service fit for heroes to grow old in.' As Brown called up the heroes of the left, however, he also conjured the spirit of unity which would lead him to avoid a divisive competition with Blair:

Never – said Aneurin Bevan, just before his death, to Michael Foot – never underestimate the passion for unity in the Labour Party. It is the instinct of all decent people. And never should our opponents forget that our passion for unity is born of an even greater passion: our passion for social justice.

So let us remember: at this critical time in our party's history:

that to everything there is a season and a time to every purpose. A time to mourn and a time to renew. A time to reflect and a time to move forward. A time to challenge and a time to come together. A time to debate and a time to unite. For us now, more than ever before, this is the time to unite.

It is difficult not to see the internal conflicts besetting Brown laid out in the biblical language of his father's pulpit. He wanted to continue himself the legacy of his old friend Smith, but also seemed to recognise that this could damagingly split the party. At no point did Blair ever express similar doubts.

Caricatures such as these are not the whole story. In some ways, Brown was less odd than Blair. Before entering Parliament, Brown was a veteran of a big family, of rugger-playing school life and prolonged hospitalisation; of student politics and of Scottish journalism; a young man who liked to argue and shared the uncertainties – on religion, on relationships – of most of his contemporaries. Blair's youth was much more detached. His childhood brought him into less contact with the outside world. The family had less secure roots and travelled a lot. His father was struck down by a stroke when Blair was just ten. At Fettes Blair rebelled against the ethos of the school. At Oxford too he preferred to be part of a small group of friends rather than participate in mainstream university life, then further set himself apart by his active Christianity.

As an indicator of relative normality, 'Who would you most like to have a drink in the pub with?' often featured in opinion polls. I have had the chance to compare the pubmanship of the two men. Visiting the Duke of Wellington in Southampton with Blair was a rather dislocated experience. We had just broadcast a live interview programme during the 1997 general election campaign from the smart new hotel Blair was based at near the harbour front, a brutally modern building with a soaring plate-glass pyramid serving as the atrium. Once it was over, Alastair Campbell said we should all have a drink. Blair was ready to order some wine from room service. Though a teetotaller, Campbell insisted that the hotel was 'too plastic' and that he wanted to go to 'a real pub'. As usual in such circumstances, we settled for the nearest hostelry and set off on foot across the greensward to a pub nestled against the medieval harbour walls. Campbell was pleased that, in spite of the modernisation of the area, the pub retained an authentic working-class dockside feel. It was quite early on a summer evening, the pub was far from packed but the barman was playing rock music at deafening disco volume. We could scarcely lose face and turn back, so we shouldered up to the bar, Blair perhaps looking the least enthusiastic member of the party. I asked the Labour leader what he wanted to drink and I would swear that I heard him say 'a Gunness [sic] please'. After several shouted enquiries I managed to order him half a pint of Guinness. Initially, conversation was impossible over the music, and the attempts of our party to get the volume lowered threatened to turn into a 'Who do you think you are?' confrontation with the landlord. Things only got worse when they realised who Blair was – most likely prime minister in a couple of weeks' time. Suddenly the music was cut and to embarrassed mutterings of 'it really is you', the entire bar staff and regulars lined up to shake Blair's hand and ask for his autograph. As soon as we decently could, both political and press parties pleaded pressure of work and skulked back to the hotel.

Drinking with Brown was a much less agonising experience. During the dead days one early January evening, some colleagues and I looked for consolation in the Marquis of Granby off Smith Square in Westminster. This time, too, the pub was just half full, and as soon as we walked through the door we noticed Brown and his party ten yards away at the end of the bar. Evidently, Brown had visited the pub of his own free will. Journalists and politicians often find themselves sharing watering holes, and the general convention is to live and let live. Brown was no particular friend of ours. We would move off to our own corner once we'd got our drinks. But he wasn't having that. He came down the bar, greeted us by name, asked about our Christmases and insisted on buying a round. We stood around chatting normally as the pub filled up and more arrivals joined our group. For what it was worth, Brown was at ease in the pub and with a random group of people around him. Blair wasn't.

★

There was a further chance to contrast the styles of the two men on 11 June 2007 when, three weeks after Tony Blair's last pointless and ill-fated trip to Iraq, Gordon Brown paid his first visit as prime minister-in-waiting. It was a legitimate fact-finding mission which would include private meetings with Iraqi, American and British officials in Baghdad and outside the capital. No joint news conferences were planned, nor would there be a morale-boosting rally at the British military base in Basra. During his months of preparation for Number 10, Brown had already made a brief trip there; to do so again so shortly after Blair's visit would have looked inappropriate.

Many of Brown's supporters were hoping that a change of prime minister would mean a change of policy and bringing troops home soon. He had not committed himself to that but he was promising to give Parliament control over the executive in 'matters of peace and war'. As for the Iraq campaign, he had supported the policy but he had also made the bald admission that there had been 'mistakes made' by the occupying powers after the war.

It was time he went then – and even if the overall strategy was not to change, Brown still wanted to show that there would be a change in style and approach. He would also be under less pressure to go to Iraq during his first few months in power, having made a pre-emptive visit during his pending period. This was especially convenient because in practice British policy was frozen until General Petraeus reported back to the US Congress on the counter-insurgency 'surge' which he was leading in Baghdad.

The expedition was low key. Brown did not take a full complement of print and electronic journalists with him. The press party was made up of just the four political editors from the national television channels (BBC, ITV, Sky News and Channel 4), and a pooled producer and camera team. Unlike print journalists, television reporters can usually be relied on to focus on the main story or issue of the day. We all travelled together in one of the cramped and ageing planes of the Queen's Flight. (Until John Major, prime ministers would always borrow one of Her Majesty's planes for their foreign visits but then the long-haul VC 10s were retired and chartered took over.

As chancellor, Brown approved the purchase of a royal/ministerial

Airbus jet. Unfairly nicknamed Blair Force One, it was not due to come into service until some years after he resigned, but Brown quietly cancelled the whole idea 'on cost grounds' soon after he became prime minister.)

Unlike Blair, Brown himself happily offered extensive briefing on the trip, before, during and after his actual meetings. His new team of officials was also on hand, including Simon MacDonald, Nigel Sheinwald's replacement as foreign policy adviser; private secretary James Bowler and special adviser Matt Cavanagh. In a sure sign that he would be keeping his job in Brown's new cabinet, the defence secretary, Des Browne, came along accompanied by his departmental private secretary, Nick Beadle. Jamie Shelley, director of news at the Ministry of Defence, was charged with media handling.

Brown visited local Iraqi leaders and US Command, and he spent some time with British special forces based to the north of Baghdad. His only public engagement was at Maud House, residence of Major General Richard Lamb, then chief British liaison officer at Command HQ. The building served as the base for the few hundred British troops rotated into Baghdad on security detail. Brown spent half an hour chatting with the forty or so troops present and posed for snaps, in a much less status- or self-conscious way than Blair. This was neither a show of force, nor a major photo opportunity. The troops had little reason to cheer the present the Chancellor of the Exchequer brought with him: a 44 pence increase in the daily operational allowance he had introduced in October 2006 for soldiers on active duty. A specially prepared press release announced that the allowance was going up by 3.6 per cent – from £12.31 to £12.75 per day. At least Brown agreed to backdate the increase to 1 April 2007.

However, the incoming prime minister had something rather more substantial to say about policy in his television interviews. In particular – without mentioning dodgy dossiers, absent weapons of mass destruction or the late Dr David Kelly – he offered concrete, if bureaucratic, changes designed to insure that such breaches of trust would not happen in future. Brown pledged to implement the proposals from Lord Butler's post-Kelly inquiry to insulate security intelligence and analysis from political interference: in future, any intelligence made public would be 'fully validated'; there would be a new post of security co-ordinator charged to act independently unlike the chairman of the Joint Intelligence Committee who was accountable to the prime minister; and parliamentary authority over intelligence would be strengthened.

Brown's recommendations for Iraq were equally dispassionate: support and praise for the troops, encouragement of political reconciliation between Iraqi factions and a, characteristically Brownian, economic dimension. He pointed out that only a fraction of committed aid was actually being spent. But veterans of his many domestic initiatives had to suppress a smile when he proposed yet another development agency, this time for Basra.

Brown made few commitments on the presence of British troops. He confirmed that the intention was still to move to UK 'overwatch' in Basra, the only province still under British security control. He stressed that the advice of military commanders would be paramount as to the presence of British troops, stating that no decision should be expected until after General Petraeus's report on the eighteen benchmarks, the criteria set by Congress for gauging the success of the Iraq 'surge'. (A month later, the US certified that less than half of these had so far been met by the Iraqi government.) Meanwhile British officials conceded that continuing reductions meant that Britain's presence was effectively coming down to the 'irreducible core' – the point at which any further cuts would mean that all the remaining contingent would have to pull out for its own security.

Within twenty minutes of Brown's arrival in the Green Zone, the Iraqi media reported his presence so the news blackout on the accompanying British media was lifted. The insurgents took a little longer to fire up than they had on Blair's last visit. The mortar alarms sounded only in the afternoon, as Brown's party was gathering at the British embassy for departure.

Brown kept up the same modest and dignified demeanour in his first months as prime minister – even when in receipt of the star invitation of international politics: a visit with the US president at Camp David.

On 30 July 2007, Brown thus found himself in the hills of Maryland as a guest of President Bush. In public, George W. Bush was an unpredictable figure. At times he seemed skittish, prepared to blurt out the first thing that came into his head. At others he could be sullen, giving the impression that he didn't really want to be there and couldn't be bothered now that he was.

Brown sent an outward signal that he did not expect or want to enjoy the same matey 'Yo Blair' intimacy with the president as his predecessor. Throughout his stay at the camp, he refused to put on casual clothes, remaining deliberately buttoned-up, in every sense, in his business suit and tie. (On the flight home, journalists were delighted to find a suit carrier containing a brand-new Camp David bomber jacket. Like Blair, Brown had been given one by the president; unlike him, Brown had refused to wear it. A diplomatic apology had to be given to the Americans after one Brown aide was reported saying the jacket was 'tacky'.)

Bush politely followed Brown's dress code at their open-air press conference, but he exuberantly pulled out all the stops from his very first sentence: 'Everybody is wondering whether or not the prime minister and I were able to find common ground. Absolutely!' He went on to heap praise on Brown: a principled man, shared values, a leader who'd proved himself after the terror attacks; 'we think the same'; not a dour Scot – a humorous Scot. Bush tried to exert his jokey charm as he bantered with journalists. He called attention to the fact that it was the thirty-eighth birthday of one *New York Times* reporter present: 'Here you are in an amazing country, Gordon. The guy is under forty years old, asking me and you questions. It's a beautiful sight.' When Brown pointed out that six members of his cabinet were also under forty, the president retorted, 'You must be feeling damn old then?'

It was all very similar to the love-bombing aimed at Tony Blair when he first visited Bush at Camp David. Blair then had smiled and played long, with a slightly embarrassed air of disbelief. Brown remained unmoved but talked repeatedly about shared values and goals and the UK's 'most important bilateral relationship' with the US. Once again, the president followed the prime minister's lead, responding that the 'relationship between Great Britain and America is our most important bilateral relationship'. This form of words went well beyond the usual non-exclusive courtesy Americans use to fob off Britons who mention the 'special relationship', that 'America has no greater friend than Great Britain.'

President Bush declared that 'failure in Iraq would be a disaster'. However, Prime Minister Brown did not adopt this passionate rhetoric, reserving his strongest words for a struggle against an undefined 'international terrorism'. Brown acknowledged Britain's obligations not to cut and run from Iraq but then pointed out that Britain had already handed three of the four provinces under its control back to the Iraqis and was making progress in the last one. He said he would wait for General Petraeus to make his report to Congress and would then make his own statement on Iraq to Parliament in October. Bush said he would, in turn, wait to hear what Brown's military advisers had to say, and expressed the wish that progress had been as fast elsewhere as in the British zones.

At the end, the president honoured Brown with his trademark commendation – 'good job' – and a handshake. British headlines immediately interpreted Brown's remarks as BROWN POINTS TO BRITISH TROOPS WITHDRAWAL FROM COMBAT IN IRAQ. The prime minister hadn't said that, but his spin team did little to dispel the impression when they stressed that Brown had not said there would be an *accelerated* withdrawal. Brown had shifted the UK government's positioning towards disengagement.

Three months after becoming prime minister, Gordon Brown made his statement on Iraq – but it was not first made to Parliament as he had promised. Instead, he went back to Iraq again after all, at the beginning of October – during the Conservative Party conference, on the day that the Tories were debating defence policy. This time Brown posed against a live backdrop of troops in desert camouflage. He talked of 1,000 troops being home by Christmas and of a phased withdrawal of all British forces. It looked like another campaigning stop in the build-up to an imminent general election, but it backfired and was widely judged to be inappropriate and exploitative. The following weekend Brown decided against an early election. He had gone from under-playing Blair to over-playing Blair.

EXIT PRIME MINISTER

27 JUNE

If you get out at this age, you've still got a lot left in you.
Tony Blair, 2008

The Queen could endure this farewell with equanimity – and not just because there would be another prime minister along in a minute. Gordon Brown would be the eleventh prime minister of her reign.

Her partnership with Tony Blair had never really been convincing. True, as his sense of decorum had stiffened with years in office, Blair had grown more correct in his praise. In his eightieth birthday tribute he had professed himself 'profoundly grateful for her wise counsel . . . superb judgement . . . intuitive empathy with people . . . and . . . unshakeable and profound sense of duty'. But New Labour had never really pretended that the monarchy was essential to the project. They showed no natural instinct for respect and Mrs Blair had never once curtseyed properly.

The first Blair administration had included avowed republicans such as Mo Mowlam, who wanted to move the royal family out of their palaces into newly built homes. And Alastair Campbell had had the cheek to stuff the mouth of the fortieth monarch since William the Conqueror with New Labour slogans for Blair's first Queen's speech. Blair had been helpful reading the public mood when Diana had died but he was also presumptuous. The events of that week in September 1997 were very sad but, as the spinners from Downing Street came to Buckingham Palace and started to kick around what roles Harry and William should play in the funeral, the Queen had relished the moment when Philip had bellowed over the speakerphone from Balmoral, 'Fuck off. We are talking about two boys who have just lost their mother.' Once the arrangements had been sorted out Blair did read the lesson very melodramatically that day in the Abbey.

Then there had been her mother's funeral. Yes, they had probably over-planned it; and it probably was true that there had been an honest misunderstanding about whether Blair would have 'a part to play'. That Easter weekend, Downing Street probably did get an old copy of 'Operation Tay Bridge' out of the safe which suggested he would speak during the ceremonies. That would explain why they told the press he would and the initial misunderstandings when the Downing Street officials phoned Black Rod who had the revised up-to-date instructions. But it certainly didn't explain the bullying way they threatened Black Rod and his journalist friends to try to get them to withdraw reports that Blair had been pushy – which he had in a way, even if he didn't mean to be.

So, it was off your knees, Mr Blair. Thank you and farewell (and no, we won't miss you that much).

The prime minister left Buckingham Palace in limbo. He had surrendered the imaginary seals of office and had his last 'audience of the Queen', but he still had his official car, avoiding the embarrassment suffered by Ted Heath who found his had already gone when he came downstairs after resigning. Now he faced one last engagement: Prime Minister's Questions. The moment he had chosen to place his thoughts on that momentous day on the record.

As a political performer, Prime Minister Blair always rose to the big occasion – he found the words for the moment; from the 'new dawn' that first morning in office, through mourning 'the People's Princess', to his last ever appearance in the House of Commons.

Blair had thought carefully about what he wanted to say, and right from his opening words at his final session of Prime Minister's Questions on 27 June 2007 he took control. From the outset the gathered MPs were promised a swan song from a virtuoso.

Blair began sombrely with what had become one of his regular innovations at PMQs: expressing condolences by name on the latest casualties from Iraq and Afghanistan. (He was also in the habit of listing policemen and firefighters who had died on active duty.) This gave him the opportunity to set the tone on the mentions of the war which were bound to follow. 'I know that some may think that they face these dangers in vain. I don't, and I never will. I believe that they are fighting for the security of this country and the wider world against people who would destroy our way of life. But whatever view people take of my decisions, I think there is only one view to take of them: they are the bravest and the best.'

Next, Blair lightened the mood. Questions to the prime minister range so freely because MPs exploit a loophole. In almost all circumstances, they ask a standard question – will the prime minister list his engagements for the day? – which then permits them to raise a matter of concern which may or, in their view, ought to be on his agenda. Prime ministers have adopted a standard form of words to parry this courtesy question, but on this exceptional occasion, Blair inverted the set formula: 'This morning, I had meetings with ministerial colleagues and others. In addition to my duties in the House, I will have no such meeting today, or any other day.' MPs burst out in appreciative laughter.

The prime minister had already dealt with Iraq, and the remaining questions he took that day, from both Labour MPs and the opposition, could have been designed to let him touch on the main themes of this administration. PMQs became a parliamentary version of a 'Greatest Hits' album.

On the NHS: '. . . People used to die on waiting lists – now those waiting lists are at record lows.'

On education: 'Our pupils are performing better as a result of the investment and changes that have been made in our school system.'

On crime, in reply to one of his home secretaries, David Blunkett:

'It is correct, of course, that crime has fallen over the period of this government . . . early years learning, the Sure Start centres, the children's centres, the extension of nursery education and the investment in primary schools will stand us in good stead for the future in creating the responsible citizens we all want to see.'

On Northern Ireland, a tribute from the Rev. Ian Paisley: 'The People of Northern Ireland felt the same way as him. They were angry and cross, lost their tempers and were sad – but we made progress.'

On socialism, Blair's rejoinder to a habitually critical Labour left-winger: '"For the many not the few" . . . I wholeheartedly agree.'

Two buffoonish MPs gave him the opening to make his point on two vexed questions of the ten years. On religion, he once again evaded a clever-clever attempt to seek his views on the Church of England and the state: 'I am really not bothered about that one.' (He wasn't in two ways: he would soon be neither PM nor C of E.) And on Europe, he produced a brilliant reply to Tory Sir Nicholas Winterton's blustering: 'I am afraid that we cannot agree on the treaty, but as for his good wishes to me, may I say to him *au revoir, auf wiedersehen* and *arrivederci*.' Sir Nicholas quaked with gratified mirth.

This was a further reminder of how skilful a performer Blair was in Parliament, even though as he now admitted in his closing remarks, 'I have never pretended to be a great House of Commons man.' Tony Blair had never been one to savour the traditions or the clubbable atmosphere of Parliament. He was no frequenter of the Tea Room. His headquarters were his executive offices in Downing Street and he came to the Commons for business only: to meet MPs, to address the Parliamentary Labour Party or to make statements to the House about his government's plans. Blair also cut down the number of times he had to attend Parliament each week, changing PMQs from a twice-weekly, fifteen-minute session on Tuesday and Thursday afternoons, to half an hour at noon on Wednesday. Many weeks that was the only time Blair was seen in the Palace of Westminster, since he also had a very poor voting record – with a parliamentary majority such as his he hardly needed to bother.

Over the ten years, other MPs took their lead from the prime minister, heading back to their constituencies as early as Wednesday night. By the end of the Blair decade, MPs were on average not at Westminster for four days out of seven when Parliament was in session.

Tony Blair could certainly debate, as he showed when he successfully argued the case for going to war in Iraq during the Commons debates of March 2003. But debates took all day and they required votes by MPs at the end. Blair took part in fewer of these exchanges than any of his predecessors in modern times. Instead, he informed MPs of his government's intentions through statements in a format which generally took well under an hour, which required no vote, and which permitted opponents to ask only brief questions to which the prime minister had the automatic right of reply.

Blair had treated Parliament more like a president would than a traditional prime minister. He had remained true to his intention to spend more time 'doing' in government than 'talking about it'. Now in his emollient farewell, he gave MPs a flattering reason for his lack of attention to them: 'I pay the House the greatest compliment I can by saying that, from first to last, I never stopped fearing it. The tingling apprehension that I felt at three minutes to twelve today I felt as much ten years ago, and every bit as acute. It is in that fear that the respect is contained.'

This was a glimpse of frankness and vulnerability. Blair dwelt on neither as he pressed on to his sentimental grand finale: 'The second thing that I would like to say is about politics and to all my colleagues from different political parties. Some may belittle politics but we who are engaged in it know that it is where people stand tall. Although I know that it has many harsh contentions, it is still the arena that sets the heart beating a little faster. If it is, on occasions, the place of low skulduggery, it is more often the place for the pursuit of noble causes . . .'

Then Blair's voice quavered a little with emotion as he delivered his final public words as prime minister – there could be no greater tribute to Parliament than that from the great showman: 'I wish everyone, friend or foe, well. That is that. The end.'

During PMQs the leader of the opposition had congratulated Blair on his decade as prime minister: 'no one can doubt his huge efforts in public service'. Now Cameron proved himself the true heir to Blair, at least as far as overturning parliamentary convention was concerned. He leapt to his feet and started clapping. His party and most of the other MPs in the chamber, with the exception of the Scottish Nationalists, joined in an unprecedented standing ovation. *Hansard* recorded the word *[Applause]* – bracketed in italics like a final stage direction.

The chamber had witnessed emotion before over departing ministers. After she withdrew from the leadership race, the election timetable had allowed Margaret Thatcher a PMQs curtain – 'I'm enjoying this.' Blair permitted Peter Mandelson to take Northern Ireland Questions on the day he was sacked from the cabinet for the second time. But no one had ever departed like Blair, head held high, in the manner and timing of their own choosing. In his leaving, he had again behaved like a president rather than observe the proprieties of a parliamentary democracy.

Later that day, he made the break with Parliament absolute by standing down as an MP. Tony Blair applied to the Chancellor of the Exchequer, appropriately enough, for the stewardship of the Chiltern Hundreds. (This is a Crown appointment which automatically disqualifies the holder from having a seat in the Commons.)

The possibility that Blair might go immediately had been raised in several newspaper reports – but had been dismissed by Blair and his allies. The *News of the World* first broke the story in 2006. I asked Blair about it at his next monthly news conference but he refused to give it credence. On 3 May 2007, London's *Evening Standard* ran the headline BLAIR 'QUITS TO MAKE MILLIONS': PM IS LIKELY TO STAND DOWN AS MP IN WEEKS. Again there was no official confirmation. On the day Blair went to Sedgefield to set his departure timetable, even his local constituency party believed he would serve out the remainder of the parliamentary term. Although when I spoke to him later that day, John Burton suggested there could perhaps be an early out 'if Tony took a big international job'. This uncertainty meant that the MPs in the Commons for Blair's last question time did not know how long he would be remaining as one of them. His departure only subsequently became clear through two indirectly related announcements – first, that Blair had agreed to become the Quartet's Middle East envoy, and secondly that Sedgefield Constituency Labour Party had called an emergency meeting which Blair would attend that evening.

Blair returned to the constituency several times in July to campaign for Labour in the by-election his standing down had caused. True to its orderly reputation, Sedgefield Labour Party chose the favourite son Phil Wilson, as the candidate to follow Blair. Wilson had been one of the 'Famous Five' party officials who spotted Blair's talent and chose him to fight Sedgefield back in 1983. Wilson had been based all his life in Sedgefield and his two sons had attended school there. The only potential issue was that, like many others, he had gone through a painful divorce. He and his new partner, Margaret, had set up a PR business locally. As just about the only non-white person present, she cut a striking figure at the declaration of the vote in the Newton Aycliffe Leisure Centre.

Blair's final break with Westminster politics came around midnight on 19 July when Phil Wilson was duly elected member for Sedgefield. There had been an 11 per cent swing to the Liberal Democrats but it was still a safe Labour seat. Wilson got 44.8 per cent of the vote, compared to the 58.9 per cent Blair had secured two years previously. The results also allowed Gordon Brown's honeymoon with the voters to continue, since David Cameron's Conservatives had been pushed into third place both in no-hope County Durham and, more importantly, in the simultaneous by-election in the London constituency of Ealing Southall, where they had campaigned vigorously.

Cash for honours

Even before he had safely passed on his seat, some equally momentous news was breaking for Tony Blair. At the end of an inquiry peppered with leaks, there was a final authoritative lead that the Crown

Prosecution Service would announce that there was insufficient evidence to proceed with any prosecutions as a result of the Metropolitan Police investigation into alleged cash for peerages arrangements.

On 28 June, the day after he left office, it emerged that Blair had been questioned for a third time by the police during his last month in office. Each time he was treated as a witness, although it was also made clear that the prime minister would have felt obliged to resign immediately had he, like several of his officials, been arrested or questioned under caution as a suspect. Such a possibility would have brought down the Blair administration.

Now the slate had been wiped clean – but even without any trials the view of Blair and his allies was that the investigation had placed a dark and debilitating pall over his last fifteen months in power.

Blair was always willing to volunteer that he found fundraising the least attractive of his jobs as party leader. He accepted it was a necessity and preferable to leaving the taxpayer to foot the cost of political parties, but he made it clear that he regarded it as an unpleasantness which he preferred to have wafted away from his sight. On the other hand, he was one of the most enthusiastic dispensers of patronage. Blair created more new members of the House of Lords than any other prime minister since Lloyd George and transformed Labour into the largest party in the Upper House. Nor could he deny the correlation which showed that those who donated significant sums to political parties, greatly increased their chances of being honoured. Blair's reply to that was that there was nothing dishonourable about making donations; indeed donors should be praised for performing a public service. Having been a donor should not be the reason for getting an honour – but it certainly should not be a bar to receiving one.

However, Blair had come to power promising to sweep away Tory 'sleaze' and insisting that he expected his government's behaviour to be 'purer than pure'. To this end, he had introduced a number of reforms in the party funding and honours systems. There was now greater compulsory transparency about donations, and independent panels were established to scrutinise the awards of honours.

As Blair tried to wean the Labour Party from the trade unions and as they grew disenchanted with him, the need for cash from other sources became pressing. Ever since Bernie Ecclestone's million-pound cheque in 1997, it was obvious that the party was open to donations from sources that were not immediately otherwise associated with Labour. The party's difficulties over cash for peerages came about when its need for money became entangled in the very regulations it had introduced.

At the centre of the entanglement was the politically naive figure of Michael Levy, a former pop impresario. The man who became Baron Levy of Mill Hill in the London Borough of Barnet in 1997 got to know Tony Blair through party fundraising and the Labour Friends of Israel group. He helped the party obtain the funds for the 1997 election victory and in so doing became a friend of Blair. Like Blair, Levy enjoyed a game of tennis, and the prime minister was among the celebrity players on Levy's private court. John Witherow, editor of the *Sunday Times*, was another.

Levy was a matey, if somewhat pushy, individual. Although well over half the cabinet turned up when he threw his sixtieth birthday party at the Banqueting Hall in Whitehall, many senior figures in the party looked a bit askance at his increasing influence. Blair appointed him not just chief fundraiser but his personal envoy to the Middle East and Latin America. Levy was given a desk in the Foreign Office and moved freely in and out of 10 Downing Street.

In late 2005, *The Times* reported that a number of millionaires who had bankrolled Labour and the Conservatives in the recent election campaign were to get peerages. There were mutterings of sleaze but few eyebrows were raised. But the names of some of those earmarked for the Lords did not pop up on the next New Year's honours list. On 5 March 2006, the *Sunday Times* reported that the Appointments Commission had warned Downing Street off some of the recommendations. Those affected included a number of known donors to Labour campaigns or causes: the food magnate Sir Gulam Noon; the proprietor of the Priory rehabilitation clinics, Dr Chai Patel; property developer Sir David Garrard; and Barry Townsley, a City financier.

Naturally, since all four men were of public standing, they resented any aspersion being cast on their names. In fact, the watchdog seems to have queried the frankness of the disclosures made on their nomination forms. In some cases, donations made in the form of loans had not been declared. Technically this was legal, but the suspicion was that Labour officials, including Lord Levy, had advised that gifts be converted into loans, so that they would not have to be mentioned on the disclosure forms.

Pressure mounted for an internal inquiry at least. On 15 March the crisis went critical for Labour when the party treasurer, Jack Dromey, a long-time Gordon Brown ally, toured the television studios complaining loudly that he knew nothing of what had gone on. It emerged subsequently that although Dromey rejoiced in the honorific of 'party treasurer', he held no such responsibility under the law. Legally the Labour Party's general secretary was also the financially accountable officer. Dromey spoke up on the evening that Labour's parliamentary majority had been reduced to ten because of a rebellion over Blair's proposals for academies and foundation schools. Many of the rebels were Brown supporters, as in private were Dromey and his wife, Harriet Harman. That day, Blair had had a tense meeting with Brown, which ended with the chancellor remarking ominously that a reconciliation over schools might be irrelevant since something 'dreadful' was going to happen that evening. Many of Blair's supporters believed that Dromey's outburst was the fulfilment of Brown's prediction.

Following Dromey's outcry, Angus MacNeil – a young first-time Scottish National Party MP – made a speculative complaint to the Metropolitan Police. He was reportedly sore that he had been unable to claim expenses for overnight stays in a hotel when his flights home to Barra were delayed. He estimated he was some £31,000 a year out of pocket as a result. Potentially, two acts of parliament could have been violated: the 1925 Honours (Prevention of Abuses) Act on the sale of peerages, brought in following the excesses of Lloyd George and Maundy Gregory; and the Political Parties, Elections and Referendums Act of 2000, party funding reforms brought in by the New Labour government.

In total the police received around twenty registered complaints about what was becoming known as the cash for peerages affair. One of the complainants was a Labour MP, Bob Marshall-Andrews, the maverick member for Medway and also a still practising QC and barrister. It fell to Deputy Assistant Commissioner John Yates to review the potential case against the Labour leadership. And there was fairly widespread astonishment when Commissioner of the Metropolitan Police Sir Ian Blair took up Yates's recommendation and decided that there was a case to answer. He placed 'Yates of the Yard' in charge of the inquiry; until then Yates had been best known for bringing the unsuccessful prosecution against Paul Burrell, Princess Diana's butler.

The police were adamant that 'the law's the law' and that it looked as though an offence might have been committed. Yet no credible explanation has ever been offered as to why they decided to act on this particular set of complaints. Perhaps Sir Ian Blair wanted to dispel the impression that he was Tony Blair's man. Perhaps he wanted others to get a taste of their own medicine, given the inquiries and criticisms he faced following the Stockwell tube station shooting by the police of an innocent Brazilian, Jean-Charles de Menezes, in 2005.

There was no way of bringing the inquiry to an early conclusion once it was launched. It was not completed in autumn 2006 as Yates said he hoped it would be to the Public Administration Committee of MPs who had to delay their own inquiry while the criminal investigation proceeded. Instead, the inquiry broadened out in 2007 to pursue conspiracy to pervert the course of justice allegations against Lord Levy and Ruth Turner, Tony Blair's director of government relations.

In the course of the investigation, Lord Levy was arrested twice; Ruth Turner was arrested; Des Smith, a fundraiser who told the *Sunday Times* that donators to city academies were likely to get honours, was arrested; Sir Christopher Evans, scientist and biotech businessman, was arrested. Jonathan Powell was questioned twice under caution; and more than a hundred other people were interviewed including Blair; Michael Howard, the former leader of the opposition;

and all members of the cabinet serving at the relevant time, up to the 2005 election. Only two ministers were said to have treated the police rudely and disobligingly – John Prescott and Peter Hain.

Sarah Helm, the journalist and partner of Jonathan Powell, wrote an article in the *Observer* complaining of 'Gestapo tactics'. She was particularly angered by the dawn raid to arrest Turner: 'As if she was some street criminal ready to scarper, Ruth's home was swooped upon by Yates' men and she was forced to dress in the presence of a female officer. Then there was a tip-off to the press.' The police version was that Turner was treated as any other suspect. The alternative would have been to have arrested her at her place of work, 10 Downing Street, and to have escorted her home. This they argued would have drawn much more media attention. Unlike with Levy, who was asked to report at a police station at a fixed time, the Yates investigators insist that no notice could be given to Turner because of the fear that documents might be destroyed. Ruth Turner's memo to Jonathan Powell has never been published. It has been reported that it suggested that she felt under pressure from Levy to change her testimony. This may well have been the strongest piece of evidence the police had, and they did not want any further potential evidence to disappear. They found nothing and, according to police sources, Turner herself did not complain of her treatment.

Throughout the investigation there were many tip-offs to the press. The vast majority of them blackened the reputation of the suspects, and therefore benefited the police inquiry. As far as I know, most of the leaks came from the police and prosecution side rather than the accused, which is hardly surprising since such leaks are commonplace in other criminal cases. John Yates denied that he was personally responsible for any of them, but he had later to correct testimony to the House of Commons Committee that he had never spoken to a parliamentary lobby correspondent on the grounds that he had been unaware that some television reporters were also members of the lobby.

All of this contributed to the general impression in most of the media that Yates would get his men and women. Many reputations were trashed in the process. For example. Sir Ken Macdonald, the

Director of Public Prosecutions, faced tabloid exposure as an adulterer even though he had stepped aside from the case because of his links to the government.

The sleaze inquiry sparked off a 'feeding frenzy' by the media, in which it was generally assumed that the key figures from Number 10 would face charges. This was explained partly by the general perception that there is indeed a history of linkage between donations to political parties and honours. Both in public and in leaks, statements from the police side were bullish and accurate, at least as far as their own inquiry was concerned. Drawing on my sources, I reported that Jonathan Powell would be interviewed as a suspect under caution, which prompted angry and worried calls from Downing Street. I was convinced that Powell had not been informed by the police of their intentions at that time, but it has subsequently been disclosed that he was interviewed three times, on two occasions as a suspect.

I became even more unpopular, but with those on the other side, including in New Scotland Yard, once I began to report in 2007 that is was most unlikely that the investigation would result in prosecutions. According to a source on the prosecution side, Yates first concluded that he should prepare for both possible outcomes and not just for prosecutions, having heard a report of mine in early July. Private accusations were made that I was a Blairite stooge. In fact I was working from my own judgement, backed up by a number of conversations with lawyers. In their excitement, many journalists forgot to seek legal opinion. If they had, they would have been told by the legal experts – both friends and foes of New Labour – that it was extremely unlikely that a prosecution would be brought. In such a highly sensitive case of white-collar crime, the Crown Prosecution Service would usually demand a 75 per cent chance of conviction before agreeing to a prosecution. This would require an unshakable piece of evidence amounting to a bill of sale stating that a peerage had been exchanged for a sum of money. Even a casual and boastful dealmaker would have been unlikely to be so stupid as to leave such evidence behind.

Discussing a peerage with a donor was not a crime and, as any Westminster veteran would tell you – and Angus MacNeil MP himself conceded – such arrangements had always been made on 'a nod and a wink'. In any case, after the initial months of the police trawl it was evident that no such evidence had been found, and that none of the suspects had turned Queen's evidence to suggest it had. In such cases, conspiracy charges without proof of an original crime were even less likely. The view of the legal profession was that the inquiry had taken so long because the buck was being passed as to who would take responsibility for calling the whole thing off. Macdonald gave way to his CPS subordinate Carmen Dowd, and she in turn called in an independent QC, David Perry, to assess the police case. On the basis of Perry's assessment, Dowd pulled the plug on 20 July. Yates was initially upset, but some months later when he appeared before a Commons Committee, he seemed to have reconciled himself to the CPS caution.

There was no case to answer, but there had already been far-reaching damage done to Blair's final months in office. The investigation quite literally made criminal suspects of senior figures in the administration, and further reinforced the growing impression post-Iraq that the government and prime minister lacked integrity. It also disrupted Blair's own policy agenda. These concerns, coupled with Blair's growing hostility to the media, explained, but did not totally excuse, his failure to keep the media up to date about his own involvement in the events. He was the first prime minister in office to be actively caught up in a criminal inquiry, and he was interviewed three times, yet the media were properly informed only of the first interview. Blair's official spokesman Tom Kelly denied that an interview had taken place for a week after the second one – 'to the best of my knowledge' was the get-out clause on that one. And the third interview was confirmed only after the fact on 28 June, the day after Blair had stood down as prime minister.

There was some surprise that Yates himself did not conduct the interrogations, but this would have been a breach of normal police practice. Yates had not conducted any formal interviews for the best part of a decade because the role of the senior officer was to supervise the investigating team and assess what they produced. The prime minister's main interviewer was in fact a relatively lowly detective sergeant, Paul Kelsey, a six-foot-four giant of a man. The legally trained Blair was charm itself and never put a foot wrong. The first two meetings were at Downing Street, but for the last Kelsey went to Chequers. Once the formal business was over, Blair offered one of his tours of the mansion. The two men paused by some swords, part of the Cromwell memorabilia in the house. Somewhat to the prime minister's alarm, the DS joked that in the old days the differences between them would have been settled by a duel.

Blairites believed that there was a direct link between Jack Dromey's intervention and opposition to the reform agenda. If so, it did not succeed. Blair was able to complete his policy review which he regarded as vital – not just as a stock-take of his own achievements, but to set the rudder for the future. He was far from certain that Brown would have automatically followed his reform agenda but, after watching Brown's first few months, Blair concluded that he had boxed his successor in conclusively.

There was one set of reforms, however, that remained completely off-limits. While his own probity had been in question, Blair was inhibited from seeking any significant rule changes on party funding and electoral reform. The prime minister also decided that it would be impossible for him to have a resignation honours list.

Out of Westminster

The established convention is for British prime ministers to stay on in Parliament as constituency MPs for a decent interval after they leave office, at the very least until the next general election. John Major was defeated in the 1997 general election but served out the full parliamentary term until 2001. Margaret Thatcher was deposed in 1990 and left Parliament in the 1992 election. Both James Callaghan and Edward Heath stayed on long enough to become Father of the House. Callaghan stood down as an MP in 1987, eight years after ceasing to be prime minister. Heath didn't leave the Commons until 2001, having served longer as an MP after he left Number 10 than he had before becoming prime minister. Harold Wilson resigned in

1976 and quit the Commons in 1983. Sir Alec Douglas-Home stayed on long enough after 1964 to become foreign secretary, leaving the Commons ten years later. Winston Churchill did not leave Parliament until 1964, the year before his death. Clement Attlee led the opposition until 1955. The only post-war prime ministers to make hasty exits were two Conservatives, Anthony Eden and Harold Macmillan. Both stood down on health grounds and neither, unlike Blair, left Parliament on the day they ceased to be in Number 10.

Like much else in Blair's exit, he chose to treat his departure from Parliament as a private matter, about which he considered himself to be accountable to no one other than those directly affected – in this case his constituency officials. But this understandable, if unusually fierce, attempt to keep matters secret had the unfortunate consequence that he was far from frank about his intentions when asked. This in turn led to some – almost certainly unfair – inferences that there was something improper about Blair's behaviour and that he was a little ashamed of it. There were, in fact, good reasons for his immediate departure from British public life, both political and personal.

In recent years, the perception had grown that the job of the prime minister was essentially an executive one. Both of Blair's immediate predecessors, Major and Thatcher, had stood down sooner than those who had been prime minister before them. Neither had tried to build a supplementary career in British politics as Heath, Callaghan and Douglas-Home had done. Provided Labour could win the by-election (and it could because it was one of the safest seats in the country, with an outgoing MP who was popular locally), Blair was doing Gordon Brown a favour by depriving himself of opportunities to interfere intimately in the affairs of the next government. The next prime minister would not have to contend with a 'back-seat driver' as Thatcher had been to Major, or 'the longest sulk in history' as Thatcher had endured from Heath. The absence of domestic political ties also increased Blair's eligibility for international employment because it meant there would be fewer complications with taking up a job associated with multilateral bodies or foreign governments, such as the role of Middle East envoy, which would have been impossible had he remained tied to the politics of one national partner in the Quartet.

It was a more difficult decision than might have been expected. Even though he no longer had friends and family from his childhood in the Northeast, he regarded it, rather than Scotland, say, as where his roots were. The associations with County Durham and his late mother were particularly strong, and it was a wrench to cut such a tie, even though he retained ownership of Myrobella.

Leaving Parliament did, though, give Blair much more freedom to exploit his market value.

From about 1980 onwards, the personal earning potential of former prime ministers and presidents ballooned in line with the sustained booms in Western economies and the media of popular culture. Greed may not have been universally regarded as good but it became widely accepted that senior politicians could become seriously wealthy after leaving office by taking on commercial contracts and by cashing in on their celebrity through memoirs and speaking engagements. The new generation of ex-politicians was better placed to take advantage of such opportunities because their main careers were ending at a younger age and because there were fewer ideological disagreements with the market economy. Under the old dispensation, a concert party of wealthy benefactors clubbed together to ensure that even Churchill in old age did not have to sell his main home, Chartwell. In contrast, John Major, Bill Clinton and Tony Blair all became multi-millionaires – dollars or pounds – after leaving office and were able to expand their personal property holdings. The new political high earners tended to develop a portfolio of activities in which massive private earnings from part-time business deals offset the costs of voluntary work, as well as seeding foundations and trusts established to benefit the former politicians' favourite causes.

In Britain, a seat in the Houses of Parliament, whether Lords or Commons, could materially hamper such money-making ambitions. Thanks to reforming laws brought in during the ten years, MPs and peers were obliged to make full and regular disclosure of their financial interests. It was much more convenient for an ex-prime minister, a potentially very high earner, not to be subjected to such extensive published and public scrutiny. They were not likely to do anything improper but each potential entry on the register would arouse fresh comment and criticism and be easily accessible to journalists and opponents by right. The wish to engage in less fettered business activity was one reason why Blair, Major and Heath were all reluctant to take up the seat in the House of Lords automatically on offer to them. Though in fairness to the three, none of them had evinced much enthusiasm for the institution of the Upper House. Heath and Major were both reticent dispensers of patronage.

Blair's first twenty-four hours as a former prime minister confirmed that he intended to follow Bill Clinton's post-White House model of remaining a high-profile international figure, with foundations and public appointments subsidised by commercial and private earnings. Blair disentangled himself from British politics and started to take up honorific posts. Each new role promoted Blair's preoccupations as prime minister. The theme uniting them was globalisation – a force which Blair believed passionately was beneficial. The Middle East job was announced on the day he quit. The following day he added to it the post of co-chair of Davos, the World Economic Forum, the world's number one schmoozing interface between politicians, big business and opinion formers. In Sedgefield, he unveiled plans for the Tony Blair Sports Foundation to be administered from Myrobella.

As anticipated when he attended the launch in Berlin in April 2007, Blair also joined the Africa Progress Panel, a group set up to monitor delivery of the Gleneagles pledges, which included amongst its members Dame Graça Machel, Mandela's wife, and Bob Geldof. The body was funded by the Bill and Melinda Gates Foundation and was chaired by ex-UN Secretary-General Kofi Annan. Believing that only better governance could chart a course of genuine progress for Africa, Blair independently took on the role of adviser to several African governments, including Rwanda. He also became international envoy for the Climate Group to keep up pressure for action on global warming.

All these appointments would keep Blair in the public eye and in contact with peers from his glory days as prime minister. They also went some way to paying the expenses for an office headquarters and staff and for international travel but none of them carried a salary. The total annual cost to the British taxpayer of Blair's Middle East post was £400,000 (the UK's share of the Quartet's £2 million Blair budget) plus four Foreign Office diplomats seconded to the former PM's team. Blair's motorcade of silver SUVs and Mercedes soon became notorious for clogging up traffic in Israel – a remarkable achievement in a country long used to disruption 'for security reasons'. He set up his envoy headquarters occupying the entire top floor of the American Colony in East Jerusalem, one of the city's most luxurious and louche hotels, run by Palestinians. The Jewish-run King David Hotel, historic HQ of the British Mandate, was much more austere. The Blair camp claimed that it was possible to move more freely from the American Colony because security would have to be heavier elsewhere.

Blair's earnings from British politics plummeted when he left Parliament. As prime minister his final salary had been £187,611 per annum, plus the Downing Street flat, plus Chequers, plus full administrative support. On quitting, he was immediately eligible to a pension of £63,468 a year and £84,000 towards the expense of running a private office. These sums hardly dented the totals he planned to spend either for personal or business expenses.

The mortgage on his main London home in Connaught Square alone was more than £16,000 a month. The Blairs' property portfolio also included an adjoining mews house, purchased to increase security, the controversial pair of flats in Bristol which led to Cherie Blair's humiliation and Myrobella in Sedgefield. 'The Office of Tony Blair' had several temporary homes before establishing itself permanently in an ambassadorial, four-storey block in Grosvenor Square. At first, Blair borrowed executive rooms in Mount Row, Mayfair which were being vacated by Matthew Freud, Rupert Murdoch's son-in-law, and his company Freud Communications. Blair then moved to 33 St James's Square, a few doors down from BP's smart executive headquarters, from which Lord Browne, the top UK businessman of Blair's era, coincidentally made a forced exit in May 2007. Rent alone on Grosvenor Square ran to £550,000 a year.

The Grosvenor Square office made an eloquent statement of how Blair saw his role after the premiership. He regarded himself as still 'a relatively young man' with 'a great deal to do' and the elegant eighteenth-century townhouse set back on one corner of the square was in practice an embassy for one man and what he described as his 'global social business'. It stood in one of London's main diplomatic areas – the Canadian and Italian official residences were down the street to the left, and at right angles to the right loomed the giant US embassy, the focus of the famous anti-Vietnam War demonstration in 1968. The square has many American associations. It was the location of Eisenhower's wartime headquarters and has a statue of FDR in its garden. In the centre is a memorial garden dedicated to those who lost their lives in the 11 September attacks (the square was the main gathering place for UK mourners in the immediate aftermath). A plaque on Blair's building notes that it served as the home for the second US president, John Adams, the first 'minister plenipotentiary', effectively ambassador, sent to Britain. Adams and his family occupied the house at his own expense from 1785 to 1788 – paying a more reasonable-sounding £160 per annum. At the time, the British foreign secretary, Lord Carmarthen, and the prime minister, Lord North, were both neighbours in the square. Adams subsequently served as president from 1797 to 1801 and was also the first occupant of the White House in Washington.

Blair's office was discreet. There was no nameplate in spite of a specially commissioned logo and colours, khaki and black, for his post-Downing Street organisation. At his own request, there was no armed or uniformed policeman visible at the door for fear of putting off visitors – in marked contrast to his new family home where neighbours complained of the intimidating presence of protection forces. Inside, the high-ceilinged rooms were freshly painted white. Modern artworks were loaned by a public foundation and there were fussy art nouveau-style energy-saving light fittings. Blair's office occupied the large square room on the first floor that the Adamses had used as a salon and dining room. The mood was much calmer and less cluttered than that of the old dens in Number 10: just a grey leather sofa facing two matching, overstuffed armchairs, a four-seater meeting table in the corner and double doors opening into a brightly lit open-plan office for his aides. Since leaving Downing Street, Blair had learned to send emails and text SMS messages. So now, unlike in Downing Street, he had his own desktop computer. On his mantelpiece there were five family portraits in clunky frames, including Blair kissing baby Leo in front of the Downing Street door – the iconic number 10 dominating the centre of the shot – and an earlier picture of the family making their way to the polling station in Sedgefield on that momentous day in 1997. In the next-door waiting room, a shelf of fresh hardback books leant against a bronze bust of one Thomas J. Dodd. Senator Dodd had been a prosecutor at the Nuremberg war trials. In September 2003, Blair and Bertie Ahern had been awarded the inaugural Dodd International Justice and Human Rights Prize by the University of Connecticut. (Blair sent John Prescott to deliver his acceptance speech!) The bookshelf reflected the variety of Blair's latest interests: Bill Clinton's *Giving*; *India's Century*; *The Second Bounce of the Ball* by Sir Ronnie Cohen, a venture capitalist rather closer to Gordon Brown than to Blair; and a biography of the American banker J. P. Morgan.

In spite of his entreaties, none of Blair's most long-standing team went to work for him. There was no dominant figure other than Blair. This was the way he and, perhaps more importantly, Cherie wanted it.

Even so, Mrs Blair did not get her way entirely. She had hoped to establish a joint working headquarters with her husband, but Tony Blair insisted that he and his wife should keep their business affairs entirely separate once he left Number 10. Cherie Blair and her American friend Martha Greene operated from the new family home in Marble Arch and not Grosvenor Square.

Of the old retainers, Anji Hunter, Sally Morgan and Alastair Campbell had long established new lives. Liz Lloyd and Jonathan Powell went into banking. PR specialists Hilary Coffman and David Hill both chose private careers, Hill returning to his old job working with Lord (Tim) Bell. Kate Garvey went to Freud Communications. Experienced 'events organiser' Jo Gibbons left the office to have a baby in early 2008. However, Blair was lucky to retain the services of Gavin Mackay, the civil service private secretary in charge of making the prime minister's engagements work.

For the rest Blair took with him from government a younger crowd of twenty- and thirty-somethings, predominantly female and with civil service backgrounds. Blair's last director of government relations, and focus of the cash for peerages inquiry, Ruth Turner, stayed with him to set up a new interfaith foundation, assisted by Parna Taylor, a former PA to James Purnell and Number 10 secretary, and by William Chapman, the civil servant who had dealt with the honours list in Downing Street. Catherine Rimmer, whose most important task had been briefings for PMQs, and Victoria Gould, former diary secretary, took up new versions of their old jobs running Blair's business interests and schedule. Katie Kay, another former diary secretary, and Maree Glass, Peter Mandelson's former PA, were brought in to help them. Nick Banner was seconded from the Foreign Office to work on the Middle East. And Matthew Doyle became political director; he had previously been the Labour Party press secretary and deputy to David Hill, the director of communications.

In the final weeks at Number 10, Doyle organised a garden party which allowed Blair's staff to bring their families to Downing Street. Blair wandered around to meet and greet them. Afterwards he asked his team if the event had not been 'a bit gay?' Aghast, some of them quietly told the prime minister that Matthew Doyle was gay. In a mark of his lack of curiosity about others, Blair said he had no idea and immediately apologised to Doyle.

Blair's so-called 'global social business' was a new manifestation of the private–public partnership ideas he had pioneered in government. He brought together his reputation and his appeal to business to help fund his continuing work and expenses dealing with chosen causes, which he had also championed while in office. His environmental advocacy, for example, was funded by the Climate Group, a not-for-profit organisation set up by international businesses to build on the watershed report by Sir Nicholas Stern on the economic implications of global warming – originally commissioned by Blair and Brown.

To underpin his planned interfaith foundation, Blair agreed to deliver a series of lectures on 'Faith and Globalisation' at Yale University's School of Management and Divinity. He wanted the foundation to supply educational material for schools and Yale would provide the groundwork for this.

None of these activities carried a salary, and almost all of them required establishments and staff which Blair would have to fund. Even before it came to taking care of himself and his family, Blair's earnings needed to be considerable. The 'Blair Rich Project' had very great expectations.

Money

All Blair had to sell was himself – as a writer, a maker of speeches and personal appearances and a corporate adviser. He never doubted that he could succeed at each and soon put his earning schemes into execution, helped by a group of wealthy friends which he had built up as prime minister but who had comparatively little overlap with his other political and social circles. One of Blair's greatest personal skills was that he was 'a user'. He knew how to get what he wanted from people and was not squeamish about who he dealt with. I once discussed this side of Blair's character with Jonathan Powell, who put it succinctly: 'You mean there are people you and I would run a mile from, but Tony would invite them to dinner and find out if they had a nice place to go on holiday.'

For Labour stalwarts, Blair's new friends were sometimes hard to take. One of his most loyal servants considered resignation when he saw reports of Blair socialising in the Caribbean with members of the Bamford family, prominent Conservative supporters in the Midlands, with a big construction vehicle manufacturing business not known for its trade union sympathies. No general election campaign was ever complete for Margaret Thatcher without a visit to pose with the 'dancing diggers' of JCB. None of this seemed to deter Blair.

On another occasion I witnessed these rivalries first hand. A party of media folk, well known to Blair, went for dinner at the River

Café. By chance, Mr and Mrs Blair were dining with the investment banker Russell Chambers a few tables away. The two groups did not acknowledge each other, except for surreptitious glares, much to the amusement of Blair's security detail. But Blair himself was typically conciliatory and secretly sent a friendly greeting of thanks to Ruthie Rogers, who was dining with the media party but as the co-owner of the restaurant had naturally welcomed all the tables, including the Blairs'.

Blair certainly made new friends thanks to his holidays at Cliff Richard's house in Barbados. He was photographed yachting with Chambers and with Charles Dunstone, CEO of the Carphone Warehouse (Blair's former aide Sally Morgan became a non-executive on the Carphone Warehouse board). Martha Greene, member of the trendy wholefood Villandry Restaurant and shop, was another friend. All of them helped Blair to expand his circle of contacts, but suggestions that this group acted as agents to secure lucrative business contracts for the ex-prime minister are wide of the mark. It was part of his job as prime minister to interact with business leaders and he got to know them well – as he demonstrated at his final appearance at a CBI conference when he spoke off-the-cuff for an hour, addressing many of his questioners by name. The ex-prime minister had no false modesty about his worth and he waited for the bids to come in. If he needed a network, and that was questionable, it was already there thanks to the Davos World Economic Forum.

As broker for his deals, Blair retained Bob Barnett, a Washington lawyer who had already acted for top political figures including the Clintons, the Ronald Reagan Foundation, Queen Noor of Jordan, Benazir Bhutto, Laura Bush, Ted Kennedy, Alan Greenspan and Dick Cheney. Barnett was not an agent taking a percentage of his clients' earnings, he was a lawyer, billing a hefty $950 an hour for any work done. He cost a lot up front but nothing afterwards. Since he billed well over 2,000 hours a year he was also a wealthy man and well connected in US politics, especially on the Democrat side, where he also acted as a debate coach.

Barnett organised a publishers' auction for Blair's autobiography; clinched his adviser deals, including his first two with JP Morgan

Chase bank and Zurich Financial Services, estimated to be worth respectively £2.5 million and £2 million a year; and helped manage Blair's speaking engagements.

Five major publishing houses were invited to bid for Blair's book: Random House (Bertelsmann), HarperCollins (News Corp), Penguin (Pearson), Bloomsbury and Simon & Schuster (Viacom). Their representatives met separately with Blair for about an hour. They were shown a synopsis but no sample chapter. Blair was not a man given to telling anecdotes. Instead, his selling point was that he planned to write the book himself without a ghost.

There was little surprise when the bidding was won by Random House – whose reported £4.6 million offer was only £100,000 higher than that of the runner-up. Random House was something of a New Labour house publisher in the UK. Its chairman and chief executive, Gail Rebuck, had become one of Britain's most successful businesswomen. She was also the wife of Philip Gould, Blair's long-time opinion pollster and one of the founding fathers of New Labour. In 2004, Gould became a member of the House of Lords on Blair's recommendation. He was also deputy chairman of Freud Communications. Rebuck had already managed the triumphant first publication of Alastair Campbell's (bowdlerized) diaries. At the same time, Random House had brought out *The Ghost* by Robert Harris, one of the publisher's most popular authors. Harris was an old friend of Peter Mandelson and the writer was given special privileges to accompany Blair on the night he came to power in 1997. But Blair called him 'a cheeky fuck' for *The Ghost*, a racy and pointed fictionalisation of the afterlife of the Blairs centred on the ghosting of the ex-prime minister's memoirs, against a brooding backdrop of war crimes charges.

By April 2008, Blair had written only one 16,000-word chapter of his planned memoirs, but he had done it quickly, in longhand, in just four days. Random House planned to publish the book in October 2009, after the party conferences – the usual season for political books. The greatest interest would be in what Blair had to say of Brown and by this timetable, the book would appear only after the British people had given their verdict in a general election, if Brown stuck to the precedent of calling a poll after a four-year Parliament.

Mrs Blair, meanwhile, signed her own million-pound book deal for publication in May 2008. Tony Blair believed that he had ensured the book would be uncontroversial and would not 'lay into Gordon'. But in the event, *Speaking for Myself* made headlines primarily because of Mrs Blair's unusual frankness about personal matters many would consider unmentionable.

Away from his book, Blair wanted his other business deals to be lucrative and low profile. Like other former politicians, he decided not to join company boards – since this could raise questions about conflicts of interest and also imposed statutory obligations on members. Instead, he preferred the private role of informal adviser on strategic and political matters to the chief executive – Jamie Dimon at Morgan Chase and James Schiro at Zurich. Both were big figures in their own right in the macho corporate world of 'Masters of the Universe', familiar to Blair from Davos and elsewhere.

Blair did not allow his reputation to grow stale before embarking on speaking engagements, and once again he looked to the United States for his main market. In the summer of 2007, the Washington Speakers Bureau posted on its website a slightly weaselly colour photograph of the former prime minister, along with a biography which revealed: 'He has always been a strong advocate of a values-based, activist and multilateralist foreign policy.' Blair's mug shot joined a gallery of luminaries including other ex-prime ministers such as John Howard of Australia; former US cabinet members, including James A. Baker III; and celebrities such as Donald Trump, Rudy Giuliani and CNN's Christiane Amanpour.

In the next few months, Blair gave a series of speeches in China as well as making repeated visits to North America. Some were charity appearances, such as for the Clinton Global Initiative and the American Catholic Church, but ticket prices usually began at around $180 rising to thousands of dollars for the best seats and the chance of a personal meeting. The Washington Speakers Bureau did not reveal Blair's scale of fees but the cost per appearance was put at between $75,000 and $300,000 He cleared more than a million pounds from public speaking in the first year of his afterlife.

Blair's pragmatic and unapologetic moves to obtain financial security for himself and his pet projects were carried out in the glare of full media attention. Some, especially Labour supporters, found his actions demeaning of the man and the office of prime minister. Des Turner, MP for Brighton Kemptown, was highly critical: 'He's cashing in big time. It's one law for some and another for the rest.'

Middle East

The former prime minister, however, gave the largest share of his time – at least ten days a month – to his most serious *pro bono* role, that of Middle East envoy. Tony Blair's predecessor as envoy for the Quartet, James Wolfensohn, had given up the position in April 2006, dismayed at the lack of progress being made and the absence of engagement from the decisive influence in the region, the United States. Blair, though, volunteered himself for the post, finally agreeing with George Bush to accept the appointment during his last prime ministerial visit to the White House. Even then, the job was not secure because of the worsening relationship between the British and Russian governments following the murder in London of the former FSB agent Alexander Litvinenko. The Kremlin held back its approval of Blair's appointment until the week he stood down as prime minister. Blair claimed that he wanted the position because it was unfinished business – not as 'atonement' for what had happened in Iraq.

Blair's fascination with the intractable problem of an Israeli–Palestinian settlement was piqued by his success in negotiating the Good Friday Agreement. He flew to the Middle East for the first time as prime minister less than a fortnight after the deal had been reached in Belfast, openly promising to bring to bear some of the lessons he had learned negotiating with republicans and unionists. In the spring of 1998 it was an over-ambitious plan. At the time, Israel was preparing to celebrate its fiftieth anniversary as a nation and British relations with the hard-line Likud government of Binyamin Netanyahu were poor.

In advance of Blair, Foreign Secretary Robin Cook had taken a confrontational attitude towards the expansion of Israeli settlements. He was jeered and pelted by settlers at Har Homa, and the Israeli government cancelled the official banquet. Blair and Netanyahu managed their meeting rather more smoothly. Blair laid a wreath at the tomb of the assassinated Israeli Prime Minister Yitzhak Rabin, and was clearly shaken after his visit to Yad Vashem, the Holocaust memorial. The two prime ministers paid tribute to each other's achievements. On this first visit, Blair outlined one of his key themes. There could be peace, he argued, only if the economies of Israel and the Palestinian territories converged, and that meant that the West, and especially the European Union, needed to give the Palestinians substantially more financial assistance. Blair was snubbed by the Israeli prime minister he would later negotiate with at the end of his administration. Ehud Olmert, then mayor of Jerusalem, refused to attend a reception for the British prime minister because Blair had refused to hold a one-on-one meeting with him.

Blair also visited Yasser Arafat in Gaza, paying him the compliment of political recognition by addressing him as President Arafat. National anthems were played, with the Palestinian military band achieving a splendidly off-key bizarre rendition of 'God Save the Queen'. Blair urged talks between leaders on both sides as soon as possible, even though Arafat's trembling lips already indicated that he was in a poor state of health.

As Bill Clinton came towards the end of his presidency he, too, craved a breakthrough in the Middle East. Hopes rose that this might be possible in June 1999 when the Israeli Labour Party's Ehud Barak was elected the new prime minister. Philip Gould, Blair's polls guru, had worked for the Barak campaign along with his then partner, the Democrat strategist Stan Greenberg. Sure enough, Barak and Arafat attended the Camp David peace talks in the final months of the Clinton presidency. But progress that summer was shattered by the start of the second intifada following the Israeli opposition leader Ariel Sharon's visit to Temple Mount – which is also the Islamic holy place called al-Haram al-Sharif. In January 2001, talks held at the border town of Taba in Egypt were inconclusive, and Israel's position hardened in March 2001 with the election of Sharon as prime minister.

September 11 2001 refocused Blair's interest in the Middle East. From the moment that he heard of the terrorist attacks, he stressed repeatedly that 'justice for the Palestinians' had to be part of the solution to the Islamist threat. A month later on 15 October, he invited Arafat to Downing Street for what would be their eleventh meeting. Blair 'applauded the president for his efforts to control violent rejectionist groups within the ranks of the Palestinian people'.

But the following April, Bush ruled out any further dealings with Arafat as he stood next to Blair during their summit meeting in Crawford, Texas: 'I was asked on British TV the other day, have I lost trust in Chairman Arafat? And I said, well, he never earned my trust, because he hasn't performed.' Blair subsequently admitted that Bush had blindsided him, since Arafat had not formed part of their main discussions about the build-up to war in Iraq. At the time, he did not rush to echo the president's words. However, Blair claimed later that he too had become disillusioned with Arafat. Private conversations that winter had left him with the impression that the Palestinian leader would never negotiate sincerely with the Israelis. Blair was particularly offended by Arafat's remark, 'Sharon, Barak they are all the same.'

Arafat became an increasingly marginalised figure in the remaining years until his death in November 2004. His political rivals drove him out of Gaza to his headquarters compound in Ramallah in the West Bank, where he was effectively confined to house arrest by the threat of Israeli bombardment. The US had declared that he was not an acceptable negotiating partner. But 2004 was a pivotal moment for Blair's Middle East diplomacy. Once again he was caught on the hop by Bush. This time, the day before a scheduled meeting with the prime minister at the White House, the president played host at short notice to Ariel Sharon. Unexpectedly, Sharon announced his peace plan for a unilateral withdrawal by Israel from the Gaza Strip. This was a departure from the 'road map' officially endorsed by the Quartet, but the president welcomed the proposal.

Blair was left in an uncomfortable quandary the next day at his news conference with the president: should he reject Sharon's take-it-or-leave-it plan or back Bush? Blair decided to welcome the initiative, though with his familiar caveats of the need for investment and for negotiations with the Palestinians:

> Now, forgive me, but I've been dealing with this for almost a decade. And it's been very, very difficult ever to get a situation where an Israeli prime minister is prepared to say, we're actually going to take these settlements away – and make that not conditional on something that the Palestinians are doing, but say, we're just going to do that.
>
> Now, of course, there's a whole string of things that, then, have to be decided. All these issues have to be negotiated. We have to get back into the road map and get on a proper process towards a resolution of those issues.
>
> But if that disengagement takes place, surely the intelligent thing, not just for the Palestinians, but for the international community, is to be ready to respond. And here's where the Quartet can play a part, the other part that's in this process. The European Union, for example. We put money into reconstruction in the Palestinian Authority. I believe that there is a real possibility if we can get the right political system there, the European Union putting money in to help reconstruct the country, to help build the proper security capability.

Blair's typically positive attempt to make the best of the situation infuriated many European policy-makers. 'Fifty-two former senior British Diplomats', including Sir Crispin Tickell (UN representative 1987–90), Sir Harold Walker (Iraq ambassador 1990–91), Francis Cornish (Israel ambassador 1998–2001), put their names to an open letter which tore into Blair over the Iraq War and the Sharon plan: 'After all those wasted months, the international community has now been confronted with the announcement by Ariel Sharon and President Bush of new policies which are one-sided and illegal and which will cost yet more Israeli and Palestinian blood. Our dismay at this backward step is heightened by the fact that you yourself seem to have endorsed it, abandoning the principles which for nearly four decades have guided international efforts to restore peace in the Holy Land . . .'

Thanks to Iraq, Blair was by now immune to such criticisms. Days before Christmas 2004, he went on a cordial visit to Sharon: 'I am a friend of Israel and proud to be so.' Sharon was unexpectedly jovial and broke with his usual practice by speaking English for much of their news conference. Both men insisted that the Sharon plan was complementary to, rather than a replacement for, the road map. And Blair assured me that withdrawal from Gaza would be only the beginning of Israel's move towards peace: 'Is disengagement really supposed to be the final word, and actually Israel doesn't want to move beyond that? . . . The answer of the prime minister has been very clear, if we can get the right measures of security in place and the terrorism stopped, he does want to move forward.'

Once again, the British prime minister's focus was on practical help for the Palestinians and he announced that he would host a pledging conference in London the following spring to bring assistance to Mahmoud Abbas's government.

After thirty-eight years of occupation, the Israeli pull-out from Gaza went ahead, but Israel also pressed on with the construction of the security fence, which amounted to a significant grab of Palestinian territory as defined by international agreement. At the start of 2006, Sharon suffered the stroke which sent him into an irreversible coma. Ehud Olmert took over as Israeli prime minister. Politically, he was much weaker than Sharon and had less leeway to depart from a hard-line 'security first' posture, at a time when hostility towards Israel was gathering along its borders.

The militant Islamist group Hamas took control of Gaza in elections, defeating the Fatah Party of Abbas and Arafat before him. At the same time, another Islamist party, Hezbollah, was gaining strength to the north in Lebanon. Hamas militants kidnapped an Israeli conscript, Corporal Gilad Shalit. Meanwhile, Hezbollah forces also took hostages during a cross-border incursion and carried out frequent rocket attacks on Israel. By late July, Israel was fighting a war on two fronts, having invaded Gaza and Southern Lebanon and initiated a bombing campaign against targets across Lebanon.

The UN and many EU nations condemned the scale of Israel's attacks, but Blair sided with Bush and called merely for restraint on all sides. At the height of the war, Blair was infamously overheard at the G8 in St Petersburg in 2006 telling the American president that he was happy to do the US's early bidding in the Levant. Don't risk America's credibility, he told Bush – send me. If I fail, it will matter less, he suggested.

At his August 2006 news conference Blair expressed his feelings in an almost comical diatribe. He urged us to

> Put yourself in Israel's place. It has a crisis in Gaza sparked by the kidnap of a soldier by Hamas. Suddenly, without warning, Hezbollah, who have been continuing to operate in Southern Lebanon for two years in defiance of UN resolution 1559, cross the blue line, kill eight Israeli soldiers and kidnap two more. They then fire rockets indiscriminately at the civilian population in Northern Israel. Hezbollah get their weapons from Iran. Iran are now also financing militant elements in Hamas. Iran's president has called for Israel to be 'wiped off the map'. And he's trying to acquire a nuclear weapon. Just to complete the picture, Israel's main neighbour along its eastern flank is Syria who support Hezbollah and house the hard-line leaders of Hamas. It's not exactly conducive to a feeling of security, is it?

Blair then gave a revealing insight into how he now perceived the problem in the Middle East: 'even the issue of Israel is just part of the same, wider struggle for the soul of the region . . . Islamic extremism's whole strategy is based on a presumed sense of grievance that can motivate people to divide against each other. Our answer has to be a set of values strong enough to unite people with each other.'

Blair's position on Lebanon that August broke the patience of the British Labour Party, stoking the discontent which resulted in the attempted coup against him on 6 September. But even after he'd been forced to announce his delayed departure, the prime minister kept up his diplomatic efforts with a zeal that was now often described as 'messianic'.

Just weeks after the Lebanese ceasefire, Blair returned to the Middle East. On 11 September 2006, he paid the first ever visit by a British prime minister to Beirut and the Lebanon. The legislative centre of the city was cut off by troops and barbed wire as thousands demonstrated against him beyond the periphery. His purpose was to support the fragile elected government of Prime Minister Siniora. And even though their news conference that day was disrupted by a banner-waving European demonstrator, Siniora did indeed manage to stay in power far longer than most of us in Beirut that day would have predicted.

The tour also took in Jerusalem. At a press conference in the orange grove behind the Israeli prime minister's residence, Blair revelled in his welcome as a 'great friend of the Jewish state', as a man who understood what it was to be on terror's frontline, to be fighting the great fight.

The following day, he visited Mahmoud Abbas in Ramallah. It was the height of the cash for honours inquiry and Michael Levy ostentatiously bustled around the meeting. Levy was rewarded with lavish public praise from both prime minister and president. One of the ironies of Levy's Middle East job was that he enjoyed much better access to Fatah and the West Bank than he did to the Israeli government, in part because his son David was an Israeli Labour Party activist, rendering his father a member of the Israeli opposition by association.

Blair appeared immune to the consequences of both his support for Israel over the war and the effusive welcome he received in Jerusalem. He seemed to reason that the Arabs would welcome him as a man doing what he could to help, just as the Israelis had done. He followed up on his Middle East obsession that autumn in his emotional final speech as leader to the Labour Party conference, telling delegates: 'From now until I leave office I will dedicate myself, with the same commitment I have given to Northern Ireland, to advancing peace between Israel and Palestine. I may not succeed. But I will try because peace in the Middle East is a defeat for terrorism.'

True to his word, but unusually for a serving prime minister, Blair went on a further mission to the Middle East before the end of the year. By now even Michael Levy was losing patience. I asked him gently what the prime minister was likely to achieve. 'Fuck all,' was the startling reply from the prime minister's own Middle East envoy.

The president of Egypt, Hosni Mubarak, refused to be seen in public with Blair, so the two men met behind closed doors during Blair's short stopover in Cairo. After Egypt, the prime ministerial delegation boarded an RAF Hercules for a tiring haul to Iraq – an almighty schlep as one of those travelling in the cargo section complained. In a clearly worsening Baghdad, Blair put his usual brave spin on it all before flying to Basra, where he was given an at best tepid reception by British troops.

Back in Israel things got quite silly. Left to twiddle his thumbs all day while Ehud Olmert met with a US congressional delegation (a clear indication of where the British prime minister figured in Israeli thinking), Blair was later ambushed and patronised by the Israeli prime minister. Emerging from talks for a press conference in the same familiar orange grove, Olmert invited Blair to don a skullcap and light a candle to mark the Jewish festival of Hanukkah. Blair obliged, he and his clueless officials apparently impervious to how such a symbolic act would be interpreted on the streets of Ramallah, Gaza, Cairo and Amman. At least the pictures got little playback in the UK, where the media were obsessing over the murders of five prostitutes in Ipswich. Asked afterwards if Olmert had made a fool of him, Blair smiled and shrugged, 'I don't have a fragile, big shining ego like most politicians.'

The next day, Blair's chartered BA jumbo left Israel for the United Arab Emirates. On the plane, his spokesman told us that the (not exactly democratic and free) Gulf states were regarded by the prime minister as an intrinsic part of an 'arc of moderation' essential to Middle East peace and prosperity. Ironically, Blair's plane was left haplessly circling in the skies over Abu Dhabi, automatically denied permission to land because it had originated in the Jewish state. Not much moderation there, then. Once on the ground, the travelling pool were surprised not to be offered food or drink all day; it appeared there was no one on the British side bright enough to point out that it was the Muslim fasting season of Ramadan.

Blair gave a speech the following day which attempted to draw together the different strands of the trip. The essential message seemed to be that if the peoples of the region could get their act together, then Basra, Baghdad and Gaza could thrive – they could be just like Dubai. It was a remarkably naive exhortation – an almost plaintive, and typically Blairite, 'Why can't you all just get along?' A reasonable mantra for that most unreasonable of places!

Conventional wisdom about the Middle East is that it is intrinsically unreasonable. Everything there is turned on its head. Where Europeans see strength, Arabs (and for that matter Israelis) see weakness; where we see compromise they invariably see concession. But Blair refused to sign up to this view. He remained convinced that with the right safeguards and reassurances, rival populations could live in peace side by side and the dispossessed could be wooed back from extremism. With hindsight, it was possible to see his repeated visits to the Middle East in his final months as prime minister as a component of the successful pitch he would make to become Middle East envoy. On either side of the Downing Street front door he sincerely wanted to do what he could for the region, but he also enjoyed the chance to continue doing the rounds of the sunny sheiks' palaces which had sheltered him as prime minister.

In Blair's view, the defining moment of breakdown in the recent peace process was the failure of Gaza to stabilise after the Israeli withdrawal under the Sharon plan. He believed it would take a long time to rebuild the confidence of Israel to make gestures for peace again. At the same time, he argued that he was well placed to restore the faith in the process on both sides – with the determination, patience and attention to detail that the task required. With some justice, Blair also pointed out that he was the first envoy to have the trust of both the official Palestinian leadership and the Israelis as well as the Americans. George W. Bush, too, identified progress in the Middle East as one of the potential saving graces of the dying year of his administration. Blair at least coaxed the White House into holding the Annapolis conference and into visits by Condoleezza Rice and the president to the region. With neither time, nor demographics nor economics on their side, Blair reckoned that the

Israelis needed to reach a settlement. In his view the pressure came as much from economics as security. For example he liked to point out that Abu Dhabi's sovereign wealth fund alone was now three times the size of Israel's entire GNP.

For all his dedication to the Middle East, to climate change, to Africa, to his new foundations, Blair remained open to other possibilities. His view was that there was a job to do as the new president of the European Council.

He let it be known that he was much happier in his afterlife than he ever had been in Downing Street, working just as hard but to his own, rather than the nation's, agenda. But he was also still a relatively young man, just fifty-four.

It was wrong to think that he found it difficult to give up Downing Street – he knew that was inevitably going to happen. His biggest strength, whether in modernising the party or international negotiations, was always that he was ready to walk away.

Blair considered himself to be a sort of anti-politician. He claimed he didn't think like other politicians and, in talking about them, he assumed they were remote from him, a completely different breed. Yet after ten years at Number 10, he was a typical politician in the way he kept as many options as possible open for his future. He had had his time at the top but there was more living to be done. Unlike the Thane of Cawdor, he did not 'throw away the dearest thing he ow'd, As 'twere a careless trifle'.

Tony Blair extracted himself from the premiership more skilfully and with less damage to his sense of his own worth than almost any previous ex-prime minister. Whatever the achievements and errors of his administration, he looked forward confidently to an opulent and prominent new phase of his life after ten years at Number 10.

DIARY OF THE LAST 100 DAYS
AND BEYOND

2007

1 May	Tenth anniversary as PM. GMTV live. Labour HQ, Westminster. Edinburgh, Scottish election campaign. Statement on Turkey's democratic future
2 May	PMQs
3 May	Elections in Scotland and Wales
4 May	Election results interview, Labour HQ
5 May	Downing Street podcast re G8, interviewer Bob Geldof
6 May	Fifty-fourth birthday dinner with family members, Chequers
7 May	Message to the French people on Sarkozy's victory, YouTube
8 May	Restoration of power-sharing government in Northern Ireland, Stormont. Speech and media interviews
9 May	PMQs – Home Office split enacted
10 May	Resignation announced to cabinet. Speech to local party supporters, Trimdon Labour Club, Sedgefield
11 May	President Talabani of Iraq, Downing Street. Chirac and Sarkozy, Paris
12 May	Labour confirms Blair to step down as party leader on 24 June
13 May	'Better Education' report released with foreword by the prime minister
14 May	Education visits – Millennium Primary School, Greenwich; Northampton Academy; Windsor High School, Halesowen; Kilton Children's Centre; and South Trafford College by helicopter

15 May	Address to joint session of the Commons and Lords by Taoiseach Bertie Ahern
16 May	PMQs. Speech, mothers from disadvantaged backgrounds. Written statement, new ministerial committees of the cabinet. Downing Street podcast with Bertie Ahern, interviewer Patrick Kielty
17–18 May	Last joint press conference with President Bush, Washington DC. To Kuwait via Heathrow
19 May	Baghdad and Basra, Iraq. Meetings with Prime Minister Maliki and visit with British troops
20 May	First Labour Party leadership election hustings
21 May	Royal Free Hospital, London
22 May	Downing Street reception, MOD civilians involved in Northern Ireland. Call for extradition of Litvinenko murder suspect
23 May	PMQs – commitment to nuclear energy
24 May	Prime ministerial statement on the Equality Act. Belgian Prime Minister Guy Verhofstadt, Downing Street. Interview, France 2
25 May	Dudley Hospital, West Midlands
26 May	Chequers – farewell party for friends and colleagues
27 May	Calls for extension to police powers to fight terrorism
28 May	Compass report 'Closer to Equality?' questions Blair's record in office
29 May	Colonel Gaddafi, Libya
30 May	Freetown, Sierra Leone. Address to British troops. Press conference with President Kabbah and the President of Liberia. Paramount Chief ceremony
31 May	Speech at UNISA (University of South Africa). Nelson Mandela, Johannesburg
1 June	President Mbeki, Pretoria
2 June	Chequers – private dinner for the 'team of '97'
3 June	Chancellor Merkel, Berlin. GLOBE legislators forum on the environment award
4 June	Speech at the 'Islam and Muslims in the World Today' conference, London
5 June	Reception for leaders from the Third Sector, Downing Street
6 June	PMQs. Nick Robinson interview, Cabinet Room
6–8 June	Heiligendamm, German G8 summit. Last meeting with Putin

9 June	Premiere of short film, *Global Cool*, in which Blair appears as a 'carbon crusader'
10 June	Plans for young people to undertake mandatory community service floated
11 June	Statement to the House on G8
12 June	Speech, 'Our Nation's Future – Public Life', Reuters News Agency
13 June	PMQs. Sky Sports News interview – London Olympics and community sport. Czech Prime Minister, Downing Street. Reception for public sector champions, Lancaster House
14 June	Community centre and Knowsley Community College, Liverpool
15 June	Carmel Roman Catholic Technology College, Darlington
16 June	Trooping the Colour
17 June	Twenty-fifth Anniversary Falklands Parade
18 June	Last appearance, Commons Liaison Committee
19 June	Statement on sixty-second birthday of Aung San Suu Kyi. Scouting Centenary reception, Downing Street
20 June	PMQs. Commemorative badge for 'Bevin Boys' announced
21 June	Statement on UK and US defence trade treaty
21–23 June	European Council, Brussels
23 June	Success on four 'red lines' in the European treaty negotiations. Vatican, private visit
24 June	Special Labour Party conference, Manchester. Gordon Brown announced leader of the party, Harriet Harman deputy leader
25 June	Statement to the House on the European Council
26 June	Joint engagements on climate change with Arnold Schwarzenegger, school visit and last press conference as PM
27 June	Handover day. Final PMQs. Middle East role as Quartet envoy announced
28 June	Trimdon Labour Club, Sedgefield
29 June	Chequers
3 July	Opens library, Sedgefield Community College
8 July	Wedding reception of Jonathan Powell and Sarah Helm, Hampshire
12–14 July	Allen & Co.'s annual media and technology conference, Sun Valley, Idaho

17–18 July	Meetings on the Middle East, Brussels, Rome and Madrid
19 July	Quartet meeting, Lisbon
20–26 July	First trip to the Middle East as Quartet envoy
20 July	Jordanian foreign minister, Amman. Minister of Defence Barak, Jerusalem
24 July	Prime Minister Olmert, Jerusalem. President Abbas and Palestinian Prime Minister Fayyad, Ramallah
26 July	Bahrain and UAE
28 July	Family holiday in Barbados followed by Mediterranean cruise
31 August	Tenth anniversary Memorial Service for Princess Diana
10 September	King Abdullah of Jordan
24 September	Update on the Middle East to the UN
26–27 September	Bill Clinton's third Global Initiative Conference, New York
1 October	Speech, 'Globalisation in Politics', Blenheim Palace
19 October	Speech attacking Iranian support for terrorism, New York
4 November	Speech to the Saban Forum on the twelth anniversary of Yitzhak Rabin's death, Jerusalem
14 November	Launch of the Tony Blair Sports Foundation
19 November	Key development projects for the Palestinian economy announced
27 November	Annapolis Conference, Maryland
29 November	Interviews, CNN and NBC networks
5 December	Opening ceremony, Madejski Academy in Whitley, Reading
10–11 December	Meeting with leaders of Saudi Arabia, Kuwait and Qatar
12 December	Second meeting with Prime Minister Fayyad and Minister of Defence Barak
17 December	Co-chair of the International Donors Conference for the Palestinian State, Paris
18 December	Africa Progress Panel meeting, Berlin

2008

10 January	Role as adviser to JP Morgan announced
23–27 January	Co-chair of the World Economic Forum, Davos
28 January	Role as adviser to Zurich Financial Services announced
7 February	Nablus, West Bank
24 February	Kigali, Rwanda
7 March	Position as Howland Distinguished Fellow, Yale University, announced
14 March	'Breaking the Climate Deadlock' initiative announced. Followed by related visits to Japan, China and India
2 April	Statement on resignation of Bertie Ahern
3 April	Lecture, 'Faith and Globalisation', Westminster Cathedral
12 April	Charity dinner marking the tenth anniversary of the Good Friday Agreement, Dublin – Bono and Bob Geldof fellow attendees
21 April	Speech to the Atlantic Council, Washington DC
25 April	Appeal for runners to join 'Great North Run Team 100' in aid of Sports Foundation
1 May	Joint appeal with Prime Ministers Gordon Brown and Salam Fayyad for private sector investment in Palestine
2 May	Middle East Quartet meeting, London
6 May	Rwandan government-building team announced
13 May	Launches paper, 'Towards a Palestinian State'
15 May	Publication of Cherie Blair's memoirs, *Speaking for Myself*
21–23 May	Palestine Investment Conference, Bethlehem
30 May	Faith Foundation launch, Time Warner Centre, New York

ACKNOWLEDGEMENTS

This book would never have existed without the encouragement and help of Andrew Wylie, my literary agent; Tom Roberts, my researcher; and the publishing team at Simon & Schuster, especially the two editors Mike Jones and Andrew Gordon.

It could not have been written without the kindness and input of: Tricia McLernon, Julian Glover, Tony and Gabriela Ball, Peter Oborne, Michael Thrasher, Pierre Hodgson, James Macintyre, David Cracknell, Jonathan Levy, Ben and Yulia Wegg-Prosser, Gary Honeyford, Liz Lloyd, Will Tricks, Nick Pisani, Matthew Doyle and Tony Blair.

Or without the forbearance of my family – especially Anji and Lucy, Hannah and Blaise – and the support and opportunities given to me to cover politics by my employers before and during the Blair years: the late Leslie Stone, TV-am and, above all, Sky News.

I humbly thank them all.

INDEX

(the initials TB in subentries denote Tony Blair)